THE CHURCH IN THE SHADOW OF THE MOSQUE

JEWS, CHRISTIANS, AND MUSLIMS
FROM THE ANCIENT TO THE MODERN WORLD

SERIES EDITORS
MICHAEL COOK, WILLIAM CHESTER JORDAN, AND PETER SCHÄFER

Imperialism and Jewish Society, 200 B.C.E. to 640 C.E.
by Seth Schwartz

A Shared World: Christians and Muslims in the Early Modern Mediterranean
by Molly Greene

Beautiful Death: Jewish Poetry and Martyrdom in Medieval France
by Susan L. Einbinder

Power in the Portrayal: Representations of Jews and Muslims in Eleventh- and Twelfth-Century Islamic Spain
by Ross Brann

Mirror of His Beauty: Feminine Images of God from the Bible to the Early Kabbalah
by Peter Schäfer

In the Shadow of the Virgin: Inquisitors, Friars, and Conversos *in Guadalupe, Spain*
by Gretchen D. Starr-LeBeau

The Curse of Ham: Race and Slavery in Early Judaism, Christianity, and Islam
by David M. Goldenberg

Resisting History: Historicism and Its Discontents in German-Jewish Thought
by David N. Myers

Mothers and Children: Jewish Family Life in Medieval Europe
by Elisheva Baumgarten

A Jewish Renaissance in Fifteenth-Century Spain
by Mark D. Meyerson

The Handless Maiden: Moriscos and the Politics of Religion in Early Modern Spain
by Mary Elizabeth Perry

Poverty and Charity in the Jewish Community of Medieval Egypt
by Mark R. Cohen

Reckless Rites: Purim and the Legacy of Jewish Violence
by Elliott Horowitz

Living Together, Living Apart: Rethinking Jewish-Christian Relations in the Middle Ages
by Jonathan Elukin

The Church in the Shadow of the Mosque: Christians and Muslims in the World of Islam
by Sidney H. Griffith

THE CHURCH IN THE SHADOW OF THE MOSQUE

CHRISTIANS AND MUSLIMS IN THE WORLD OF ISLAM

Sidney H. Griffith

PRINCETON UNIVERSITY PRESS

PRINCETON AND OXFORD

PUBLISHED BY PRINCETON UNIVERSITY PRESS, 41 WILLIAM STREET,
PRINCETON, NEW JERSEY 08540
IN THE UNITED KINGDOM: PRINCETON UNIVERSITY PRESS,
3 MARKET PLACE, WOODSTOCK, OXFORDSHIRE OX20 1SY

LIBRARY OF CONGRESS CATALOGING-IN-PUBLICATION DATA
GRIFFITH, SIDNEY HARRISON.
THE CHURCH IN THE SHADOW OF THE MOSQUE : CHRISTIANS
AND MUSLIMS IN THE WORLD OF ISLAM / SIDNEY H. GRIFFITH.
P. CM. — (JEWS, CHRISTIANS, AND MUSLIMS
FROM THE ANCIENT TO THE MODERN WORLD)
INCLUDES BIBLIOGRAPHICAL REFERENCES (P.) AND INDEX.
ISBN 978-0-691-13015-6 (CLOTH : ALK. PAPER)
1. ARAB COUNTRIES—CHURCH HISTORY. 2. CHRISTIANITY
AND CULTURE—ARAB COUNTRIES—HISTORY. 3. CHRISTIANITY
AND OTHER RELIGIONS—ISLAM—HISTORY.
4. ISLAM—RELATIONS—CHRISTIANITY—HISTORY. I. TITLE.
BR1067.A7G75 2008 270.0917′4927—DC22 2007005577

BRITISH LIBRARY CATALOGING-IN-PUBLICATION DATA IS AVAILABLE

THIS BOOK HAS BEEN COMPOSED IN GALLIARD

PRINTED ON ACID-FREE PAPER. ∞

PRESS.PRINCETON.EDU
PRINTED IN THE UNITED STATES OF AMERICA

3 5 7 9 10 8 6 4 2

For my mother, Catherine Sappington Griffith,
and in memory of my father, H. Gloyd Griffith

CONTENTS

ILLUSTRATIONS

PREFACE

THIS BOOK HAS BEEN in the making for many years. It all began when more than twenty-five years ago I was a fellow at Dumbarton Oaks and in regular conversations with the Byzantinists who were my constant conversation partners there, and with Professor Irfan Shahid in particular, the master of Byzantine/Arab studies, who has continued to give me constant encouragement and help. In those days, Professor Giles Constable was the benevolent and broadminded director of Dumbarton Oaks, to whom I herewith acknowledge my gratitude for his unstinting advocacy and support. At that time I had proposed to write an account of the responses of the Christians in the so-called Oriental Patriarchates, as the Greeks called the Episcopal sees of Alexandria, Antioch, and Jerusalem, to the challenges posed for them by the Muslims under whose hegemony most of the Coptic, Syriac, and Arabic-speaking Christians lived. Little did I know how long it would take me to accomplish the project; at that time there were few scholarly studies of the relevant materials in Greek, Syriac, and Arabic to which I could turn for help. I spent many years writing articles about individual Christian Arabic and Syriac writers and their compositions, translating and commenting on some texts and editing others. In the fall semester of the academic year 1991–92, I profited immensely from a semester's stay in the Institute for Advanced Study at the Hebrew University in Jerusalem, at the invitation of Professor R. J. Zwi Werblowsky and the late Professor Hava Lazarus-Yafeh; the community of scholars in Jerusalem in my fields of interest is unequalled anywhere. Finally, in the fall of 2004 I was appointed to John Carroll University's Walter and Mary Tuohy Chair of interreligious studies, a situation that allowed me the opportunity to write as public lectures the general essays that, after much revision, would become the chapters of this book. I am most grateful to Professor David Mason, the director of the chair, and to all my erstwhile colleagues in the university's department of religious studies, particularly Dr. Zeki Saritoprak, for their warm welcome and unstinting hospitality during my time in Cleveland.

For more than thirty years I have been a member of the faculty in the Department of Semitic and Egyptian Languages and Literatures at the Catholic University of America in Washington, DC, where I took my own graduate degree under the guidance of the late Msgr. Patrick W. Skehan and now retired Professor Richard M. Frank. Needless to say, my debt to them is beyond calculation and well beyond what a simple acknowledgment here can adequately repay. For all of these years I have had the privilege to work in the incomparable library of the university's Semitics Department and its Institute of Christian Oriental Research; again I am much indebted to the library's curator, Dr. Monica J. Blanchard, who for many years has gone well beyond the call of either duty or friendship to provide me with the often hard to find resources I have needed for my researches. Over these same years I have received much support from my colleagues and students, too numerous to list individually here; they, and our current chairman, Professor Michael Patrick O'Connor, have offered me their friendship and scholarly companionship, without which I surely would not have been able to work so happily for so long.

A number of people have read some or all of this book's chapters and have offered many helpful comments, not to mention their very welcome corrections of my unwitting errors of fact or interpretation. Among them I wish particularly to thank Professor Christopher Blum of Christendom College in Front Royal, Virginia; Professor Robert L. Wilken of the University of Virginia; Dr. Norbert Hintersteiner of the Catholic University of America; Fred Appel and Meera Vaidyanathan of the Princeton University Press; Dawn Hall, my copyeditor; and the two anonymous readers whom the press appointed to evaluate my work; their remarks and suggestions have very much improved the final product. I am particularly grateful to the Institute of Christian Oriental Research at the Catholic University of America; Professor Joseph Patrich of the Hebrew University, Jerusalem; and the British Library for permission to reproduce here the illustrations that belong to them.

Finally I wish to express here my gratitude for the support of my family, friends, and confreres, all of whom, again too numerous to mention here, have patiently, willingly, and supportively endured the vagaries of one absorbed for so long in the preoccupations of research and writing. I owe special thanks to Marlene Debole for her support and her skillful help in the assembly of the text, and to Professor Christine M. Bochen of Nazareth College of Rochester, New York, for long years of personal solicitude and inspiration.

This book is not a comprehensive presentation of its subject. Rather, I conceive it to be a general introduction to the study of Christian cultural and intellectual life in the world of Islam, from the time of the prophet Muḥammad to the time of the Crusades and the Mongol conquest of the Middle East in the middle of the thirteenth century. For this reason, and to lead the reader to further sources of study, I have included copious bibliographical annotations in the text. It is my hope that the book may thus become something of a reference source for the study of the Christian Middle East among English speakers, who are not yet well served with an abundant literature in this field. I, and all who work in Christian Arabic studies, owe much to the pioneering work in our time of Fr. Samir Khalil

Samir, S.J., whose many editions of texts and numerous scholarly studies, mostly in Arabic and French, have brought new life to the study of an often-overlooked portion of the Christian heritage; to him I offer the homage of a grateful colleague.

Washington, DC
September 2006

THE CHURCH IN THE SHADOW OF THE MOSQUE

Frontispiece. St. Catherine's Monastery at Mount Sinai
While the monastery at Sinai was dedicated to the martyr St. Catherine of Alexandria (fourth century) after the ninth century, it was founded in 527 CE and dedicated originally to the Mother of God. The monastery's library now houses one of the largest collections of Christian Arabic manuscripts, a number of them written in the monasteries of Palestine, the earliest of them dating from the second half of the eighth century CE. (Courtesy of Professor Joseph Patrich, The Hebrew University of Jerusalem.)

INTRODUCTION

THE STORY OF THE CHRISTIANS who are at home in the world of Islam has seldom been told in terms that highlight how their intellectual culture and even their denominational identities came to be expressed in the Arabic idiom of the Islamic culture of which they were for centuries an integral part. In the heyday of the classical world of Arabo-Islamic civilization in the Middle East, from the middle of the eighth century to the middle of the thirteenth century, Arabic-speaking Christians not only made major contributions to Islamic culture, but they also wrote philosophical and theological texts of their own in Arabic; they translated much of their several ecclesiastical traditions from Greek, Syriac, and Coptic into Arabic; and they produced scholars, scientists, and churchmen who in their own day gained enviable reputations in the Arab world. This book tells their story in broad outline, with copious bibliographical annotations for those who would like to learn more about this exciting and little-known chapter in the history of Christianity.[1]

A number of first-rate studies of Christians in the Middle East have been published in recent years, but they have not been so much concerned with the history of the development and expression of Christian culture and learning in Arabic. Rather, their concern has been, for the most part, to set forth the internal history and fortunes of the several "Oriental" churches, the perilous demographic state of these communities since the fourteenth century, and to provide the historical statistics that chart their decline.[2] There have also been recent studies of the multiple hardships endured by Jews, Christians, and other "People of the Book" in their experience of life in the special status stipulated for them in Islamic law, a status that has recently been designated by the neologism, *Dhimmitude*, a term that echoes the Arabic word designating their legal standing.[3] But another dimension

[1] Kenneth Cragg's well received study of Arab Christian history largely ignores the intellectual and cultural accomplishments of the several Arabic-speaking churches, concentrating more on what he perceived to be their failure, successfully to meet the religious challenge of Islam. See Kenneth Cragg, *The Arab Christian: A History in the Middle East* (London: Mowbray, 1992). See also Sidney H. Griffith, "Kenneth Cragg on Christians and the Call to Islam," *Religious Studies Review* 20 (1994): 29–35.

[2] See, e.g., Jean-Pierre Valognes, *Vie et mort des chrétiens d'Orient: Des origines à nos jours* (Paris: Fayard, 1994); Andrea Pacini, *Christian Communities in the Arab Middle East: The Challenge of the Future* (Oxford: Clarendon Press, 1998). There are also numerous, more popular works, such as Betty Jane Bailey and J. Martin Bailey, *Who Are the Christians in the Middle East?* (Grand Rapids, MI: William B. Eerdmans, 2003).

[3] The several works of Giselle Littmann, writing under the pen name Bat Ye'or, have helped to popularize the neologism, *Dhimmitude*. See, e.g., Bat Ye'or, *The Decline of Eastern Chris-*

to the life of the Christians in the world of Islam also deserves attention and has often been neglected by westerners. It is the story of the religious, cultural, and intellectual achievements of the Arabophone Christians.

Many well-informed westerners are still completely unaware of the fact that there is a large archive of texts in Arabic composed by Christians from as early as the eighth century of the Christian era and continuing right up to today. Arabic is often thought to be simply the language of the Muslims.[4] And hand in hand with the unawareness of Christian Arabic there has gone the concomitant unawareness of the considerable cultural and intellectual achievements of the Christians who have for more than a millennium been an integral part of the societies of the Arabic-speaking Muslims in the Middle East. It is almost as if in the western imagination the religious discourse and the intellectual concerns of Middle Eastern Christians were frozen in time, in the form they had at the time when the Islamic hegemony came over them in the seventh century. This unawareness of the continuing vitality of Christian life and culture in the world of Islam after the Islamic conquest is no doubt due in large part to the slow pace of the academic study of Christian Arabic in the West. It did not really become a going concern until the twentieth century,[5] and then often only by riding on the coattails of other academic disciplines. The situation is almost a complete contrast with that of the study of Judeo-Arabic[6] and the cultural and intellectual achievements of the Jews of Islam during the centuries when there were large Jewish populations in the Islamic world, not only in the East but also in North Africa and al-Andalus.[7]

By contrast with the case of the Arabic-speaking Christians, many of the seminal Jewish thinkers of the Middle Ages who lived among the Muslims and wrote in Arabic are now well known to many educated westerners.

---

tianity under Islam: From Jihad to Dhimmitude; Seventh–Twentieth Century (Madison, NJ: Fairleigh Dickinson University Press, 1996); *Islam and Dhimmitude: Where Civilizations Collide* (Madison, NJ: Fairleigh Dickinson University Press, 2002). More on these works below.

[4] See Mark N. Swanson, "Arabic as a Christian Language?" available at http://www.luthersem.edu/faculty/fac_home.asp?contact_id=mswanson. At the same Web site see also the author's companion piece, "Early Christian-Muslim Theological Conversation among Arabic-Speaking Intellectuals."

[5] The standard reference book is still Georg Graf, *Geschichte der christlichen arabischen Literatur*, 5 vols. (Vatican City: Biblioteca Apostolica Vaticana, 1944–53).

[6] See Joshua Blau, *The Emergence and Linguistic Background of Judaeo-Arabic* (Jerusalem: Ben-Zvi Institute, 1999).

[7] See Norman Stillman, comp., *The Jews of Arab Lands: A History and Source Book* (Philadelphia: Jewish Publication Society of America, 1979); Bernard Lewis, *The Jews of Islam* (Princeton, NJ: Princeton University Press, 1984); Mark R. Cohen, *Under Crescent and Cross: The Jews in the Middle Ages* (Princeton, NJ: Princeton University Press, 1994). On the three traditions intertwined in the Middle Ages, see Roger Arnaldez, *À la croisée des trois monotheismes: Une communauté de pensée au Moyen Age* (Paris: Albin Michel, 1993), esp. 153–275.

Their works and their languages have been studied in western universities for generations. Many readers, on the one hand, will probably recognize such names as: Saʿadyah ben Yosef Gaʾon (882–942), Yehudah Ha-Levi (ca. 1075–1141), Avraham ibn Ezra (1089–1164), or Moses Maimonides (1135–1204). Who, on the other hand, even among Christian medievalists, has heard of Ḥunayn ibn Isḥāq (808–873), Theodore Abū Qurrah (ca. 755–ca. 830), ʿAmmār al-Baṣrī (fl. ca. 850), Yaḥyā ibn ʿAdī (893–974), Bar Hebraeus (d. 1286), or al-Muʿtaman ibn al-ʿAssāl (fl. 1230–1260)? Strangely, there is one Arab Christian scholar of early ʿAbbasid times whose name readers of the works of the Irish poet William Butler Yeats (1865–1939) might recognize. He was the Syrian "Melkite" Qusṭā ibn Lūqā al-Baʿalbakī (d. 912); Yeats used his name, under the form Kusta Ben Luka, to designate a mysterious interlocutor in his esoteric work, *A Vision*.[8] But no one seems to know how Yeats came upon the name of this distinguished Arab Christian scholar, or indeed if he even knew much about his background.[9]

In the West, Christendom is often thought of as coterminous with the lands and cultures of the Latin Middle Ages, and many people nowadays are also unaware of the names of even the neighboring medieval Byzantine Christian writers and thinkers whose language was Greek or Slavonic, let alone the names of any Arabic or Syriac writers among the Christians who lived in the world of Islam. Latin Christians in particular have historically been inclined to think of the Christians of the Orient as schismatic or even heretical and so as people who left the church centuries ago. Now is the time to take steps to remedy this situation, first of all because the intellectual heritage of the eastern Christians belongs to the whole church and we are the poorer without any knowledge of it.[10] But it is also the case that in the multicultural world of the twenty-first century, when Muslim/Christian relations are becoming daily more important worldwide, the experience of the Christians of the Orient who have lived with Muslims for centuries, and who have immigrated to the West together with the Muslims, is immediately relevant for those of us in the West who would be in dialogue with Muslims today and who would welcome some deeper knowledge of

[8] William Butler Yeats, *A Vision* (London: Macmillan, 1937). See Suheil B. Bushrui, "Yeats' Arabic Interests," in *In Excited Reverie: A Centenary Tribute to William Butler Yeats, 1856–1939*, ed. A. Norman Jeffares and K. G. W. Cross (London: Macmillan, 1965).

[9] In another place Yeats spoke of "Kusta ben Luka himself once so learned and so eloquent could now, lacking me but twitter like a swallow." Quoted from George Mills Harper, *The Making of Yeats's* A Vision: *A Study of the Automatic Script*, 2 vols. (Carbondale, IL: Southern Illinois University Press, 1987), 2: 408.

[10] Typically of the western, Latin Christian attitude, even so sympathetic a figure as Louis Massignon (1883–1962) spoke of Islam, seemingly with approval, as the "vainqueur des chrétientés schismatiques d'Orient, qu'il encapsula dans sa gangue, comme 'des insects dans l'ambre.'" Louis Massignon, *Les trois prières d'Abraham* (Paris: Cerf, 1997), 112.

the history of our shared religious and intellectual heritage.[11] The time is long overdue for the Christians of the West to extend their modern ecumenical concerns to their coreligionists of the Islamic world.

The purpose of this book is to provide a succinct overview of the cultural and intellectual achievements, including the theological posture vis-à-vis Islam, of the Christians who spoke and wrote in Syriac and in Arabic and who lived in the world of Islam from the time of the prophet Muḥammad (ca. 570–632) up to the time of the Crusades at the end of the eleventh century and even beyond that time to the era of the very destructive Mongol invasions of the Middle East in the mid-thirteenth century. The title of the work, *The Church in the Shadow of the Mosque*, is meant to evoke both the overshadowing effects, as well as the protective shade, afforded by the shadow cast by the mosque over all other institutions in the Islamic world. It is seldom recognized that the establishment of Islamic, Arabic-speaking culture in the caliphate by the end of the ninth century, albeit that it eventually led to the declension of the local Christian communities and finally brought them to their modern demographic insignificance in the Middle East, nevertheless also provided the circumstances for two important developments in Christian life in early Islamic times. It fostered the articulation of a new cultural expression of Christian doctrine, this time in Arabic, and it provided the cultural framework within which the several Christian denominations of the Orient ultimately came to define their mature ecclesial identities. These unsung developments hold within them the seeds of a hope that once again, within a sphere of a religious freedom now unfortunately widely unavailable in Islamic countries, a Christian voice can once again be heard where Islam holds sway, in the very idiom of the dominant Islamic religious discourse. It could pave the way for the Christians of the world of Islam to lead their coreligionists in the rest of the world into a renewed Muslim/Christian dialogue and to hasten the general recognition of the fact that there is indeed an "Islamo-Christian" heritage on which both Muslims and Christians can draw in their efforts to promote a peaceful and mutually respectful *convivencia* in the future.

Almost exactly one century ago, first at Princeton Theological Seminary in Princeton, New Jersey, and then at seminaries in Chicago, Illinois, and Louisville, Kentucky, during the academic year 1902–3, William Ambrose

[11] This shared intellectual heritage is discussed in a comprehensive but summary way in the previously mentioned work of Roger Arnaldez, *À la croisée de trois monotheismes*. See also Richard W. Bulliet, *The Case for Islamo-Christian Civilization* (New York: Columbia University Press, 2004); Stephen O'Shea, *Sea of Faith: Islam and Christianity in the Medieval Mediterranean World* (New York: Walker, 2006).

Shedd of the American Presbyterian Church delivered a series of six lectures on the general theme of Islam and the Oriental churches.[12] His topics closely parallel those of the following chapters of the present book, with the difference that the scholarship of the intervening century has considerably enhanced our knowledge of the history and culture of the Christians who have lived with Muslims. And there is another important difference. Shedd's final chapter concerns the missionary heritage of the indigenous churches of the Islamic world, and he speaks of the campaign of the Christians of the West to conquer Islam. Now, a century later, while western Christians are still no less devoted to proclaiming the Good News, there is also a recognition of the right to religious freedom for all and the imperative for interreligious dialogue and comparative theology, important steps toward peace in the twenty-first century. My own final chapter searches for the theological, historical, and cultural postures Christians might now reasonably assume in their continuing encounter with Muslims, in the light of the lessons learned from the thought and experience of the Arabic-speaking Oriental churches in the early centuries of Islam. From this perspective one might think that modern advances in the world of Islamic scholarship and the current Christian readiness to dialogue with members of other religious communities, the times would offer a new opportunity for a measure of Christian/Muslim rapprochement, and for a renewal of mutual respect, rather than for continued confrontation and mutual recrimination. It is true that the lessons of history on this point do not offer grounds for heightened expectations, but the alternative to not making the effort to make things better is already well known and mutually destructive.

[12] W. A. Shedd, *Islam and the Oriental Churches: Their Historical Relations* (Philadelphia: Presbyterian Board of Publication and Sabbath-School Work, 1904; repr., Piscataway, NJ: Gorgias Press, 2004).

I

"PEOPLE OF THE GOSPEL," "PEOPLE OF THE BOOK"

CHRISTIANS AND CHRISTIANITY IN THE WORLD OF ISLAM

Jews and Christians in the Qur'ān

Arabic-speaking Jews and Christians were no doubt in the audience to whom the Qur'ān first addressed the word of God in "a clear Arabic tongue" (16:103 and 26:105), as the Qur'ān itself says of its message. Indeed, on its own terms the Qur'ān presumes the precedence of the Torah and the Gospel in the consciousness of its audience, and insists that in reference to the earlier divine revelations it is itself "a corroborating scripture in Arabic language to warn wrong doers and to announce good news to those who do well." (46:12) In the Qur'ān, the voice of God even advises the Muslims, "If you are in doubt about what We have sent down to you, ask those who were reading scripture before you" (10:94).

Just a brief acquaintance with the text of the Qur'ān is sufficient to convince any reader that it presumes in its audience a ready familiarity with the stories of many of the principal narrative figures of the Old and New Testaments, as well as with an impressive array of Jewish and Christian lore.[1] It offers a critique of Jewish and Christian faith and practice and in many ways contests the Jewish and Christian understandings of the Torah, the Prophets, the Psalms, and the Gospel, to cite the parts of the Bible the Qur'ān mentions by name. So the question naturally arises in connection with this state of affairs: Who were the Christians in the Arabic-speaking milieu of Muḥammad and the Qur'ān, and what were their affiliations with Christian groups elsewhere? The Qur'ān does not really offer much explicit

[1] See, e.g., the early studies by Abraham Geiger, *Was hat Mohanned aus dem Judenthume aufgenommen?* Eine von der königliche preussisschen Rheinuniversität gekrönte Preisschrift, 2nd ed. (Leipzig: M. W. Kaufmann, 1902) and J. Henninger, "Spuren christlicher Glaubenswahrheiten im Koran," *Neue Zeitschrift für Missionswissenschaft/Nouvelle Revue de Science Missionnaire*, 1 (1945): 135–40, 304–14; 2 (1946): 56–65, 109–22, 289–304; 3 (1947): 128–40, 293–301; 4 (1948): 129–41, 284–93; 5 (1949): 127–40, 290–300; 6 (1950): 207–17, 284–97. More recent scholars have, of course, added abundantly to the fund of knowledge about Jewish and Christian traditions perceptible in the Qur'ān.

help in this inquiry, confining itself for the most part to admonishing the followers of Jesus.[2] But in the terms in which it addresses the Christians in its Arabic-speaking audience about their religious formulas, their beliefs and practices, the Qur'ān does offer scholars some tantalizing clues about the ecclesial identities of the Christians of pre-Islamic Arabia.[3] These often-enigmatic pieces of evidence have in fact become ample grist for the academic mill that grinds out hypotheses on the subject with great regularity. So it is important first of all briefly to review some of the terms in question.

Although the Qur'ān addresses Christians directly and speaks about them in a number of places, ironically it never actually mentions the name "Christians." For the most part, Christians in the Qur'ān are included among those whom the text calls the "People of the Book," the "Scripture People," or "scriptuaries" (*ahl al-kitāb*), a general expression that occurs some fifty-four times and in addition to Christians includes Jews and to some extent Zoroastrians.[4] Once, the particular designation "Gospel People" appears (5:47). But more interestingly, the name for Christians that is used some fourteen times in the Qur'ān, and which all modern interpreters translate as "Christians," is the Arabic term *an-Naṣārā*. There is some controversy about its etymology and exact significance, but the modern scholarly consensus is that it is simply the Arabic form of the name "Nazoreans" or "Nazarenes," adjectives that are normally taken to refer to people from Jesus's hometown of Nazareth in Galilee. In the singular it is applied to Jesus in the Gospels (cf. Matthew 2:23), and in the plural, already in the New Testament (Acts 24:5), it is a name referring to Jesus's followers. While the term "Christians" early on became the primary designation for Jesus's followers (Acts 11:26), the name "Nazarenes" apparently continued in use in the Aramaic-speaking milieu of early Christianity for some time. It appears as a name for "Christians" in Syriac texts, written by east Syrian writers living in the Persian empire in pre-Islamic times, particularly when they report references made by non-Christians to Christians.[5]

[2] See Jane Dammen McAuliffe, *Qur'ānic Christians: An Analysis of Classical and Modern Exegesis* (Cambridge: Cambridge University Press, 1991; McAuliffe, "Christians in the Qur'ān and Tafsīr," in *Muslim Perceptions of Other Religions: A Historical Survey*, ed. Jacques Waardenburg (New York and Oxford: Oxford University Press, 1999).

[3] For a general discussion, see J. Spencer Trimingham, *Christianity among the Arabs in Pre-Islamic Times* (London and New York: Longman, 1979).

[4] See Yohanan Friedmann, "Classification of Unbelievers in Sunnī Muslim Law and Tradition," *Jerusalem Studies in Arabic and Islam* 22 (1998): 164, 179–82.

[5] See Sebastian P. Brock, "Christians in the Sasanid Empire: A Case of Divided Loyalties," in *Religion and National Identity*, ed. Stuart Mews, 1–19, Studies in Church History, 18 (Oxford: Oxford University Press, 1982); Simon C. Mimouni, "Les Nazoréens: Recherche étymologique et historique," *Revue Biblique* 105 (1998): 208–65; François De Blois, "*Naṣrānī* (ναζωραιος) and *ḥanīf* (εθνικος): Studies on the Religious Vocabulary of Christianity and Islam," *Bulletin of the School of Oriental and African Studies* 65 (2002): 1–30.

Granted then that the "Nazarenes" in the Qur'ān really are "Christians" by another scriptural name, which the Qur'ān doubtless uses for its own rhetorical purposes, one next wants to know more about their Christian, theological profiles. And this too is a matter of considerable controversy among scholars. Suffice it to say for the present purpose that in the opinion of this writer the community identity of the Christians in the Qur'ān's audience must be determined in reference to the whole profile of Christians and Christianity that emerges from the Qur'ān's references and allusions to their scriptures, beliefs, and practices. The matter should not be determined just on the basis of the etymologies of particular terms and phrases taken in conjunction with certain theological constructions that modern interpreters think they can plausibly impose on them.[6] When approached from the broader perspective that I advocate, it seems reasonable to propose that the Christians to whom the Qur'ān refers, whose doctrines and ecclesiastical lore the text actually reflects, are none other than those who would in due course be subsumed under the three names later Muslim Arab writers would regularly use for the Christians in their midst: the "Nestorians," the "Jacobites," and the "Melkites."[7]

In Muḥammad's lifetime, Christians who may reasonably be associated with these denominations, albeit somewhat anachronistically, were certainly making inroads from the surrounding peripheries into Arabia along trade routes and other well-established pathways, spreading Christianity among the Arabic-speaking tribesmen, even into the Hijāz. And while the documentation for this activity is sparse, it is not nonexistent. The Qur'ān, with its wealth of biblical allusion and evocation of Christian themes, is a principal piece of the evidence, notwithstanding the contemporary, revisionist, scholarly theories that posit its compilation in its final form well over a century after Muḥammad and outside of Arabia.

Greek, Syriac, Coptic, Armenian, and Ethiopic were the languages of the Christian communities on the edges of Arabia; over the preceding centuries they all had relationships with the Arabic-speaking tribesmen of the inte-

[6] This seems to me to be the flaw in the otherwise brilliant article by F. De Blois, "*Naṣrānī* and *ḥanīf*," where, in agreement with earlier commentators, the author takes the term *an-Naṣārā* in the Qur'ān to refer to a community that early Christian heresiographers called Nazarenes, on whom, see Ray A. Pritz, *Nazarene Jewish Christianity: From the End of the New Testament Period until Its Disappearance in the Fourth Century* (Jerusalem: Magnes Press, and Leiden: Brill, 1988); Édouard-Marie Gallez, *La messie et son prophète: Aux origines de l'islam*, 2 vols. Studia Arabia, 1 and 2, 2nd ed. (Paris: Éditions de Paris, 2005).

[7] This line of thinking, which considers both the rhetoric of the Qur'ān and the etymology of its words and phrases in its historical context, is proposed in two forthcoming studies: Sidney H. Griffith, "Syriacisms in the Arabic Qur'ān: Who Were 'Those who said that Allāh is Third of Three' according to *al-Mā'idah* 73?" in press, and Griffith, "Christian Lore and the Arabic Qur'ān: A Comparative Study of the Narratives of the 'Companions of the Cave' in the Qur'ān and in Syriac Tradition," to appear.

rior and these continued into the time of Muḥammad. But there is every reason to believe that Arabic was nevertheless the language of the Christian communities that in their several ecclesial identities were among the tribesmen of Arabia,[8] albeit that their characteristic confessional formulas would have been originally phrased in other languages.[9] The original liturgical and confessional languages of their communities would have been the languages of the periphery of Arabia, and especially Syriac as the evidence suggests, echoes of which can yet be heard in the very diction of the Qur'ān.[10] So by the time the Qur'ān was addressing the Christians in its audience in what it called "a clear Arabic tongue," (16:103) these Christians were themselves already speaking and praying in Arabic, albeit that in all likelihood they did not yet have their scriptures and liturgies in written Arabic texts.[11]

The Qur'ān's message to the Arabic-speaking Christians in its audience was a critique of their religious faith and practice; it meant to call them to its rule of right belief. The most comprehensive verse addressed directly to Christians in this vein says:

> O People of the Book, do not exaggerate in your religion, and do not say about God anything but the truth. The Messiah, Jesus, Mary's son, is only God's messenger, and His Word He imparted to Mary, and a Spirit from Him. Believe in God and in His messengers, and do not say, "Three." Stop it! It is better for you. God is but a single God; He is too exalted for anything to become a son to Him, anything in the heavens or anything on the earth. God suffices as a guardian. (4:171)

The Qur'ān also objected to certain aspects of Christian behavior. For, while on the one hand it says to Muḥammad and his followers, "You shall

[8] See especially the studies of Irfan Shahid, *Rome and the Arabs: A Prolegomenon to the Study of Byzantium and the Arabs* (Washington, DC: Dumbarton Oaks, 1984); *Byzantium and the Arabs in the Fourth Century* (Washington, DC: Dumbarton Oaks, 1984); *Byzantium and the Arabs in the Fifth Century* (Washington, DC: Dumbarton Oaks, 1989); *Byzantium and the Arabs in the Sixth Century* (Washington, DC: Dumbarton Oaks, 1995).

[9] Hence the charge of Muḥammad's adversaries recorded in the Qur'ān: "We know that they say only a human being teaches him. The language of the one to whom they point is foreign; this is a clear Arabic language," 16 *an-Naḥl* 103. See Claude Gilliot, "Les 'informateurs' juifs et chrétiens de Muḥammad," *Jerusalem Studies in Arabic and Islam* 22 (1998): 84–126.

[10] No plea is made here for the far-reaching proposals of Christoph Luxenberg, *Die syro-aramäische Lesart des Koran* (Berlin: Das arabische Buch, 2000). For my thoughts on the subject, see Griffith, "Syriacisms in the Arabic Qur'ān" and "Christian Lore and the Arabic Qur'ān."

[11] See Sidney H. Griffith, "The Gospel in Arabic: An Inquiry into Its Appearance in the First Abbasid Century," *Oriens Christianus* 69 (1985): 126–67; Griffith, "From Aramaic to Arabic: The Languages of the Monasteries of Palestine in the Byzantine and Early Islamic Periods," *Dumbarton Oaks Papers* 51 (1997): 11–31.

find the closest in affection to the believers to be those who say: 'We are Nazarenes,' for among them are priests and monks, and they are not arrogant" (5:82), the text also says in another place, "Neither the Jews nor the Nazarenes will be pleased with you until you follow their religion" (2:120). What is more, it accuses these "Scripture People" of changing the words of the Bible, concealing them and distorting their meaning (2:75–59; 3:78; 5:12–19).[12] Clearly then, the Qur'ān speaks to a measure of estrangement among the believers in its audience,[13] between those who will be Muslims on the one side, and the Christians, along with the Jews, on the other side, granted that the greatest number of the Qur'ān's religious adversaries would have been the native Arab polytheists, who are never called "believers." Even before Muḥammad's death in Medina in the year 632, relationships between the burgeoning Muslim community and the "People of the Book" in Arabia had come to the point that the Qur'ān itself had to dictate a principle to govern the relationship between the Muslims, and the Jews and Christians. The text tells the Muslims: "Fight those among the 'People of the Book' who do not believe in Allāh and the Last Day, who do not forbid what Allāh and His Messenger have forbidden and do not profess the true religion, till they pay the poll-tax (*jizyah*) out of hand and submissively (9:29)."

Nevertheless, in spite of this charge, which in later Islamic times would become the statutory principle behind the social policy of discrimination between Muslims and the "People of the Book" in the world of Islam, the Qur'ān still envisions dialogue between Jews, Christians, and Muslims. The text goes so far as to advise the Muslims, "If you are in doubt about what We have sent down to you, ask those who were reading scripture before you" (10:94). And the Qur'ān further says, "Do not dispute with the 'People of the Book' save in the fairest way;[14] except for those of them who are evildoers. And say: 'We believe in what has been sent down to us and what has been sent down to you. Our God and your God is one and to Him we are submissive'" (29:46).

Given these considerations, it is clear that already in the lifetime of Muḥammad, and in the very provisions of the Qur'ān, Jews, Christians, and Muslims have had a warrant for dialogue with one another since the

[12] See Jean-Marie Gaudeul and Robert Caspar, "Textes de la tradition musulmane concernant le *taḥrīf* (falsification) des écritures," *Islamochristiana* 6 (1980): 61–104.

[13] On the more comprehensive sense of the term "believers" (*al-mu'minūn*) as it is used in the Qur'ān and early Islamic tradition, see Fred M. Donner, "From Believers to Muslims, Patterns of Communal Identity in Early Islam," *Al-Abhath* (2003), in press; F. M. Donner, *Narratives of Islamic Origins: The Beginnings of Islamic Historical Writing* (Princeton, NJ: Darwin Press, 1998), esp. 98ff.

[14] See Jane Dammen McAuliffe, "'Debate with them in the better way': The Construction of a Qur'ānic Commonplace," in *Myths, Historical Archetypes, and Symbolic Figures in Arabic Literature: Towards a New Hermeneutic Approach*, ed. Angelika Neuwirth et al., 163–88 (Beirut: In Kommission bei Franz Steiner Verlag Stuttgart, 1999).

very birth of Islam. But, as we all too readily also recall, the dialogue has not normally been a happy or even a productive one, especially if we study its history only from the perspective of the Christians who lived outside of the world of Islam, who never participated in any meaningful way in the culture of the Islamic world or ever engaged in real conversations with Muslims.

The Arab Occupation of the Levant

By the year 732, just one hundred years after the death of the prophet Muḥammad, Arab military forces, mightily inspired by Islam, had consolidated their hegemony over a large stretch of territory outside of Arabia, which thereafter would become the heartland of the enduring "Commonwealth of Islam." This expanse of territory, embracing major portions of the Roman and Persian empires of Late Antiquity, included numerous Christians. They were by far the majority of the population in the former Roman provinces, in the three so-called Oriental Patriarchates of Alexandria, Antioch, and Jerusalem, as well as in North Africa and Spain, where the government had been officially Christian. The Christians also constituted a numerically respectable, demographic minority in the land of the Persians, where for all their numbers they never in fact enjoyed any significant political preferment.[15]

It is important to take cognizance of the seldom acknowledged fact that after the consolidation of the Islamic conquest and the consequent withdrawal of "Roman"/"Byzantine" forces from the Fertile Crescent in the first half of the seventh century, perhaps 50 percent of the world's confessing Christians from the mid-seventh to the end of the eleventh centuries found themselves living under Muslim rule.[16] Conversely, during these same first four centuries of the Muslim government of these large territories, roughly up to the time of the Crusades, the very centuries during which the classical Islamic culture was coming into its own, the Muslims themselves still did not make up the absolute majority of the population everywhere in the caliphate, not even in Mesopotamia, Syria, Palestine, and Egypt, where by the end of the ninth century the largest populations of the speakers of Arabic lived.[17] The recognition of this situation prepares us to see how a new opportunity for cultural and intellectual accomplishment

[15] See Garth Fowden, *Empire to Commonwealth: Consequences of Monotheism in Late Antiquity* (Princeton, NJ: Princeton University Press, 1993); Hugh Kennedy, "The Decline and Fall of the First Muslim Empire," *Der Islam* 81 (2004): 3–30.

[16] See Jean-Pierre Valognes, *Vie et mort des chrétiens d'orient: Des origines à nos jours* (Paris: Fayard, 1994).

[17] See Richard W. Bulliet, *Conversion to Islam in the Medieval Period: An Essay in Quantitative History* (Cambridge, MA: Harvard University Press, 1979).

presented itself, even for the Christians who lived under the rule of Islam during this period.

The Christian communities—who were in a position the most immediately to interact with the Muslims in the centers of Islamic culture and power outside of the Arabian peninsula after the conquest, first in Damascus in Syria, and then more significantly in Baghdad in Iraq after the foundation of the city in the year 767—were for the most part Arameans, in the sense that their ecclesiastical languages were Aramaic, albeit with a constant reference to conciliar and doctrinal developments that had found their first expressions in Greek in the Roman Empire in the fourth and fifth centuries. In the case of Christians living in Sinai, Palestine, or Trans-Jordan, where the "Byzantine" Orthodoxy of the council of Chalcedon (451) held sway from the mid-fifth century onward, and where Greek was the dominant ecclesiastical language in the numerous international monastic communities, the Aramaic dialect of the local churches was Christian Palestinian Aramaic.[18] In Syria and Mesopotamia, where the local Christian communities straddled the former frontiers of the Roman and Persian empires, and where "Byzantine," Roman imperial Orthodoxy was widely rejected,[19] Syriac was the Aramaic dialect that served as the dominant ecclesiastical language.

Most Syriac-speaking Christians at the time of the Islamic conquest accepted Christological formulas articulated the most effectively either originally in Greek by Severus of Antioch (ca. 465–538) and in Syriac by Philoxenus of Mabbug (ca. 440–523), echoing the earlier theology of St. Cyril of Alexandria (d. 444) (the so-called Jacobites or Monophysites), or they accepted formulas articulated in Syriac by Narsai (d. 503) and Babai the Great (551/2–628), reflecting the positions of Theodore of Mopsuestia (ca. 350–428), composed originally in Greek a hundred years earlier (the so-called Nestorians).[20] In other words, already at the time of the Islamic conquest and throughout the early Islamic period, most Aramean Christians, along with the Copts in Egypt and the Armenians in the Caucasus, did not accept the "Byzantine" imperial orthodoxy of the first six ecumenical councils. The resulting schisms had already estranged the ma-

[18] See Griffith, "From Aramaic to Arabic"; Griffith, "The Signs and Wonders of Orthodoxy: Miracles and Monks' Lives in Sixth-Century Palestine," in *Miracles in Jewish and Christian Antiquity: Imagining Truth*, ed. John Cavadini, 139–68, Notre Dame Studies in Theology, vol. 3 (Notre Dame: IN: University of Notre Dame Press, 1999).

[19] See Wilhelm Baum and Dietmar Winkler, *The Church of the East: A Concise History* (New York: Routledge Curzon, 2003); Sebastian Brock and David G. K. Taylor, *The Hidden Pearl: The Syrian Orthodox Church and Its Aramaic Heritage* (Rome: Trans World Film Italia, 2001).

[20] See D. S. Wallace-Hadrill, *Christian Antioch: A Study of Early Christian Thought in the East* (Cambridge: Cambridge University Press, 1982).

jority of Christians in the Oriental Patriarchates from both Rome and Constantinople by Muḥammad's day. Nevertheless, there remained among them, in Alexandria, Antioch, and Jerusalem, communities who did accept the orthodoxy of the "six councils," enforced by the Byzantine emperors. In consequence of this loyalty, those who accepted Byzantine orthodoxy who lived in the newly conquered Islamic world came soon after the sixth council (III Constantinople, 681) to be called "Melkites" ("imperialists," "royalists") by their "Jacobite" and "Nestorian" adversaries.[21]

So it was that the Muslim conquerors of the eastern homelands of Christianity, when they assumed control of the Levant, found the Christians there in a state of theological and cultural diversity and in the very process of division into the ecclesiastical communities that would remain the dominant ones for Christians in the Islamic world for centuries to come. Indeed, as we shall see, the several communities continued to articulate their differences with one another when they came under Muslim domination, and in due course they came eventually to define the final terms of their separate ecclesial identities in Arabic, the language of the commonwealth of Islam. This very fact in itself, together with their gradual incorporation into the ways of life of the Islamic polity, which, as we shall see, they helped create, meant that culturally they belonged to the new world of Islam. They became more and more isolated from and in large part estranged from western Christians, both Latin- and Greek-speaking. Tellingly, when the latter did come into the world of Islam, as they did increasingly after the time of the Crusades, they lived apart from and often in tension with the local Christians, lodging in enclaves of their own or in the *funduqs* and the *fondacos* of the western strangers who were already bent on exploiting every commercial opportunity in the East.[22] For by then the indigenous Christians living among the Muslims had begun their long slide into that demographic insignificance in the Middle East that is the fate of their communities in modern times.[23]

[21] See Sidney H. Griffith, "'Melkites,' 'Jacobites,' and the Christological Controversies in Arabic in Third/Ninth-Century Syria," in *Syrian Christians under Islam: The First Thousand Years*, ed. David Thomas, 9–55 (Leiden: Brill, 2001).

[22] See in this connection, Olivia Remie Constable, *Housing the Stranger in the Mediterranean World: Lodging, Trade, and Travel in Late Antiquity and the Middle Ages* (Cambridge: Cambridge University Press, 2003), esp., "Colonies before Colonialism: Western Christian Trade and the Evolution of the *fondaco*," 107–57.

[23] See Valognes, *Vie et mort des chrétiens d'orient*; Andrea Pacini, ed., *Christian Communities in the Arab Middle East: The Challenge of the Future* (New York: Oxford University Press, 1998).

Christians under Muslim Rule

The history of Christians under Muslim rule is a history of continuous, if gradual, diminishment; over the centuries the numbers declined from a substantial majority of the population in many places in the conquered territories in the times before the Crusades, to significant minorities in most of the Islamic world by Ottoman times. It is hard to pinpoint the proximate causes of this gradual Christian diminishment, beyond the natural attrition that the attractiveness of a new religious allegiance would have held out to socially, upwardly mobile individuals in the subject, Christian communities. One factor was certainly the social condition of Christians under Muslim rule. For not only did the Muslims rule, and their Arabic language become the medium of public discourse, but also the public space, the cityscape, the landscape, and the public institutions all conspired to display the public culture of Islam in its formative period.[24] The situation was evocatively described by the late Oxford historian, Albert Hourani:

> By the third and fourth Islamic centuries (the ninth or tenth century AD) something which was recognizably an "Islamic World" had emerged. A traveler around the world would have been able to tell, by what he saw and heard, whether a land was ruled and peopled by Muslims. . . . By the tenth century, then, men and women in the Near East and the Maghrib lived in a universe which was defined in terms of Islam. . . . Time was marked by the five daily prayers, the weekly sermon in the Mosque, the annual fast in the month of Ramadan and the pilgrimage to Mecca, and the Muslim calendar.[25]

Already in the first third of the eighth Christian century, in the time of the caliph ʿAbd al-Malik (685–707), Muslim authorities had begun definitively and symbolically to appropriate the Arab-occupied territories outside of Arabia for the new political reality in the world, the burgeoning Islamic commonwealth. From the religious perspective, the program for the display of Islam had two principal features. Positively, there were the efforts in stone, mortar, and coinage to declare everywhere the Islamic *shahādah*, the testimony of faith in one God and His messenger Muḥammad, throughout the land; negatively, there was the correlative campaign to erase the public symbols of Christianity, especially the previously ubiquitous sign of the cross. Positively, the most dramatic enactment was

[24] See Jonathan P. Berkey, *The Formation of Islam: Religion and Society in the Near East, 600–1800* (Cambridge: Cambridge University Press, 2003); Patricia Crone, *God's Rule: Government and Islam* (New York: Columbia University Press, 2004).

[25] Albert Hourani, *A History of the Arab Peoples* (New York: Warner Books, 1992), 54–57.

the building of the caliph ʿAbd al-Malik's monument to Islam in Jerusalem, the Dome of the Rock, with its explicitly anti-Christian inscriptions, taken substantially from the Qurʾān.[26] But perhaps the policy with the most far-reaching subsequent effects was the caliph ʿUmar ibn ʿAbd al-ʿAzīz's (717–720) program for promoting the equality of all Muslims, be they Arab conquerors or new converts to Islam.[27] This policy would in due course become a plank in the political platform of the movement that by the middle of the eighth century brought about the ʿAbbasid revolution and ushered in the era of the growth and development of the classical culture of the Islamic world. Socially speaking, these developments had their effects among the Christians living under the caliphs' rule; they may well have made conversion to Islam a more attractive option than heretofore, especially among the socially more upwardly mobile Christian families. They certainly made the Muslim authorities more attentive to the development of policies for regulating the social lives of Jews, Christians, and other non-Muslims living within the Muslim polity.

Earlier mention was made of the special poll tax (*al-jizyah*), which according to the Qurʾān is to be demanded of the "People of the Book" living among the Muslims, and of the appropriately submissive, low social profile Christians should assume in paying it (9:29). Historically, after the conquest and the consolidation of Islamic rule in the conquered territories, over a period of time a legal instrument known as the Covenant of ʿUmar gradually came into being to govern this low social profile expected of the Christians, Jews, and others who paid the tax. The stipulations came originally from the treaties concluded between the Muslims and the cities and garrisons they conquered in the seventh century in the time of the second caliph, ʿUmar I (r. 634–644), hence the name of the compilation of these and later stipulations, the Covenant of ʿUmar.[28] Over time, other considerations dictated a more ideal approach to the matter, and by the middle of the ninth century, when the Covenant seems to have reached its classical form, legal scholars had elaborated several theoretical schemes for

[26] See the discussion of these matters in Sidney H. Griffith, "Images, Islam, and Christian Icons: A Moment in the Christian/Muslim Encounter in Early Islamic Times," in *La Syrie de Byzance à l'Islam VIIe–VIIe siècles*, ed. P. Canivet and J.-P. Rey-Coquais, 121–38, Actes du Colloque International Lyon-Maison de l'Orient Mediterranéen, Paris—Institut du Monde Arabe, September 11–15, 1990 (Damascus: Institut Français de Damas, 1992). See also Fowden, *Empire to Commonwealth.*

[27] See Daniel C. Dennett, *Conversion and the Poll Tax in Early Islam* (Cambridge, MA: Harvard University Press, 1950).

[28] See A. S. Tritton, *The Caliphs and Their Non-Muslim Subjects: A Critical Study of the Covenant of ʿUmar* (London: Oxford University Press, 1930); Antoine Fattal, *Le statut légal des non-musulmans en pays d'Islam* (Beirut: Imprimerie Catholique, 1958); Yohanan Friedmann, *Tolerance and Coercion in Islam: Interfaith Relations in the Muslim Tradition* (Cambridge: Cambridge University Press, 2003).

the governance of non-Muslims in Islamic society, some of which included a whole series of stipulated civic and personal disabilities thought to be appropriate to the status of those who by then were being called the *dhimmī* populations.[29]

Classically, the tax (*al-jizyah*) came to be considered the price to be paid by the "People of the Book" for the special "protection" or "covenant of protection" (*adh-dhimmah*) the Islamic government would then assume for them. It was thought of as a kind of answerability, even responsibility for dependent persons on the part of the government, not without a note of dispraise in the verbal root of the Arabic word, which basically means "to affix blame" or "to find fault." Persons in this situation are then described by the Arabic adjective *dhimmī*, meaning someone under the protection and responsibility of the Islamic government. In modern discourse on the subject, the neologism *dhimmitude* has come to express this theoretical, social condition of Jews, Christians, and others under Muslim rule.[30] In classical Islamic times the *dhimmī* populations were to be governed through the offices of their own leaders, who were then held responsible for both the taxes and the good behavior of those under their care. In later Ottoman times, this arrangement came to be called the *millet* system, a term frequently used for it by modern scholars.[31]

There is no doubt then that in view of the stipulations of the Covenant of ʿUmar the *dhimmī* populations of Christians in the Islamic world were what we would now call "second class citizens," if the term "citizen" can even be meaningfully used of people whose presence in the body politic is merely tolerated. The legal disabilities that governed their lives required subservience, often accompanied by prescriptions to wear distinctive clothing and to cease from the public display of their religion, and, of course, to refrain from inviting converts from among the Muslims. Christian wealth, buildings, institutions, and properties were often subject to seizure.

[29] See the important study of Milka Levy-Rubin, "*Shurūṭ ʿUmar* and Its Alternatives: The Legal Debate on the Status of the *Dhimmīs*," *Jerusalem Studies in Arabic and Islam* 30 (2005): 170–206.

[30] In English the originally French neologism has been popularized in the work of Bat Yeʾor, *The Decline of Eastern Christianity under Islam: From Jihad to Dhimmitude; Seventh–Twentieth Century* (Madison, NJ: Fairleigh Dickinson University Press, 1996); Yeʾor, *Islam and Dhimmitude: Where Civilizations Collide* (Madison, NJ: Fairleigh Dickinson University Press, 2002).

[31] See C. E. Bosworth, "The 'Protected Peoples' (Christians and Jews) in Medieval Egypt and Syria," *Bulletin of the John Rylands University Library of Manchester* 62 (1979): 11–36; Bosworth, "The Concept of *dhimma* in Early Islam," in *Christians and Jews in the Ottoman Empire: The Functioning of a Plural Society*, 2 vols., ed. B. Braude and B. Lewis, 1: 37–51 (New York: Holmes and Meier, 1982); Mahmoud Ayoub, "Dhimmah in Qurʾan and Hadith," *Arab Studies Quarterly* 5 (1983): 172–82. See also M. O. H. Ursinus, "Millet," in *The Encyclopaedia of Islam: New Edition*, ed. C. E. Bosworth et al., 7: 61–64 (Leiden: Brill, 1993).

As a consequence, over the course of time, the number of bishoprics, churches, monasteries, and schools gradually decreased, having fallen victim to the very conditions of the official establishment of Islam. These circumstances of a necessity put *dhimmī* groups such as the Christian communities at risk; in spite of their numbers they became sociological minorities, subaltern populations subject to discrimination, disability, and at times even persecution.[32] In response, their disadvantaged situation in life under Muslim rule inevitably elicited from the subject Christians both a discourse of accommodation and a discourse of resistance.[33] On the one hand they attempted to compose a philosophical or religious discourse in Arabic for the sake of a clearer and more effective, apologetic statement of their Christian faith in their Islamic circumstances, and on the other hand they also produced a Christian Arabic literature of resistance and of martyrdom, with a more polemical intent. These genres of writing will all be discussed in some detail in the following chapters.

Dhimmitude

Dhimmitude brought hardship and eventual demographic diminution, but it also for a time brought with it a new cultural opportunity for the articulation and defense of Christianity in Arabic, within the world of Islam. Materially speaking, Christians in many Muslim communities before the time of the Crusades and the Mongol invasions of the thirteenth century found and exploited positions in various professions and even in the civil service of the Islamic government. Some Christians, like some Jews in the same circumstances, became successful physicians, merchants, scribes, and chancery officials.[34] Some Christians became active in intellectual enterprises, like the Graeco-Arabic translation movement in Baghdad from the eighth to the tenth centuries, which would play such an important role in the growth and development of Muslim intellectual life.[35] Some Christians

[32] See Youssef Courbage and Philippe Fargues, *Christians and Jews under Islam*, trans. Judy Mabro (London and New York: I. B. Tauris, 1997).

[33] The same phenomenon, mutatis mutandis, appeared among the Jews and even the Zoroastrians. See, e.g., the studies included in Norman Golb, ed., *Judeo-Arabic Studies: Proceedings of the Founding Conference of the Society for Judaeo-Arabic Studies*, Studies in Muslim-Jewish Relations, 3 (Amsterdam: Harwood Academic Publishers, 1997), esp. Sarah Stroumsa, "Jewish Polemics against Islam and Christianity in the Light of Judaeo-Arabic Texts," 241–50; Jamsheed K. Choksy, *Conflict and Cooperation: Zoroastrian Subalterns and Muslim Elites in Medieval Iranian Society* (New York: Columbia University Press, 1997).

[34] See Bernard Lewis, *The Jews of Islam* (Princeton, NJ: Princeton University Press, 1984).

[35] See Dimitri Gutas, *Greek Thought, Arabic Culture: The Graeco-Arabic Translation Movement in Baghdad and Early ʿAbbāsid Society (2nd–4th/8th–10th Centuries)* (London: Routledge, 1998).

even became philosophers in their own right who would then be the teachers of Muslims, who in due course would themselves become world-class philosophers whose names and works are to this day discussed in the histories of philosophy and whose ideas are taken seriously in ongoing philosophical discourse. Al-Farabī (870–950), Ibn Sīnā/Avicenna (980–1037), and Ibn Rushd/Averroes (1126–1198) are the Muslim philosophers with the most immediate name recognition in this connection, but they were far from being the only ones.[36] And, of course, their accomplishments sparked yet another translation movement in the eleventh and twelfth centuries, this time in the Islamo-Christian west, in places like Bologna, Toledo, and Barcelona, where eager minds translated philosophical texts from Arabic into Latin and provided the impetus for the flowering of scholastic philosophy and theology in the works of Thomas Aquinas, Bonaventure, and Duns Scotus, through the earlier achievements of scholars such as Abelard and Albert the Great.[37]

But beyond unalloyed philosophy, which for all its intellectual importance never actually took a commanding position in Islamic thought, and from the perspective of the contents of Arabic texts surviving from the early Islamic period, it is in the realm of what one might call intertextual or interreligious thinking and writing, or even comparative theology and exegesis, that for our present purposes the most interesting material is to be found in the works of Jewish, Christian, and Muslim authors. For in what has been called "the sectarian milieu"[38] of the early Islamic period, Muslim, Christian, and Jewish thinkers were all struggling to present their distinctive religious claims in relationship to the challenges posed by one another, and often in what one can only call a "Judaizing," "Christianizing," or "Islamicizing" discourse, depending on the individual case. For example, in the realm of scriptural exegesis, early Muslim commentators can be seen simultaneously to be engaged in "Biblicizing" their presentations of Qur'ānic figures or elements from the biography of the prophet Muḥammad, while at the same time they are "Islamicizing" their accounts of bib-

[36] See Majid Fakhry, *A History of Islamic Philosophy*, 3rd ed. (New York: Columbia University Press, 2004).

[37] See Fernand van Steenberghen, *Aristotle in the West: The Origins of Latin Aristotelianism*, trans. Leonard Johnston (New York: Humanities Press, 1970); Charles Burnett, "The Translating Activity in Medieval Spain," in *The Legacy of Muslim Spain*, 2 vols., ed. Salma Khadra Jayyusi, 2: 1036–58 (Leiden: Brill, 1994); Burnett, "Arabic into Latin: The Reception of Arabic Philosophy into Western Europe," in *The Cambridge Companion to Arabic Philosophy*, ed. Peter Adamson and Richard C. Taylor, 370–404 (Cambridge: Cambridge University Press, 2005); Jean Jolivet, *La théologie et les arabes* (Paris: Cerf, 2002).

[38] See John E. Wansbrough, *The Sectarian Milieu: Content and Composition of Islamic Salvation History* (Oxford: Oxford University Press, 1978).

lical themes or personae. Sometimes modern researchers can identify earlier or even contemporary Jewish or Christian texts featuring the same traditions with which the Muslim scholars were working in their own distinctive way.[39]

Similarly, in the origins and full flowering of the distinctively Islamic *ʿilm al-kalām*, or reasoned discourse on important themes in the religious worldview, be it of the Muʿtazilite or Asharite traditions, one can often discern not only formal, methodological points of comparison with the discourse of earlier or contemporary Christian thinkers, in Greek, Syriac, or even Arabic texts, but also thematic continuities.[40] Of course, in the end the Islamic "take" on these common religious themes and exegetical traditions was distinctively Islamic, to the degree that they cannot truthfully be called influences or borrowings. Rather, they were parallel exercises in wrestling with the same conceptual problems, within the same or comparable scriptural horizons, with which earlier traditions had wrestled. There were also issues in the current discourse of the same contemporary, rival communities whose positions had to be bested, or even falsified, in the Muslim effort to commend to contemporaries the verisimilitude of, in this instance, a distinctively Islamic doctrine.[41]

Conversely, within the social context and time frame of these very developments in early Islamic thought, which were undertaken not in Arabia but in the Islamic centers of the conquered territories, where the "People of the Book" with their well-developed intellectual traditions were still very much in the demographic majority, the way was opened for a comparable discourse of opportunity for both Jewish and Christian theology and apologetics, newly under siege by challenging Muslims. For, beginning in the second half of the eighth century in Palestine, continuing into the ninth century in the rest of Syria and in Mesopotamia, and finally getting under way in the tenth century in Egypt, Christians in the world of Islam eventually came to adopt Arabic not only as the lingua franca of daily life in the caliphate, but even as an ecclesiastical language.[42] Of course, by this time the religious lexicon in Arabic had already been co-opted by Islam, and unlike the earlier situation in pre-Islamic Arabia, the newly Arabic-speaking Jews and Christians outside of Arabia in the ninth and tenth centuries in

[39] See Hava Lazarus-Yafeh, *Intertwined Worlds: Medieval Islam and Bible Criticism* (Princeton, NJ: Princeton University Press, 1992).

[40] See, e.g., the classic study by C. H. Becker, "Christliche Polemik und islamische Dogmenbildung," *Zeitschrift für Assyriologie* 25 (1911): 175–95.

[41] See the masterful survey by Josef Van Ess, *Theologie und Gesellschaft im 2. und 3. Jahrhundert Hidschra*, 6 vols. (Berlin: De Gruyter, 1991–97).

[42] See Sidney H. Griffith, "From Aramaic to Arabic"; Griffith, "The Monks of Palestine and the Growth of Christian Literature in Arabic," *The Muslim World* 78 (1988): 1–28.

the conquered territories were faced with the imperative of translating their teachings into and commending their faith in a religious vocabulary that had now become suffused with explicitly Islamic connotations, insinuated there in no small part by the Qurʾān's and the Islamic tradition's earlier critique of Jewish and Christian beliefs and practices. In other words, the Jews and Christians living in the Islamic world were faced with the apologetic necessity, one might also call it an opportunity, both for Islamicizing, so to speak, the Arabic expression of their Jewish and Christian teachings and for both Judaizing and Christianizing the current Islamic discourse devoted to reasoned argumentation (*ʿilm al-kalām*) in defense of the true religion. Christian writers in Arabic who exercised this double option would have had two audiences in mind, the first of them being their own Arabic-speaking fellow Christians, whose conversion to Islam they would have hoped to forestall. Their second audience was the Muslim, and eventually the Jewish, scholars with whom they were often engaged in controversy, and whom they would have hoped to persuade of the reasonableness, if not of the truth, of Christian doctrines in spite of their apparent rejection in Jewish sources, in the Qurʾān, and in early Islamic tradition.

Christian Responses to Challenge

Historically, whenever Christians have come into new cultural circumstances it has been their constant practice to translate their scriptures and other ecclesiastical books into a new target language and to proclaim the Gospel message in the idiom and thought patterns of their new circumstances. It was no different in this respect when the Christian communities of the Middle East and Spain faced the multiple challenges of life under Muslim rule in the years when Arabic became the language of public life in the caliphate. But there was this one big difference: this was the first time, and historically so far the only time, when Christians have been faced with the necessity of translating, defending, and commending their religion in a new language and in new cultural circumstances, still within the borders of their own conquered homelands, where in due course, over a period of centuries, most Christians eventually either emigrated or converted to another religion, in this instance Islam. Only in Spain, and then only amid great social upheavals and multiple historical injustices, was the situation eventually reversed.

This historically unique set of circumstances helps to explain why it came about, after the Christians began to decline precipitously in numbers in the Islamic world after the time of the Crusades and the Mongol invasions of the thirteenth century, when Muslim anti-Christian policies became more pronounced under the influence of rigorously strict constructionists of the

Covenant of ʿUmar like Ibn Taymiyya (1263–1328),[43] that many Christians lost interest in renewing the Arabic expression of their faith. They continued to use the Arabic language of course, and to copy the texts produced in earlier times, as they do to this very day. But after the thirteenth century the creative genius for borrowing the cultural and linguistic idiom of the Muslim Arabs for the proclamation and defense of Christianity seems to have waned. In some places, such as among the Coptic Orthodox of Egypt, a certain resentment of the Islamic tone of the traditional language of Christian theology in Arabic has come about in more recent times. More and more, especially in the Diaspora communities, the energies of Christian scholars have turned away from the Medieval, Arabic expressions of their theologies, with their accompanying Islamic nuances, to the study of the patristic and liturgical sources of their several confessions, in the original languages of those sources.[44] Some communities, such as the Armenians and the Ethiopians, never made any significant move to Arabic in the first place, having all along preferred to preserve their own traditions in their own ancestral languages, albeit with many texts translated from pre-Islamic, Syriac sources. Their histories are beyond the purview of the present study.

For a time, from the late eighth century to the twelfth century, Christians in the Arabic-speaking world of the Muslims did produce an impressive archive of translations and original compositions in Arabic that amounted to a new expression of Christian faith in new, religiously challenging circumstances. It truly had within it the seeds of a new theological development, perhaps even in the manner described by John Henry Newman in his nineteenth-century classic *The Development of Christian Doctrine*. Ultimately, however, this new set of theological efforts fell short of the goal and eventually they disappeared into history, hardly to be remembered today except by those learned in the lore of the Oriental Christian communities. The question before us now is why should we in the western world in the first decade of the twenty-first century be interested in these Christian Arabic texts from the early Middle Ages?

The answer to this question is twofold. In the first place, from a strictly scholarly point of view, it has become clear that for a fuller picture of the growth and development of Islam in its early years, it is imperative to consider not only Islamic sources, often composed many years after the events they describe, but also to see it from the perspective of those non-Muslims

[43] See Thomas Michel, *A Muslim Theologian's Response to Christianity: Ibn Taymiyya's al-Jawāb al-Ṣaḥīḥ* (Delmar, NY: Caravan Books, 1984). See also Paul L. Heck, "*Jihād* Revisited," *Journal of Religious Ethics* 32 (2004): 95–128.

[44] See, e.g., Mark N. Swanson, "Are Hypostases Attributes? An Investigation into the Modern Egyptian Christian Appropriation of the Medieval Arabic Apologetic Heritage," *Parole de l'Orient* 16 (1990–91): 239–50.

who witnessed Islam's rise in the world and wrestled with its challenges in contemporary texts that are still accessible to us.[45] Second, in the world of the twenty-first century, Muslims are no longer just "over there," in another world from the one inhabited by western Christians and Jews. They are here among us, our neighbors, friends, co-workers and cobelievers in the one God, creator of all that is, with whom we are engaged on a daily basis both at home and abroad, both in struggle and in dialogue. Surely then we have much usefully to learn from the study of the works of the Jews and Christians who first seriously engaged the Muslims in their own world so long ago, and in their own language of faith, long before the intervening times of colonialism and imperialism, with their accompanying mutual invective and recrimination, the rhetoric of which to this day characterizes and distorts many western views of the challenge of Islam.

The following chapters will in turn explore the first Christian responses to Islam, the birth of Christian theology in Arabic, the hopes on the part of some Christians who lived in the Islamic world that the cultivation of a philosophical way of life would provide a space for a harmonious *convivencia* between Jews, Christians, and Muslims. There will also be some discussion of how Christian self-definition continued to develop even in the world of Islam. The studies are put forward with the hope that today Jews, Christians, and Muslims might be inspired to undertake the unlikely task of turning the historical clash of theologies between Islam, Christianity, and Judaism into an exercise in comparative theology, which will hopefully be more successful in promoting a mutually tolerant interreligious dialogue than has proved possible heretofore.[46]

[45] For the very beginnings of Islamic history, an invaluable survey of early, non-Islamic sources is provided in Robert Hoyland, *Seeing Islam as Others Saw It: A Survey and Evaluation of Christian, Jewish, and Zoroastrian Writings on Early Islam*, Studies in Late Antiquity and Early Islam, 13 (Princeton, NJ: Darwin Press, 1997).

[46] In this connection, see the interesting collection of studies in Barbara Roggema et al., eds., *The Three Rings: Textual Studies in the Historical Trialogue of Judaism, Christianity, and Islam* (Leuven, Belgium: Peeters, 2005).

II

APOCALYPSE AND THE ARABS

THE FIRST CHRISTIAN RESPONSES TO THE CHALLENGE OF ISLAM

First Notices

The first notices in texts written by Christians in the Roman and Persian territories neighboring Arabia that refer to incursions of marauding Arabs in the years immediately following the death of Muḥammad in the year 632 show little or no awareness that these raids were part of the larger military campaign that would in due course be recognized as the Islamic conquest. Rather, the writers of the few texts from the seventh century we have in hand that refer to these events seem initially to have considered the depredations we now recognize as constituting the first phase of the conquest as little more than incursions by Arab tribesmen from the desert, of the sort with which they were long familiar whenever the rule of the Roman or Persian emperors was weak in the lands bordering the deserts of Arabia.[1] And as a matter of fact, in the fateful decade of the 630s imperial control in the area could not have been weaker; both Rome and Persia were still reeling from the debilitating effects of their decades-long war (609–28), a struggle that had just concluded with the Roman emperor Heraclius's (r. 610–41) signal victory over the Persians in the year 628.[2] Less than a decade later, at the battle of the Yarmuk in Syria in 636, where the invading Arabs defeated the Roman army, and at the battle of Qadisiyya just west of the Euphrates in what is now Iraq in 637, where they defeated the Persian army, symbolically, as later chroniclers would think of it, the Arab forces won victories that in times to come would be seen to have marked the beginning of the demise of both Roman and Persian rule for good in the territories stretching east from the eastern shore of the

[1] See Walter E. Kaegi, "Initial Byzantine Reactions to the Arab Invasions," *Church History* 10 (1969): 139–49. See also some of the most pertinent texts from beyond Byzantium in Andrew Palmer, ed., *The Seventh Century in the West-Syrian Chronicles*, Translated Texts for Historians, vol. 15 (Liverpool: Liverpool University Press, 1993).

[2] See Geoffrey Regan, *First Crusader: Byzantium's Holy Wars* (Stroud, UK: Sutton, 2001); Walter E. Kaegi, *Heraclius, Emperor of Byzantium* (Cambridge: Cambridge University Press, 2003).

Mediterranean.[3] In a reoriented configuration, these very regions were destined to become the heartland of a newly inaugurated "Islamic empire," and in due course the spiritual homeland of an "Islamic commonwealth" of nations in the centuries to come.[4]

In the wake of the first stunning military exploits, the major centers of Christian life in the East came quickly one by one under the hegemony of the invading Arabs: first Damascus (635), Jerusalem (637),[5] and Antioch (637); and then Edessa in Syria (640), Alexandria in Egypt (642), and Seleucia/Ctesiphon, the capital of Sasanid Persia, just beyond the Tigris (645). So within just a dozen years after the death of Muḥammad, three of the five patriarchates of the Roman Christians, plus the Persian seat of the *catholicos* of the "Church of the East," had come under the rule of the Arabian prophet's enthusiastic followers.

The Christian writers who first took notice of the Bedouin invasions in the 630s registered their alarm at the approach of the Arabs, whom they as often as not called "Saracens," "Hagarenes," or "Ishmaelites,"[6] and from the beginning they seem to have been aware of the fact that novel religious motivations inspired the invaders. For example, in a text written in Greek by a recently converted Palestinian Jew, probably in the year 634, the author tells of the incursions of the Arabs and of a "false prophet" who had appeared among them, and of the inquiries that were made about him. The text reports a question put to a learned Jew, "What can you tell me

[3] See Fred M. Donner, *The Early Islamic Conquests* (Princeton, NJ: Princeton University Press, 1981); Walter E. Kaegi, *Byzantium and the Early Islamic Conquests* (Cambridge: Cambridge University Press, 1992).

[4] On the significance of these terms, see Garth Fowden, *Empire to Commonwealth: Consequences of Monotheism in Late Antiquity* (Princeton, NJ: Princeton University Press, 1991); Hugh Kennedy, "The Decline and Fall of the First Muslim Empire," *Der Islam* 81 (2004): 3–29.

[5] On the various dates proposed for the Arab occupation of Jerusalem, see Robert G. Hoyland, *Seeing Islam as Others Saw It: A Survey and Evaluation of Christian, Jewish, and Zoroastrian Writings on Early Islam*, Studies in Late Antiquity and Early Islam, 13 (Princeton, NJ: Darwin Press, 1997), 64, n. 31.

[6] These terms had long been used by Christian writers from the early Christian period onward to refer somewhat fearfully to the Bedouin Arab tribesmen of the desert; in Islamic times they were transferred to the Muslims. The etymology and basic sense of the term "Saracen" is disputed. The terms "Hagarene" and "Ishmaelite" refer respectively to Abraham's concubine Hagar and their son Ishmael (Genesis 16), conceived as the biblical ancestors of the Bedouin Arabs. The scripture says of the infant Ishmael, "He shall be a wild ass of a man, his hand against every man and every man's hand against him; and he shall dwell over against all his kinsmen" (Genesis 16:12). Of the grown Ishmael, the text says, "God was with the lad, and he grew up; he lived in the desert and became an expert with the bow" (Genesis 21:20). In the Islamic context, the religious sense of rejection implied in the terms as they were used by Christians to refer to Muslims is heightened by allusion to St. Paul's comments about Hagar and Ishmael, in his epistle to the Galatians 4:21–31: "Hagar is Mount Sinai in Arabia" (v. 25), and "Cast out the slave and her son" (v. 30).

about the prophet who has appeared with the Saracens?" To which he replied, "He is false, for the prophets do not come armed with a sword," and the learned man avers that the prophet may in fact be the Antichrist. Then, according to the text, the questioner made further inquiries and he "heard from those who had met him that there was no truth to be found in the so-called prophet, only the shedding of men's blood. He says also that he has the keys of paradise, which is incredible."[7] This earliest known Jewish Christian polemic against Islam here attributed to Jewish observers, thus voices negative themes, which will reappear constantly in later Christian texts, that evaluate the religion of the Arabs from a Christian point of view: bloodshed, Antichrist, the sensual nature of paradise. The earliest known Christian reference to Muḥammad by name occurs in a Syriac chronicle composed around the year 640, where the text mentions "a battle between the Romans and the Arabs of Muḥammad in Palestine twelve miles east of Gaza" in the year 634.[8]

Of particular interest for our present purposes are texts that refer to the Arab occupation of Jerusalem and the establishment of a Muslim place of prayer on the Temple Mount. As we shall see, from the very beginning of the confrontation between the Muslims and the Christians outside of Arabia, Jerusalem quickly became the symbolic location of their rival statements of scriptural faith. And it began already at the conquest, in the time of Patriarch Sophronius of Jerusalem (d. ca. 639) and Caliph ʿUmar I (r. 634–44), who quickly became the literary figures of record in both the Christian and the Muslim narratives of the surrender of Jerusalem.[9]

In Patriarch Sophronius's sermons on holy days like Christmas and the Epiphany in the years between 634 and 637 we find his remarks about those whom he took to be marauding Arabs. Giving voice to a theme that would often occur in Christian homilies of the period, already in his synodical letter on the occasion of taking possession of his see the patriarch had spoken of the fear of the Saracens, "who, on account of our sins, have now risen up against us unexpectedly and ravage all with cruel and feral design, with impious and godless audacity."[10] But it is in his sermon on the Epiphany, probably in the year 636, that Sophronius gave a description of

[7] Quoted from the *Doctrina Jacobi Nuperbaptizati*, as translated in Hoyland, *Seeing Islam as Others Saw It*, 57. For further discussion of this text, see David M. Olster, *Roman Defeat, Christian Response, and the Literary Construction of the Jew* (Philadelphia: University of Pennsylvania Press, 1994), esp. 158–79.

[8] Hoyland, *Seeing Islam as Others Saw It*, 120. On this chronicle, see Palmer, *The Seventh Century*, 5–24.

[9] See Christoph von Schönborn, *Sophrone de Jérusalem: Vie monastique et confession dogmatique* (Paris: Beauchesne, 1972); Heribert Busse, "ʿOmar b. al-Ḫaṭṭāb in Jerusalem," *Jerusalem Studies in Arabic and Islam* 5 (1984): 73–119; Busse, "ʿOmar's Image as the Conqueror of Jerusalem," *Jerusalem Studies in Arabic and Islam* 8 (1986): 149–68.

[10] Hoyland, *Seeing Islam as Others Saw It*, 69.

events that are more easily recognizable as campaigns in the Jerusalem area in service of the Islamic conquest. And once again he spoke of the sins of the Christians as having brought on the depredations. He said,

> That is why the vengeful and God-hating Saracens, the abomination of desolation clearly foretold to us by the prophets, overrun the places which are not allowed to them, plunder cities, devastate fields, burn down villages, set on fire the holy churches, overturn the sacred monasteries, oppose the Byzantine armies arrayed against them, and in fighting raise up the trophies [of war] and add victory to victory. Moreover, they are raised up more and more against us and increase their blasphemy of Christ and the church, and utter wicked blasphemies against God.[11]

One recognizes in these last remarks the patriarch's incensed reaction to what he must by then have come to recognize as a rival religious critique of Christian faith and practice. In the end, of course, the Muslim forces took the city of Jerusalem in the year 637, and in due course they established a mosque there, most probably on the Temple Mount.[12] There is a Christian account of the event appended to the original text of a book called *The Spiritual Meadow* (*Pratum spirituale*), in its Georgian version, written years previously by Patriarch Sophronius's friend John Moschus (d. 619 or 634). The author of this additional passage wrote:

> The godless Saracens entered the holy city of Christ our Lord, Jerusalem, with the permission of God and in punishment for our negligence, which is considerable, and immediately proceeded in haste to the place which is called the Capitol.[13] They took with them men, some by force, others by their own will, in order to clean that place and to build that cursed thing, intended for their prayer and which they call a mosque.[14]

[11] Quoted in the translation of Hoyland, *Seeing Islam as Others Saw It*, 73.

[12] See Heribert Busse, "Zur Geschichte und Deutung der frühislamischen *Ḥaram*bauten in Jerusalem," *Zeitschrift des deutschen Palästina-Vereins* 107 (1991): 144–54; Busse, "Die ʿUmar-Moschee im östlichen Atrium der Grabeskirche," *Zeitschrift des deutschen Palästina-Vereins* 109 (1993): 73–82.

[13] There is some difference of opinion among modern scholars about the location of "the Capitol." One scholar argues that at first it was on the site of the Holy Sepulchre and only later was it thought to have been on the Temple Mount. See Jerome Murphy-O'Connor, "The Location of the Capitol in Aelia Capitolina," *Revue Biblique* 101 (1994): 407–15. Arguably, *The Spiritual Meadow* had the Temple Mount in mind.

[14] Hoyland, *Seeing Islam as Others Saw It*, 63. See also Bernard Flusin, "L'esplanade du temple a l'arrivée des arabes, d'après deux récits byzantins," in *Bayt al-Maqdis: ʿAbd al-Malik's Jerusalem*, part 1, ed. Julian Raby and Jeremy Johns, 17–31, esp. 17–22 (Oxford: Oxford University Press, 1992).

Christian legend says of the surrender of Jerusalem to the Muslims that Patriarch Sophronius insisted on handing over the city only to the Arab "king," the caliph ʿUmar, in person. Islamic legend in its turn presents ʿUmar's entry into Jerusalem as a humbly solemn affair, in which the pious Muslim caliph upstages the haughty Christian patriarch in religious fervor. As the story goes, ʿUmar refused the patriarch's invitation to pray in the church of the Anastasis/Holy Sepulchre lest the Muslims later expropriate it. Rather, he repairs to the Temple Mount, left abandoned amid ruins by the Christians, and there offers his prayers and leaves instructions for the construction of a mosque, the Mosque of ʿUmar, to mark the Islamic respect for and claim to the Holy City.[15] It seems obvious that these legendary accounts owe much to the later role of Jerusalem in the discourse of Muslims and Christians about the sanctity of the Holy City and its symbolic importance in the relationships between the two communities.

While the city of Jerusalem thus became in the course of time both the site and the symbol par excellence of the confrontation between Christianity and Islam from the very beginnings of Islamic rule outside of Arabia, a symbolism that would be enhanced not only in the accruing legends of later times but even in the architecture of the Islamic appropriation of the Holy City in the late seventh century, in other places the conquest sometimes received what modern scholars are often tempted to interpret as mixed reviews, if not positive commendations in Syriac, Coptic, or Armenian Christian sources. In Syria, for example, while most texts from the seventh century speak of the depredations of the Arabs and of the destruction and mayhem they wrought, some are seen to put a happier construction on events. The patriarch of the Church of the East, for example, Ishoʿyabh III (d. 659), wrote a letter not long after the year 637 in which the following passage occurs, often, as here, quoted out of context. "As for the Arabs, to whom God has at this time given rule over the world, you know well how they act towards us. Not only do they not oppose Christianity, but they praise our faith, honor the priests and saints of our Lord, and give aid to the churches and monasteries."[16]

Similarly, Coptic or Jacobite Syriac, texts are sometimes quoted by modern historians, in which the authors refer to the relief from heavy Byzantine taxes or the escape from religious persecution their communities are alleged to have achieved as a result of the Arab conquests. However, in their contexts, as in the case of the passage just quoted from Patriarch Ishoʿyabh's letter, closer inspection reveals that the writers were not so much

[15] For a quick résumé of these legends and a caveat regarding their verisimilitude, see Oleg Grabar, *The Shape of the Holy: Early Islamic Jerusalem* (Princeton, NJ: Princeton University Press, 1996), 46–49 and 198, n. 64.

[16] Quoted from Hoyland, *Islam as Others Saw It*, 181.

voicing a welcome for what we recognize in hindsight as the onset of the Islamic conquest, as they were invidiously comparing even Arab rule, which they disdained, to the oppressive conduct of their previous governors. They viewed their erstwhile Roman rulers as unorthodox Christians or, as in the case of Ishoʿyabh, their Persian rulers as supporters of their Christian rivals. In other words, already at the time of the Arab conquest the theme of intra-Christian, rivalry and intercommunal polemic found its way into the discourse of the Christian response to Islam.[17] Otherwise, the Christians of all communities unanimously regarded the conquest as a disaster, and when they were not blaming it on their own sinfulness they were citing the sins of their Christian adversaries, whom they regarded as heretics, as the proximate cause of the conquest and of the death and destruction it brought in its wake.[18]

First Responses

As the seventh century came to an end, and the Arab invaders showed no signs of returning to the desert as they had done so many times in the past, Christian writers began to pay more attention to the religious ideas of the conquering tribesmen. It was not long before the first, piecemeal Christian religious and theological assessments of what the Arabs believed began to appear. At first the references to what we recognize as Islamic ideas are oblique, and they are mentioned by way of contrast. For example, in the 690s a monk in the monastic communities of Sinai, Anastasios of Sinai (d. ca. 700) by name, who was a staunch supporter of the teachings of the six councils of Byzantine orthodoxy, wrote a book in Greek called *Hodēgos* (*The Guide*). His purpose was to support the teachings of the councils against those whom he regarded as "Monophysites," and particularly against the teachings to be found in the works of Severus of Antioch (ca. 465–538). In the course of his work he refers a number of times to what he calls the "false notions of the Arabs," notions the reader easily recognizes as Islamic ideas, for Anastasios makes no explicit reference to Muḥammad, the Qurʾān, or to Islam.[19]

[17] For the Syriac-speaking milieu, see Michael G. Morony, *Iraq after the Muslim Conquest* (Princeton, NJ: Princeton University Press, 1984), esp. 332–83; and the author's "History and Identity in the Syrian Churches," in *Redefining Christian Identity: Cultural Interaction in the Middle East since the Rise of Islam*, ed. J. J. van Ginkel et al., 1–33, Orientalia Lovaniensia Analecta, 134 (Leuven, Belgium: Peeters, 2005).

[18] See the survey of the immediate reactions of the several Christian communities to the Islamic conquest in Francisco Javier Martínez, "La literatura apocalíptica y las primeras reacciones cristianas a la conquista islámica en Oriente," in *Europa y el Islam*, ed. Gonzalo Anes y Álvarez de Castrillón, esp. 155–81 (Madrid: Real Academia de la Historia, 2003).

[19] See Sidney H. Griffith, "Anastasios of Sinai, the *Hodēgos* and the Muslims," *Greek Orthodox Theological Review* 32 (1987): 341–58.

By way of example, we may briefly examine here just one of the several passages in which Anastasios of Sinai shows his familiarity with Islamic ideas and furnishes evidence that already in his time Christians were engaging in religious controversy with Muslim Arabs. In the preface to the *Hodēgos* Anastasios sets forth his reasons for writing the book. Having already listed ten reasons, he finally offers the following one:

> Because, prior to any discussion at all, we must condemn however many false notions about us the opponent has, as when we set out to converse with Arabs we have first to condemn anyone who says, "Two gods," or anyone who says, "God has carnally begotten a son," or anyone who makes prostration as to God, to any creature whatever, in heaven or on earth. Likewise, in regard to the rest of the heresies, it is necessary first to condemn however many false opinions about the faith they have. For, giving heed to these things, they accept the rest more eagerly.[20]

The first thing to notice in this passage is that religious controversy with Arabs, and its already customary procedure, is put forward as an example of the procedure that Anastasios is proposing to use in his *Hodēgos*. Further, it is clear that what should first be rebutted, in Anastasios's view, are the false notions the opponent already harbors. He gives three examples of such notions, from what his reader is expected easily to recognize as false Arab notions about what Christians believe. On examination it quickly appears that these "notions" about Christian beliefs can all be found in the Qur'ān, in the very terms in which Anastasios mentions them.

Already in the context of *sūrat an-Naḥl* (16), which contains a clear rejection of the polytheism of the pagan Arabs, one finds the explicit injunction: "God said, 'Do not accept two gods. There is but a single God. So, fear me'" (16:51). Then, in the later *sūrat al-Mā'idah* (5), precisely this language is used again to reject what the Qur'ān perceives to be the erroneous core of Christian preaching about Jesus, son of Mary. In the context of 5:109 to 114, where the Qur'ān presents a fairly comprehensive sketch of the Islamic view of Jesus and his mission, and a threat of eternal punishment to any one of Jesus's followers who would later disbelieve (vs. 115), there is the description of a scene in which Jesus stands in judgment before God: "God said, 'O Jesus, son of Mary, did you tell people, "Take me and my mother for two gods instead of God?" '" (vs. 116).

Surely the standard Christian proclamation that Jesus is God, the son of God, and Mary his mother, is the mother of God, would have been sufficient to elicit the Qur'ān's adverse judgment. Whoever among the Arabs who invaded Syria/Palestine, who had heard the Qur'ān proclaimed, would

[20] Karl-Heinz Uthemann, *Anastasii Sinaitae Viae dux*, Corpus Christianorum, Series Graeca, 8 (Leuven, Belgium: University Press, 1981), 9.

certainly have thought, on the basis of *al-Mā'idah* 5:116, that Jesus's disbelieving followers taught that he and his mother were two gods. Accordingly, Anastasios reminds his reader: this is a false notion about Christians that one must condemn before engaging in controversy with Arabs.

The false Arab notion that what Christians believe involves God in the carnal generation of a son also has its roots in the Qur'ān. A constant feature of Muḥammad's reaction against Christian teaching is the phrase, "They say God has taken a son; praised be He. Nay, whatever is in the heavens or on the earth is His, all are subservient to Him" (*al-Baqarah* 2:116; and cf. *an-Nisā'* 4:171). Anastasios's very wording of this false Arab notion, as he would have it, once again ties the rejection of a Christian doctrine in with the Qur'ān's earlier rejection of pagan ideas, as in *al-An'ām* 6:101, where the assumption that God has offspring is explicitly associated with the unacceptable notion that such a proposal would involve God with a female consort: "The Creator of heaven and earth—how does He have offspring? He did not have a female consort. He created everything." Clearly then, in the Qur'ān's view, to say that God has a son, or that Jesus Christ is God's son, would involve God in a twofold impossibility: it posits Mary as God's consort; and Jesus and Mary as two gods instead of God. These are precisely the false notions about what Christians teach that Anastasios says one must clearly anathematize before arguing with Arabs.

In the Qur'ān's view, as is already clear from the passages quoted above, for example, in *al-Baqarah* 2:116, to make a prostration to Jesus, son of Mary as to God, would automatically involve one in the pagan worship of creatures. The Qur'ān's constant admonition is: "The Lord of the heavens and the earth and what is between them, worship Him, and be constant in worshipping Him. Do you know any other worthy of His name?" (*Maryam* 19:65). Accordingly, Anastasios notes that before arguing with Arabs, one must anathematize whoever worships any creature in heaven or on earth. He assumes it is a false notion of the Arabs that Christians are guilty of such misguided worship.

For our purposes, what we have to learn from analyzing this and other passages in Anastasios's *Hodēgos* is both that he, a Greek-speaking Christian in the Sinai in the late seventh century, was aware of the Qur'ānic terms of Muslim religious teaching, and that he was accustomed to having conversations with Muslim Arabs, presumably in Arabic, about ways in which he thinks they are mistaken in what they believe about Christian doctrine.[21] Furthermore, it is interesting to note in passing, and the issue will come up again below when we speak about St. John of Damascus's ideas about Islam, Anastasios obviously thought that it was appropriate to consider

[21] See Griffith, "Anastasios of Sinai."

Islam a kind of Christian heresy, for having spoken of the false notions of the Arabs he went on to say, "Likewise, in regard to the rest of the heresies, it is necessary first to condemn however many false opinions about the faith they have."[22]

Similarly, Syriac writers of the same time period were also aware of problems involving the interactions of Christians and Muslims in religious matters, and they even spoke of instances in which Christians and Muslims shared the same religious ideas. A case in point is provided by passages in the works of the Syrian Orthodox bishop, Jacob of Edessa (d. 708), who wrote canonical legislation about relations between Muslims and Christians, and who spoke about Islamic religious ideas in some of his letters. For example, he stipulated that one need not rebaptize a Christian who became a Muslim and then returned to the profession of Christianity, and that it is legitimate to offer the holy Eucharist to a woman who is married to a Muslim and who threatens to apostatize otherwise.[23]

The most striking evidence of Jacob of Edessa's awareness of Muslim religious thought, and even of passages in the Qur'ān, comes in a letter he wrote to one John the Stylite about the fact that the Virgin Mary was of the house of David. Jacob wrote as follows:

> That, therefore, the Messiah is in the flesh of the line of David . . . is professed and considered fundamental by all of them: Jews, Muslims and Christians. . . . To the Jews . . . it is fundamental, although they deny the true Messiah who has indeed come. . . . The Muslims, too, although they do not know nor wish to say that this true Messiah, who came and is acknowledged by the Christians, is God and the son of God, they nevertheless confess firmly that he is the true Messiah who was to come and who was foretold by the prophets; on this they have no dispute with us. . . . They say to all at all times that Jesus son of Mary is in truth the Messiah and they call him the Word of God, as do the holy scriptures. They also add, in their ignorance, that he is the Spirit of God, for they are not able to distinguish between word and spirit, just as they do not assent to call the Messiah God or son of God.[24]

The last sentence in this quotation clearly shows Jacob of Edessa's awareness of the passage in the Qur'ān that says, "The Messiah, Jesus son of Mary, is only Allāh's Messenger and His Word, which He imparted to

[22] Uthemann, *Viae dux*, 9.

[23] See the texts quoted in Hoyland, *Seeing Islam as Others Saw It*, 162–63.

[24] Quoted from Hoyland, *Seeing Islam as Others Saw It*, 166. See also F. Nau, "Traduction des lettres XII et XIII de Jacques d'Édesse," *Revue de l'Orient Chrétien* 10 (1905): 197–208, 258–82; Nau, "Cinq lettres de Jacques d'Édesse à Jean le Stylite (traduction et analyse)," *Revue de l'Orient Chrétien* 14 (1909): 427–40.

Mary, and is a spirit from Him" (*an-Nisā* 4:171). In later times many Christian writers would quote this passage and build their apologetic arguments on it. But the reference to it in Jacob of Edessa's letter shows that already by the last decade of the seventh century, Christians in the newly occupied territories outside of Arabia were aware of the teachings of Islam and of the Qur'ān already before most people there were speaking Arabic or had adopted it as a church language.

Apocalypse Now

Roughly in the time of the Umayyad caliph ʿAbd al-Malik (685–707) and during the reigns of his sons and successors (707–50), Christian writers in the caliphate turned their attention from merely recording the vicissitudes of the conquest and making note of what to them were the eccentric, new beliefs of the Arabs, to the long task of articulating a theological and apologetic response to the religious challenge the Muslims now posed to the Christians in the occupied territories. And it may well have been the case that a precipitating cause of this defensive, apologetic undertaking was the assertive campaign launched by ʿAbd al-Malik and his successors publicly and monumentally to proclaim the permanent hegemony of Islam in the land and in the public sphere generally.[25] In this connection, the most notable enterprise of the campaign was undoubtedly the building of the Dome of the Rock in Jerusalem. The building was begun around the year 692 and presumably was completed by the turn of the eighth century.[26] At least two previous caliphs, ʿUmar I (r. 634–44) and Muʿāwiya (r. 661–80), in recognition of the religious significance of Jerusalem and of the Temple Mount in particular for Jews, Christians, and Muslims alike, had been engaged in building activities on the same site. But ʿAbd al-Malik's structure, striking in its architectural statement to this very day, was in a class apart. In the cityscape of Jerusalem in the late seventh century, the Dome of the Rock stood seemingly by design over against the Church of the Anastasis/Holy Sepulchre and other Christian structures in the Holy City,[27] and it monumentally proclaimed the Islamic appropriation of the

[25] See Sidney H. Griffith, "Images, Islam, and Christian Icons: A Moment in the Christian/Muslim Encounter in Early Islamic Times," in *La Syrie de Byzance à l'islam; VIIe–VIIIe siècles*, ed. Pierre Canivet and Jean-Paul Rey-Coquais, 121–38 (Damascus: Institut Français de Damas, 1992).

[26] See Amikam Elad, "Why Did ʿAbd al-Malik Build the Dome of the Rock? A Re-Examination of the Muslim Sources"; Sheila Blair, "What Is the Date of the Dome of the Rock"; Josef van Ess, "ʿAbd al-Malik and the Dome of the Rock: An Analysis of Some Texts," all in Raby and Johns, *Bayt al-Maqdis* 1, 33–103.

[27] See Grabar, *The Shape of the Holy*, 52–116.

city the local Christians called the "Mother of the Churches."[28] But there is more.

The beautiful Kufic inscription in gold leaf that goes around the base of the dome, on both its inner and outer faces, using passages from the Qur'ān, over and over again proclaims among other things, "There is no god but God alone. . . . He did not beget and was not begotten. . . . Muḥammad is the messenger of God. Such too was Jesus son of Mary. . . . Praise be to God who has not taken a son. . . . Religion with God is Islam. . . . Those who had been given the scripture differed only after knowledge came to them, out of envy for one another."[29] The import of these repeated Qur'ānic phrases is crystal clear: Islam has supplanted Christianity even in Jerusalem on the Temple Mount where previously Christians had seen the signs of their own succession to the Jews.[30] Symbolically and chronologically, the construction of the Dome of the Rock marked the beginning of the era when Christians living in the caliphate seriously undertook the task of rebutting the Muslims' charges against them.

Apocalypse was the earliest genre in which Christians initially expressed their most sustained response to the religious challenge of Islam, and as we shall see, even here symbolically Jerusalem still stood at the high point of the narrative.[31] While a number of writers spoke of turmoil, natural disasters, and plagues as portents of what they thought of as the scourge of the Arabs, some inevitably were concerned with these events as signs of the end times. By far the most well known text in this vein is the one that has come down to us under the somewhat mystifying title *The Apocalypse of Pseudo-Methodius.*[32] The Methodius of the title refers to the ancient Methodius, martyr, prolific writer, and bishop of Olympus in Lycia (d. 312), who according to the narrative foresees the troublesome interlude of the kingdom of the Arabs in the eschatological calculus Christians had projected for the history of the world on the basis of the prophecies in the biblical book of Daniel. In the *Apocalypse*, the Methodius character explains how the interlude of Arab domination, all immediate evidence to the contrary notwithstanding, will not really disrupt the unfolding sequence of the four

[28] See Robert L. Wilken, *The Land Called Holy: Palestine in Christian History and Thought* (New Haven, CT: Yale University Press, 1992), 171.

[29] See Christel Kessler, "ʿAbd al-Malik's Inscription in the Dome of the Rock: A Reconsideration," *Journal of the Royal Asiatic Society* (1970): 2–14; Grabar, *The Shape of the Holy*, 56–71, 184–85.

[30] See Heribert Busse, "Monotheismus und islamische Christologie in der Bauinschrift der Felsendoms in Jerusalem," *Theologische Quartalschrift* 161 (1981): 168–78.

[31] See Harald Suermann, *Die geschichtstheologische Reaktion auf die einfallenden Muslime in der edessenischen Apokalyptic des 7. Jahrhunderts* (Frankfurt: Peter Lang, 1985); Martínez, "La literatura apocalíptica."

[32] See Gerrit J. Reinink, *Die syrische Apokalypse des Pseudo-Methodios*, CSCO, vols. 540 and 541 (Louvain, Belgium: Peeters, 1993).

kingdoms of the prophecies in the book of Daniel, destined to end with the kingdom of the Greeks. Rather, he says, the depredations of the Arabs are part of God's plan for the era of punishment for sin that is destined to usher in the final days of world history.[33]

Methodius of Olympus was not in fact the author of the *Apocalypse*, hence the epithet "pseudo" attached to his name in modern references to this work; the text was composed originally in Syriac in northern Syria, during the time of the caliph ʿAbd al-Malik and probably around the year 691. The author was most likely a Jacobite, or perhaps even a "Chalcedonian" Christian, one of those soon to be called Melkites; he described an apocalyptic vision that reconciled the evident fact of the Islamic conquest with the earlier Christian eschatological expectation, based on the visions of Daniel, of four world empires leading up through six millennia to the last days of the world in the seventh millennium. In the end, Pseudo-Methodius assured his readers, after many vicissitudes and catastrophes, including the punishing rule of the Arabs, the sons of Ishmael, the last Roman emperor, the leader of the final kingdom of the Greeks, really would, after a time of confusion and cleansing suffering, place his crown on the cross of Christ on Golgatha, in Jerusalem, and offer his kingdom to God the Father.

The *Apocalypse of Pseudo-Methodius* was soon translated from Syriac into Greek and very soon thereafter into all the other languages of early and medieval Christianity.[34] It inspired hope in Christians under Muslim rule for a millennium and more. But it was only one of a number of such works composed in Syriac in the first decades of the eighth century.[35] There were other apocalypses and there were works in other genres as well, particularly apologetic compositions designed to staunch the initial flow of Christian conversions to Islam in these years of the consolidation of Muslim rule. For, as one Syriac chronicler very poignantly put it,

> The gates were opened to them to [enter] Islam. The wanton and the dissolute slipped towards the pit and the abyss of perdition, and lost their souls as well as their bodies—all, that is, that we possess. . . .

[33] See Gerrit J. Reinink, "Ps.-Methodius: A Concept of History in Response to the Rise of Islam," in *The Byzantine and Early Islamic Near East, vol. 1: Problems in the Literary Source Material*, ed. Averil Cameron and Lawrence I. Conrad, 149–87, Studies in Late Antiquity and Early Islam, 1 (Princeton, NJ: Darwin Press, 1992).

[34] See Paul J. Alexander, *The Byzantine Apocalyptic Tradition* (Berkeley: University of California Press, 1985).

[35] See, e.g., Suermann, *Die geschichtstheologische Reaktion*; S. P. Brock, "North Mesopotamia in the Late Seventh Century: Book XV of John Bar Penkāyō's *Rīš Mellō*," *Jerusalem Studies in Arabic and Islam* 9 (1987): 51–75; Han J. W. Drijvers, "The Gospel of the Twelve Apostles: A Syriac Apocalypse from the Early Islamic Period," in Cameron and Conrad, *Byzantine and Early Islamic Near East,* 1: 189–213; Drijvers, "The Testament of Our Lord: Jacob of Edessa's Response to Islam," *ARAM* 6 (1994): 104–14.

> Without blows or tortures they slipped towards apostasy in great precipitancy; they formed groups of ten or twenty or thirty or a hundred or two hundred or three hundred without any sort of compulsion . . . going down to Ḥarrān and becoming Muslims in the presence of [government] officials. A great crowd did so . . . from the districts of Edessa and of Ḥarrān and of Ṭella and of RêshʿAyna.[36]

It was this social circumstance, the dawning attractiveness of conversion to Islam in the first decades of the eighth century, that no doubt prompted the composition of the first Christian apologetic tracts in the Islamic milieu.[37] The first of them were written in Syriac and they took on a literary form and included a line of argumentation that would in due course become standard features in the Christian response to the challenge of Islam in later times.

First Apologies

The two earliest Syriac apologetic tracts that have come down to us from early Islamic times both feature a literary scenario in which a Christian spokesman finds himself in a setting in which he is being interrogated about his faith by a prominent Muslim. The Christian supplies satisfying answers to provocative questions in ways that not only justify the reasonableness of Christian faith but also that suggest that Christianity is in fact the true religion according to which God wills to be worshipped. It is difficult to avoid the conclusion that the anonymous writers of these works intended to furnish Christian readers with ready answers to the challenges that must often have been posed to them by Muslims in the course of their daily lives.

Probably the earliest such text is the one in which a now unknown writer presents an account in the form of a letter on the alleged occasion when the Jacobite Patriarch John Sedra (r. 631–48) was interrogated by a Muslim emir, perhaps ʿUmayr ibn Saʿd al-Anṣārī, on Sunday, May 9, AD 644.[38] It is typical of such compositions that the authors furnish enough details

[36] Amir Harrak, trans., *The Chronicle of Zuqnīn: Parts III and IV; A.D. 488–775*, Mediaeval Sources in Translation, 36 (Toronto: Pontifical Institute of Mediaeval Studies, 1999), 324, quoted here in the trans. of J. G. Segal, *Edessa, "the Blessed City"* (Oxford: Oxford University Press, 1970), 206.

[37] See Gerrit J. Reinink, "The Beginnings of Syriac Apologetic Literature in Response to Islam," *Oriens Christianus* 77 (1993): 165–87.

[38] See F. Nau, "Un colloque du patriarche Jean avec l'émir des Agaréens," *Journal Asiatique*, 11th series, 5 (1915): 225–79; Samir Khalil Samir, "Qui est l'interlocuteur musulman du patriarche syrien Jean III (631–648)?" in *IV Symposium Syriacum—1984*, ed. H. J. W. Drijvers et al., 387–400, Orientalia Christiana Analecta, 229 (Rome: Pont. Institutum Studiorum Orientalium, 1987).

to suggest historical verisimilitude for their narratives without supplying the particulars that would allow any further specification. In all probability the present text was first composed by a Syriac writer during the first third of the eighth century, although it comes down to us in a manuscript copied in the year 874.[39] The body of the text is concerned with reporting the patriarch's replies to leading questions that were posed by the emir. The questions, seven in number, are such as one would expect to have often been posed to Christians by Muslim interrogators, given the Qur'ān's known critique of Christian faith and practice. The emir's questions are as follows:

> "Is there just one Gospel which does not vary in any way and which is held to by all those who are and call themselves Christians?"
>
> "Why, if the Gospel is one, does the faith differ?"
>
> "What do you say Christ was: God or not?"
>
> "When Christ was in the womb of Mary, he being God as you say, who was bearing and managing heaven and earth?"
>
> "What doctrine and faith did Abraham and Moses have?" and, if Christian, "why did they not on that account write and inform clearly about Christ?"
>
> The emir demands that "if Christ is God and born of Mary and if God has a son, this be shown to him literally and from the Law."
>
> The emir asks "about the laws of the Christians: what and after what fashion are they, and if they are written in the Gospel or not," and he inquires about the particular case of inheritance law.[40]

These queries actually embody the substance of the Islamic critique of Christianity and in one form or another they would be the questions Christian apologists in the world of Islam would be answering for centuries to come. Similarly, the patriarch's replies voice the first lines of response that later Christian apologists would eventually develop into a new articulation of the Christian articles of faith, suitable for the particular requirements of those who lived with Muslims. We will study these developments in some detail in the next chapter.

Meanwhile, we should mention another anonymous, early Syriac composition that also features the dialogue format involving a Muslim interrogator and a Christian respondent. This one is normally described as the dialogue of the monk of Bêt Ḥālê and a Muslim notable. The scene is set almost a century after the time of Patriarch John Sedra (d. 648), most likely

[39] See Sidney H. Griffith, "Disputes with Muslims in Syriac Christian Texts: From Patriarch John (d. 648) to Bar Hebraeus (d. 1286)," in *Religionsgespräche im Mittelalter*, ed. B. Lewis and F. Niewöhner, 257–59, Wolfenbütteler Mittelalter-Studien, 4 (Wiesbaden: Harrassowitz, 1992).

[40] Quoted from Hoyland, *Seeing Islam as Others Saw It*, 459–60.

in the monastery of Dayr Mār ʿAbdâ near Kufa and Ḥira in Iraq. In the preface, the monk says that his Muslim interlocutor is an Arab in the entourage of the emir Maslama, who due to sickness had sought hospitality in the monastery for about ten days. This detail allows us to suppose that the emir was Maslama ibn ʿAbd al-Malik, who was in fact governor for a brief time in Iraq in the early 720s. So while the text survives only in manuscript copies of the eighteenth and nineteenth centuries, we can with some confidence suppose that it was first composed in the first third of the eighth century.[41] And once again, while the names of the actual dramatis personae are not mentioned, the scant details given are sufficient to suggest a certain social verisimilitude; the emir Maslama was in fact in Iraq at the appropriate time and it was a custom for Muslims to seek the hospitality of monasteries in this period for a variety of purposes, ranging from recreation to rehabilitation.[42]

At the beginning of his narrative the monk says that the Muslim was a man interested in religion, "learned in our scriptures as well as in their own Qurʾān." This detail then sets the frame of reference for the conversation, which begins in earnest when the Muslim, observing how astute the monks of the monastery were in prayer, remarks that it is too bad that "your creed does not allow your prayer to be acceptable." And he goes on to claim that in following the teachings of Abraham and Muḥammad the Muslims avoid the religious excesses of the Christians. And he adds: "Here is the sign that God loves us and is pleased with our religion: He has given us authority over all religions and all peoples; they are slaves subject to us." To this allegation the monk immediately retorts, "You Ishmaelites are holding only the smallest portion of the earth. All of creation is not subject to your authority." And from this beginning the Muslim poses all the customary objections to Christian beliefs and practices already brought up in the Qurʾān, plus some others that in the course of time would become standard, such as: why do you worship the cross; why do you honor images; why do you pay respect to the bones of dead men; why do you pray facing toward the east? The monk deftly disposes of these and other questions in succinct, pointed replies. He does concede a point that will become a commonplace

[41] See Griffith, "Disputes with Muslims," 259–61; Griffith, *Syriac Writers on Muslims and the Religious Challenge of Islam*, Mōrān ʾEthʾō, 7 (Kottayam, Kerala, India: St. Ephraem Ecumenical Research Institute, 1995); S. H. Griffith, "Disputing with Islam in Syriac: The Case of the Monk of Bêt Ḥālê with a Muslim Emir," *Hugoye* 3, no. 1 (2000), http://syrcom.cua.edu/Hugoye/Vol3No1/HV3N1/Griffith.html.

[42] See Hilary Kilpatrick, "Monasteries through Muslim Eyes: The *Diyārāt* Books," in *Christians at the Heart of Islamic Rule: Church Live and Scholarship in ʿAbbasid Iraq*, ed. David Thomas, 19–37, The History of Christian-Muslim Relations, vol. 1 (Leiden: Brill, 2003); G. Troupeau, "Les couvents chrétiens dans la literature arabe musulman," *La Nouvelle Revue de Caire* 1 (1975): 265–79.

in later texts composed by Christians who live in the world of Islam; the monk gives it as his opinion that Muḥammad "was a wise man and a God-fearer, who freed you [Arabs] from the worship of demons and made you acknowledge that the true God is one." At the end of his account of their dialogue, the monk reports that the Arab notable offered this final testimony: "I testify that were it not for the fear of the government and of shame before men, many would become Christians. But you are blessed of God to have given me satisfaction by your conversation with me."[43]

Clearly this Syriac text was written for a Christian audience, and its purpose was surely to communicate a certain confidence to Christians who may have been tempted to convert to Islam. The message was that Christians really did have satisfactory answers to the religious objections Muslims posed for them. Indeed, the text goes even further to suggest that Muslims could see the reasonableness of Christian faith; only the possession of political and military power, the author suggests, and social convention, prevented the Muslims' conversion to Christianity. It is rhetoric of a sort well suited to instill a sense of hidden superiority in subaltern, socially subject populations, not only in the world of Islam but in many other historical circumstances as well.

Syriac-speaking, Christian writers in early Islamic times were also adept at borrowing elements from Islamic religious tradition and turning them to a Christian purpose. An example is the work begun by a now anonymous Syriac author of the late eighth or early ninth century called by its modern editor, "a Christian Baḥîrâ Legend."[44] Baḥîrâ is the name of a Christian monk who, according to Islamic tradition, recognized the mark of prophethood on the body of the young teen-aged Muḥammad when the boy once came with a caravan from Mecca to Syria. The Christian author of the legend composed a work made up of equal parts of apocalyptic material on the order of that to be found in the *Apocalypse of Pseudo-Methodius* and a section purporting to tell the story of the monk's catechesis of Muḥammad. The monk, now known as Sargîs/Sergius Baḥîrâ, the term *baḥîrâ* in Syriac being a reverential title for a monk on the order of the English term "venerable," is said to have been a renegade monk who out of compunction for his sins undertook the task of instructing Muḥammad in Christian teachings and even of composing them into a book of revelations for him to be called the Qur'ān. Unfortunately, according to the legend, Muḥammad's later followers, and especially the Jews among them, distorted the original Qur'ān into the form in which the Muslims now have it. Their subsequent triumph in the Islamic conquest then, according to the legend, brought on the horrors detailed in the apocalyptic section of

[43] All the quotations are from Griffith, *Syriac Writers on Muslims*, 27–37.

[44] Richard Gottheil, "A Christian Bahira Legend," *Zeitschrift für Assyriologie* 13 (1898), 189–242; 14 (1899), 203–68; 15 (1900), 56–102; 17 (1903), 125–66.

the work, calamities allowed by God, the Christian monk supposed, in punishment for the sins of the Christians.[45]

There has been much controversy in modern times about this kind of literature, composed anonymously as it was, and initially in the indigenous languages of the Christians in the Islamic world like Syriac, Coptic, or Armenian. Scholars have been eager to point out its fictive qualities and to deny its historicity.[46] While this judgment is certainly true on a literal level, it is also irrelevant to the original, socioreligious purpose of such compositions. All the details in such texts that seem to make an appeal for historical verisimilitude are surely intended to lend the narratives a measure of authenticity, not so much from the perspective of the historical record as such, but from the point of view of a now publicly disenfranchised, religious worldview that is nevertheless sure of its own veracity, which it represents as unknowingly acknowledged even by those who publicly contest it. The anonymous authorship of these compositions also testifies to their relevance as underground literature, with an "insider" readership, whose confidence it was this literature's main purpose to bolster.[47] The Christian, *dhimmī* population was helped by these texts to savor a sense of seemingly rightful superiority in the face of all the evidence to the contrary in their daily circumstances of life. Between the lines of all these texts there lurked the question that in the no doubt fictional story of their encounter, the Muslim notable is made to put straightforwardly to the monk of Bêt Ḥālê: "While I know your religion is right, and your way of thinking is even preferable to ours, what is the reason why God handed you over into our hands and you are driven by us like sheep to the slaughter, and your bishops and your priests are killed, and the rest are subjugated and enslaved with the king's impositions night and day, more bitter than death?"[48]

The Sectarian Milieu

Apocalypse and legend were not the only Christian literary responses to the challenge of Islam that the Muslim campaign for the appropriation of the public sphere in the conquered territories elicited in the eighth century.

[45] See Sidney H. Griffith, "Muḥammad and the Monk Baḥîrâ: Reflections on a Syriac and Arabic Text from Early Abbasid Times," *Oriens Christianus* 79 (1995): 146–74; Barbara Roggema, "A Christian Reading of the Qur'ān: The Legend of Sergius-Baḥīrā and Its Use of the Qur'ān and Sīra," in *Syrian Christians under Islam: The First Thousand Years*, ed. David Thomas, 57–73 (Leiden: Brill, 2001).

[46] See especially Reinink, "The Beginnings of Syriac Apologetic Literature."

[47] See the insightful comments in Leo Strauss's essay, "Persecution and the Art of Writing," which mutatis mutandis may provide some help in interpreting the fuller sense of the texts under discussion here. See Leo Strauss, *Persecution and the Art of Writing* (Chicago: University of Chicago Press, 1952), 22–37.

[48] Diyarbekir MS 95, private typescript, p. 15.

This was also the period, after the time of the early "traditionists" of the seventh century, of the burgeoning Islamic intellectual life that in the ninth century would flower into the classical intellectual culture of early ʿAbbasid times. One has in mind here the groundbreaking work of figures such as Wahb ibn Munabbih (d. ca. 728), Ḥasan al-Baṣrī (d. 728), Muḥammad ibn Isḥāq (d. ca. 767), and al-Wāqidī (747–822), to name only four. The works of these Muslim scholars contributed substantially to the shape of the new Islamic, religious discourse, produced in the social context of the encounter between Jewish, Christian, and Muslim claimants to religious verisimilitude, which John Wansbrough has so challengingly and aptly called "the sectarian milieu."[49] These exciting developments in Islamic scholarship provided the challenging background for yet another intellectual development in the presentation of Christian thinking in the world of Islam. The seemingly comprehensive challenge to Christian faith prompted at least two important Christian writers, one in Greek and the other in Syriac, to produce the first ever comprehensive, summary compendia of Christian doctrine.

Arguably, the very first *summa theologiae* in Christian intellectual history was St. John of Damascus's (d. 749/764) composite work *Pēgē Gnoseōs*, or *The Fount of Knowledge*. He wrote it in Greek, perhaps as a monk of Mar Sabas monastery in the Judean desert,[50] in the first half of the eighth century, the very years of the burgeoning of Islamic religious scholarship just mentioned. Most Christian scholars have taken his work to represent the last of the patristic era in the East and to have been addressed to a largely monastic audience whose eyes and hearts were turned toward Constantinople in Byzantium.[51] But that is to read John of Damascus's works entirely from the point of view of Byzantium, where John never lived and where his writings on subjects other than the veneration of the holy icons made no notable impression until some centuries after his lifetime.[52] In his own time he was called "Saracen-minded" by the Iconoclasts in Constan-

[49] See J. Wansbrough, *The Sectarian Milieu: Content and Composition of Islamic Salvation History*, London Oriental Series, vol. 34 (Oxford: Oxford University Press, 1978).

[50] Some modern scholars have doubted that John of Damascus was ever a monk of Mar Sabas; see, e.g., M.-F. Auzepy, "De la Palestine à Constantinople (VIIIe–IXe siècles): Étienne le Sabaïte et Jean Damascène," *Travaux et Mémoires* 12 (1994) : 183–218. Andrew Louth has cited evidence that John of Damascus may have been a monk of the "Old Lavra," i.e., Mar Chariton, in Andrew Louth, "St. John Damascene: Preacher and Poet," in *Preacher and Audience: Studies in Early Christian and Byzantine Homiletics*, ed. P. Allen and M. Cunningham (Leiden: Brill, 1998), 249.

[51] This is the position adopted by Andrew Louth, *St. John Damascene: Tradition and Originality in Byzantine Theology*, Oxford Early Christian Studies (Oxford: Oxford University Press, 2002).

[52] See Basil Studer, *Die theologische Arbeitsweise des Johannes von Damaskus*, Studia Patristica et Byzantina, 2 (Ettal, Germany: Buch-Kunstverlag, 1956), 131.

tinople[53] who were concerned about his support of the Christian practice of venerating icons and who made no reference at all to any part of his masterpiece, *The Fount of Knowledge*. The fact is that John of Damascus, called Manṣūr ibn Sarjūn in the Arabic-speaking world of Islam, lived all his life among Muslims, and Arabic was the language of his early employment, albeit that all of his surviving writings are in Greek, the theological and liturgical language of the burgeoning Melkite Christian community, whose chief spokesperson he was to become. When one considers his entire literary output from the point of view of the intellectual concerns of the Christians in the world of Islam, it becomes immediately evident how well they fit into the scheme of the issues that prevailed in the controversies among the Melkites, Jacobites, and Nestorians of the Islamic milieu, and how ill-suited they are for all practical purposes to the immediate concerns of the theologians of Constantinople in his day.[54]

In his masterpiece, *The Fount of Knowledge*, John of Damascus presented what he considered to be a compendium of the "teachings of the fathers" of Christian orthodoxy on the articles of Christian faith. The work is in three parts: definitions of philosophical terms that are used in the formulas of Christian doctrinal statements; a list and description of the principal Christian heresies; and, finally, a systematic presentation of Christian dogma according to the teachings of the six councils of Byzantine orthodoxy.[55] As we shall see in a later chapter, not only the topics of John's great work, but in large part its methodology as well, came to have a powerful influence on subsequent presentations of Christian theology in Arabic. But what is of most immediate interest for our present purpose is to note that as the last of the one hundred heresies John of Damascus discusses in the second part of his book is the one he calls, "the heresy of the Ishmaelites."[56]

For John of Damascus, as for the other Christian writers of his day, the Ishmaelites were the Arab descendants of the biblical Hagar, whose religion, he says, leads people astray and, sounding his own apocalyptic note,

[53] The acts of the Iconoclast council of Hiereia in 754 speak of John of Damascus as, "Mansur, the one with a vile-sounding name and of Saracen opinion." Quoted in Daniel J. Sahas, *Icon and Logos: Sources in Eighth-Century Iconoclasm*, Toronto Medieval Texts and Translations, 4 (Toronto: University of Toronto Press, 1986), 168.

[54] See Sidney H. Griffith, "'Melkites,' 'Jacobites,' and the Christological Controversies in Arabic in Third/Ninth-Century Syria," in *Syrian Christians under Islam: The First Thousand Years*, ed. David Thomas, 9–55 (Leiden: Brill, 2001).

[55] While it is clear that John of Damascus himself considered *The Fount of Knowledge* to be an integral work, albeit composed of three distinct parts, it seems from manuscript and other evidence that the components seldom if ever actually circulated together; the *De Haeresibus* in particular circulated apart. See Louth, *St. John Damascene*, 31–37.

[56] See Daniel J. Sahas, *John of Damascus on Islam: The "Heresy of the Ishmaelites"* (Leiden: Brill, 1972); Raymond Le Coz, ed., *Jean Damascène: Écrits sur Islam*, Sources Chrétiens, 383 (Paris: Cerf, 1992).

he calls it the forerunner of the Antichrist.[57] John applies their name to the Muslims.[58] His discussion of Islam is obviously well informed; for example, one can easily discern his allusions to passages in the Qurʾān. But John's approach is entirely polemical, and in accordance with this purpose he actually caricatures those aspects of Islamic teaching and practice that he mentions. His purpose is to discredit the religious and intellectual claims of Islam in the eyes of inquiring Christians. But the interesting thing to notice for the modern scholar of the history of the relations between the Muslims and the Christians over the centuries is the fact that John of Damascus includes Islam as the last in his list of Christian heresies.[59] Indeed he speaks of Muḥammad as having been one who, "having happened upon the Old and New Testament, likewise having probably been in conversation with an Arian monk, contrived his own heresy."[60] John's use of the word "heresy" here amounts to an admission that the Muslims for all their differences are after all in the same world of discourse with the Christians when it comes to religious matters, albeit that the differences are substantial. John's critique of the heresy of Islam may be seen as a reply to the Qurʾān's own polemical critique of Christianity, which in Christian eyes is simply wrong. But what one wants to emphasize in the present context is the fact that John of Damascus's response to the challenge of Islam was not confined to just the polemical passage against "the heresy" contrived by Muḥammad that John included in the *De Haeresibus*. Rather, the response to the commanding intellectual challenge of Islam across the board must be considered to have been a motivating factor behind John's whole conception of *The Fount of Knowledge*. His larger purpose would have been to provide the Christian teachers of the burgeoning Melkite community with a compendium of orthodox doctrine useful for their response to the whole range of challenges facing them, the attacks of their Christian rivals, the Jacobites, the Nestorians, and the Manichaeans as well as the Muslims, whose rule allowed the Christian rivals of the Melkites also to flourish.

Similarly, in the Syriac-speaking community of the Church of the East in the waning years of the eighth century another scholar also composed a summary presentation of Christian teaching for the instruction of those of

[57] Le Coz, *Jean Damascène*, 210.

[58] See the discussion of the significance of the epithet "Ishmaelites" in n. 6 above.

[59] The idea that Islam is a heresy, even the epitome of all heresies, would become popular not only in Byzantium, but even in western anti-Islamic Christian treatises. See Hartmut Bobzin, "A Treasury of Heresies": Christian Polemics against the Koran," in Stefan Wild (ed.), *The Qurʾān as Text*, ed. Stefan Wild, 157–75 (Leiden: Brill, 1996).

[60] Le Coz, *Jean Damascène*, 210–12. Given the language of this passage, it is difficult to understand how Le Coz, pointing to John's earlier use of the word θρησκεια to designate the ancient "religion of the Ishmaelites" can say without further nuance in his introduction to the text, "Jean appelle l'Islam 'Religion des Ismaélites,' et l'utilisation du mot religion montre bien que, pour lui, ce n'est pas un simple hérésie chrétienne" (p. 89).

his denomination who were faced with intellectual challenges similar to those facing the Melkites, for whom St. John of Damascus wrote *The Fount of Knowledge*. Theodore bar Kônî (fl. ca. 792) wrote a summary presentation of the doctrine of the Church of the East in the form of an extended commentary on the whole Bible, the Old Testament and the New Testament. He called it simply *Scholion* because it is in the form of *scholia*, or commentaries, on what are taken to be difficult passages in the several biblical books.[61] In fact it also includes numerous definitions of philosophical terms that are important for the proper understanding of church doctrines and creedal statements. There are eleven chapters in the book, the first nine of them follow the order of the biblical books, presenting doctrine in the catechetical style of questions posed by a student and answered by a master. The same literary style appears also in chapter 10, which is a Christian response to objections to Christian doctrines customarily posed by Muslims.[62] Chapter 11 is an appendix to the *Scholion*, containing a list of heresies and heresiarchs, along with brief statements of their teachings. In the preface Bar Kônî states the purpose of the chapter, and in a single sentence he rather pithily states the pastoral problem the Christians face in the Islamic milieu of his day. He says he is writing "against those who while professing to accept the Old Testament, and acknowledging the coming of Christ our Lord, are nevertheless far removed from both of them, and now they demand from us an apology for our faith, not from all of the scriptures, but only from those which they acknowledge."[63] Clearly he had the Muslims in mind.

In chapter 10 of the *Scholion*, the chapter devoted to the response to the challenges of the Muslims, the topics that come up for discussion are as follows: the Scriptures and Christ; Baptism; the Eucharistic mystery; the veneration of the Cross; sacramental practice in general; the Son of God; and, of course, interwoven with all of them, the all-embracing doctrine of the Trinity. These same issues are the ones that will appear in the topical outlines of almost all of the apologetic tracts written by Christians living among the Muslims for the next five hundred years. What is evident in the list of

[61] See Sidney H. Griffith, "Theodore bar Kônî's *Scholion*: A Nestorian *Summa contra Gentiles* from the First Abbasid Century," in *East of Byzantium: Syria and Armenia in the Formative Period*, ed. N. Garsoïan, T. Mathews, and R. Thomson, 53–72 (Washington, DC: Dumbarton Oaks, 1982).

[62] See Sidney H. Griffith, "Chapter Ten of the Scholion: Theodore bar Kônî's Apology for Christianity," *Orientalia Christiana Analecta* 218 (1982): 169–91. Theodore bar Kônî customarily calls the Muslims *ḥanpê*, a Syriac term which means roughly "pagans," but it is cognate to the Arabic term *ḥanīf* (pl. *ḥunafāʾ*), which is used in the Qurʾān as virtually a synonym for the adjective *muslim*. See, e.g., *Āl ʿImrān* 3:67. It is likely that Bar Kônî was fully aware of the double entendre inherent in the term.

[63] Addai Scher, *Theodorus bar Kônî Liber Scholiorum*, CSCO, vols. 55 and 69 (Paris: E Typographeo Reipublicae, 1910 and 1912), 69: 231.

them is the obvious intermingling of questions of faith and practice in such a way that it is also clear that the shape of theology itself is determined in this milieu by the apologetic imperative to justify the reasonableness of religious beliefs in virtue of the public practices they entail. This feature of the apologetic enterprise will become especially evident when we turn our attention in the next chapters to the discussion of Christian theology in Arabic. Meanwhile, it seems clear from both St. John of Damascus's *The Fount of Knowledge*, written in Greek, and Theodore bar Kônî's *Scholion*, written in Syriac, that by the end of the eighth century, the intellectual challenge that Islam posed for Christians had already imposed upon Christian writers in that milieu the task of turning their attention to the comprehensive presentation and defense of the reasonableness of Christian faith in response to a new and virtually comprehensive rejection of its major tenets. This development would affect the shape and style of Christian theology in all of its phases forever thereafter, even well beyond the confines of the world of Islam.

III

CHRISTIAN THEOLOGY IN ARABIC

A NEW DEVELOPMENT IN CHURCH LIFE

Syriac Beginnings

By the end of the eighth century, Christian thinkers who lived among the Muslims were already doing theology with the challenges of Islam uppermost in their minds. One of the earliest and most interesting of them was the long-lived Patriarch Timothy I (727/8–823), who served as catholicos/patriarch of the Church of the East for the last forty-three years (780–823) of his life.[1] Patriarch Timothy's transfer of his see from its traditional location in Seleucia/Ctesiphon, the erstwhile capital of the Persian emperors, to Baghdad, the seat of the Muslim caliphs since the city's foundation in 767, symbolically expressed the new orientation in Christian thinking. The move gave the patriarch much more ready access to the centers of power in the new world order. This was important to him not only for the sake of the administration of the dioceses of his far-flung church, but also for the support of the church's missionary enterprises, which in his time, even under Muslim rule, extended eastward far into Central Asia along the so-called silk road and southward into India. But Patriarch Timothy was more than an able church administrator. He was an accomplished scholar whose interests brought him even into contact with the Muslim intellectuals of the caliph's court.

The fruit of Patriarch Timothy's scholarly concerns is preserved in a large collection of letters, really letter-treatises, which he addressed to monks and fellow bishops on any number of topics of interest to him or of importance to the life of the church.[2] Timothy wrote in Syriac, but it is clear that he was competent in Greek and, of course, fluent in Arabic. Several of his letter-treatises enjoyed a wide circulation and afford us now a precious insight into how Christian intellectual life in the caliphate developed in tandem

[1] See Hans Putman, *L'église et l'islam sous Timothée I (780–823): Étude sur l'église nestorienne au temps des premiers ʿAbbāsides avec nouvelle edition et traduction du dialogue entre Timothée et al-Mahdī* (Beirut: Dar el-Machreq, 1975); Bénédicte Landron, *Chrétiens et musulmans en Irak: Attitudes nestoriennes vis-à-vis de l'islam* (Paris: Cariscript, 1994), 46–54.

[2] See Raphael Bidawid, *Les lettres du patriarche nestorien Timothée*, Studi e Testi, 187 (Vatican City: Biblioteca Apostolica Vaticana, 1956). See also Thomas R. Hurst, "The Syriac Letters of Timothy I (727–823): A Study in Christian-Muslim Controversy" (PhD diss., Catholic University of America, 1986).

with the interests of Muslim intellectuals. Timothy's Letter 40 provides a case in point.[3] Ostensibly it is an account of a discussion the patriarch says he had with an Aristotelian philosopher at the caliph's court about the definitions of logical terms and their proper deployment in Christian theology. In fact, the text contains an exercise in a style of religiously inspired reasoning that would soon become standard fare in apologetic treatises written by both Muslims and Christians in Arabic. In the introduction, which clearly states Timothy's apologetic purpose in writing the letter-treatise, Timothy very interestingly describes the Muslims as "the new Jews."[4] He says, "In the days of Herod, Pilate and the old Jews there was both defeat and victory, and truth and falsehood. So also, now, in the days of the present princes, in our own time and in the days of the new Jews among us, there is the same struggle and the same contest to distinguish falsehood and truth."[5]

What makes Letter 40 especially important for our inquiry is its topical outline. Not only are a number of the standard topics of religious controversy between Muslims and Christians mentioned, but also Timothy reports that his conversation with the philosopher at court began with a discussion of the modes of human knowledge in general and then moved on to a disquisition on the terms one should use to express knowledge about God. In short, what would much later and in another place be called theodicy and the theory of knowledge, in the early Islamic period in the Arabic-speaking milieu often prefaced interreligious conversations about the controversial doctrinal issues that separated Muslims and Christians. This procedure would in the coming years develop into a standard feature of both Christian and Muslim *kalām* treatises in Arabic. In this context, the Arabic term *kalām*, which literally means simply "speech" or "talk," came to articulate the formal, intellectual exercise in the systematic defense of the credibility of religious doctrines,[6] developed originally by Muslim apologists, but not without some debt to earlier, even Syriac-speaking Christians.[7] Eventually, *kalām*-style treatises in Arabic became the medium for theological development, even in Christian thought in the world of Islam.

[3] See Thomas R. Hurst, "Letter 40 of the Nestorian Patriarch Timothy I (727/8–823): An Edition and Translation" (master's thesis, Catholic University of America, 1981); Hanna Cheikho, *Dialectique du langage sur Dieu de Timothée I (728–823) à Serge* (Rome: Pont. Institutum Studiorum Orientalium, 1983).

[4] For more on this theme see Sidney H. Griffith, "Jews and Muslims in Christian Syriac and Arabic Texts of the Ninth Century," *Jewish History* 3 (1988): 65–94.

[5] Hurst, "Letter 40," 48.

[6] See Richard M. Frank, "The Science of Kalām," *Arabic Science and Philosophy* 2 (1992): 9–37.

[7] See Michael Cook, "The Origins of Kalam," *Bulletin of the School of Oriental and African Languages* 43 (1980): 32–43; Cook, *Early Muslim Dogma* (Cambridge: Cambridge University Press, 1981).

The mention of the Aristotelian philosopher at the caliph's court with whom Patriarch Timothy says he had his conversation reminds one that the patriarch himself was one of the first of a long line of Christians to be commissioned by a caliph to produce an Arabic translation of a work of Aristotle. Around the year 782 the caliph al-Mahdī (r. 775–85) commissioned Timothy to make a translation of Aristotle's *Topics*, the book of the *Organon* that deals with dialectical reasoning. He worked from an earlier Syriac version, but with consultation of the original Greek. The patriarch accomplished this task with the help of his associate and coreligionist, Abū Nūḥ al-Anbārī, who at the time was the Christian secretary of the Muslim governor of Mosul.[8] This detail helps us to notice how already by this time a network of Christian scholars, dependent on their own earlier school traditions, were prepared to participate with Muslims in the development, especially in Baghdad, of what during the next two centuries would become the remarkably inclusive culture of early Islamic intellectual life, based largely on the Graeco-Arabic translation movement. As for Patriarch Timothy, his own scholarly endeavors brought him to the point of reaching beyond the boundaries of the institutions of his own Church of the East in his search for books and manuscripts. He is on record as having made use of the services of an intermediary to borrow materials even from the Jacobite monastery of Mār Mattī near Takrit, midway between Baghdad and Mosul.[9] But this is not all; Patriarch Timothy was also one of the first Christian apologists to bring the defense of Christian beliefs and practices right into the caliph's court.

The most well known text from the pen of Patriarch Timothy I is undoubtedly the account he composed originally in Syriac some time after the occasion when on two successive days he was summoned to the presence of the caliph al-Mahdī to engage in a debate on the relative merits of Islam and Christianity.[10] As Timothy reported them, the issues discussed all had to do with the standard topics of conversation between Muslims and Christians on religious matters. The caliph raises the standard Islamic objections to Christian doctrines and practices, and the patriarch provides suitable apologetic replies. In literary form, the patriarch's Syriac text is a

[8] See Dimitri Gutas, *Greek Thought, Arabic Culture: The Graeco-Arabic Translation Movement in Baghdad and Early ʿAbbāsid Society (2nd–4th/8th–10th Centuries)* (London: Routledge, 1998), 61 and n. 1; Georg Graf, *Geschichte der christlichen arabischen Literatur*, 5 vols., Studi e Testi, 118, 133, 146, 147, 172 (Vatican City: Biblioteca Apostolica Vaticana, 1944–53), 2: 118.

[9] See Sebastian P. Brock, "Two Letters of the Patriarch Timothy from the Late Eighth Century on Translations from Greek," *Arabic Sciences and Philosophy* 9 (1999): 233–46.

[10] The Syriac text and English translation are included in Alphonse Mingana, *Woodbrooke Studies: Christian Documents in Syriac, Arabic, and Garshūni; Edited and Translated with a Critical Apparatus*, vol. 2 (Cambridge: Heffer, 1928), 1–162.

letter addressed to an unnamed correspondent. The preface is in a florid style, and it is highly rhetorical, but not devoid of interest. In it Timothy voices some diffidence about the "vain labor" involved in such a composition, and he complains that he is carrying out the task of writing it, "not without difficulty, nor without unwillingness."[11] What may have proved daunting to the patriarch was the knowledge that his best apologetic efforts would carry little conviction for Muslims, nor would they do much to prevent upwardly mobile Christians from converting to Islam, especially from within his own Church of the East. Several times in his report of the two sessions during which Timothy says he answered the caliph's questions, he alludes to the Muslim's desire for arguments from nature or from the scriptures, and his wariness of arguments based on reasoning processes, or his caution in the face of the logic-chopping rebuttals in debate style that were the normal apologists' stock in trade.[12]

Patriarch Timothy's letter, which amounts to an apologetic catechism for Syriac-speaking Christians living with Muslims, was an immediate success in the Syriac-speaking Christian communities. It seems to have circulated widely and for a long time in its original Syriac recension. There was even a Syriac epitome in circulation of the report of Timothy's first session with the caliph, presented in a simple question and answer format, which for a long time in the manuscript tradition was attributed to another author.[13] But very soon the whole work was also translated into Arabic in a somewhat augmented form, and in this language Patriarch Timothy's report of his days in debate with the caliph al-Mahdī has enjoyed a large popularity among all the communities of Arabophone Christians.[14] For by the last years of the eighth century Arabic was itself becoming an ecclesiastical language.

Ecclesiastical Arabic

The earliest surviving evidence for the use of written Arabic by Christians living under Islamic rule in the conquered territories comes from the last third of the eighth century. By that date, Arabicization, as it is called, or the spread of Arabic as the public language of business in the caliphate, brought about the circumstance that members of the Christian communities living within the *dār al-islām* themselves had to embrace Arabic not only as their daily language but in the ecclesiastical sphere as well. This

[11] Mingana, *Woodbrooke Studies*, 2: 91.

[12] See, e.g., Ibid., 2: 154 and 156.

[13] See A. Van Roey, "Une apologie syriaque attribuée à Elie de Nisibe," *Le Muséon* 59 (1946): 381–97.

[14] See Putman, *L'église et l'islam sous Timothée I.*

Fig. 1. Monastery of St. George at Choziba in the Judean Desert
Located in the Wadi Qelt east of Jerusalem, the monastery of St. George at Choziba was founded in the late fifth century; it followed the traditions of St. Gerasimus (d. 475) and the monasteries of the Jordan valley and became one of the most important centers of Palestinian monasticism well into the Islamic period. Many of its buildings survive to this day. (Courtesy of Professor Joseph Patrich, The Hebrew University of Jerusalem.)

move, the adoption of Arabic as a church language, happened first in the community that would be called "Melkite," whose patristic and liturgical tradition had been and would remain Greek.[15] But increasingly from the eighth century onward, as the Melkite ecclesial identity grew into full maturity, Arabic in fact became this community's language of communal identity. Beginning in the second half of the eighth century, if not somewhat earlier, and reaching its stride in the ninth century, the Melkites, largely in the monasteries of Jerusalem, the Sinai, and the Judean desert of Palestine, produced an archive of Christian Arabic texts in a distinctive Arabic idiom,

[15] See Sidney H. Griffith, "From Aramaic to Arabic: The Languages of the Monasteries of Palestine in the Byzantine and Early Islamic Periods," *Dumbarton Oaks Papers* 51 (1997): 11–31.

and even in the beginning in a characteristic manuscript hand, which included translations of the scriptures, lives of the saints, and other classical texts of the church, as well as original compositions in Arabic. This community's enculturation into the world of Islam, therefore, was principally accomplished by their adoption of the by now thoroughly Islamicized Arabic language as an ecclesiastical language.[16]

The earliest translations of the Bible into Arabic for which we have any clear documentary evidence come from this period. While there undoubtedly was a pre-Islamic, proto-Arab Christian culture among the Arabic-speaking Christians who were in the Qur'ān's original audience, it seems to have been the case that in due course it was entirely subsumed into the nascent culture of Islam, or it disappeared at an early date in the Islamic era, along with the Christian allegiance of many of the Arab tribesmen who made up the early armies of the conquest. The evidence for any translations of the Bible or of liturgical texts into Arabic that they may have produced either has not survived or has not yet been discovered.[17] Rather, the earliest extant texts of the Bible in Arabic translation belong to a family of Palestinian, Melkite manuscripts, the earliest of which can in all probability be dated to the late seventh century, and they contain the four Gospels, translated from Greek, with hints of a relationship to earlier translations from Greek into Christian Palestinian Aramaic. They are equipped with rubricated notations marking the pericopes to be read during the several liturgical seasons of the year, according to the calendar of the old Jerusalem liturgy that persisted in use in the Syro-Palestinian communities until the Byzantinization of the Holy City's liturgical usages replaced it at the time of the return of Constantinopolitan influence over the see of Jerusalem from the eleventh century onward.[18]

Most of the works surviving in the archive of "old south Palestinian" Arabic manuscripts, as these early Melkite texts have been called by Joshua Blau, the modern scholar who has studied them most closely from a grammatical point of view,[19] are translations. Out of the sixty some works in the archive that Blau studied closely, he is sure of only five of them as original compositions.[20] All of these are apologetic works. The remaining works,

[16] See Sidney H. Griffith, "The Monks of Palestine and the Growth of Christian Literature in Arabic," *The Muslim World* 78 (1988): 1–28.

[17] It seems not improbable that Arabic-speaking, Christian priests, preachers, and teachers in pre-Islamic times may have had private notes or texts, even in Arabic, which would have served them as *aides de mémoire*. See Gregor Schoeler, *Écrire et transmettre dans les débuts de l'islam* (Paris: Presses Universitaires de France, 2002), 26–29.

[18] See Sidney H. Griffith, "The Gospel in Arabic: An Inquiry into Its Appearance in the First Abbasid Century," *Oriens Christianus* 69 (1985): 126–67.

[19] See Joshua Blau, *A Grammar of Christian Arabic*, CSCO, vols. 267, 276, and 279 (Louvain, Belgium: Peeters, 1966–67).

[20] Blau, *Grammar*, 267: 42–54, with the original compositions described on pp. 21–23. One suspects that the number should really be six, if not seven.

that is to say the translations, fall into the category of "church books," texts that Christians require for the ordinary conduct of their internal religious affairs. Among them is a group of thirty-five items, consisting mainly of homilies, saints' lives, martyrdoms, patristic selections, and so forth, while twenty-one pieces are Arabic versions of parts of the scriptures. This ratio of original compositions to translations, leaving room for the reassignment of some of the hagiographical items to the status of originals, accords well with what one otherwise knows of the sociohistorical situation of Christians in Syria/Palestine in the ninth and tenth centuries; the new cultural circumstances were forcing them to spend most of their energies translating their religious heritage into the new public idiom of the Islamic world. Beginning somewhat earlier, and continuing haphazardly even well into the Islamic period, these same Palestinian monasteries had also sponsored translations of many similar texts into Christian Palestinian Aramaic.[21] But, whereas the texts in this Aramaic dialect were intended totally for local use, the Arabic texts potentially spoke to a much wider world. In fact, a survey of the colophons of many of them reveals the fact that their network included communities in Palestine, Edessa/Ḥarrān, Antioch, Baghdad, Damascus, Sinai, and Alexandria in Egypt. The best way to get a sense of the range and significance of this translation movement is briefly to consider the activity of two of the translators whose names we happen to know. Their work may serve as a model for the accomplishments of their numerous colleagues, who are now known only by the many anonymous texts that happen to have survived until our times.

Anthony David of Baghdad, a monk and scribe of Mar Sabas monastery in the Judean desert in the late ninth century, is known from the colophons of two Arabic manuscripts he wrote in the year 885/6 for Abba Isaac of Mount Sinai.[22] These manuscripts, Vatican Arabic MS 71 and Strasbourg Oriental MS 4226 (Arabic 151), contain translations from Greek into Arabic of a number of patristic texts, such as the life of Epiphanius of Salamis by John of Constantinople, the lives of the monks Euthymius and Sabas by Cyril of Schythopolis, along with works by Anastasios of Sinai, Ephraem Graecus, Basil of Caesarea, Gregory of Nyssa, Athanasius of Alexandria, Isaac of Nineveh, and others. The case of the last-named writer, Isaac of Nineveh, is particularly interesting because his ascetic works had in the previous century been translated from Syriac to Greek by the monks Patrikios and Abramios at Mar Sabas monastery, testifying to an already flour-

[21] See Griffith, "From Aramaic to Arabic." See also Milka Rubin, "Arabization versus Islamization in the Palestinian Melkite Community during the Early Muslim Period," in *Sharing the Sacred: Religious Contacts and Conflicts in the Holy Land*, ed. Arieh Kofsky and Guy G. Stroumsa, 149–62 (Jerusalem: Yad Izhak Ben Zvi, 1998).

[22] See Sidney H. Griffith, "Anthony David of Baghdad, Scribe and Monk of Mar Sabas: Arabic in the Monasteries of Palestine," *Church History* 58 (1989): 7–19.

Fig. 2. Mar Sabas Monastery in the Judean Desert
Established in the year 483 CE by St. Sabas (439–532) and long known as the "Great Laura," Mar Sabas was home to many of the Greek, Syriac, Christian, Palestinian, Aramaic, and Arabic-speaking monks who contributed so much to Christian intellectual culture in Islamic times. The monastery flourishes to this day. (Courtesy of Professor Joseph Patrich, The Hebrew University of Jerusalem.)

ishing translation culture in the Judean desert monasteries in the eighth century.[23]

Stephen of Ramla was a monk of the monastery of Mar Chariton in the Judean desert in the last quarter of the ninth century. He worked on two manuscripts that have survived to modern times, British Library Oriental MS 4950, which he copied in the year 877, and Sinai Arabic MS 72, which he finished in the year 897.[24] The first of these texts contains two compositions originally written in Arabic, the one a summary presentation of Melkite theology in Arabic called *The Summary of the Ways of Faith in the Trinity of the Unity of God, and in the Incarnation of God the Word from*

[23] See Hilarion Alfeyev, *The Spiritual World of Isaac the Syrian*, Cistercian Studies, no. 175 (Kalamazoo, MI: Cistercian Publications, 2000), 30.

[24] See Sidney H. Griffith, "Stephen of Ramlah and the Christian Kerygma in Arabic in Ninth-Century Palestine," *Journal of Ecclesiastical History* 36 (1985): 23–45.

the Pure Virgin Mary,[25] and the other Theodore Abū Qurrah's Arabic tract on the veneration of the holy icons.[26] The second manuscript Stephen of Ramla wrote contains an Arabic translation of a Gospel lectionary that belongs to the family of Arabic texts of the four Gospels mentioned above; it is one of the earliest dated manuscripts of the Gospels in Arabic.

The "church books" translated by these monks and their colleagues would have served the ongoing needs of the members of the Melkite community, whose vernacular language would increasingly have been Arabic. The apologetic, original compositions in Arabic that they copied represent the first steps taken by the Melkites to address themselves to issues beyond their own internal community life, issues that take into account questions raised by Muslims and others, and which inevitably would by the late eighth century have been raised in Arabic.[27] In the subsequent centuries of Christian Arabic literature, this proportion of a large number of translations of Christian texts in other languages, relative to a small but steady output of original compositions in Arabic, would be maintained.

The Earliest Arab Christian Theologian

With the possible exception of two texts now preserved only in several papyrus fragments,[28] the oldest apology for Christianity in Arabic, and thus the earliest original Christian composition in Arabic now known, is undoubtedly the work preserved in an old parchment manuscript from Sinai (Sinai Arabic MS 154). In 1899 most of it was published and translated into English under the title *On the Triune Nature of God*.[29] Subsequent studies have expanded our knowledge of this important work, allowing one the opportunity now to review it from the point of view of its interface with

[25] See Samir Khalil Samir, "La 'Somme des aspects de la foi': Oeuvre d'Abū Qurrah?" and Sidney H. Griffith, "A Ninth Century *Summa Theologiae Arabica*," in *Actes du Deuxième Congrès International d'Études Arabes Chrétiennes (Oosterhesselen, septembre 1984)*, ed. Samir Khalil Samir, 93–121 and 123–41, Orientalia Christiana Analecta, 226 (Rome: Pontificio Istituto degli Studii Orientali, 1986).

[26] See Sidney H. Griffith, trans., *A Treatise on the Veneration of the Holy Icons Written in Arabic by Theodore Abū Qurrah, Bishop of Ḥarrān; Translated into English, with Introduction and Notes*, Eastern Christian Texts in Translation, 1 (Leuven, Belgium: Peeters, 1997).

[27] See Griffith, "The Monks of Palestine."

[28] See Georg Graf, "Christliche-arabische Texte; Zwei Disputationen zwischen Muslimen und Christen," in *Griechische, koptische und arabische Texte zur Religion und religiösen Literatur in Ägyptens Spätzeit*, ed. Friedrich Bilabel and Adolf Grohmann, 1–31 (Heidelberg: Verlag der Universitätsbibliothek, 1934).

[29] Margaret Dunlop Gibson, *An Arabic Version of the Acts of the Apostles and the Seven Catholic Epistles, with a Treatise on the Triune Nature of God*, Studia Sinaitica, 7 (London: C. J. Clay and Sons, 1899), 74–107 (Arabic), 2–36 (English).

Islam and, in particular, with the Qur'ān.[30] Indeed, the evocation of the Qur'ān and its religious categories is never far below the surface in any of the texts written in Arabic by Christian thinkers, however resolutely abstract and philosophical they may at times seem to be.

The treatise *On the Triune Nature of God* is anonymous as it has come down to us, and some of the last pages are missing, but at one point in the text the author provided an indication of the date of his writing. Speaking of the stable endurance of Christianity against all odds, even up to his own day, he wrote: "If this religion were not truly from God it would not have stood so unshakably for seven hundred and forty-six years."[31] If we reckon the beginning of the Christian era from the beginning of the year of the Incarnation, according to the computation of the Alexandrian world era, which Palestinian scribes were likely to use prior to the tenth century, we arrive at a date not too far removed from AD 755 for the composition of the treatise.[32] This date makes it the oldest known work of Christian theology originally composed in Arabic.

The treatise *On the Triune Nature of God*, to continue using the name Margaret Dunlop Gibson gave it in 1899, in fact discusses the following main issues: the doctrine of the Trinity, the Messiah in the history of salvation, the doctrine of the Incarnation, and the mission of the Apostles to preach the news of the coming of the Messiah in the person of Jesus of Nazareth to all nations. It closes with a long list of quotations from the books of the prophets that the author interprets as biblical testimonies to the works of the Messiah manifest in the life and ministry of Jesus. Near the beginning of the treatise, as he begins the discussion of the doctrine of the Trinity, the author makes a statement that may well serve as an expression of his purpose in the whole work. He says,

> We praise you, O God, and we adore you and we glorify you in your creative Word and your holy, life-giving Spirit, one God, and one Lord, and one Creator. We do not separate God from his Word and his Spirit. God showed his power and his light in the Law and the Prophets, and the Psalms and the Gospel, that God and his Word and his Spirit are one God and one Lord. We will show this, if God will,

[30] See Samir Khalil Samir, "The Earliest Arab Apology for Christianity (c. 750)," in *Christian Arabic Apologetics during the Abbasid Period (750–1258)*, ed. Samir Khalil Samir and Jørgen S. Nielsen, 57–114 (Leiden: Brill, 1994); Maria Gallo, trans., *Palestinese anonimo: Omelia arabo-cristiana dell'VIII secolo* (Rome: Città Nuova Editrice, 1994).

[31] Sinai Arabic MS 154, f. 100v. Unaccountably, Gibson omitted this leaf from her edition of the text.

[32] See Mark N. Swanson, "Some Considerations for the Dating of *Fī tathlīth Allāh al-wāḥid* (Sinai Ar. 154) and *Al-Jāmiʿ wujūh al-imān* (London British Library Or. 4950)," in *Actes du quatrième congrès international d'études arabes chrétiennes*, ed. Samir Khalil Samir, published in *Parole de l'Orient* 18 (1993): 117–41.

> in these revealed scriptures, to anyone who wants insight, [who] understands things, recognizes the truth, and opens his breast to believe in God and his scriptures.[33]

One notices straightaway the apologist's intention to make his case for the Christian teaching from the scriptures; he names the Law, the Prophets, the Psalms, and the Gospel. Reading his words with the Qur'ān in mind, as the author himself surely had it, one notices that these are precisely the biblical books the Qur'ān names, and what is more, the author's statement "that God and his Word and his Spirit are one God," is surely in this context an evocation of the passage in the Qur'ān that is most comprehensively critical of Christian doctrine, that is *sūrat an-Nisā'* 4:171. It is a passage to which later Christian apologists return again and again because it explicitly speaks of the Messiah, Jesus, son of Mary, as "God's Word" and as "a Spirit from Him." But what is truly surprising is to notice that as the text goes on the author is willing to include the Qur'ān by name among the scriptures from which he is prepared to quote in testimony to the credibility of the doctrine of the Trinity! At one point in the development of his argument, in search of testimonies for a notion of plurality comprehended within the affirmation of the oneness of the Godhead, he turns to the scriptures for citations of passages in which the one God speaks in the first person plural. He says,

> You will find it also in the Qur'ān that "We created man in misery [90:4], and We have opened the gates of heaven with water pouring down [54:11], and have said, and now you come unto us alone, as We created you at first [6:94]." He said also, "Believe in God, and in his Word; and also in the Holy Spirit [4:171]," but the Holy Spirit has brought it down "a mercy and a guidance from thy Lord [16:64, 102]," but why should I prove it from this and enlighten [you] when we find in the Law and the Prophets and the Psalms and the Gospel, and you find it in the Qur'ān that God and his Word and his Spirit are one God and one Lord? You have said that you believe in God and his Word and the Holy Spirit, so do not reproach us, O men, that we believe in God and his Word and his Spirit: and we worship God in his Word and his Spirit, one God and one Lord and one Creator.[34]

It is relatively rare in Christian Arabic texts from the early Islamic period to find passages quoted from the Qur'ān and directly attributed to the Is-

33 Gibson, *An Arabic Version*, 3 (English), 75 (Arabic). Here the English translation has been adapted from Gibson's version.

34 Gibson, *An Arabic Version*, 5–6 (English), 77–78 (Arabic). The awkward English translation has been slightly altered and while awkwardness remains, hopefully the point is clear; phrases from the Qur'ān are included in the passage.

lamic scripture by name. In the present treatise, the author not only quotes from it explicitly, but he regularly uses both the vocabulary and the thought-patterns of the Qur'ān throughout his work. In an important way the Islamic idiom of the Qur'ān has become his religious lexicon.[35] Furthermore, it is evident in the passage just quoted that the Christian author is addressing himself directly, at least in part, to devotees of the Qur'ān as well as to those of the Christian Bible. He speaks of what "we find in the Law and the Prophets and the Psalms and the Gospel" and of what "you find . . . in the Qur'ān." While this form of address in the second person may be rhetorical, in that the intended audience of the tract was probably those Arabophone Christians in the Melkite world of Palestine who at the time were tempted to convert to Islam, the fact remains that the writer does address himself to Muslims, albeit perhaps only in a literary flourish. So the question arises, does he consider the Qur'ān a revealed scripture on a par with the Law, the Prophets, the Psalms, and the Gospel? While the answer to this question is surely "No," given the fact that throughout the treatise arguments from the Bible and Christian tradition are adduced expressly to respond to the challenge of Islamic teaching, nevertheless the fact remains that the prominence of the Qur'ān's influence in the work does testify to the Muslim scripture's active currency even among the Christians in the Arabic-speaking community of eighth-century Palestine. And the author obviously thought that his quotations from the Qur'ān would have some probative value for his apologetic purposes. Indeed it seems clear that the Qur'ān has in important ways even set the agenda in this and all subsequent works of Christian theology in Arabic.

Another prominent feature of the tract *On the Triune Nature of God* is the high frequency in it of quotations from the Bible, especially from the books of the Old Testament. The author comments on these passages in such a way as to argue that they find their full meaning, and their fulfillment, in what one learns from the Gospel. This was, of course, the traditional mode of Christian thinking. What one should not fail to notice in the present context, however, is its immediate relevance to the Christian-Muslim dialogue in the early Islamic period. For in many ways the Qur'ān itself, particularly in what one might call its "prophetology," is a statement on how the scriptures of the Torah, the Prophets, the Psalms, and the Gospel are to be read and understood. Accordingly, a large part of the Arab Christian response to the challenge of Islam, in this work and in many others, consists of *scholia* and commentary on biblical passages.[36]

[35] For more on Qur'ānic language and style in this work, see Mark N. Swanson, "Beyond Prooftexting: Approaches to the Qur'ān in Some Early Arabic Christian Apologies," *The Muslim World* 88 (1998): esp. 305–8.

[36] See Sidney H. Griffith, "Arguing from Scripture: The Bible in the Christian/Muslim Encounter in the Middle Ages," in *Scripture and Pluralism: Reading the Bible in the Reli-*

In the context of the Melkite milieu of Palestine in the eighth century, the Arabic tract *On the Triune Nature of God* exhibits an attitude toward the world of Islam that finds in it not only a major challenge to Christian faith but also a cultural transformation that furnishes both a new idiom in which that faith must be articulated if it is to continue to carry conviction and a new opportunity for the proclamation of the Gospel. The writer did not argue against Islam directly. Rather, his intention was to commend the truth of Christianity to his readers, some of whom may have been Muslims, but who were most probably Arabic-speaking Melkite Christians, who may or may not have found conversion to Islam an attractive religious option. We do not know the name of the writer of this tract, nor do we know where he composed it. He was most probably a monk in one of the monasteries of the Judean desert, Mar Sabas or Mar Chariton. He wrote the treatise because in his day there was a pressing need for an effective catechesis in Arabic to support the faith of the Christians and to take advantage of the opportunity to proclaim the Gospel in a new social and political context. He was the first of a long line of Christian theologians to write in Arabic.

Pastoral Problems of Christians among Muslims

We may learn something of the social circumstances among the Christians under Islamic rule, which made the composition of tracts in Christian theology in Arabic a practical necessity, from the writer of another anonymous Christian Arabic text from the early Islamic period. It is the *Summary of the Ways of Faith* mentioned earlier as one of the works copied by Stephen of Ramla in the year 877 at the monastery of Mar Chariton in Palestine. The now unknown author spoke very concretely of the changing cultural and religious circumstances that prompted his own apologetic work. The *Summary* consists of twenty-five chapters, many of them comprised of preexisting pieces put together into a well-articulated ensemble. In the opening chapter, after a recitation of the Nicene/Constantinopolitan creed, the author remarks that ever since its publication it has been the task of Christian scholars to defend this creed vigorously against adversaries who would subvert it, and he mentions that no past adversary has been as formidable as the Muslims. He says that the present problem is that while the religious language of people in the past was over-subtle in theological matters, "the language of this community about God is a clear language which the broad mass of people understands." He means Arabic and he goes on to specify:

giously Plural Worlds of the Middle Ages and Renaissance, ed. T. J. Heffernan and T. E. Burman, 29–58, Studies in the History of Christian Traditions, 123 (Leiden: Brill, 2006).

> I mean their saying, *lā ilāha illa Allāh*. By *lā ilāha illa Allāh* they mean a God other than the Father, the Son and the Holy Spirit. According to what they say, God is neither a generator nor is He generated;[37] nor, according to what they say, is the Holy Spirit anything but a creature among creatures. So their saying *lā ilāha illa Allāh* and what we say is one in words but very different in meaning. That is because when we, the assembly of Christians (*an-Naṣārā*) say *lā ilāha illa Allāh* we mean by it a living God, endowed with a living Spirit (*rūḥ*) which enlivens and lets die, an intellect (*ʿaql*) which gives determination to whatever it wills, and a Word by means of which all being comes to be.[38]

So it appears from this remark that some contemporaneous Arabic-speaking Christians were making the first phrase of the Islamic *shahādah* their own; that they did so at all is a measure of their enculturation into the world of Islam. It also appears that some of the Arabic-speaking Christians were using Islamic language to conceal their Christian faith and to protect themselves from the reproach of the Muslims. The author says of these hesitant, Arabic-speaking Christians that they are a race living in the midst of the Muslims who rule over them, "a race born among them, grown up with them, and educated in their culture. They conceal their faith and disclose of it only what suits them."[39] The author then has this to say of these dissimulating Christians:

> They are the hypocrites (*munāfiqīn*) among us, marked with our mark, standing in our congregations, contradicting our faith, forfeiters of themselves (*al-khāsirīn*), who are Christians (*Naṣārā*) in name only. They disbelieve in their Lord and their God, Jesus Christ, the son of Mary; due to the disparagement of strangers they are ashamed to describe for them any of their Lord's actions in the flesh.[40]

The author of the *Summary of the Ways of Faith* pinpoints Christology as the decisive issue in Christian/Muslim relations in his day. He contends that once Christians have given way on this issue, the distinctiveness of their faith is eclipsed, and he describes the situation of such "wavering," Arabic-speaking Christians, whose ways he opposes, as follows. He says,

> If you ask them about Christ our Lord, they maintain that he is a messenger like one of the messengers;[41] they do not favor him in any way over them, save in the pardon he brought and in the taking of precedence. They are not concerned to go to church, nor do they do any

[37] See the Qur'ān, *Ikhlāṣ* 112:3.
[38] British Library Oriental MS 4950, f. 5v.
[39] Ibid., f. 6r.
[40] Ibid., f. 6v.
[41] See the Qur'ān, *al-Māidah* 5:75.

> of the things which Christians do in their churches. Openly declaring themselves to be in opposition to the trinity of the oneness of God and His incarnation, they disparage the messengers, the fathers, and the teachers of the New Testament. They say, "What compels us to say 'Father,' 'Son,' and 'Spirit,' and to maintain that the Messiah is God? We are content with that with which the Israelites were content, God is one (Deuteronomy 6:4). We have no need for the hypostases, nor for what mere human beings deem impermissible."[42]

The author warns such Christians, "Beware, the group you applaud is too smart for you and too bright for your arguments."[43] So he proposes to offer them a better way of thinking in his *Summary of the Ways of Faith*. One supposes that other writers of apologies for Christianity in Arabic were similarly motivated by the same kind of pastoral necessity that prompted this anonymous author to take up his pen and to write Christian theology in Arabic.

In this same connection, another text from the early ninth century, which also offers an insight into the social circumstances obtaining among the Christians at the time and which similarly prompted the author's response, is Theodore Abū Qurrah's (ca. 755–ca. 830) Arabic tract in defense of the Christian practice of venerating the holy icons. Abū Qurrah wrote the tract soon after the year 800; the circumstance that elicited it was a situation that manifested itself in the behavior of some Christians at the Church of the Icon of Christ, in the metropolitan city of Edessa. The problem was, as Abū Qurrah put it,

> Many Christians are abandoning prostration to the icon of Christ our God. . . . Anti-Christians, especially ones claiming to have in hand a scripture sent down from God, are reprimanding them for their prostration to these icons, and because of it they are imputing to them the worship of idols, and the transgression of what God commanded in the Torah and the Prophets, and they sneer at them.[44]

It is clear in the context that Muslims are the principal "anti-Christians" involved in the obloquy so many Christians feared. After having presented his arguments from scripture and reason in substantiation of the practice of venerating icons, Abū Qurrah cites some of the taunts the non-Christians voiced. For example, some people said, "If the icons of the saints are entitled to prostration by way of honor, make prostration to me; I am, they

[42] British Library Oriental MS 4950, f. 7v.

[43] Ibid., f. 7v–8r.

[44] Sidney H. Griffith, trans., *A Treatise on the Veneration of the Holy Icons Written in Arabic by Theodore Abū Qurrah, Bishop of Ḥarrān (c. 755–c. 800 A.D.)*, Eastern Christian Texts in Translation, 1 (Leuven, Belgium: Peeters, 1997), 29.

maintain, someone who is the image of God."[45] Others were afraid that if non-Christians saw "an icon of Christ shamefully crucified, they would say to us, 'Woe unto you! Are you not ashamed that this is your God?'"[46] Abū Qurrah argued that the icons are public proclamations of the truths for which authentic Christians are willing to bear the consequences for their testimony to their veracity. The pastoral problem was that some Christians were seeking to make accommodations with their oppressors in the matter of their public behavior regarding the icons, and this was the occasion for Abū Qurrah's treatise. This situation, writ large, was the circumstance that prompted the beginnings of Christian theology in Arabic.

Arabic-Speaking, Christian Theologians

Theodore Abū Qurrah is actually the first writer, whose name we know, who regularly wrote Christian theology in Arabic. He was a Melkite from Edessa in Syria, and he was perhaps for a time a monk in the monastery of Mar Sabas in the Judean desert. He was certainly in frequent association with the monastic establishment in Jerusalem. He was bishop of Ḥarrān in Syria in the early years of the ninth century.[47] A prolific writer, Abū Qurrah wrote both in Syriac and in Arabic, although none of his work in Syriac is known to have survived to our time. In Arabic almost twenty of his compositions are known and published.[48] And there are some forty-three, mostly very

[45] Griffith, *A Treatise on the Veneration of the Holy Icons*, 88.

[46] Ibid., 94.

[47] See Ignace Dick, "Un continuateur arabe de saint Jean Damascène: Théodore Abuqurra, évêque melkite de Harran," *Proche-Orient Chrétien* 12 (1962), 209–23, 319–32; 13 (1963), 114–29; Sidney H. Griffith, "Reflections on the Biography of Theodore Abū Qurrah," *Parole de l'Orient* 18 (1993): 143–70. But see also John C. Lamoreaux, "The Biography of Theodore Abū Qurrah Revisited," *Dumbarton Oaks Papers* 56 (2002): 25–40.

[48] The Arabic works of Abū Qurrah are published as follows: Constantine Bacha, *Les oeuvres arabes de Theodore Abou-Kurra, évêque d'Haran* (Beirut: Maṭbaʿat al-Fawāʾid li Ṣāḥibha li Ḥalīl al-Badawī, 1904); Bacha, *Un traité des oeuvres arabes de Theodore Abou-Kurra, évêque de Haran* (Tripoli, Syria, and Rome: L'Éevêché Grec-Catholique and Procureur des Basiliens de Saint-Sauveur, 1905); G. Graf, *Die arabischen Schriften des Theodor Abu Qurra, Bischofs von Ḥarrān (ca. 740–820)* (Paderborn, Germany: Ferdinand Schöningh, 1910); Louis Cheikho, "Mīmar li Tadūrūs Abū Qurrah fī wujūd al-Khāliq wa d-dīn al-qawīm" *al-Machriq* 15 (1912), 757–74; 825–42; G. Graf, *Des Theodor Abu Kurra Traktat über den Schöpfer und die wahre Religion*, Beiträge zur Geschichte der Philosophie des Mittelalters, Texte und Untersuchungen, Band XIV, Heft 1 (Münster, Germany: W. Aschendorf, 1913); I. Dick, "Deux écrits inédits de Théodore Abuqurra," *Le Muséon* 72 (1959): 53–67; S. H. Griffith, "Some Unpublished Arabic Sayings Attributed to Theodore Abū Qurrah," *Le Muséon* 92 (1979): 29–35; I. Dick, *Théodore Abuqurra, Traité de l'existence du createur et de la vraie religion; introduction et texte critique*, Patrimoine Arabe Chrétien, 3 (Jounieh and Rome, 1982); Dick, *Théodore Abuqurra, Traité du culte des icons; introduction et texte critique*, Patrimoine Arabe Chrétien, 10 (Jounieh and Rome, 1986). See also the selection of Abū Qurrah's Arabic works

brief compositions, preserved in Greek that are ascribed to Abū Qurrah.[49] All indications are that the Greek texts have been translated from Arabic. It is doubtful if Abū Qurrah himself wrote in Greek, although he certainly knew the language. At some point between 813 and 820, when he was in Ḥarrān, Abū Qurrah made an Arabic translation of the pseudo-Aristotelian treatise *De virtutibus animae* for Ṭāhir ibn al-Ḥusayn, the caliph al-Maʾmūn's (r. 813–33) general from Khorasan.[50] The last we hear of him in the historical record is in connection with a debate about the verisimilitude of the Christian religion, which took place between Abū Qurrah, the caliph al-Maʾmūn, and a number of Muslim scholars, in Ḥarrān in the year 829, when the caliph passed through the city on his way to battle on the Byzantine frontier.[51] Since by our reckoning Abū Qurrah would have been about seventy-five years old in that year, presumably he died not long afterward.

We have lingered over some of the details of Theodore Abū Qurrah's biography, skimpy as they are, because we actually know more about the course of his life than we do about the lives of most other Arabic-speaking Christian intellectuals of his era. One supposes that his career, mutatis mutandis, was not much different from that of others of his contemporaries whose names we know in ecclesiastical ministry. The Melkite Abū Qurrah, and the two earliest Arabic-speaking theologians of the other two mainline communities, the Jacobite Ḥabīb ibn Khidmah Abū Rāʾiṭah (d. ca. 851)[52] and the Nestorian ʿAmmār al-Baṣrī (fl. ca. 850),[53] both of whom were active in the generation after Abū Qurrah, may be taken altogether to repre-

translated into English by John C. Lamoreaux, *Theodore Abū Qurrah* (Provo, UT: Brigham Young University Press, 2006).

[49] The Greek texts attributed to Abū Qurrah were collected by Jakob Gretser in 1606 and republished by J. P. Migne, *Patrologia Graeca*, vol. 97, cols. 1445–1610. Few of them have been systematically studied.

[50] This information is contained in a statement appended to an Arabic version of the treatise. See Fuʾad Sayyid, *Fihris al-Makhṭūṭāt al-muṣawwarah*, part 2, *at-tāʾrīkh* (Cairo: Maṭbaʿat as Sunnah al-Muḥammadiyyah, 1954), no. 298, p. 59. See also M. Kellermann-Rost, "Ein pseudoaristotelischer traktat über die Tugend: Edition und Übersetzung der arabischen Fassungen des Abū Qurra und des Ibn aṭ-Ṭayyib" (unpublished PhD diss., Erlangen, 1965).

[51] See the report that derives from the lost chronicle of the Jacobite patriarch Dionysius of Tell Maḥrē, now included in the thirteenth-century Syriac chronicle *Ad Annum 1234 Pertinens*. See I.-B. Chabot, *Anonymi Auctoris Chronicon ad Annum Christi 1234 Pertinens*, CSCO, vol. 15 (Paris, 1916), 23. A later Arab Christian author composed an account of Abū Qurrah's replies on this occasion. See Ignace Dick, *La discussion d'Abū Qurrah avec les ulémas musulmans devant le calife al-Maʾmūn: Étude et edition critique* (Aleppo, Syria: Privately printed, 1999).

[52] See Sandra Toenies Keating, "Dialogue between Muslims and Christians in the Early 9th Century: The Example of Ḥabīb ibn Khidmah Abū Rāʾiṭah al-Takrī tī's Theology of the Trinity," (PhD diss., Catholic University of America, 2001).

[53] See Sidney H. Griffith, "ʿAmmār al-Baṣrī's *Kitāb al-burhān*: Christian *Kalām* in the First Abbasid Century," *Le Muséon* 96 (1983): 145–81.

sent the first full generation of creative thinkers among the Arabic-speaking Christian writers.[54] There were many other writers, of course, whose names have not come down to us even when their works have survived anonymously in the manuscript tradition. While responding to the challenges of Islam was high on their agendas, the first Arabic-speaking theologians, like the major Christian thinkers in the caliphate in the following generations, were also in a major way concerned with arguing in Arabic on behalf of the orthodoxy of the Christological formulas of their own confessional communities. In this way it came about that it was only in the early Islamic period, and in the Arabic language, that the three principal Christian churches of the world of Islam, the Melkites, the Jacobites, and the Nestorians, came to the full statement of their confessional identities.

In their more direct responses to the religious challenge of Islam, Abū Qurrah, Abū Rāʾiṭah, ʿAmmār al-Baṣrī, and their anonymous colleagues all wrote tracts in Arabic in which they addressed themselves to the intellectual search for the true religion and the signs that would verify it, as they often put the matter. This effort was in large part shaped in response to the contemporary program of Muslim scholars to commend the religious credibility of Islam, and to demonstrate that the signs of true prophecy and religion are verified in the career of Muḥammad, the teachings of the Qurʾān, and in the religion of Islam. The Christian writers of later generations in Syria and Iraq in all three of the mainline communities, such as the Jacobite Yaḥyā ibn ʿAdī (893–974),[55] the Nestorian Elias of Nisibis (975–1046),[56] the Melkite Paul of Antioch (ca. 1180),[57] again to name only the most well known of them, all followed suit.[58]

In the meantime, Muslim scholars and writers were taking note of the

[54] See Seppo Rissanen, *Theological Encounter of Oriental Christians with Islam during Early Abbasid Rule* (Åbo, Finland: Åbo Adademis Förlag, 1993). See also the essays on these and other contemporary writers collected in Sidney H. Griffith, *The Beginnings of Christian Theology in Arabic: Muslim-Christian Encounters in the Early Islamic Period*, Variorum Collected Studies Series, 746 (Aldershot, England: Ashgate, 2002).

[55] On Yaḥyā the religious writer, see Emilio Platti, "Yaḥyā ibn ʿAdī, philosophe et théologien," *MIDEO* 14 (1980): 167–84; Platti, "Une cosmologie chrétienne," *MIDEO* 15 (1982): 75–118; Platti, *Yaḥyā ibn ʿAdī: Théologien chrétien et philosophe arabe; sa théologie de l'incarnation*, Orientalia Lovaniensia Analecta, 14 (Leuven, Belgium: Katholieke Universiteit Leuven, Departement Orientalistiek, 1983).

[56] See Samir Khalil Samir, *Foi et culture en Irak au XIe siècle: Elie de Nisibe et l'Islam*, Collected Studies Series, 544 (Aldershot, England: Variorum/Ashgate, 1996).

[57] See Paul Khoury, *Paul d'Antioche: Évêque melkite de Sidon* (Beirut: Imprimerie Catholique, 1964).

[58] For a comprehensive list and description of the Christian Arabic writers and their works in all three of the principal denominations up to the middle of the fifteenth century, see Georg Graf, *Geschichte der christlichen arabischen Literatur*, vol. 2, Studi e Testi, 133 (Vatican City: Biblioteca Apostolica Vaticana, 1947). See also the systematic bibliographies in R. Caspar et al., eds., "Bibliographie du dialogue islamo-chrétien," *Islamochristiana* 1 (1975) to 7 (1981).

works of the Christian Arabic writers.[59] Some Muslims wrote against the Christian authors by name. For example, the Muʿtazilī Abū Mūsā ʿĪsā ibn Ṣubayḥ al-Murdār (d. ca. 840) is on record as having written a tract, *Against Abū Qurrah, the Christian*,[60] and among Abū Hudhayl al-ʿAllāf's works is one titled, *Against ʿAmmār the Christian, in Refutation of the Christians.*[61] Some of them, such as Abū ʿĪsā al-Warrāq (d. ca. 860)[62] and the Muʿtazilī *mutakallim* ʿAbd al-Jabbār (d. 1025),[63] the Andalūsī polemicist Ibn Ḥazm (994–1064),[64] and, somewhat later, the traditionalist Ibn Taymiyya (1263–1328),[65] set out to take account of the religious claims of the Christians in their midst in a major way and to refute their claims to religious liberty, their allegations of doctrinal verity, and the authenticity of their scriptures. As time went on many Muslims became unhappy with the seemingly easy relationships some Christian intellectuals enjoyed in the highest levels of Islamic society, especially in Baghdad and some other seats of Islamic government. What they wrote in response to this state of affairs testifies as well, albeit indirectly, to the entrée Christian and other intellectuals sometimes in fact enjoyed at the highest levels of society in the early Islamic period.

In this connection, one may cite an interesting passage from the biographical dictionary of the Spanish Arabs by the eleventh-century author Abū ʿAbd Allāh ibn Muḥammad al-Ḥumaydī (d. 1095). He tells the story of a certain Abū ʿUmar Aḥmad ibn Muḥammad ibn Saʿdī, who visited Baghdad at the end of the tenth century, not long after the death of the

[59] See Erdman Fritsch, *Islam und Christentum im Mittelalter* (Breslau: Müller and Seiffert, 1930); Ali Bouamama, *La littérature polémique musulmane contre le christianisme depuis ses origines jusqu'au XIIIe siècle* (Algiers: Enterprise Nationale du Livre, 1988).

[60] J. W. Fück, "Some Hitherto Unpublished Texts on the Muʿtazilite Movement from Ibn-al-Nadim's Kitāb-al-Fihrist," in *Professor Muhammad Shafi Presentation Volume*, ed. S. M. Abdullah, 62 (Lahore, Pakistan: Punjab University Press, 1955); Bayard Dodge, ed. and trans., *The Fihrist of al-Nadīm: A Tenth-Century Survey of Muslim Culture*, 2 vols. (New York: Columbia University Press, 1970), 1: 394.

[61] Fück, "Some Hitherto Unpublished Texts," 57–58; Dodge, *A Tenth-Century Survey*, 1: 388.

[62] See David Thomas, ed. and trans., *Anti-Christian Polemic in Early Islam: Abū ʿĪsā al-Warrāq's "Against the Trinity,"* University of Cambridge Oriental Publications, 45 (Cambridge: Cambridge University Press, 1992); David Thomas, ed. and trans., *Early Muslim Polemic against Christianity: Abū ʿĪsā al-Warrāq's "Against the Incarnation,"* University of Cambridge Oriental Publications, 59 (Cambridge: Cambridge University Press, 2002).

[63] See Gabriel Said Reynolds, *A Muslim Theologian in the Sectarian Milieu: ʿAbd al-Jabbār and the Critique of Christian Origins*, Islamic History and Civilization, Studies and Texts, vol. 56 (Leiden: Brill, 2004).

[64] See Theodore Pulcini, *Exegesis as Polemical Discourse: Ibn Ḥazm on Jewish and Christian Scriptures* (Atlanta: Scholars Press, 1998).

[65] See Thomas F. Michel, *A Muslim Theologian's Response to Christianity: Ibn Taymiyya's al-Jawāb al-ṣaḥīḥ* (Delmar, NY: Caravan Books, 1984).

Christian philosopher and apologist Yaḥyā ibn ʿAdī (d. 974). While he was there, Abū ʿUmar twice visited the sessions of some famous Muslim scholars of the city, but he vowed he would never attend them again. He was shocked at what he found in them. He is reported to have given the following account of his experience:

> At the first session I attended I witnessed a meeting which included every kind of group: *Sunnī* Muslims and heretics, and all kinds of infidels: Majūs, materialists, atheists, Jews and Christians. Each group had a leader who would speak on its doctrine and debate about it. Whenever one of these leaders arrived, from whichever of the groups he came, the assembly rose up for him, standing on their feet until he would sit down, then they would take their seats after he was seated. When the meeting was jammed with its participants, and they saw that no one else was expected, one of the infidels said, "You have all agreed to the debate, so the Muslims should not argue against us on the basis of their scripture, nor on the basis of the sayings of their prophet, since we put no credence in these things, and we do not acknowledge him. Let us dispute with one another only on the basis of arguments from reason, and what observation and deduction will support." Then they would all say, "Agreed." Abū ʿUmar said, "When I heard that, I did not return to that meeting. Later someone told me there was to be another meeting for discussion, so I went to it and I found them engaging in the same practices as their colleagues. So I stopped going to the meetings of the disputants, and I never went back.[66]

Clearly, Abū ʿUmar can be taken as a spokesman for the Muslim traditionalists in the later ʿAbbasid era, who may well have been in the majority already in Yaḥyā ibn ʿAdī's day. The visitor from Spain clearly disapproved of the very easy exchanges between the intellectuals of the several religious communities as he observed them in Baghdad at the very time that Yaḥyā himself was so fond of promoting them.

In the twelfth and thirteenth centuries, the center of gravity in the evolution of Christian Arabic literature shifted from Baghdad and the East, westward into Egypt. The Copts, who included some Melkites in their number, were by this time mostly Jacobites, that is, Monophysites in their confessional identity. They had begun to write theology in Arabic and to translate their church books into the new language of the dominant Islamic culture only in the tenth century. They did not summarily abandon their own Coptic language, as scholars have sometimes suggested,[67] but it was

[66] Abū ʿAbd Allāh al-Ḥumaydī, *Jadhwat al-Muqtabis*, ed. Muḥammad ibn Tāwīt al-Ṭanjī (Cairo: Dār al-Miṣriyyah, 1953), 101–2.

[67] See, in this connection, the findings of Jason R. Zaborowski, *The Coptic Martyrdom of*

certainly the case that by the thirteenth century Arabic had become as much and more so an ecclesiastical language in Egypt as it was already in Syria/Palestine and in Mesopotamia.

The earliest Coptic Orthodox author regularly to write in Arabic, whose name we know, is Severus ibn al-Muqaffaʿ (ca. 905–987). In the Arabic-speaking world Severus's apologetic works have been among the most frequently copied and the most widely disseminated of all Christian texts in the Arabic language.[68] After the time of Severus ibn al-Muqaffaʿ, Arabic quickly became the principal language of the Copts, and they went on to produce more texts in Arabic than all the other Christian communities in the caliphate put together; the list of the known authors and their works in our period is extensive.[69] In addition to numerous *florilegia* of patristic texts and translations from the scriptures and the works of earlier Christian writers, historical texts are among the more well known Christian Arabic works produced in Egypt. In this connection one might mention in particular the *Annals* of the Melkite patriarch, Eutychius of Alexandria (877–940),[70] and the famous, multiauthored *History of the Patriarchs of Alexandria*.[71]

In the thirteenth century in Egypt there dawned what some scholars have called a golden age in Christian Arabic literature.[72] It is symbolized by the activities of a remarkable family of Christian scribes and writers who are altogether called the *Awlād al-ʿAssāl*, the sons of ʿAssāl, who flourished during the middle years of the thirteenth century, 1230–60.[73] They were principally three, aṣ-Ṣafī, Hibatallāh, and al-Muʿtaman, who undertook impressive programs of manuscript discovery, copying, translating, and original composition of Christian theology in Arabic.[74] One of the notable features of their work is the obviously ecumenical character it assumed; they

John of Phanijōit: Assimilation and Conversion to Islam in Thirteenth-Century Egypt, The History of Christian-Muslim Relations, vol. 3 (Leiden: Brill, 2005), esp. 3–5, 133–35.

[68] See Sidney H. Griffith, "The *Kitāb miṣbāḥ al-ʿaql* of Severus ibn al-Muqaffaʿ: A Profile of the Christian Creed in Arabic in Tenth Century Egypt," *Medieval Encounters* 2 (1996): 15–42.

[69] See Graf, *Geschichte der christlichen arabischen Literatur*, 2: 294–468.

[70] See Sidney H. Griffith, "Apologetics and Historiography in the Annals of Eutychios of Alexandria: Christian Self-Definition in the World of Islam," in *Studies on the Christian Arabic Heritage*, ed. R. Ebied and H. Teule, 65–89, Eastern Christian Studies, 5 (Leuven, Belgium: Peeters, 2004).

[71] See Johannes den Heijer, *Mawhūb ibn Manṣūr ibn Mufarrij et l'historiographie copto-arabe: Étude sur la composition de l'Histoire des Patriarches d'Alexandrie*, CSCO, vol. 513 (Louvain, Belgium: Peeters, 1989).

[72] See, e.g., Samuel Rubenson, "Translating the Tradition: Some Remarks on the Arabicization of the Patristic Heritage in Egypt," *Medieval Encounters* 2 (1996): 4–14.

[73] See Georg Graf, "Die Koptische Gelehrtenfamilie der *Aulād al-ʿAssāl* und ihr Schrifttum," *Orientalia*, n.s. 1 (1932): 34–56, 129–48, 193–204.

[74] Graf, *Geschichte der christlichen arabischen Literatur*, 2: 387–414.

relentlessly sought out the best Christian tracts in Arabic from earlier times wherever they could find them, be their authors Nestorians, Jacobites, or Melkites. One of the family members, al-Muʿtaman, probably taking his cue from an earlier writer named Abū ʿAlī Naẓīf ibn Yumn (d. after 983), a Melkite in the circle of the Jacobite Yaḥyā ibn ʿAdī in Baghdad,[75] spoke in his magisterial *Summary of the Principles of Religion* of how all the Christian communities and denominations professed the same faith in Christ, albeit that they differed in their theologies.[76]

Finally, among the Copts there was Shams ar-Riʾāsa Abū al-Barakāt, often known under the name Ibn Kabar (d. after 1321). He wrote a virtual encyclopedia of Christian theology in Arabic, into which he subsumed texts of many earlier writers from the several communities, to the extent that his work is almost a reference book for Christian theology and ecclesiastical practice in Arabic, from its beginnings to the thirteenth century.[77] He called it *A Lamp in the Darkness*, a title that might well evoke a sense of the many difficulties and disabilities that Christians under Muslim rule in the Middle East increasingly came to experience, especially in the wake of the Crusades, the Mongol invasions of the mid-thirteenth century, and the long years of Mamlūk rule (1254–1517) in Egypt and in the Arabic-speaking world of Islam more generally.

In spite of the steady crescendo of scholarship in the area of Christian Arabic theology in the Middle East, especially in the twentieth century, it remains true that most of the writers of the early Islamic period remain unknown, and an even larger number of their texts remain unedited in their manuscripts, which are often hidden away in monastic libraries in the Levant, as well as in the major libraries of the Middle East and Europe. Scholarly labor has for the most part concentrated on the difficult task of providing critical editions and translations of individual works by the most important authors. A few anthologies have appeared, including brief selections from the writings of the major authors over the centuries,[78] but

[75] See Samir Khalil Samir, "Un traité du cheikh Abū ʿAlī Naẓīf ibn Yumn sur l'accord des chrétiens entre eux malgré leur disaccord dans l'expression," *Mélanges de l'Université Saint-Joseph* 51 (1990): 329–43.

[76] See A. Wadi, *Studio su al-Muʾtaman Ibn al-ʿAssāl* [Arabic], Studia Orientalia Christiana Monographiae, 5 (Cairo and Jerusalem: The Franciscan Centre of Christian Oriental Studies/Franciscan Printing Press, 1997). See also Al-Muʾtaman Ibn al-ʿAssāl, *Summa dei Principi della Religione*, ed. A. Wadi, Studia Orientalia Christiana Monographiae, 6a–b and 7a–b (Cairo and Jerusalem: The Franciscan Centre of Christian Oriental Studies/Franciscan Printing Press, 1998–99).

[77] See Graf, *Geschichte der christlichen arabischen Litertur*, 2: 438–45. For the text, see Samir Khalil Samir, ed., *Miṣbāḥ aẓ-ẓulma fī īḍāḥ al-khidma* (Cairo: Maktabat al-Kārūz, 1971).

[78] See, e.g., Louis Cheikho, *Seize traités théologiques d'auteurs arabes chrétiens* (Beirut: Dar al-Machreq, 1906); Cheikho, *Vingt traités théologiques d'auteurs arabes chrétiens* (Beirut: Dar

the texts remain in Arabic, with very few translations into western languages.[79] The field of study is ripe for further development.

It remains only to mention that in al-Andalus, Islamic Spain, there were also Arabic-speaking Christian theologians.[80] By the ninth century they too were translating the scriptures and other church books from Latin into Arabic and writing Christian theology and apologetics in the public language of the caliphate.[81] The earliest such writer whose name we know is Ḥafṣ ibn Albar al-Qūṭī (d. 889),[82] the son of the very Paulus Alvarus of Cordoba (d. 861), who in the previous generation wrote so vehemently against the Muslims in Latin and decried the adoption of Arabic on the part of young Spanish Christians. Ḥafṣ both translated the Psalms from the Latin Vulgate into Arabic and composed an apologetic treatise in Arabic against the Muslims. Unfortunately, the latter work survives only in portions quoted from it by a later, thirteenth-century Muslim writer of polemics against Christianity, known only as Imam al-Qurṭubī.[83] After Ḥafṣ ibn Albar, both because of a dearth of such material from the intervening period and the vicissitudes of time and history, modern scholarship knows of no other apologetic or polemic works written originally in Arabic by Spanish Christians until late in the eleventh century. For the later period, three important texts from the environs of Toledo, produced between the years 1120 and 1200, have been studied by Thomas E. Burman; he has edited the surviving Latin translation of the now lost Arabic original of the longest and most important of them, the so called *Liber De-*

---

al-Machreq, 1920); P. Paul Sbath, *Vingt traités philosophiques et apologétiques d'auteurs arabes chrétiens du IXe au XIVe siècle* (Cairo: H. Friedrich, 1929).

[79] There is at least one anthology of texts by multiple authors in English translation: N. A. Newman, *The Early Christian-Muslim Dialogue: A Collection of Documents from the First Three Islamic Centuries (632–900 A.D.); Translations with Commentary* (Hatfield, PA: Interdisciplinary Biblical Research Institute, 1993).

[80] For general orientation, see Dominique Millet-Gérard, *Chrétiens mozarabes et culture islamique dans l'Espagne des VIIe–IXe siècles* (Paris: Études Augustiniennes, 1984); Ann Christys, *Christians in al-Andalus (711–1000)* (Richmond, UK: Curzon Press, 2002).

[81] See H. Goussen, *Die christlich-arabische Literatur der Mozaraber*, Beiträge zur christlich-arabischen Literaturgeschichte, Heft, IV (Leipzig, 1909); Pieter Sjoerd van Koningsveld, "La literature cristiano-árabe de la España Medieval y el significado de la transmission textual en árabe de la Collectio Conciliorum," in *Concilio III de Toledo: XIV Centenario, 589–1989*, 695–710 (Toledo: Arzobispado de Toledo, 1991); Marie-Thérèse Urvoy, "La culture et la littérature arabe des chrétiens d'al-Andalus," *Bulletin de Littérature Ecclésiastique* 92 (1991): 259–75. See also Ioannes Gil, ed., *Corpus Scriptorum Muzarabicorum*, 2 vols. (Madrid: Instituto Antonio de Nebrija, 1973).

[82] See D. Dunlop, "Ḥafṣ b. Albar—the Last of the Goths?" *Journal of the Royal Asiatic Society* (1954): 136–51; D. Dunlop, "Sobre Ḥafṣ ibn Albar al-Qūṭ ī al-Qurṭubī," *Al-Andalus* 20 (1955): 211–13.

[83] See Thomas E. Burman, *Religious Polemic and the Intellectual History of the Mozarabs, c. 1050–1200*, Brill's Studies in Intellectual History, vol. 52 (Leiden: Brill, 1994), 14–15, 35–36.

nudationis.[84] For the rest, the Christian Arabic theological heritage of Islamic Spain is known mostly from reports of long lost works, rather than from any surviving manuscripts that contain them.

Arabic-Speaking Jews and Christian Theology in Arabic

Just as the Christian communities living under Islamic hegemony eventually adopted Arabic as an ecclesiastical language, as well as their language of everyday communication in the caliphate, so too did the Jewish communities in the several parts of the world of Islam follow in the same path at just about the same time. Like the Christians, Jews too, from the late eighth century onward, had important institutions in Baghdad, the seat of the Exilarch, and the scholarly center for the earliest Arabic-speaking scholars in the community.[85] As in the Christian case, no Jewish text in Arabic is known to have survived from pre-Islamic times. But in due course, once Jews widely adopted the public language of the world of Islam, Arabic eventually became one of the most important vehicles of Jewish thought in the Middle Ages, not only in the Middle East but perhaps more importantly in North Africa and Spain,[86] a circumstance that helps explain the fact that Jewish Arabic texts have received much more scholarly attention in the West in modern times than have Christian Arabic ones.

The earliest Jewish texts in Arabic in all probability appeared in the very period in which Arabic-speaking Christian theologians were beginning to write theology and to compose apologetic and polemical tracts to counter the religious challenges posed by both Jews and Muslims in the Islamic milieu. Significantly, the earliest Jewish Arabic texts reflect the same social and interreligious concerns, mutatis mutandis, as the ones with which the Christian writers were concerned.[87] In fact, the most prominent early Jew-

[84] See Burman, *Religious Polemic and the Intellectual History of the Mozarabs.*

[85] See Georges Vajda, "Le milieu juif à Baghdad," *Arabica* 9 (1962): 389–93.

[86] See the groundbreaking work of Moritz Steinschneider, *Die arabische Literatur der Juden: Ein Beitrag zur Literaturgeschichte der Araber; grossenteils aus handschriftlichen Quellen* (Frankfurt: J. Kaufmann, 1902). See also the general essay by Paul B. Fenton, "Judaeo-Arabic Literature," in *Religion, Learning, and Science in the ʿAbbasid Period*, ed. M. J. L. Young et al., 461–76, The Cambridge History of Arabic Literature (Cambridge: Cambridge University Press, 1990); Arthur Hyman, "Jewish Philosophy in the Islamic World," in *History of Islamic Philosophy*, ed. Seyyed Hossein Nasr and Arthur Leaman, 677–95, Routledge History of World Philosophies, vol. 1 (London: Routledge, 1996); Steven Harvey, "Islamic Philosophy and Jewish Philosophy," in *The Cambridge Companion to Arabic Philosophy*, ed. Peter Adamson and Richard C. Taylor, 349–69 (Cambridge: Cambridge University Press, 2005). See also Steven M. Wasserstrom, *Between Muslim and Jew: The Problem of Symbiosis under Early Islam* (Princeton, NJ: Princeton University Press, 1995).

[87] See, e.g., the study by David Sklare, "Responses to Islamic Polemics by Jewish Mu-

ish texts in Arabic were written not explicitly against the Muslims but against the Christians. This is the case with the famous *ʿIshrūn Maqālah,* the work of Dāwūd ibn Marwān al-Muqammiṣ, who in all probability flourished in the first half of the ninth century.[88] He was a Christian convert who reconverted to Judaism, who wrote in pointed detail, with the exact knowledge of a former "insider," against the doctrines and practices of his erstwhile Christian colleagues. His case reminds one of the roughly contemporary Muslim, anti-Christian polemicist, ʿAlī Rabbān aṭ-Ṭabarī, who was a Christian convert to Islam and the author of both a "Refutation of the Christians" (*radd ʿalā n-naṣārā*)[89] and a book demonstrating the truth of Islam called the "Book of Religion and Empire" (*Kitāb ad-dīn wa d-dawlah*).[90] The careers of these two converts from Christianity in the ninth century, the one to Judaism, and the other to Islam, readily testify to the multidimensional nature of the interreligious apologetic and polemical enterprise of the period, dominated as it was, in Arabic, by the contemporary growth and development of the Islamic *ʿilm al-kalām.*

Another Jewish text of a similar nature, which in its present form probably has its roots in the same ninth century, Arabic-speaking milieu, is the anonymous, anti-Christian work called in Arabic, *Qiṣṣat mujādalat al-usquf,* and in its later Hebrew translation, *Sefer Nestor ha-Komer.*[91] A *kalām* work in its form and style, like its Christian and Muslim counterparts in the same era, it argues in defense of the credibility of Judaism as the true religion, against the claims of contemporary Christian and even Muslim controversialists. Centuries later, in its Hebrew translation this work brought the religious controversies of the world of Islam in ʿAbbasid times into the polemical milieu of the Latin Middle Ages.

These two texts, the *Ishrūn maqālah* and the *Qiṣṣat mujādalat al-usquf,*

takallimūn in the Tenth Century," in *The Majlis: Interreligious Encounters in Medieval Islam,* ed. H. Lazarus-Yafeh et al., 135–61, Studies in Arabic Language and Literature, 4 (Wiesbaden: Harrassowitz, 1999).

88 See Sarah Stroumsa, ed. and trans., *Dāwūd ibn Marwān al-Muqammiṣ's Twenty Chapters (ʿIshrūn Maqālah),* Études sur le Judaïsme Médiéval, vol. 13 (Leiden: Brill, 1989).

89 See A. Khalifé and W. Kutsch, "Ar-radd ʿalā-n-naṣārā de ʿAlī aṭ-Ṭabarī," *Mélanges de Université de Saint Joseph* 36 (1959): 115–48. Translated into French by J. M. Gaudeul, *Riposte aux Chrétiens* (Rome: Pontifical Institute of Arabic and Islamic Studies, 1995).

90 See the Arabic text published in A. Mingana, ed., *Kitāb ad-d īn wa d-dawlah* (Beirut: Dār al fāq al-Jadīdah, 1982) and the English translation by A. Mingana, *The Book of Religion and Empire: A Semi-Official Defense and Exposition of Islam Written by Order at the Court and with the Assistance of the Caliph Mutawakkil (A.D. 847–861),* Manchester: Manchester University Press, and New York: Longmans Green, 1922). Regarding the controversies surrounding this text, see David Thomas, "Ṭabarī's Book of Religion and Empire," *Bulletin of the John Rylands Library* 69 (1986): 1–7.

91 See Daniel J. Lasker and Sarah Stroumsa, eds. and trans., *The Polemic of Nestor the Priest: Qiṣṣat Mujādalat al-Usquf and Sefer Nestor Ha-Komer,* 2 vols. (Jerusalem: Ben-Zvi Institute, 1996).

may be seen as examples of a newly enfranchised, Jewish, anti-Christian polemic, in response to the ongoing Christian, anti-Jewish invective, which seems to have actually increased in quantity and intensity just prior to the time of the rise of Islam.[92] Under Muslim rule the old *Adversus Judaeos* tradition continued among Christian writers in Syriac and Arabic, with the difference that no longer was the Jewish response muted. Rather, the adoption of Arabic in Jewish communities, and the gradual development of Judaeo-Arabic as a distinct state of the language,[93] opened new vistas for Jewish intellectual life in the world of Islam, including a role in the intercommunal, religious controversies of the time.

Along with the standard tropes of anti-Judaism inherited from an earlier era, one finds some newer motifs in the Syriac and Arabic texts written by Christians in the early Islamic period.[94] For example, some writers, and in this connection Theodore Abū Qurrah comes to mind, sometimes directed their polemics against Jews in such a way that it quickly appears they are stand-ins for the Muslims, who are the real adversaries of the piece.[95] Presumably, in the Islamic context it was safer to attack the Jews. One recalls in this connection too that in one of his Syriac letters, in which he reports a debate with a Muslim adversary at the caliph's court, the Nestorian Patriarch Timothy I refers to the Muslims not by name but as "the new Jews among us."[96] And in yet another twist on an older theme, in a number of literary dialogues written in Arabic by Christians and featuring a debate between Christian and Muslim adversaries, a Jewish character is sometimes introduced to vouch for the textual authenticity of the scripture passages cited by the Christian spokesman from the Old Testament.[97] But the real difference in the relationship between the Jews and Christians in the Is-

[92] See David M. Olster, *Roman Defeat, Christian Response, and the Literary Construction of the Jew* (Philadelphia: University of Pennsylvania Press, 1994); V. Déroche, "La polémique anti-judaique au Ve et au VIIe siècle: Un memento inédit, les *Képhalia*," *Travaux et Mémoires* 11 (1991): 275–312.

[93] See Joshua Blau, *The Emergence and Linguistic Background of Judaeo-Arabic*, 3rd rev. ed. (Jerusalem: Ben-Zvi Institute, 1999).

[94] See Sidney H. Griffith, "Jews and Muslims in Christian Syriac and Arabic Texts of the Ninth Century," *Jewish History* 3 (1988): 65–94.

[95] This is notably the case in Abū Qurrah's Arabic tract in defense of the veneration of icons. See Sidney H. Griffith, intro. and trans., *A Treatise on the Veneration of the Holy Icons Written in Arabic by Theodore Abū Qurrah, Bishop of Ḥarrān; Translated into English, with Introduction and Notes*, Eastern Christian Texts in Translation, 1 (Leuven, Belgium: Peeters, 1997).

[96] See Hanna Cheikho, *Dialectique du langage sur Dieu de Timothée I (728–823) à Serge* (Rome: Pontificium Institutum Studiorum Orientalium, 1983), 186 and n. 4.

[97] See Sidney H. Griffith, "The Monk in the Emir's *Majlis*: Reflections on a Popular Genre of Christian Literary Apologetics in Arabic in the Early Islamic Period," in *The Majlis: Interreligious Encounters in Medieval Islam*, ed. Hava Lazarus-Yafeh et al., 13–65, Studies in Arabic Language and Literature, vol. 4 (Wiesbaden: Harrassowitz, 1999).

lamic world was that now they participated in the religious controversies among themselves, and between the two of them and the Muslims, on an equal footing as members of subaltern, theoretically protected, minority groups, subsumed under the common religio-sociological label in the Islamic polity as "People of the Book" or "Scripture People." In these circumstances the Jews and Christians developed independent discourses in Arabic that nevertheless were intertwined with one another in many ways, and with the evolving Islamic discourses in the same linguistic and cultural milieu.[98]

The earliest major author of Jewish thought in Arabic whose name we know was doubtless Saʿadyah Gaʾōn ibn Yūsuf al-Fayyūmī (882–942), who was Egyptian by origin but who moved to Baghdad as an adult,[99] where he was a contemporary of noted Christian thinkers such as Abū Bishr Mattā ibn Yūnus (d. 940) and Yaḥyā ibn ʿAdī (893–974), along with the Muslims, Abū l-Ḥasan ʿAlī ibn Ismāʿīl al-Ashʿarī (873–935), the famous Sunnī *mutakallim*, Abū Naṣr al-Fārābiī (ca. 870–950), and Muḥammad ibn Zakariyyā ar-Rāzī (864–925), to mention only the most prominent Muslim philosophers of the time. Saʿadyah, like several of the earliest Arab Christian writers, held a prominent position in his own Jewish community; he translated the scriptures and other important Jewish texts into Arabic, he commented on parts of the scriptures, and in addition to many other intra-Jewish scholarly undertakings, he wrote original works in Arabic that reflect the controversies and concerns of Jewish, Christian, and Muslim thinkers of the era, most notably for the present purpose, in his *Book of Beliefs and Opinions.*[100] But his philosophical acumen was also much in evidence even in biblical commentary, as is evident in his Arabic translation of and commentary on the book of Job.[101]

Like the earliest Christian thinkers who wrote in Arabic, so too was Saʿadyah involved in intracommunal, virtually denominational controversies that had their roots in earlier history, but which came to the fore in a newly insistent way in early Islamic times. In the Jewish instance, in ninth-century Baghdad, this was particularly the controversy between the "Rab-

[98] See, e.g., Hava Lazarus-Yafeh, *Intertwined Worlds: Medieval Islam and Bible Criticism* (Princeton, NJ: Princeton University Press, 1992).

[99] See P.-B. Fenton, "Saʿadyā ben Yūsuf," *EI*, new ed., 7 (1993): 661–62; Lenn E. Goodman, "Saadiah Gaon al-Fayyumi," in Nasr and Leaman, *History of Islamic Philosophy*, 696–711.

[100] See Samuel Landauer, ed., *Kitâb al-amânât wa l-itiqâdât von Saʾadja b. Jûsuf al-Fajjûmî* (Leiden: Brill, 1880) and the English translation by Samuel Rosenblatt, trans., *Saadia Gaon: The Book of Beliefs and Opinions*, Yale Judaica Series (New Haven, CT: Yale University Press, 1948).

[101] See L. E. Goodman, trans. and commentator, *The Book of Theodicy: Translation and Commentary on the Book of Job by Saadiah ben Joseph al-Fayyūmī*, Yale Judaica Series (New Haven, CT: Yale University Press, 1988).

banites" and the "Karaites," in which Saʿadyah championed the Rabbanites.[102] In the next century in the Baghdad milieu, the Karaite scholar, Yaʿqūb ibn Isḥāq al-Qirqisānī, similarly composed works in Arabic that not only championed the opposite side in the intra-Jewish controversy, but which also engaged the thinking of Christians and Muslims writing in the same milieu.[103]

Meanwhile in North Africa, Isaac Israeli (850–932), like the Christian philosopher/physicians in Baghdad in the same era, was wrestling in his Arabic works with the tensions between the Aristotelian Neoplatonism of the early Muslim philosophers and the requirements of biblical faith.[104] But it was farther to the west, in Andalusia, that a Jewish thinker first systematically compared the religious claims of Judaism, Christianity, and Islam, with a view to commending Judaism as the true religion. The poet, Abū l'Ḥasan, Judah Halevi (ca. 1075–1141), did just this in his now famous book, the *Kuzari*, which he wrote originally in Arabic.[105] In Toledo the philosopher Abraham ibn Daʾud (1089–1164) took seriously the objections of Christians and Muslims in his book, *The Exalted Faith*, a systematic defense of the central institutions of Judaism that Ibn Daʾud originally wrote in Arabic but which has survived only in Hebrew and other translations.[106] At virtually the same time, and in much the same milieu, the polymath Abraham ibn Ezra (1089–1164) was producing the biblical commentaries that were to have long-lasting effects both within and beyond the world of Islam, not only among Jews but in the works of Christians and Muslims as well.[107]

No doubt the high point of Jewish thinking in the Arabic-speaking mi-

[102] See Daniel Lasker, "Rabbinism and Karaism: The Contest for Supremacy," in *Great Schisms in Jewish History*, ed. R. Jospe and S. M. Wagner, 47–72 (New York: Ktav Publishing House, 1981); Meira Polliack, "Rethinking Karaism: Between Judaism and Islam," *AJS Review* 30 (2006): 67–93.

[103] See Haggai ben Shammai, "Qirqisani on the Oneness of God," *Jewish Quarterly Review* 73 (1982): 105–11; Bruno Chiesa and Wilfrid Lockwood, eds. and trans., *Yaʿqūb al-Qirqisānī on Jewish Sects and Christianity* (Frankfurt: Peter Lang, 1984).

[104] See A. Altmann and S. M. Stern, *Isaac Israeli: A Neoplatonic Philosopher of the Tenth Century; His Works Translated with Comments and an Outline of His Philosophy*, Scripta Judaica, vol. 1 (London: Oxford University Press, 1958).

[105] See David Baneth and Haggai Ben-Shammai, eds., *Kitāb ar-radd wa d-dalīl fī d-dīn adh-dhalīl (al-kitāb al-Khazarī)* (Jerusalem: Magnes Press, 1977). See also Wout Jac. Van Bekkum, "The *Kuzari* of Judah Halevi and Its Reflection on Life, Faith, and Philosophy," in *The Three Rings: Textual Studies in the Historical Trialogue of Judaism, Christianity and Islam*, ed. Barbara Roggema et al., 3–18 (Leuven, Belgium: Peeters, 2005).

[106] See Norbert M. Samuelson, ed. and trans., *The Exalted Faith: Abraham ibn Daud*, ed. Gershon Weiss (Rutherford, NJ: Fairleigh Dickinson University Press, 1986). See also Resianne Fontaine, "Abraham ibn Daud's Polemics against Muslims and Christians," in Roggema, *The Three Rings*, 19–34.

[107] See Lazarus-Yafeh, *Intertwined Worlds.*

lieu, which is the focus of our present concern, was achieved by Moses Maimonides (1135–1204), who was originally from Andalusia but who spent most of his working life in Egypt.[108] Maimonides's *Guide for the Perplexed*,[109] to name only his most famous book outside the Jewish community, addresses from the Jewish perspective, and in the same Arabic language, many of the philosophical and theological issues that concerned the contemporary and earlier Christian and Muslim thinkers. Indeed, in the *Guide* Maimonides is one of the few Jewish writers in Arabic actually to mention by name earlier Muslim and Christian authors who discussed the same issues that concerned him in his famous book. Of the Christians, he mentions particularly John Philoponos (ca. 490–ca. 570) and Yaḥyā ibn ʿAdī (893–974);[110] Yaḥyā would have been appalled to know that Maimonides named him as one of those from whom the Muslim *mutakallimūn* learned the arts of the *ʿilm al-kalām*. Yaḥyā prided himself on being an Aristotelian logician, and in his own work he disparaged the methods of the *mutakallimūn*.[111] It was just a generation after Maimonides's lifetime that the golden age of Christian Arabic literature dawned in Egypt, highlighted, as we have seen, in the works of the so-called *awlād al-ʿAssāl*, who flourished in the environs of Cairo between the years 1230 and 1260.

Finally, among the Arabic-speaking Jewish writers who flourished in the time of those who inaugurated Christian theology in Arabic in the world of Islam, we must mention Saʿd ibn Manṣūr ibn Kammūna (ca. 1215–ca. 1285), a little-known Jewish philosopher who lived in Baghdad in a politically catastrophic period, who nevertheless around the year 1285 wrote a well-known book in Arabic in comparative apologetics. He called it *Tanqīḥ al-abḥāth li l-milal ath-thalāth*, a title usually translated into English as "Examination of the Inquiries into the Three Faiths."[112] In it, Ibn Kammūna follows closely the arguments of the Muslim *mutakallimūn* in connection with their efforts to show the authenticity of Muḥammad's prophetic mission; he compares their arguments with those put forward by Jews and Christians, concluding that the case for the claims of Judaism is

[108] See the magisterial work of Herbert A. Davidson, *Moses Maimonides: The Man and His Works* (Oxford: Oxford University Press, 2005).

[109] See the version of Shlomo Pines, trans., *Moses Maimonides: The Guide of the Perplexed*, 2 vols. (Chicago: University of Chicago Press, 1963).

[110] See Pines, *Moses Maimonides: The Guide*, 1: 177–78.

[111] See, e.g., Shlomo Pines and Michael Schwarz, "Yaḥyā ibn ʿAdī's Refutation of the Doctrine of Acquisition (*iktisāb*)," in *Studia Orientalia Memoriae D. H. Baneth Dedicata*, ed. J. Blau et al., 49–94 (Jerusalem: Magnes Press/Hebrew University, 1979).

[112] See Moshe Perlmann, ed., *Saʿd B. Manṣūr ibn Kammūna's Examination of the Inquiries into the Three Faiths: A Thirteenth-Century Essay in Comparative Religion* (Berkeley: University of California Press, 1967); Perlmann, *Ibn Kammūna's Examination of the Three Faiths: A Thirteenth-Century Essay in the Comparative Study of Religion, Translated from the Arabic, with an Introduction and Notes* (Berkeley: University of California Press, 1971).

the strongest.[113] The very title of his book testifies that as late as the thirteenth century in Baghdad, religious and philosophical inquiry was still in many ways conceived by the local scholars as featuring a colloquy between the "three faiths (*milal*)": Judaism, Christianity, and Islam. But Ibn Kammūna's own experience was a harbinger of things to come; he was attacked by a mob in Baghdad, furious at the treatment of Islam in his book, a development that precipitated his flight from the city.[114] Subsequently, several Muslims composed tracts against Ibn Kammūna's book, and in the early fourteenth century a Jacobite Christian writer, Abū l-Ḥasan ibn al-Maḥrūma, wrote a series of critical marginal notes (*al-ḥawāshī*) appended to Ibn Kammūna's chapters on the Jews and the Christians.[115]

While modern commentators speak rather easily of a colloquy between the scholars of the three faiths in early Islamic times, and indeed the works of the Arabic-speaking Jews, Christians, and Muslims of the period do regularly cite one another's beliefs and practices, one must nevertheless point out that evidence for actual conversations between the scholars of the three communities, either literary or viva voce, is rare. Seldom are the Christian scholars mentioned in the works by Jewish authors we have mentioned, nor are the contemporary Jewish scholars, with the notable exception of Ibn Kammūna, mentioned by the Christian writers. They and the contemporary Muslims lived and wrote in the same milieu and responded to one another's arguments, often in a caricatured fashion. But the colloquy can now only be traced by a comparative study of their texts, a difficult and very specialized task that requires a rare expertise in at least two of the three traditions, not to mention uncommon linguistic skills.

[113] See the analyses of Barbara Roggema, "Epistemology as Polemics: Ivn Kammūna's Examination of the Apologetics of the Three Faiths," in Roggema, *The Three Rings*, 47–68.

[114] See Roggema, "Epistemology as Politics," 50.

[115] See Ḥabīb Bacha, ed., *Ḥawāshī (Notes) d'ibn al-Maḥrūma sur le Tanqīḥ d'ibn Kammūna*, Patrimoine Arabe Chrétien, 6 (Jounieh, Lebanon: Librairie Saint-Paul and Rome: Pontificio Istituto Orientale, 1984).

IV

THE SHAPE OF CHRISTIAN THEOLOGY IN ARABIC

THE GENRES AND STRATEGIES OF CHRISTIAN DISCOURSE IN THE WORLD OF ISLAM

The Genres of Christian Arabic Theology

One can discern a theological development in the works of the Christian authors who wrote in Arabic in the early Islamic period. This development comes into view in the ways in which these writers articulated their Christian doctrines in parallel, almost in tandem, with the evolving patterns of Islamic religious thought in the same period. The same might be said of many of the works of the contemporary Jewish writers whom we have mentioned. In this context, Christians sought to defend the reasonableness of their distinctive doctrines in terms of the same religious idiom as that employed by their Muslim interlocutors and counterparts, who, in accord with the teachings of the Qurʾān, often rejected the central Christian doctrines. In contrast with the previously standard modes of Christian discourse in Greek or Syriac, for example, the Arabic-speaking Christian writers often built their arguments on ways of thinking that the Muslims had initially elaborated in view of commending their own faith in the Qurʾān and in the traditions of the prophet Muḥammad. As a result, the discourse of the Christian apologists in Arabic presents a conceptual profile that cannot easily be mistaken for Christian theology in any other community of Christian discourse. For example, their approach to the reasoned articulation in Arabic of the doctrines of the Trinity and the Incarnation involved the effort to express the former in terms of the contemporary Islamic discussion of the ontological status of the divine attributes, the Qurʾān's "beautiful names of God," and the latter in terms of the Islamic discussion of the signs of authentic prophecy and true religion.[1] This theological development be-

[1] For a detailed discussion of prophecy and its signs from the perspective of a Jewish scholar in the Islamic milieu, see the work of Ibn Kammūna: Moshe Perlmann, trans., *Ibn Kammūn's Examination of the Three Faiths: A Thirteenth-Century Essay in the Comparative Study of Religion* (Berkeley: University of California Press, 1971).

came traditional in Christian religious discourse in Arabic in the Islamic world; it was improved over the centuries by many writers in different times and places, but scarcely ever abandoned until the modern era.[2] It makes sense and carries intelligibility and conviction, the most readily only in the Arabic-speaking Islamic milieu; it is not a discourse easily translated into the theological idioms of the West.

The principal genres of Christian theology and apology in Arabic had their origins in texts composed by Syriac-speaking, Christian writers in the early years of Islamic times.[3] All of them, it is interesting to note, are dialogical in form and literary structure. The earliest texts we know, all of them written in the eighth century, are: "the interrogation of Patriarch John I (r. 631–48) by a Muslim Emir";[4] "The Debate of a Monk of Beth Ḥālê with an Arab Notable";[5] "Chapter X of the *Scholion* of Theodore bar Kônî (fl. ca. 792)";[6] and the "Epistle" of Patriarch Timothy I (r. 780–823) in which he recounts his debate with Caliph al-Mahdī (r. 775–85).[7] In these, and other early texts, both in Syriac and eventually Arabic, the principal

[2] In this connection, see Daniel Gimaret, *Les noms divins en Islam: Exégèse lexicographique et théologique* (Paris: Cerf, 1988); Mark N. Swanson, "Are Hypostases Attributes? An Investigation into the Modern Egyptian Christian Appropriation of the Medieval Arabic Apologetic Heritage," *Parole de l'Orient* 16 (1990–91): 239–50.

[3] For a general survey of these texts, see Sidney H. Griffith, "Disputes with Muslims in Syriac Christian Texts: From Patriarch John (d. 648) to Bar Hebraeus (d. 1286)," in *Religionsgespräche im Mittelalter*, ed. Bernard Lewis and Friedrich Niewöhner, 251–273, 25. Wolfenbütteler Symposion, 1989 (Wiesbaden: Harrassowitz, 1992). See also Michael Penn, "Syriac Sources for the Study of Early Christian-Muslim Relations," *Islamochristiana* 29 (2003): 59–78.

[4] See François Nau, "Un colloque du patriarche Jean avec l'émir des Agaréens et faits divers des années 712 à 716," *Journal Asiatique*, series 11, 5 (1995): 225–79. See the English translation in N. A. Newman, ed., *The Early Christian-Muslim Dialogue; a Collection of Documents from the First Three Islamic Centuries (632–900 A.D.); Translations with Commentary* (Hatfield, PA: Interdisciplinary Biblical Research Institute, 1993), 7–46. See also Samir Khalil Samir, "Qui est l'interlocuteur musulman du patriarche syrien Jean III (631–648)?" in *IV Symposiium Syriacum 1984*, ed. Han J. W. Drijvers et al., 387–400, Orientalia Christiana Analecta, 229 (Rome: Pontifical Institute of Oriental Studies, 1987).

[5] See the very brief descriptions of this still unpublished text in Peter Jager, "Intended Edition of a Disputation between a Monk of the Monastery of Bêt Ḥālê and One of the Ṭayôyê," in Drijvers, *IV Symposium Syriacum*, 401–2; Sidney H. Griffith, "Disputing with Islam in Syriac: The Case of the Monk of Bêt Ḥālê and a Muslim Emir," *Hugoye* 3 (2000), http://syrcom.cua.edu/Hugoye/Vol3No1/HV3N1Griffith.html. See also Hoyland, *Seeing Islam*, 465–72.

[6] See A. Scher, *Theodorus bar Kônî Liber Scholiorum*, CSCO, vols. 55 and 69 (Paris, 1910 and 1912), 69: 231–84. See also Sidney H. Griffith, "Theodore bar Kônî's Apology for Christianity," *Orientalia Christiana Periodica* 47 (1981): 158–88.

[7] See the text published in Alphonse Mingana, *Woodbrooke Studies; Christian Documents in Syriac, Arabic, and Garshūni, Edited and Translated with a Critical Apparatus*, vol. 2 (Cambridge: Heffer, 1928), 1–162. English translation alone in Newman, *The Early Christian-Muslim Dialogue*, 163–267.

genres of Christian apology in the world of Islam are already in evidence. One may categorize them under the following four descriptive headings: "the monk in the emir's *majlis*," "the master and the disciple," the epistolary exchange, and the formally systematic treatise.

The Monk in the Emir's Majlis

Three of these texts, excluding Theodore bar Kônî's work, are the earliest examples of a distinct genre of Christian apologetic literature, which, in Arabic, became the most popular of all the apologetic genres: "The Monk in the Emir's *Majlis*."[8] Typically, as the name implies, the texts in this genre feature accounts of monks or other ecclesiastics summoned into the presence of Muslim authorities and required to defend their faith in open debate with a caliph, an emir, and/or a phalanx of Muslim scholars. The narrator tells the story of their encounter and details the course of the conversations. In the case of Patriarch John I and the Muslim emir, the narrative is in the form of a letter, sent as if from the patriarch himself by a member of his entourage. It tells of the occasion, on Sunday, May 9, probably in the year 644, when the patriarch was allegedly summoned to appear before the emir ʿUmayr ibn Saʿd al-Anṣārī to answer questions about Christian faith and practice. According to the narrator, the letter was composed in the first place to allay fears in the Christian community about the patriarch's safety. But there are other issues as well, including an intra-Christian agenda. For example, the narrator says that the patriarch spoke to the emir in behalf of all the Christians, not just for his own Jacobite community; even the Melkites are said to have prayed for him. What is more, although the encounter between the patriarch and the emir is said to have taken place at a very definite time in the first half of the seventh century, all indications are that the text, in the form in which we have it, was written in the early eighth century.[9] This circumstance calls attention to the fact that the narrative has a literary and social function of its own, independent of its historical point of reference. It is an apologetic text, intended for circulation in the Syriac-speaking, Christian community. In its narrative the reader is invited to participate imaginatively with the narrator in a scenario into which a Christian has been brought to give an account of himself and his ways of faith, both to himself and to an inquisitive, domineering Muslim, in a context that mirrors with some verisimilitude the very religiously challenging milieu in which he, the reader, actually lives. The

[8] See Sidney H. Griffith, "The Monk in the Emir's *Majlis*," in *The Majlis; Interreligious Encounters in Medieval Islam*, ed. Hava Lazarus Yafeh et al., 13–65, Studies in Arabic Language and Literature, 4 (Wiesbaden: Harrassowitz, 1999).

[9] For a slightly different view, see Gerrit J. Reinink, "The Beginnings of Syriac Apologetic Literature in Response to Islam," *Oriens Christianus* 77 (1993): 165–87.

narrative details furnish this scenario of verisimilitude; its social function, in the context of the story's composition, extends beyond a simply documentary purpose to an exemplary one.

The same can be said with even more confidence about the account of the debate between the monk of Bêt Ḥālê and a Muslim notable. In this narrative the background details are kept to a minimum; there is no real chance of learning anything concrete about the interlocutors, other than the fact that it is surely plausible that a monk in a monastery in the environs of Antioch in the first third of the eighth century could well have had the opportunity to get into a conversation about religion with a disabled Muslim soldier. In the narrative the emphasis is on the debate itself, on the topics that two men are said to have discussed, and on the fact that in each instance the monk could give such satisfactory answers to the Muslim Arab's questions that were it not for social pressure, as the narrative has him say in conclusion, the Muslim would have become a Christian. The topics are those that would be the standard ones in Christian apologetic literature produced in the Islamic world for the next millennium and more. They include: the faith of Abraham; the doctrines of the Trinity and the Incarnation; the Christian estimation of the status of Muḥammad as a prophet, and of the Qur'ān as a revelatory scripture; the Christian practice of venerating crosses and icons; and how to recognize the true religion. The action in the story is in the monk's deft handling of the Muslim's questions; he always scores the debater's point, and thus shows the Syriac reader how the religious challenge of Islam in arguments about religion can best be met.[10]

In Patriarch Timothy's account of his conversations with the caliph al-Mahdī, the same topics are discussed. The patriarch himself composed the letter in which the account is given, addressed to his friend Sergius. He was in the habit of writing public letters of this sort; one might even call them letter-treatises, the epistolary conventions being just that, a matter of conventional literary style.[11] The reader is invited to observe the patriarch giving brilliantly satisfactory answers to the Islamic challenge to Christian teachings in a way that not only commended the veracity of the Christian doctrines and practices, but did so in a style of writing that subtly discounted the claims of Islam in seemingly inoffensive language as well. It is no wonder that this text circulated in the Christian communities for centuries in its own language, in its entirety and also in an abbreviated form, and eventually in Arabic translation.[12]

[10] See Hoyland, *Seeing Islam*, 465–72. See also Griffith, "Disputing with Islam in Syriac."

[11] See Eva Riad, *Studies in the Syriac Preface*, Studia Semitica Upsaliensia, 11 (Uppsala, Sweden: Almqvist and Wiksell, 1988).

[12] See Hans Putman, *L'Église et l'islam sous Timothée I (780–823)* (Beirut: Dar El-Machreq, 1975).

Fig. 3. Ibn Bakhtishūʿ and the Emir Saʾl ad-Dīn in Discussion
In the thirteenth-century Arabic manuscript containing the work by Ibn Bakhtishūʿ called *Animals and Their Uses*, the illustration portrays the author, who was from a famous Christian family, in a colloquy with his Muslim patron. Such conversations between the members of the intelligentsia of the several religious communities were common in ʿAbbasid Baghdad. (British Library Oriental Manuscript 2984, thirteenth-century Arabic, ff. 101v–102. Arabic translation of Aristotle's "Animals and Their Uses," by permission of the British Library.)

From the ninth century onward, the genre "The Monk in the Emir's *Majlis*" flourished, especially in Arabic. One finds the names of some of the most well known Arab Christian apologists associated with it. In this connection, after the account of Patriarch Timothy's encounter with al-Mahdī, one thinks most immediately of the dialogue of the monk Abraham of Tiberias with the emir ʿAbd ar-Raḥmān al-Hāshimī in Jerusalem around the year 820;[13] of the story of the debate of Theodore Abū Qurrah (ca. 755—

[13] See Giacinto Bulus Marcuzzo, *Le dialogue d'Abraham de Tibériade avec ʿAbd al-Raḥmān*

ca. 830) in the *majlis* of the caliph al-Ma'mūn (r. 813–33);[14] of the *Kitāb al-majālis*, or "Book of Sessions," of Elias bar Shināyâ (975–1046);[15] and of the debate of the monk George as-Sim'ānī with the Muslim scholars of Aleppo in the twelfth century.[16] To judge by the number of the surviving manuscripts, these texts had a wide popularity in the Arab Christian world.

One might also include in this category one of the most popular of all the Christian apologetic texts in the world of Islam, the so-called Christian Baḥîrâ Legend.[17] While it does not, strictly speaking, feature a monk answering for Christianity in an emir's *majlis*, the central scene in the story is not so far removed from this setting. Within the context of an apocalyptical narrative explaining the rise and early history of Islam, the text includes an account of a series of meetings between Muḥammad and the monk Baḥîrâ, in which the reader learns that whatever is good and true in the teachings of Islam and in the Qur'ān, Muḥammad learned from the monk. The story circulated widely in all the Christian communities; in its original form it was composed in Syriac, but it was soon translated and somewhat transposed into Arabic. In the Syriac recension, the apocalyptic narrative is more pronounced; in the Arabic recension, in which the story

---

al-Hāšimī à Jérusalem vers 820, Textes et Études sur l'Orient Chretien, 3 (Rome: Pontifico Istituto Orientale, 1986).

[14] See the brief summary in Alfred Guillaume, "A Debate between Christian and Muslim Doctors," *Journal of the Royal Asiatic Society*, centenary supplement (October 1924): 233–44; A. Guillaume, "Theodore Abu Qurra as Apologist," *The Moslem World* 15 (1925): 42–51: Sidney H. Griffith, "The Qur'ān in Arab Christian Texts: The Development of an Apologetical Argument: Abū Qurrah in the *Maǧlis* of al-Ma'mūn," *Parole de l'Orient* 24 (1999): 203–33.

[15] The Arabic text is published in Louis Cheikho, "Majālis Ilīyā Muṭrān Nusaybīn," *al-Machriq* 20 (1922): 33–44, 112–17, 117–22, 267–70, 270–72, 366–77, 425–34. See also the detailed study in Samir Khalil Samir, "Entretien d'Elie de Nisibe avec le vizir Ibn 'Alī al-Maghribī, su l'Unité et la Trinité," *Islamochristiana* 5 (1979): 31–117. See also Samir, *Foi et culture en Irak au XIe siècle; Elie de Nisibe et l'Islam* (Aldershot, UK: Variorum, 1996).

[16] The text was published by Paul Carali, *Le Christianisme et l'Islam. Controverse attribuée au moine Georges du Couvent de St. Siméon (Séeucie) soutenue devant le Prince El-Mouchammar Fils de Saladin en 1207* (Beit Chebab, Lebanon: Imprimerie Al-Alam, 1933). English translation in Alex Nicoll, "Account of a Disputation between a Christian Monk and Three Learned Mohammedans on the Subject of Religion," in *The Edinburgh Annual Register for 1816*, vol. 9, parts 1 and 2 (Edinburgh: A. Richbald Constable, 1820), ccccv–ccccxlii.

[17] Syriac and Arabic recensions of the story are published in Richard Gottheil, "A Christian Bahira Legend," *Zeitschrift für Assyriologie* 13 (1898): 189–242; 14 (1899), 203–68; 15 (1900), 56–102; 17 (1903), 125–66. See also Sidney H. Griffith, "Muḥammad and the Monk Baḥîrâ: Reflections on a Syriac and Arabic Text from Early Abbasid Times," *Oriens Christianus* 79 (1995): 146–74; Barbara Roggema, "A Christian Reading of the Qur'ān: The Legend of Sergius-Baḥīrā and Its Use of the Qur'ān and Sīra," in *Syrian Christians under Islam: The First Thousand Years*, ed. David Thomas, 57–73 (Leiden: Brill, 2001). It is pertinent to note in passing that there was also a Jewish version of the Baḥīrā story. See Moshe Gil, *A History of Palestine, 634–1099* (Cambridge: Cambridge University Press, 1992), 690.

seems to have had its widest circulation, the central scenario of the catechizing of Muḥammad by the monk is enhanced, in line, it seems, with the heightened interest in debate and apologetics among Arabic-speaking Christians from the ninth century onward. The point of the narrative is to maintain that in its original form, the Qur'ān, as Baḥîrâ is supposed to have taught it to Muḥammad, proclaimed the truth, as Christians see it, about all the issues in controversy between Muslims and Christians. According to the story, Jews and others subsequently corrupted this true Islamic scripture into the form in which the Islamic community now actually has the Qur'ān.[18] In the narrative the monk is the principal character who artfully commends the truths of Christianity. In this way his role approximates that of the principal characters in the works that more properly compose the apologetic genre, "the Monk in the Emir's *Majlis*."

Questions and Answers

Theodore bar Kônî (fl. ca. 792) seems to have been the first Syriac writer to employ the genre, "the Master and his Disciple," in a Christian apologetic work written in response to the religious challenge of Islam. At the heart of the genre is the "Question and Answer" style of textual presentation. In time to come the literary conventions of this scholarly style would contribute much to the development of the formalities of the Christian and Islamic science of *kalām*, the systematic discipline of interreligious disputation in Arabic.[19] Bar Kônî used this "Question and Answer" style throughout his summary presentation of the doctrines of the so-called Nestorians,[20] the ecclesial community we now call the Assyrian Church of the East, in the book he entitled simply *Scholion*.[21] In it he included a chapter, chapter 10, specifically dedicated to the apology for Christianity in response to questions posed by a would-be Muslim.[22] In the preface of the chapter, Bar Kônî explained his choice of genre in the chapter this way: "Although

[18] On this theme see Griffith, "The Qur'ān in Arab Christian Text."

[19] See Michael Cook, "The Origins of *Kalām*," *Bulletin of the School of Oriental and African Studies* 43 (1980): 32–43; Hans Daiber, "Masā'il wa-Adjwiba," in *EI*, 2nd ed., vol. 6, 636–39.

[20] See Sebastian P. Brock, "The 'Nestorian' Church: A Lamentable Misnomer," *Bulletin of the John Rylands University Library of Manchester* 78 (1996): 23–35.

[21] A. Scher, *Theodorus bar Kônî Liber Scholiorum*, CSCO, vols. 55 and 69 (Paris: E Typographeo Reipublicae, 1910 and 1912); R. Hespel and R. Draguet, *Theodore bar Koni Livre des Scolies*, CSCO, vols. 431 and 432 (Louvain, Belgium: Peeters, 1981 and 1982). See also Sidney H. Griffith, "Theodore bar Kônî's *Scholion*: A Nestorian *Summa Contra Gentiles* from the First Abbasid Century," in *East of Byzantium: Syria and Armenia in the Formative Period*, ed. N. Garsoïan et al., 53–72 (Washington, DC: Dumbarton Oaks, 1982).

[22] See Sidney H. Griffith, "Chapter Ten of the *Scholion*: Theodore bar Kônî's Apology for Christianity," *Orientalia Christiana Periodica* 47 (1981): 158–88.

it is a full refutation against the *ḥanpê*,[23] and a ratification of the faith, we are putting it in questions [and answers] according to our custom in the whole book; the student takes the part of the *ḥanpê*, and the teacher the part of the Christians."[24]

Within the framework of the questions and answers in this "Master" and "Disciple" scheme, Bar Kônî discusses the principal topics of controversy between Christians and Muslims, beginning with Christian usages that have a public face, such as the rite of Baptism, the Eucharist, and the practice of venerating the cross. Then he moves on to the doctrines that are always at issue, the Trinity and the Incarnation. The Master's answers to the Disciple's questions are clever defenses of the doctrines and practices under challenge. The persuasive quotients of the arguments that are advanced are vouched for in the conclusion, where the Disciple/Muslim is made to declare: "Even though I believe that these things are so, I cannot abandon the tradition (*mashlmānûtâ*) that I hold and become a convert because I am ashamed of the reproach which is in human disgrace."[25]

This Question and Answer format went on to become quite popular among later Arabic-speaking Christian apologists, even when they dispensed with the literary *dramatis personae* of the more popular Master and Disciple dialogues and adopted a very systematic, almost academic tone. An example of this genre in one stage of its evolution may be seen in the Question and Answer dialogue included in chapter 18 in the comprehensive, apologetic work in Arabic I call the *Summa Theologiae Arabica*; its given title is: "Summary of the Ways of Faith in the Trinity of the Unity of God, and in the Incarnation of God the Word from the Pure Virgin Mary."[26] The table of contents of this work gives the following description of the chapter:

> In chapter eighteen, in our answer to their questions to us about the Trinity, about Christ, our Lord, and his incarnation, about baptism,

[23] The *ḥanpê* are the Muslims, the Syriac term being cognate to the Arabic term *ḥanīf* (pl. *ḥunafā'*). See the discussion in Sidney H. Griffith, "The Prophet Muḥammad, His Scripture and His Message According to the Christian Apologies in Arabic and Syriac from the First Abbasid Century," in *La vie du prophète Mahomet; colloque de Strasbourg—1980*, ed. T. Fahd, 118–122 (Paris: Presses Universitaires de France, 1983). See also François De Blois, "*Naṣrānī* (ναζωραιος) and *ḥanīf* (εθνικος): Studies on the Religious Vocabulary of Christianity and Islam," *Bulletin of the School of Oriental and African Studies* 65 (2002), 1–30.

[24] Scher, *Liber Scholiorum*, 69: 232.

[25] Ibid., 283.

[26] This important work is still unpublished, but it is available in its entirety in British Library Oriental MS 4950, written by Stephen ar-Ramlī in the year AD 877 at the monastery of Mar Chariton in the Judean desert. See Sidney H. Griffith, "Greek into Arabic: Life and Letters in the Monasteries of Palestine in the 9th Century; the Example of the *Summa Theologiae Arabica*," *Orientalia Christiana Analecta* 226 (1986): 123–41; Griffith, "Islam and the Summa Theologiae Arabica; *Rabī'* I, 264 A.H.," *Jerusalem Studies in Arabic and Islam* 13 (1990): 225–64.

ablutions, marriage, and the rest of their questions about those features of Christianity concerning which we are in disagreement with them, we have cited from their own theology (*kalām*) and descriptions (*ṣifāt*) of Christ, our Lord, what will give the believers the advantage over them in their questions to them—to the effect that Christ is God, the Word, the uncreated Creator of creation; he is prior to the worlds (*ʿālamīn*), and his origin is not from the virgin Mary.[27]

The text is disposed in the form of thirty-four questions, to which the writer gives answers along the lines set forth in the paragraph just quoted. One notices the author's avowed intention to quote from Islamic sources in his text, thereby making a bid for credibility in the interreligious context. The popular character of the discourse is still evident, even though the "dialogue" has been included as a chapter in a much more systematic work. But it is noteworthy that in fact this composition circulated independently of the *Summa Theologiae Arabica* in several other manuscripts.[28] And among the many unpublished Arab Christian manuscripts there are yet other examples of texts in this genre awaiting study and publication. A good case in point is a work contained in a twelfth-century Sinai manuscript, purporting to be a monk's replies to a Muslim *shaykh*'s questions about the doctrines of the Trinity and the Incarnation, which the Muslim poses after having read a work titled simply "Refutation of Christians" (*ar-radd ʿalā n-naṣārā*). As the title paragraph announces, the work is presented as a reply to questions put to a priest-monk by a Muslim *shaykh* in Jerusalem, and it is titled, *Questions and Answers, Rational and Divine* (*masāʾil wa ajwibah ʿaqliyyah wa ilāhiyyah*).[29]

By the first half of the ninth century this genre of apologetic literature had become highly developed among the Christians who were participating with Muslim intellectuals in the *ʿilm al-kalām*, or the science of discoursing about religion. A good example of it may be seen in the work called *Kitāb al-masāʾil wa l-ajwibah*, the "Book of Questions and Answers," by the Nestorian writer of the ninth century, ʿAmmār al-Baṣrī.[30] As the title indicates, the substance of the work is a sequence of questions

[27] Quoted from Griffith, "Islam and the Summa Theologiae Arabica," 247–48.

[28] See Griffith, "Islam and the Summa Theologiae Arabica," 235.

[29] Sinai Arabic MS 434, AD 1137–39, f. 171r. For a further description see Rachid Haddad, *La Trinité divine chez les théologiens arabes (750–1050)* (Paris: Beauchesne, 1985), 38; Sidney H. Griffith, "Answers for the Shaykh: A 'Melkite' Arabic Text from Sinai and the Doctrines of the Trinity and the Incarnation in 'Arab Orthodox' Apologetics," in *The Encounter of Eastern Christianity with Early Islam*, ed. E. Grypeou, M. Swanson, and D. Thomas, 277–309 (Leiden: Brill, 2006).

[30] See Michel Hayek, *ʿAmmār al-Baṣrī; apologie et controverses* (Beirut: Dar el-Machreq, 1977). See also Sidney H. Griffith, "ʿAmmār al-Baṣrī's *Kitāb al-burhān*: Christian *Kalām* in the First Abbasid Century," *Le Muséon* 96 (1983): 145–181; Bénédicte Landron, *Chrétiens et Musulmans en Irak*: *Attitudes nestoriennes vis-à-vis de l'Islam*, Études Chrétiennes Arabes (Paris: Cariscript, 1994), 60–66.

(*masāʾil*) and answers (*ajwibah*), which are arranged numerically under four topical chapter headings (*maqālāt*). But the questions and answers themselves are not now disposed in the text according to the old *Erotapokriseis* style of the Master and Disciple dialogues. Rather, they are phrased in the conditional style familiar from Islamic *kalām* texts. Here the "question" is the protasis of the statement, and the "answer" is its apodosis, for example, "If someone says (*in qāla qāʾilun*) or asks (*saʾala sāʾilun*) such and such, we say (*qulna*) thus and so." With this device ʿAmmār proceeds to develop his argument in defense of Christian doctrines in a system of consecutive dilemmas designed to thwart the views of his adversaries.

ʿAmmār introduces the *Kitāb al-masāʾil wa l-ajwibah* with a preface that is in the form of a prayer for the reigning caliph, whom he does not name, and for himself, that he might accomplish the task before him. His view of the caliph's responsibilities, as revealed in the preface, is instructive. The "Commander of the Faithful" (*amīr al-muʾminīn*), as the Muslims customarily called the caliph, is the one who in their view has the care of God's religion. ʿAmmār says that his role in religion is:

> To exert an effort to strengthen it, to certify the knowledge of it, to set up the argument (*al-ḥujjah*) against those who disclaim it, or deny it, or differ from it, or turn away from it . . . so that he may thereby encourage the Muslims, hold them together, scrutinize their opinions, exercise discernment, in the balance of the mind with which God has graced him, when something comes to his ears which departs from their doctrine, or the meanings of their arguments.[31]

ʿAmmār prays that in his own weakness and deficiency in the face of the task before him, God will encourage him "to attempt that for which my ability is too little, before which my power of reflection falls short of the burden that has been put upon me in this matter, to bring it to completion for the *amīr al-muʾminīn*."[32] It is noteworthy that ʿAmmār supposes that the caliph's writ extends to a concern for the right exposition of the truths of religion as set out by a Christian. Then ʿAmmār states the purpose for the composition of his book. He says:

> What I have set out upon in this book, God strengthen and aid the *amīr al-muʾminīn*, is the advancement of argumentation concerning the Creator, be He blessed and exalted; a statement concerning the attestation of the oneness of His lordship, praise and glory be to Him, and holy be His names; the establishment of an argument against those who deny Him; and, in behalf of His economy (*litadbīrihi*), the endorsement of a proof, the truthfulness of which cannot be refuted,

[31] Hayek, *ʿAmmār al-Baṣrī,* 93–94.
[32] Ibid., 94.

and a process of reasoning (*qiyās*), the verity of which cannot be invalidated.[33]

If the reader did not know otherwise, thus far he would certainly think that the author of this piece was a Muslim. Michel Hayek, the text's modern editor, argues that ʿAmmār's prefatory dedication of his work to the caliph, as if in composing it he were complying with an official request, was a ploy on the author's part "to assure himself of a *captatio benevolentiae* from the Muslim reader."[34] But, since such dedications were conventional also in the works of Muslim scholars, one may just as well understand it to be an intentional bid on ʿAmmār's part to be taken seriously as a participant in the ongoing dialogue of the *mutakallimūn* of his time, the Arabic-speaking Muslim and Christian controversialists concerned with defending religious credibility. One gathers as much from his statement of the book's purpose. His concern with demonstrating the existence and oneness of the Creator, along with the presentation of arguments geared to refute "deniers," certainly accords with similar concerns on the part of contemporary Muslim controversialists. It is only when he comes to his reasoning about God's economy, as revealed in the sacred scriptures, that ʿAmmār launches into his specifically Christian apology. He attempts to show that the basic Christian doctrines are logically consequent upon the conclusions reached earlier, in the first part of his treatise. There is no reason to doubt that with this methodology, ʿAmmār intended to commend belief in Christianity, in the scholarly idiom of the day, to the intellectuals who were the adepts of the Islamic *ʿilm al-kalām*, as well as to those Arabic-speaking Christians who may have been liable to be convinced by Islamic arguments. His work represents the high point of the development of the scholarly, literary genre of the "Master" and his "Disciple," in the service of Christian apologetics.

The Epistolary Exchange

A very popular genre in Christian apologetics in the Islamic world in early ʿAbbasid times was the epistolary exchange. Typically there is an initial letter in which a Muslim correspondent is represented as calling a Christian to Islam, detailing the reasons why he should consider Islam the true religion; in reply, there follows a text attributed to a Christian correspondent, whose much longer letter defends the veracity of Christian doctrines, and attacks the claims of Islam to be the true religion. The correspondents may be well-known persons in the world of early Islam, or their names may be devised by the authors of such pieces to signify their religious confessions.

[33] Ibid., 94 and 95.
[34] Ibid., 17.

In either case, it is important to remember that in the forms in which these kinds of texts have come down to us, the letters attributed to both parties may be thought to make up a single apologetic work. In other words, the text may well not be the transcript of an actual correspondence, but a unified composition, perhaps based on the report of an alleged correspondence between the parties.

Three such epistolary exchanges in the Christian Arabic repertory have received much scholarly attention in modern times. They are: the correspondence between the Byzantine emperor Leo III (r. 717–41) and the caliph ʿUmar II (r. 717–20);[35] the correspondence between the Muslim character ʿAbd Allāh ibn Ismāʿīl al-Hāshimī and the Christian character ʿAbd al-Masīḥ ibn Isḥāq al-Kindī;[36] and the correspondence between a Muslim astronomer at the caliphal court in Baghdad, Abū ʿIsā Yaḥyā ibn al-Munajjim, and two well-known Christian scholars and courtiers, Ḥunayn ibn Isḥāq and Qusṭā ibn Lūqā.[37] There is also the case of the letter of the caliph Hārūn ar-Rashīd (r. 786–809) to the Byzantine emperor Constantine VI (r. 780–97) summoning him to Islam, but no reply from the emperor seems to have survived.[38] Of the three complete exchanges of letters, by far the most influential one has been the so-called al-Hāshimī/al-Kindī correspondence.

ʿAbd Allāh's letter on the one hand is a very summary statement of the Islamic creed as expressed in the *shahādah*, the formula of faith in the one God and in the prophethood of Muḥammad, along with the other four of the five pillars of Islam. ʿAbd al-Masīḥ's reply on the other hand is a long defense of the standard Christian doctrines and practices, according to the customary outline of topics in the more popular apologies for Christianity, along with a vigorous polemic against the Qurʾān, the prophet Muḥammad, and the teachings and practices of Islam. The two letters circulated as units of a single work, the correspondents are presented as members of the

[35] See Jean-Marie Gaudeul, *La correspondence de ʿUmar et Leon (vers 900)*, Studi arabo-islamici del PISAI, no. 6 (Rome: Pontificio Istituto di Studi Arabi e d'Islamistica, 1995). See also the discussion and further bibliography in Hoyland, *Seeing Islam*, 490–501.

[36] See the discussion and bibliography in Landron, *Chrétiens et Musulmans en Irak*, 78–89; Arabic text with French translation in Georges Tartar, *Dialogue islamo-chrétien sous le calife al-Maʾmūn; les épîtres d'al-Hashimî et d'al-Kindî*, 2 vols. (Combs-la-Ville: Centre Évangélique de Témoignage et de Dialogue, 1982); English translation in Newman, *Early Christian-Muslim Dialogue*, 355–545; Laura Bottini, *Al-Kindī: Apologia Del Cristianesimo; traduzione dall'arabo, introduzione*, Patrimonio Culturale Arabo Cristiano, 4 (Milan: Jaca Book, 1998).

[37] See Samir Khalil Samir and Paul Nwyia, *Une correspondance islamo-chrétienne entre ibn al-Munaggim, Ḥunayn ibn Isḥāq et Qusṭā ibn Lūqā*, Patrologia Orientalis, tome 40, fasc. 4, no. 185 (Turnhout, Belgium: Brepols, 1981).

[38] See Hadi Eid, *Lettre du calife Hârûn al-Rašîd à l'empereur Constantin VI: Texte présenté, commenté et traduit*, Études Chrétiennes Arabes (Paris: Cariscript, 1992).

court of the caliph al-Maʾmūn (r. 813–33). The author of the al-Hāshimī/al-Kindī correspondence is completely anonymous. In all likelihood, he was a Nestorian, that is, a member of the Assyrian Church of the East. Moreover, it is highly unlikely that the names of the correspondents are authentic names of historical persons. All three elements of each name amount to a neat, confessional statement of the two creeds, Christianity and Islam. While all of the elements of each name are quite commonly found among the names of contemporaries, their neat symmetry in the present instance suggests that they go together to form the names of literary personae. Furthermore, it is hardly credible that any Muslim intellectual, even in the court of al-Maʾmūn,[39] would have been party to the summary portrayal of Islam found here, a mere preface to al-Kindī's rebuttal; or who would be in any way associated with a work which so negatively depicts Islam, the Qurʾān, and the prophet Muḥammad. A distinguishing feature of the al-Kindī apology for Christianity, which makes it somewhat unique among the Syriac or Arabic apologies of the first ʿAbbasid century, is the bluntness with which it dismisses the religious claims of Muslims, in an impudent tone of voice that disparages the Qurʾān and Muḥammad in a way that is reminiscent of the Byzantine anti-Islamic polemical treatises written in Greek from the ninth century onward.[40] In this connection, one recalls as well the blunt language of certain writers from within the Islamic community, such as the notorious "freethinker," Ibn Rāwandī (ca. 820–ca. 860).[41]

The al-Hāshimī/al-Kindī correspondence has circulated widely among Christians in medieval and modern times. It was popular among the Melkites, Jacobites, and Nestorians in the Middle East; it was adopted by Mozarab Christians in Spain, where it was translated into Latin on the commission of Peter the Venerable (d. 1156) in the twelfth century,[42] and it

[39] The caliph al-Maʾmūn was a well-known sponsor of free interreligious debates; for this reason among others he was often highly esteemed by Christians in the caliphate and a tradition even grew up among them that he was a crypto-Christian. See Mark Swanson, "The Christian al-Maʾmūn Tradition," in *Christians at the Heart of Islamic Rule: Church Life and Scholarship in ʿAbbasid Iraq*, ed. David Thomas, 63–92, The History of Christian-Muslim Relations, vol. 1 (Leiden: Brill, 2003).

[40] On Byzantine anti-Islamic literature see the comprehensive surveys of Adel-Théodore Khoury, *Les théologiens Byzantins et l'islam: Texts et auteurs (VIIIe–XIIIe siècles)* (Louvain, Belgium, and Paris: Nauwelaerts, 1969); Khoury, *Polémique Byzantine contre l'islam; VIIIe–XIIIe siècles* (Leiden: Brill, 1972); Khoury, *Apologétique Byzantine contre l'Islam; VIIIe–XIIIe siècles* (Altenberge, Germany: Verlag für christlich-islamisches Schrifttum, 1982).

[41] See Sarah Stroumsa, *Freethinkers of Medieval Islam, Ibn al-Rāwandī, Abū Bakr al-Rāzī and Their Impact on Islamic Thought* (Leiden: Brill, 1999). See also Dominique Urvoy, *Les penseurs libres dans l'Islam classique* (Paris: Albin Michel, 1996).

[42] See Jose Muñoz Sendino, "Al-Kindi, Apologia del Christianismo," *Miscelanea Comillas* 11 and 12 (1949): 339–460; James Krtizeck, *Peter the Venerable and Islam* (Princeton, NJ: Princeton University Press, 1964).

has been used in English and French translations in the nineteenth and twentieth centuries by Christian missionaries in the West seeking to convert Muslims.[43] By its very popularity it has somewhat overshadowed the other works in this genre of apologetic writing, a circumstance that should not mask the fact that the genre was a popular one among Christians living in the Islamic world from the ninth century onward.

Unlike the al-Hāshimī/al-Kindī correspondence, the other two works mentioned in this category, the Leo/ʿUmar correspondence, and the correspondence of al-Munajjim with Ḥunayn ibn Isḥāq and Qusṭā ibn Lūqā, involve historical characters. Nevertheless, as the texts have circulated in the Christian communities they have taken on a literary life of their own, independently of any actual events that may have inspired their composition in the first place. In them the letter (*ar-risālah*), an important literary genre in its own right in Islamic Arabic, became an apologetic treatise in the literary format of an epistolary exchange, one that made its bid for verisimilitude in the world of Islam by reason of the fact that in Islamic history there was already the literary precedent, recorded in the *sīrah* or biographical literature, that in his day Muḥammad had himself provided for letters to be sent out by messengers from him to Roman, Persian, and Abyssinian leaders, among others, summoning them to Islam.[44]

Already long before the rise of Islam, in Greek and Syriac texts among others, it had become conventional to use the formalities of letter writing in composing the prefaces to treatises on a wide variety of subjects. Typically, the writer would address his treatise to someone who is represented as having written to him requesting information on the subject to be discussed. After modestly protesting his inabilities, and soliciting prayers, the writer would then carry on with the treatise. It was a convention that could easily be combined with many other literary genres, including all the ones being discussed in this chapter.[45] What makes it distinctive in the present context is that the claim of letters actually sent and received, to or from known or totally fictional characters, is an important literary feature of the apologetic narrative of the genre I am calling here the "Epistolary Exchange."

[43] See, e.g., the edition and French translation published by Pasteur Georges Tartar, *Dialogue islamo-chrétien sous le calife al-Maʾmūn (813–834); les épîtres d'al-Hashimî et d'al-Kindî*, 2 vols. (Combs-la-Ville, France: Centre Évangélique de Témoignage et de Dialogue, 1977).

[44] See A. Guillaume, *The Life of Muhammad: A Translation of Ibn Ishaq's Sirat Rasul Allah* (Karachi: Oxford University Press, 1978), 652–59. On the apologetic and literary character of this work, see J. Wansbrough, *The Sectarian Milieu: Content and Composition of Islamic Salvation History*, London Oriental Series, vol. 34 (Oxford: Oxford University Press, 1978).

[45] See Riad, *The Syriac Preface*.

The Systematic Treatise

While the most well known and colorful works of Christian apologetics written in Syriac and Arabic in the Islamic world were anonymous and composed in the literary genres already discussed, the major apologists and theologians whose names we mentioned in the previous chapter more often wrote tracts of a less dramatic and a more expository character. They were sometimes letter-treatises, with prefaces of the kind described above, called *ʾegartâ* in Syriac, or *risālah* in Arabic. Alternatively, many of them bear the simple names, "treatise," or "tract" (*mêmrâ* in Syriac, *maymar/mīmar*, or simply *kitāb* or *maqālah* in Arabic), and they discuss all the topics at issue between Christians and Muslims. As often as not they are exercises in Christian *kalām*, the characteristically Islamic style of religious discourse in Arabic, in which the authors make a bid to defend Christian beliefs and practices utilizing the apologetic conventions in which the Muslim controversialists of the early Islamic period were in the habit of commending Islamic faith and life. Alternatively, some of these Christian writers, as we shall see, proceeded in a more philosophical and formally logical mode, again, in the manner of the philosophers in the world of Islam.

The earliest Christian apologetic treatise of this sort is a now anonymous one, called by its modern editor, "On the Triune Nature of God."[46] It was written in Arabic in the eighth century, most probably around the year AD 755.[47] It is an essay in which the author proposes to defend the truth of

[46] Margaret Dunlop Gibson, *An Arabic Version of the Acts of the Apostles and the Seven Catholic Epistles, with a Treatise on the Triune Nature of God*, Studia Sinaitica, no. 7 (Cambridge: C. J. Clay, 1899), 1–36 (English); 74–107 (Arabic). See Samir Khalil Samir, "The Earliest Arab Apology for Christianity," in *Christian Arabic Apologetics during the Abbasid Period (750–1258)*, ed. Samir Khalil Samir and Jørgen S. Nielsen, 57–114 (Leiden: Brill, 1994).

[47] There is some scholarly disagreement about the date. See Mark N. Swanson, "Some Considerations for the Dating of *Fī tathlīth Allāh al-wāḥid* (Sinai Ar. 154) and *Al-Jāmiʿ wujūh al-īmān* (London, British Library or. 4950)," in *Actes du 4e Congrès international d'études arabes chrétiennes*, ed. Samir Khalil Samir, published in *Parole de l'Orient* 18 (1993): 117–41. A line in the text says, "If this religion were not truly from God it would not have stood so unshakably for seven hundred and forty-six years" (Sinai Arabic MS 154, f. 110v.). Swanson convincingly makes the point that the author would most likely have counted the years according to the Alexandrian world era. But he then goes on to suppose that the lapse of 746 years should be counted from the year of Christ's crucifixion, which theologically might have been taken by the writer to mark the end of Judaism and the beginning of Christianity. Accordingly, Swanson dates the text to the year AD 788, or 746 years from the crucifixion, which, according to the computation of the Alexandrian world era, would have taken place in the year AD 42. It seems more likely to me that whatever his theological view may have been, the writer would have meant to compute 746 years from the beginning of the calendar sequence of Christian years, which begins with the Incarnation in all systems. According to the computation of the Alexandrian world era, the Incarnation would have happened in the year AD 9. Therefore, in my opinion, one should add 746 years to 9, in order to ar-

the Christian doctrines of the Trinity and the Incarnation on the basis of scriptural testimonies, including the Qurʾān. At the beginning of the work the author wrote:

> We do not separate God from his Word and his Spirit. We worship no other god with God in his Word and his Spirit. God showed his power and his light in the Law and the Prophets and the Psalms and the Gospel, that God and his Word and his Spirit are one God and one Lord. We will make this clear, if God wills, in these revealed scriptures, to anyone who wants understanding, [who] perceives things and recognizes the truth, and opens his breast to believe in God and his scriptures.[48]

Another work, written in Syriac, which may well be the second oldest Christian apologetic treatise from the early Islamic period, takes a completely different approach. It is a letter-treatise, written by Patriarch Timothy I in the year 780/1, and addressed to a man named Sergius, the future metropolitan of Elam. In it the patriarch defends the veracity of the doctrines of the Trinity and of the Incarnation, and justifies several Christian religious practices, on the basis of the proper definition of philosophical terms and the deployment of Aristotelian logic. In fact, he says that in the letter he is reporting the gist of his conversations on these matters with an Aristotelian philosopher whom he met at the caliph's court.[49]

The earliest writer of systematic, Christian apologetic treatises in Arabic whose name we know is Theodore Abū Qurrah (ca. 755–ca. 830). He flourished in the first decades of the ninth century and wrote some sixteen treatises in Arabic on topics of Christian theology, with Muslims always among his silent dialogue partners. His purpose was to explain the tenets of Melkite theology in the Arabic idiom of the contemporary discussions about religion among the Muslim *mutakallimūn*, as well as to defend the proposition that Christianity is the true religion.[50] In the first generation of Christian theology in Arabic, Abū Qurrah was joined by fellow Melkite writers, such as the author of the now anonymous *Summa Theologiae Arabica*, and Peter of Bayt Ra's, author of a long apologetical work called

---

rive at the year AD 755, as the most likely year for the composition of the work. See also Hoyland, *Seeing Islam*, 503, no. 9, who accepts Swanson's date.

[48] Gibson, *An Arabic Version*, 3. I have slightly adapted the translation.

[49] The letter is published in Hanna Cheikho, *Dialectique du langage sur Dieu de Timothée I (728–823)* (Rome: Pont. Institutum Studiorum Orientalium, 1983). See Thomas R. Hurst, "The Syriac Letters of Timothy I (727–823): A Study in Christian-Muslim Controversy" (unpublished PhD diss., Catholic University of America, 1986).

[50] For discussion and further bibliography see Sidney H. Griffith, "Faith and Reason In Christian Kalām: Theodore Abū Qurrah on Discerning the True Religion," in *Christian Arabic Apologetics during the Abbasid Period (750–1258)*, ed. Samir and Nielsen, 1–43.

Kitāb al-burhān or "Book of Proof."[51] Among the Jacobites the first apologist to write treatises in Arabic was Ḥabīb ibn Khidmah Abū Rāʾiṭah, a contemporary and debating partner of Theodore Abū Qurrah. His works include defenses of the Jacobite Christology of Severus of Antioch (ca. 465–538) against the attacks of the Melkites, as well as arguments in behalf of the doctrines of the Trinity and of the Incarnation against the challenges of Islam.[52] In the Nestorian community, after Patriarch Timothy I, whose works have been discussed above, the most notable apologist and theologian, also mentioned earlier, was ʿAmmār al-Baṣrī, who flourished in the ninth century. In addition to the *Kitāb masāʾil wa l-ajwibah*, which we have already discussed, ʿAmmār also wrote a very closely reasoned tract on the discernment of the true religion called, like the comparable work of Peter of Bayt Ra's, *Kitāb al-burhān* or "Book of Proof."[53]

For the later generations of apologists, it will be sufficient for the present purpose simply to mention some of their names. A number of them are immediately recognizable by reason of their major contributions to the intellectual life of the early ʿAbbasid caliphate. Among them were Israel of Kashkar (d. 872), the author of a popular treatise, "On the Unity and Trinity of God";[54] Ḥunayn ibn Isḥāq (d. 873), well known for his role in the translation of Greek philosophical and scientific texts into Arabic;[55] Yaḥyā ibn ʿAdī (d. 974), a Jacobite from Taqrit, who was both a famous logician and a formidable apologist for Christianity;[56] Severus ibn al-Muqaffaʿ (d. 1000), the first Copt whose name we know who wrote Christian theology in Arabic;[57] Elias of Nisibis (d. ca. 1049), a controversialist whose works

[51] For more discussion and bibliography on these two works, see Sidney H. Griffith, "The View of Islam from the Monasteries of Palestine in the Early ʿAbbāsid Period," *Islam and Christian-Muslim Relations* 7 (1996): 9–28.

[52] See Georg Graf, *Die Schriften des Jacobiten Ḥabīb Ibn Ḫidma Abū Rāʾiṭa*, CSCO, vols. 130 and 131 (Louvain, Belgium: Peeters, 1951). See also Sidney H. Griffith, "Ḥabīb ibn Ḥidmah Abū Rāʾiṭah, A Christian *mutakallim* of the First Abbasid Century," *Oriens Christianus* 64 (1980): 161–201; Sandra Toenies Keating, "Dialogue between Muslims and Christians in the Early 9th Century: The Example of Ḥabīb ibn Khidmah Abū Rāʾiṭah al-Takrītī's Theology of the Trinity" (PhD diss., Catholic University of America, 2001).

[53] See the discussion in Sidney H. Griffith, "ʿAmmār al-Baṣrī's *Kitāb al-Burhān*: Christian *Kalām* in the First Abbasid Century," *Le Muséon* 96 (1983): 145–81.

[54] See Bo Holmberg, *A Treatise on the Unity and Trinity of God by Israel of Kashkar (d. 872)* (Lund, Sweden: Plus Ultra, 1989).

[55] On Ḥunayn, see Landron, *Chrétiens et Musulmans en Irak*, 66–71. See also Dimitri Gutas, *Greek Thought, Arabic Culture; the Graeco-Arabic Translation Movement in Baghdad and Early ʿAbbāsid Society (2nd–4th/8th–10th Centuries)* (London: Routledge, 1998), esp. 133–45.

[56] For discussion and bibliography, see E. Platti, *Yaḥyā ibn ʿAdī, théologien chrétien et philosophe arabe*, Orientalia Lovaniensia Analecta, 14 (Leuven, Belgium: Katholieke Universiteit Leuven, Departement Orientalistiek, 1983). See also Gerhard Endress, *The Works of Yaḥyā ibn ʿAdī: An Analytical Inventory* (Wiesbaden: Reichert, 1977).

[57] For discussion and bibliography, see Sidney H. Griffith, "The *Kitāb Miṣbāḥ al-ʿAql* of

were widely distributed in the Christian communities in the eleventh and twelfth centuries,[58] and Paul of Antioch, a twelfth-century Melkite bishop whose efforts to defend Christianity and its teachings on the basis of texts cited from the Qur'ān elicited a strong Islamic reaction.[59] Many more names could be mentioned, but perhaps these will suffice to call to mind the range of works produced by Christian apologists in the Islamic world in the Middle Ages. The enterprise reached its apogee, as we mentioned in the previous chapter, in Egypt in the thirteenth century, with the activities of the remarkable ʿAssāl family of scholars who worked in Ayyubid times not only to produce their own treatises but also to compile collections of the works of many of the earlier apologists and theologians who wrote in Arabic, from all the church communities.

The Apologetic Agenda

The apologetic agenda for Christian controversialists in the Islamic world was largely set in response to the challenges to Christian faith voiced by Muslims in the early Islamic period, as they are now found recorded in two kinds of early Islamic texts: first, the Qur'ān, and second, in the traditions of the prophet's biography and the early literature pertinent to the establishment of Islam as the religion of a new community, the "community of believers" (*al-ummah*). It is particularly important in this connection to take account of the issues that emerged in the project to define the biography of Muḥammad the prophet, from the time of Muḥammad Ibn Isḥāq (d. 768), whose name is associated with the first systematic efforts in this enterprise, to that of ʿAbd al-Malik ibn Hishām (d. 834), whose recension of Ibn Isḥāq's biography of Muḥammad gained almost canonical status among Muslims under the title *Sirat rasūl Allāh*. The sixty some years during which this work was coming to its maturity correspond to the years during which the Christian apologetic undertaking in the Islamic world was finding its first expression, as we have seen.

As Uri Rubin has recently shown, the prophetic profile of Muḥammad that emerges from the fully developed *Sīrah*, or biography of the prophet, rests basically on an Islamic adaptation of the scriptural themes of attestation, preparation, revelation, persecution, and salvation, as they are found in the biblical profiles of the prophetic figures in the contemporary reli-

Severus ibn al-Muqaffaʿ: A Profile of the Christian Creed in Arabic in Tenth Century Egypt," *Medieval Encounters* 2 (1996): 15–42.

[58] See Samir, *Foi et culture en Irak*.

[59] See Paul Khoury, *Paul d'Antioche, évêque melkite de Sidon (XIIe s.)*, Recherches, t. 24 (Beirut: Imprimerie Catholique, 1964).

gious discourse of Judaism and Christianity.[60] Moreover, in his study of this same *Sīrah* literature almost twenty years earlier John Wansbrough had already shown that the Islamic development of these themes, in the period he so aptly styled *The Sectarian Milieu*, can be seen to express the inner Islamic, apologetic, and polemical response to the religious claims of Judaism and Christianity, as they would have been marshaled against nascent Islam at that time.[61] In this connection Wansbrough identified a dozen or so "polemical topoi," the origin of which, he said, "was interconfessional polemic and . . . their selection was imposed upon the early Muslim community from outside."[62] The same may be said, mutatis mutandis, of both the topics and the modes of expression in Arabic of Jewish and Christian theology, apology, and polemic in the early Islamic period. One may think of the situation of the three Arabic-speaking religious communities in the early Islamic period as one in which mutually reactive thinking was the intellectual order of the day.

For convenience's sake one may list the topics of Christian theology in Arabic under two headings: topics developed in response to the teachings of the Qur'ān, as they were interpreted by the Muslim *mufassirūn*, the exegetes of the Islamic scripture, and systematized by the *mutakallimūn*, the Muslim controversial theologians; and the topics designed to rebut the claims of the Islamic prophetology, as it was elaborated in the *Sīrah* literature just described. In general, the more popular works of Christian apology featured a heavier concentration on topics under the latter heading (i.e., the Islamic prophetology), while the authors of the systematic treatises tended to concentrate their attention on the defense of the Christian doctrines directly challenged by the Qur'ān.[63]

Responding to the Qur'ān's Critique

The principal Christian articles of faith directly challenged by the Qur'ān are the doctrine of the Trinity and the Incarnation. Virtually every Christian theological or apologetic work written in Syriac or Arabic in the early

[60] See Uri Rubin, *The Eye of the Beholder: The Life of Muḥammad as Viewed by the Early Muslims; a Textual Analysis,* Studies in Late Antiquity and Early Islam, 5 (Princeton, NJ: Darwin Press, 1995).

[61] J. Wansbrough, *The Sectarian Milieu; Content and Composition of Islamic Salvation History*, London Oriental Series, vol. 34 (Oxford: Oxford University Press, 1978).

[62] Wansbrough, *The Sectarian Milieu*, 14. For the list of topoi, see 40–42.

[63] For a systematic survey of the topics of controversy and the Christian response to them in the broad range of Arab Christian literature in the early Islamic period, see the comprehensive study of Paul Khoury, *Materiaux pour servir a l'étude de la controverse théologique islamo-chrétienne de langue arabe du VIIIe au XIIe siècle*, 3 vols., Religionswissenschaftliche Studien, vols. 11/1, 2, 3 (Würzburg, Germany: Echter Verlag, and Altenberge, Germany: Telos-Verlag, 1989, 1991, 1997).

Islamic period included a defense of these doctrines. Often the agenda was broadened to include such other issues as the authenticity of the canonical Gospels, the doctrine of the freedom of the will in moral choices, and issues in Christian life and worship, such as the sacraments of Baptism and the Eucharist, the veneration of the cross, and the holy icons.

The authors of the systematic, apologetic treatises typically approached the discussion of the Trinity and the Incarnation in two ways: they argued either from scripture, or from reason;[64] sometimes they employed a combination of the two strategies. But in these texts there is often a marked preference for arguments from reason. In one text, for example, now preserved only in Greek, Theodore Abū Qurrah recalled the challenge of his Muslim adversary as follows: "Persuade me not from your Isaiah or Matthew, for whom I have not the slightest regard, but from compelling, acknowledged, common conceptions."[65]

Always the efforts of the apologists were to show that the standard Christian doctrines reflect the teachings of the uncorrupted scriptures[66] and that the dogmatic formulas used by Christians were not really vulnerable to the charges leveled against them by Muslim polemicists, such as the charge that they are not scriptural but the product of church councils held under the auspices of the Byzantine emperors.[67] Special efforts were expended to find an appropriate Arabic vocabulary in terms of which to translate the technical expressions of Christian theology as they had been deployed earlier in Greek and Syriac. This enterprise often involved the further effort to define certain Arabic terms in a technical way for the purpose of theological discussion, even when the ordinary connotations of the terms in common Arabic-speaking usage militated against the senses intended in doctrinal

[64] These are the two modes of argument that both Muslims and Christians recognized. Theodore Abū Qurrah, for example, actually distinguished three modes of inquiry: from the scriptures, from the works of the traditional teachers, and from reason. See the detailed discussion in Sidney H. Griffith, "The Controversial Theology of Theodore Abū Qurrah: A Methodological, Comparative Study in Christian Arabic Literature" (PhD diss., Catholic University of America, 1978), 86–133.

[65] Theodore Abū Qurrah, Greek *Opusculum* 24, *PG*, vol. 97, col. 1556B.

[66] Muslim scholars, following the prompting of the Qurʾān, maintained that the scriptures as the Jews and Christians actually have them have been distorted and corrupted. See Jean-Marie Gaudeul and Robert Caspar, "Textes de la tradition musulmane concernant le *taḥrīf* (falsification) des écritures," *Islamochristiana* 6 (1980): 61–104. See also Sidney H. Griffith, "Arguing from Scripture: The Bible in the Christian/Muslim Encounter in the Middle Ages," in *Scripture and Pluralism: Reading the Bible in the Religiously Plural Worlds of the Middle Ages and Renaissance*, ed. Thomas Heffernan and Thomas Burman, 29-58, Studies in the History of Christian Traditions, vol. 123 (Leiden: Brill, 2006).

[67] On this topic, see Sidney H. Griffith, "Muslims and Church Councils: The Apology of Theodore Abū Qurrah," in *Studia Patristica*, ed. E. A. Livingstone, 25: 270–299 (Louvain, Belgium: Peeters, 1993).

contexts.[68] This was to remain a major problem for Christian theology in Arabic; by the time of the earliest Arabic-speaking Christian apologists, all of the religious vocabulary in Arabic had already been co-opted by Islamic religious discourse, which often systematically excluded the very meanings wanted by Christians, or at the very least Muslims Islamicized the terms in a way contrary to Christian thinking.

In defense of the doctrine of the Trinity, most Christian apologists who wrote in Arabic adopted the strategy first encountered in the Greek works of St. John of Damascus,[69] who situated the discussion in the context of the debate soon to be underway among Muslim controversialists, the *mutakallimūn*, about the ontological status of the divine attributes (*ṣifāt Allah*) as expressed in the "beautiful names" (*al-asmāʾ al-ḥusnā*) of God culled from the Qurʾān.[70] Typically this involved the Christian claim that all of the attributes of essence and action, as both Christians and Muslims distinguished them, can reasonably be shown to presume the presence of three irreducible, substantial attributes: "existing" (*mawjūd*), "living" (*ḥayy*), and "speaking" (*nāṭiq*),[71] on which all the other attributes can then logically be argued to depend. The apologists then proposed that these three substantial attributes indicate the three persons or *hypostases* (*qnômê/aqānīm*) of the one God, who is one in *ousia* (*jawhar*) as the Christians teach, and three in the divine *personae* (*parṣôpê/wujūh, ashkhāṣ*), Father, Son, and Holy Spirit, of which, according to the Christians, the Bible so clearly speaks.[72] Different Arabic-speaking theologians approached this discussion in different ways, often favoring different Arabic terms as equivalents for the traditional Christian technical vocabulary, but all of them inevitably employed the basic strategy of presenting the doctrine of the Trinity in the

[68] By way of illustration, one need only mention the term *jawhar*, used by philosophers and theologians to translate the Greek term *ousia*, but which in Arabic inevitably suggests a concrete nugget like a jewel, or an atom. On this problem, see Sidney H. Griffith, "Theology and the Arab Christian: The Case of the 'Melkite' Creed," in *A Faithful Presence: Essays for Kenneth Cragg*, ed. David Thomas, 184–200 (London: Melisende, 2003).

[69] See Miquel Beltran, "Los atributos divinos en Juan de Damasco y su influencia en el islam," *Collectanea Christiana Orientalia* 2 (2005): 25–42; Harry A. Wolfson, "The Muslim Attributes and the Christian Trinity," *Harvard Theological Review* 49 (1956): 1–18.

[70] See Richard M. Frank, *Beings and Their Attributes: The Teaching of the Basrian School of the Muʿtazila in the Classical Period* (Albany: State University of New York Press, 1978); Gimaret, *Les noms divins en islam.*

[71] Different Christian authors at different times and places used different vocabulary to identify the three substantial attributes. See Khoury, *Matériaux pour servir à l'étude de la controverse théologique*, vol. 2, esp. 13–113.

[72] See the discussion of ʿAmmār al-Baṣrī's deployment of this line of reasoning in Sidney H. Griffith, "The Concept of *al-uqnūm* in ʿAmmār al-Baṣrī's Apology for the Doctrine of the Trinity," in *Actes du premier congrès international d'études arabes chrétiennes (Goslar, septembre 1980)*, ed. Samir Khalil Samir, 169–91, Orientalia Christiana Analecta, 218 (Rome: Pontificium Institutum Studiorum Orientalium, 1982).

context of the Islamic discussion of the ontological status of the divine attributes.[73] This approach, while not totally unknown in earlier Christian discourse, nevertheless retained the stamp of the Islamic milieu in which it was articulated.

Often in the more systematic treatises the apologists embedded this kind of argumentation in the larger context of a theory of human knowledge and a theodicy that shared all the characteristics of a typical exercise in Islamic *kalām*.[74] It can be seen that in this way the intentions of the Christian writers were to commend the credibility of the Christian doctrine of the Trinity, and other doctrines as well, in the very idiom of the Islamic religious discourse of their day. In this novel form of discourse traditional Christian Trinitarian theology, originally articulated in Greek or Syriac, came to be translated and transposed into the Arabic discourse of the intellectual world of Islam, in a design and vocabulary very different from that of the Patristic era and largely unfamiliar to Christians outside of the Islamic world. It is for this reason that in modern times some Arabic-speaking Christian theologians in Egypt have called into question the authenticity of the development of doctrine that took place in the Islamic milieu, and they have proposed a return to the traditional Christian discourse of the patristic era.[75]

Responding to the Claims of Islamic Prophetology

In the religious literature of the early Islamic period, Muslim scholars elaborated a Qur'ān-based history of salvation that enabled the controversialists, the *mutakallimūn* of their community, to develop an apologetic line of argument in defense of the true prophethood of Muḥammad based on what they called the *dalā'il an-nubuwwah*, or the "indications of prophecy." In the context of the controversy with Christian apologists, the claims of this "prophetology" were marshaled in arguments about the identity of the true religion. The topics that were always included under this heading were the integrity of the scriptures; the teachings about God and the messengers who claimed to have been sent by God; the signs by which the messengers might be recognized; the religious practices of the followers of the

[73] See, e.g., the influential treatise of Yaḥyā ibn ʿAdī, published by Samir Khalil Samir, *Le traité de l'unité de Yaḥyā ibn ʿAdī (893–974)* [Arabic], Patrimoine Arabe Chrétien, 2 (Jounieh, Lebanon: Librairie Saint-Paul, and Rome: Pontificio Istituto Orientale, 1980). See also Bo Holmberg, "Notes on a Treatise on the Unity and Trinity of God Attributed to Yaḥyā ibn ʿAdī," in *Actes du deuxième congrès international d'études arabes chrétiennes*, ed. Samir Khalil Samir, 235–45, Orientalia Christiana Analecta, 226 (Rome: Pont. Institutum Studiorum Orientalium, 1986).

[74] See the discussion in Griffith, "Faith and Reason in Christian *Kalām*."

[75] See Swanson, "Are Hypostases Attributes?"

true religion, such as the direction they faced when at prayer; the moral teachings of the messengers; the character of the rewards and punishments awaiting human beings at the end of this life; and the true status of Muḥammad, the Qurʾān, and Islam.

This list of topics can be found in almost all of the more popular genres of Christian apologetics in Syriac and Arabic written in the early Islamic period. While it is evident that Christian apologists and polemicists were engaged in rejecting the claims of Muslims under all of these headings, and that they were bent on proving that Christianity alone is the true religion that promotes the true teaching on all of these subjects, the list of topics itself is a distinctly Islamic one. This outline of topics, and the prophetology on which it rests, would not be found in a Christian apologetic work outside of the context of the dialogue with Islam. Two issues in particular are worth special attention in connection with this topical outline.

The first issue is that almost all of the Christian apologists argued that the decisive factor in proof of the claim of Christianity to be the true religion is the attestation provided by the evidentiary miracles worked in testimony to its veracity by Jesus of Nazareth, and those worked in Jesus's name by his apostles and disciples.[76] The apologists came back to this theme again and again, and they often contrasted it with the situation in Islam. A number of them even quote the Qurʾān passages that seem to dissociate Muḥammad himself from any claim to be a Thaumatourgos, and they attack the Islamic appeal to the miraculous inimitability of the Qurʾān (*iʿjāz al-qurʾān*), sometimes going to great lengths in the attempt to demonstrate that the text of the Islamic scripture is anything but inimitable, and claiming greater admiration for other Arabic compositions.[77] It is interesting to observe in this connection that it is precisely in the ninth century, the era of the first appearance of some of the most polemical Christian attacks in Arabic against the Qurʾān,[78] that one finds the earliest systematic development of the doctrine of the miraculous inimitability of the language of the Qurʾān, the *iʿjāz al-qurʾān*, among the Muslim *mutakallimūn*.[79]

The second issue worth special attention in connection with the Chris-

[76] Only one Christian apologist from the early period, and then only in one work, argued that Christianity could be proved to be the true religion solely on rational grounds, without the appeal to the evidentiary force of the miracles worked by Jesus and the disciples. He was Theodore Abū Qurrah. See Griffith, "Faith and Reason in Christian Kalām," 1–43.

[77] In this connection, see in particular the appropriate passages in the "Apology of al-Kindī," in the texts cited in Landron, *Chrétiens et Musulmans en Irak*, 78–89; Newman, *The Early Christian-Muslim Dialogue*, 355–545; Tartar, *Dialogue islamo-chrétien*.

[78] For more on this theme, see Griffith, "The Qurʾān in Arab Christian Texts."

[79] See Richard Martin, "The Role of the Basrah Muʿtazilah in Formulating the Doctrine of the Apologetic Miracle," *Journal of Near Eastern Studies* 39 (1980): 175–89.

tian effort to argue, in the context of Islamic prophetology, that Christianity is the true religion, is the scheme of negative criteria the Christian apologists devised specifically in the effort to exclude Islam from any claim to be the true religion, at least to their own satisfaction. It is a unique contribution to the apologetic/polemical enterprise in Christian thought, and so deserves a special mention here. While several of the apologists whom we have mentioned employed this argument, it was perhaps the most succinctly expressed by ʿAmmār al-Baṣrī in his "Book of Proof," *Kitāb al-burhān*.[80] He put it as follows, in the context of his discussion of the necessity of miraculous signs as indicators of the true religion. He said,

> Intelligent people will be obliged to confess one of the religions because it was established in the world on account of God's signs, only when they do not find in it any one of the motives of this world (*asbāb ad-dunyah*), which by its persistence, could enable it [i.e., the religion] to be established.[81]

ʿAmmār's list of seven unworthy, worldly motives for espousing a religion includes the following items: the sword (*as-sayf*), bribes and cajolery (*ar-rishan wa l-muṣānaʿah*), ethnic bigotry (*al-ʿaṣabiyyah*), personal preference (*al-istiḥsān*), tribal collusion (*at-tawāṭuʾ*), and licentious laws and practices (*at-tarkhīṣ fī sh-sharāʾiʿ*).[82] He and other Christian apologists argued that they could reasonably show that in their day people had been enticed to embrace Islam and other non-Christian religions for one or more of these unworthy reasons, whereas, these apologists contended, no one can be shown to have chosen Christianity, nor to have remained a faithful Christian, for any of these same unworthy motives or invalid reasons. Rather, they argued, Christians can be shown on the one hand to have embraced their religion in the face of considerable difficulties and disabilities, and on the other hand to have accepted Christian doctrines and practices because they alone best accord with what the human mind can show to be closest to the truth.[83]

Some Christian apologists, most notably the author of the letter (*risālah*) of al-Kindī in the fictional al-Kindī/al-Hāshimī correspondence, but a

[80] Perhaps the earliest Christian thinker to devise such a scheme was Ḥunayn ibn Isḥāq (808–73). See his tract, "How to Discern the True Religion," in Paul Sbath, *Vingt traits philosophiques et apologétiques*, 181–200. A new, critical edition of this short text has been published by Samir Khalil Samir, "Maqālah Ḥunayn ibn Isḥāq fī kayfiyyah idrāk ḥaqīqah ad-diyānah," *al-Machriq* 71 (1997): 345–63.

[81] Hayek, *ʿAmmār al-Baṣrī*, 29.

[82] See ibid., 30–33.

[83] For more discussion of this apologetic line of reasoning, see Sidney H. Griffith, "Comparative Religion in the Apologetics of the First Christian Arabic Theologians," *Proceedings of the PMR Conference: Annual Publication of the Patristic, Mediaeval and Renaissance Conference* 4 (1979): 63–87; Griffith, "Faith and Reason in Christian Kalām."

number of others as well, echoing these same modes of thought argued at a considerable length that by reason of their worldly qualities, Muḥammad cannot be considered a prophet, nor can the Qur᾽ān be esteemed to be a book of divine revelation, nor can Islam be the true religion. These writers present their case as graphically as possible, and they highlight every trait they can portray as morally objectionable from a Christian perspective. Most of the popular works of Christian apology and polemic that develop these themes are anonymous. In addition to the al-Hāshimī/al-Kindī correspondence, one thinks particularly in this connection of a number of the works in the genre "The Monk in the Emir's *Majlis*";[84] at the end of some of them even the Muslim emir or the caliph is sometimes made to agree with the Christian protagonist in the narrative, even to the point of saying that only social pressure prevents his becoming a Christian. For example, at the end of the "Dialogue of the Monk of Bêt Ḥālê with an Arab Notable," the latter is made to say: "I testify that were it not for the fear of the government and of shame before men, many would become Christians. But you are blessed of God to have given me satisfaction by your conversation with me."[85]

Generally speaking, the works of popular apologetics written in Arabic by Christians, such as the purported transcripts of interviews between monks and emirs, survive in a greater number of manuscript witnesses than do the other, more systematic apologetic and polemical tracts written by Christian authors in Arabic or Syriac in the early Islamic period. It seems clear that the primary intention of the writers of the more popular works was to dissuade their Christian readers from acceding to the ever-present temptation to convert to Islam; and second that they also intended to give these same Christian readers a sense of the superiority of their religion over Islam. As for any potential Muslim readers of their works, the Christian authors' intent must have been to induce a sense of unease about his religion in any one of them who might pick up the work. But this observation brings up the whole issue of the audience for whom the Christian apologists wrote.

The Audience for Christian Arabic Texts

Broadly speaking, one may think of the audience of the Christian apologists who wrote in the world of Islam as being made up of both Christians and Muslims, and as ranging from the general population of the literate to

[84] See Griffith, "The Monk in the Emir's *Majlis*."

[85] Translated from the original Syriac, as contained in a private transcript of Diyarbakir MS 95, 16.

the intellectually and socially elite in both communities. The circumstances vary from work to work.

The earliest texts were clearly addressed to the Christian community. Certainly this was the case with works composed in Syriac, which very few if any Muslims would have been prepared to read. As for the works composed in Arabic, by the very nature of the case they would be open to perusal of any person literate in the Arabic language. But given the prefatory remarks of many of the authors it is clear that Christians themselves were the primary audience for the apologetic texts, in all the genres. Often the texts are addressed to inquirers whose names are mentioned, or they are presented as reports of how a particular monk or bishop fared when he was interrogated about his religion in an emir's or caliph's *majlis*. Presumably these works were addressed to the Christian community.

Yet some Christian Arabic texts did find Muslim readers. And the more formal treatises, which deal with philosophical or theological topics, sometimes even elicited a response from a Muslim writer. One recalls, for example, the Muʿtazilī controversialist (*mutakallim*) ʿĪsā ibn Ṣabīḥ al-Murdār (d. 840), mentioned in the previous chapter, who wrote against Theodore Abū Qurrah;[86] of the caliph, probably al-Maʾmūn, to whom ʿAmmār al-Baṣrī all but dedicated his *Kitāb masāʾil wa l-ajwibah*;[87] and of the *mutakallim* Abū Hudhayl al-ʿAllāf (d. ca. 840), who wrote a tract against ʿAmmār al-Baṣrī by name.[88] Perhaps the most famous instance of a Christian apologetic work that attracted the attention of Muslim readers is Paul of Antioch's letter-treatise (*risālah*) to a Muslim friend in Sidon,[89] in which the author argues in behalf of the veracity of Christianity from the Qurʾān. No less a figure than Ibn Taymiyyah (1263–1328), so authoritative a figure among many modern Muslims, wrote his famous work *al-Jawāb aṣ-saḥīḥ*, "The Right Answer," specifically against an abbreviated form of Paul of Antioch's *risālah*.[90]

[86] See Johann W. Fück, "Some Hitherto Unpublished Texts on the Muʿtazilite Movement from Ibn-al-Nadim's Kitāb-al-Fihrist," in *Professor Muhammad Shafi Presentation Volume*, ed. S. J. Abdullah, 62 (Lahore, Pakistan: Punjab University Press, 1955). The later Muʿtazili scholar ʿAbd al-Jabbār (d. 1025) also mentioned Abū Qurrah's name in connection with a report of the beliefs of the Melkites. See ʿAbd al-Jabbār al-Hamdhūnī, *Al-Mughnī fī abwūb at-tawḥīd wa-l-ʿadl*, 14 vols. (Cairo: al-Dār al-Miṣriyya li l-Taʾlīf wa l-Tarjama, 1958–65), 5: 144.

[87] See Hayek, *ʿAmmār al-Baṣrī*, 93–94.

[88] See Fück, "Some Hitherto Unpublished Texts," 57–58.

[89] See Khoury, *Paul d'Antioche*, 169–87 (French); 59–83 (Arabic).

[90] See the discussion, edition, and English translation of Ibn Taymiyyah's work in Thomas F. Michel, *A Muslim Theologian's Response to Christianity: Ibn Taymiyya's al-jawab al-sahih* (Delmar, NY: Caravan Books, 1984). See also R. Ebied and D. Thomas, eds., *Muslim-Christian Polemic during the Crusades: The Letter from the People of Cyprus and Ibn Abī Ṭālib al-Dimashqī's Response*, History of Christian-Muslim Relations, vol. 2 (Leiden: Brill, 2005).

Clearly, therefore, at least some Muslims took cognizance of Christian apologetic and polemical works. Nevertheless, there can be little doubt that Christians themselves were the primary audience for such works. But a consideration of their broader potential audience raises two other issues, one literary and the other historical. The literary question inquires about a given author's intentions in composing his work; how did he put it together in view of his intended audience? The historical question is concerned with what can be learned about the actual relations between Muslims and Christians in the early Islamic period from the works included in these several genres of apologetics and polemics that have been reviewed in this chapter. In other words, do their narratives have a historical *fundamentum in re* or a basis in real life?

From the literary perspective, one must distinguish between the popular genres of apologetics and the more scholarly exercises in controversial theology, the *kalām* texts, and the works of philosophical theology. The latter are instances of a formal, almost academic discourse, in which both Muslims and Christians engaged. While they are dialogical in character, and serious in their apologetic intent, they are didactic and logically systematic in their presentation of material. Their authors do not, by and large, seem to have attempted to engage the reader's imagination; they do not seem to have intended to instill an attitude in the reader, nor to affect his mood, nor to prompt him to a course of action. Rather, with a show of rational demonstration, their purpose was to make an appeal to the authority either of reason or of divine revelation, or both. The authors seem always to have been seriously earnest in their intentions. They wanted to convince their readers of the truth of the matters under discussion as they saw it.

The more popular genres of discourse, in contrast, have about them an air of imaginative engagement, even entertainment. They have serious points to make and important truths to communicate, but they also bespeak an attitude of an assumed superiority, almost in disguise, that they want to suggest to the reader. To wit, Christians really do have the true answers to religious questions, all appearances to the contrary notwithstanding, and Muslims are somehow radically mistaken. The characters in the narratives of the popular genres of apologetics and polemics are often types, on the order of dramatis personae; they are usually not recognizable personally, but they suggest readily recognizable personae in the society; their names are most often symbolic, even when they are the names of real persons. In the narratives they are playing a role, not representing themselves in any real way. And the role is most often that of a Christian who cannot be bested in an argument about religion by a Muslim, even by a highly placed person or a well-known scholar. Subliminally, the details of the narratives themselves then suggest the superiority of Christianity to Islam. In the repartee of debate in the narrative the characters bring delight to the reader in their one-upmanship, and in the cleverness and acuity of their responses to provocative questions. If only it were so in real life! But what can be learned from these texts about the conditions of real life in the caliphate? Do these texts reflect it in any significant way? Here we come to the historical questions.

Many modern scholars are skeptical about the idea that there is much of a historical basis for the fictional scenarios of the more popular genres of Christian apologetics in the early Islamic period. For example, Gerrit J. Reinink, in an article considering the Syriac report of the conversation between Patriarch John III and the emir ʿUmayr ib Saʿd mentioned above, says the following:

> The oldest examples of Syriac apologetics in response to Islam are not the result of actual Muslim-Christian dialogue or disputation, but have to be considered as literary fictions written by Christians for the members of their own communities, with the purpose of warding off the increasing danger of apostasy. It is *au fond* "reactive" literature.[91]

Other scholars have registered similar judgments about the historicity of the encounters between Muslims and Christians that the more popular apologetic works written by Christians in Arabic in the early Islamic period seem to report. At the very most, the more skeptical commentators are prepared to concede only that in some instances there may have been encounters between the Christian spokesman and the Muslim official named in a given text, but that later writers, mostly now anonymous, have simply used these well-known occasions as settings for their literary exercises in religious apologetics and polemics. What leads scholars to this judgment are a number of factors, chief among them being two considerations: most such narratives were written by unnamed writers long after the events they claim to narrate; and most of them deal with the prophet Muḥammad, the Qurʾān, and Islam in such a negative and openly polemical way that it hardly seems possible that such statements could ever have been uttered in Arabic in an emir's *majlis*, or in any other public forum. It is further remarkable that such negative texts by Jews and Christians written in Arabic have circulated at all, let alone seemingly so prolifically, over so many centuries within the world of Islam.[92] It all seems so unlikely to modern scholars, given their ideas about what medieval Muslim authorities would or would not tolerate. Moreover, there is scarcely any mention of any of these events in Islamic sources. Nevertheless, when all is said and done, we do

[91] Gerrit J. Reinink, "The Beginnings of Syriac Apologetic Literature in Response to Islam," *Oriens Christianus* 77 (1993): 186.

[92] See Moritz Steinschneider, *Polemische und apologetische Literatur in arabischer Sprache zwischen Muslimen, Christen und Juden* (Leipzig: Brockhaus, 1877).

have these Christian texts in Arabic and we must come to some understanding about their historical verisimilitude, or lack of it.

In this connection it may serve the historian well to consider the role of the institution of the formal "salon of inquiry" (*majlis al-munāẓarah*) in Arabic-speaking high society in the early Islamic period, as the conventional setting in the courts of caliphs and emirs for free discussions about religion and many other topics.[93] One knows from many reports how popular such sessions were among numerous medieval Muslim scholars and officials. What is more, there are also reports about how some more pious Muslims in those days were themselves shocked and offended when they attended such sessions for the first time. In this connection one should recall the interesting passage from the biographical dictionary of the Andalusī writer Abū ʿAbd Allāh al-Ḥumaydī, quoted in the previous chapter, in which the author tells the story of Abū ʿUmar Aḥmad ibn Muḥammad ibn Ṣaʿdī. He visited Baghdad at the end of the tenth century and twice attended sessions of interreligious conversations held at the homes of prominent men. The experience shocked him, and he vowed that he would never attend such sessions again. But the report of the conventions followed in the sessions Abū ʿUmar attended sheds light on the historical circumstances evoked in many of the popular Christian apologetic texts.

Considering such a report, the modern scholar would perhaps be well advised to be cautious in his judgments about what might or might not have been allowed in public scholarly discussions in the world of Islam in medieval Baghdad and elsewhere. The well-known practice of open debate may have provided the real-life basis for many of the literary compositions of the popular Christian apologies written in Arabic and Syriac in the early Islamic period. Their often undoubtedly fictional narrative, to be successful, would nevertheless seem to have required at least that measure of verisimilitude provided by the evocation of a recognizable social behavior of their own time and place. Incorporating such a scenario, an author could transmit in his narrative the signals his reader would need, successfully to imagine a situation not irrelevant to his own as a Christian in an Islamic society, who wanted to be reassured that while it was not widely recognized, he still might be convinced that his own Christian religion really was the true one, and that it could be shown to be so, even in the idiom of the social conventions of the Arabic-speaking world of Islam.

[93] See the remarks of Joel L. Kraemer, *Humanism in the Renaissance of Islam: The Cultural Revival during the Buyid Age* (Leiden: Brill, 1986), esp. 58–60.

The Profile of Islam in Christian Arabic Texts

The Christian apologetic texts in Syriac and Arabic from the early Islamic period reflect the fact that their authors had a detailed knowledge of the teachings of Islam, the Qur'ān, and the *ḥadīth* literature, as well as of the biography of the prophet, and the history of the caliphate. However, for the most part, the ways in which they used this information, to present a profile of Islam, its institutions and teachings, in a manner that made it particularly vulnerable to Christian polemic, was not exactly true to what could reasonably be considered a fair view of Islam on its own terms. At its best Islam was presented in these texts as a teaching "on the way" to the truth, or even as in some way fulfilling some biblical promises. For example, in the account of the monk Abraham's performance in the *majlis* of the Muslim emir in Jerusalem in the early ninth century, the unknown author says of the Qur'ān's claim that Muḥammad was the "seal of the prophets" (*al-Aḥzāb* 33:40): "He is not a prophet (God preserve you); he is only a king with whom God was pleased, by means of whom and in whom God fulfilled his promise to Abraham regarding Ishmael."[94]

Christians in the early Islamic period not infrequently spoke of Muḥammad as a king pleasing to God for having saved the Arabs from idolatry. The further idea voiced in the passage quoted here, that in the person of Muḥammad and in his mission God fulfilled a promise to Abraham in regard to Ishmael (Genesis 17:20), is singular. It shows a deeper sensitivity to Islamic religious claims than these texts normally recognize. It sounds a theme that one does not hear again in so many words in Christian responses to Islam until the interreligious writings of Louis Massignon in the twentieth century.[95]

Regarding the person of Muḥammad, Patriarch Timothy I was perhaps the most generous of all the Christian apologists. In the Arabic account of his session in the *majlis* of the caliph al-Mahdī, the patriarch is made to declare:

> Muḥammad deserves the praise of all reasonable men because his walk was on the way of the prophets and of the lovers of God. Whereas the rest of the prophets taught about the oneness of God, Muḥammad also taught about it. So he too walked on the way of the prophets. Then, just as all the prophets moved people away from evil and sin, and drew them to what is right and virtuous, so also did Muḥammad

[94] Marcuzzo, *Le dialogue d'Abraham de Tibériade*, #110.

[95] See Louis Massignon, *Trois prières d'Abraham*, Patrimoines (Paris: Cerf, 1997), esp. 61–118; Sidney H. Griffith, "Sharing the Faith of Abraham: The 'Credo' of Louis Massignon," *Islam and Christian-Muslim Relations* 8 (1997): 193–210.

move the sons of his community away from evil and draw them to what is right and virtuous. Therefore, he too walked on the way of the prophets.[96]

As for the Qur'ān, again we may quote from the account of Patriarch Timothy's encounter with the caliph. This time we quote from the presumably original Syriac text, where we find the following statement:

> Our King said to me: "Do you believe that our Book was given by God?" And I replied to him: "It is not my business to decide whether it is from God or not. But I will say something of which your majesty is well aware, and that is that all the words of God found in the Torah and in the Prophets, and those of them found in the Gospel and in the writings of the Apostles, have been confirmed by signs and miracles; as to the words of your Book, they have not been corroborated by a single sign or miracle. . . . Since signs and miracles are proofs from the will of God, the conclusion to be drawn from their absence in your Book is well known to your Majesty."[97]

So we see that even the friendliest of Christian apologists who lived in the world of Islam in the early Islamic period stopped short of accepting Muḥammad as a prophet in any canonical sense, and of accepting the Qur'ān as a canonical book of divine revelation. Nevertheless, the portrait of Islam as it is found in the writings of the Syriac- and Arabic-speaking apologists in this milieu is recognizably true to the reality, albeit somewhat out of focus from an Islamic perspective. And the apologetic works themselves are obviously products of the Islamic world; they could not be confused with Christian texts written in any other cultural milieu of the early medieval period. For one thing, these works lack the extremely negative rhetoric of contemporary Greek or Latin anti-Islamic texts, and they are singularly lacking in the customary invective these compositions directed against Muḥammad or the Qur'ān. Rather, in the Arabic texts written by Christians in the world of Islam it is clear that the intention of their authors was to compose a Christian discourse in the Arabic language, sufficient both to sustain the faith of Christians living in that world and to commend the reasonable credibility of Christianity to their Muslim neighbors in their own religious idiom.

[96] Robert Caspar, "Les versions arabes du dialogue entre le Catholicos Timothée I et le calife al-Mahdī (IIe/VIIIe siècle), *Islamochristiana* 3 (1977): 150 (Arabic). See also Samir Khalil Samir, "The Prophet Muḥammad as Seen by Timothy I and Other Arab Christian Authors," in *Syrian Christians under Islam: The First Thousand Years*, ed. David Thomas, 75–106 (Leiden: Brill, 2001).

[97] A. Mingana, "Timothy's Apology for Christianity," *Woodbrooke Studies* 2 (1928): 36–37.

V

CHRISTIAN PHILOSOPHY IN BAGHDAD AND BEYOND

A MAJOR PARTNER IN THE DEVELOPMENT OF CLASSICAL ISLAMIC INTELLECTUAL CULTURE

Philosophy and the Christians

While the Christian theologians who wrote in Arabic in the early Islamic period, whose works have been our concern up to this point, were for the most part associated with monasteries and other ecclesiastical institutions, many of them, along with other Christian intellectuals in the caliphate prior to the time of the Crusades, also played a role in the burgeoning intellectual life in the caliph's own capital city of Baghdad and beyond. Some were physicians, some were philosophers, and some were logicians, mathematicians, copyists, or translators. Some were also Christian apologists and theologians, as we have seen. All of them contributed something to the newly flowering culture of the classical period of Islamic civilization. But in no society-wide enterprise did Christians take a more prominent role than they did in the famed translation movement undertaken in Baghdad from the eighth to the tenth centuries, when philosophical, scientific, and sapiential texts from the Hellenistic and Persian worlds were systematically being translated from Greek, Syriac, and Pahlavi into Arabic. This enterprise not only brought the learning of ancient Greece and Persia to the new world of Islam, it also became the impetus for new developments in philosophy itself in the Arab world, and for a new appreciation of the philosophical way of life, which some Christian and Muslim intellectuals together thought could become the vehicle for a more fruitful dialogue between members of different religious communities in the caliphate.

It has often been acknowledged by scholars, as Dimitri Gutas has recently pointed out, that the vast majority of the translators of Greek and Syriac texts into Arabic in the early ʿAbbasid translation movement were

Christians.[1] Their names are duly recorded and their contributions to the movement are amply described,[2] but hardly anyone discusses the work of these scholars and translators as having a part to play in the Islamic translation movement and also in the intellectual life of the churches to which they belonged. Rather, one gets the impression from most discussions that it was simply a matter of these Christian scholars hiring out their translation services to Muslim patrons who brought their contributions to Islamic scientific and philosophical interests, but that the translators themselves had little or no interest in or use for the texts they transmitted. Modern scholars of the translation movement often fail to mention other works by the translators, especially if they are religious texts, or sometimes they fail to mention even translations of philosophical texts made for Muslim patrons by translators who are otherwise known only as theologians or scholars of religion. For example, in the previous chapter we mentioned the fact that Patriarch Timothy I (r. 780–823) translated Aristotle's *Topics* at the behest of the caliph al-Mahdī (r. 775–85), a fact duly noted by Dimitri Gutas in his magisterial study of the translation movement,[3] but he makes only passing mention of the patriarch's other works and ignores altogether Timothy's account of his conversation with an Aristotelian philosopher at the caliph's court about the ways of knowledge and the doctrine of God. Similarly, in the previous chapter we mentioned that Theodore Abū Qurrah (ca. 755–ca. 830), who is otherwise known primarily as a religious writer in Greek, Syriac, and Arabic, nevertheless did make an Arabic translation of the pseudo-Aristotelian treatise *De virtutibus animae* for Ṭāhir ibn al-Ḥusayn, the caliph al-Maʾmūn's (r. 813–33) famous general from Khorasan.[4] But Gutas makes no mention of this translator or of the translations of philosophical texts attributed to him.

[1] See Dimitri Gutas, *Greek Thought, Arabic Culture: The Graeco-Arabic Translation Movement in Baghdad and Early ʿAbbāsid Society (2nd–4th/8th–10th Centuries)* (London: Routledge, 1998), 136.

[2] See, e.g., Bénédicte Landron, "Les chrétiens arabes et les disciplines philosophiques," *Proche Orient Chrétien* 36 (1986): 23–45; Gérard Troupeau, "Le role des Syriaques dans la transmission et l'exploitation du patrimoine philosophique et scientifique grec," *Arabica* 38 (1991): 1–10; John W. Watt, "Eastward and Westward Transmission of Classical Rhetoric," in *Centres of Learning: Learning and Location in Pre-Modern Europe and the Near East*, ed. J. W. Drijvers and A. A. MacDonald, Brill's Studies in Intellectual History, vol. 61 (Leiden: Brill, 1995); Ephrem-Isa Yousif, *Les philosophes et traducteurs syriaques: D'Athènes à Bagdad* (Paris and Montreal: L'Harmattan, 1997); Mirella Cassarino, *Traduzioni e Traduttori Arabi dall' VIII all' XI Secolo* (Rome: Salerno Editrice, 1998).

[3] See Gutas, *Greek Thought, Arabic Culture*, 61 and n. 1.

[4] See Mechtild Kellermann-Rost, "Ein pseudoaristotelischer Traktat über die Tugend" (unpublished Ph.D. diss., University of Erlangen, 1965). For more on this text and other translations by Christian religious thinkers, see Sidney H. Griffith, "Arab Christian Culture

To be fair, one of Gutas's concerns in his landmark book was to argue that the translations themselves were not what inspired Muslim interest in Greek science and philosophy. Rather, he says, it was the other way around; the scientific and philosophical interests of Muslims provided the impetus that created the market for the translators. He goes so far as to say the following:

> It is therefore inaccurate to say or infer that Greek culture "flourished" in the monasteries and Christian centers before and during the first century of Islam, and that the Graeco-Arabic translation movement simply drew upon the pre-existing knowledge of Greek of the Christians. . . . The Greek of the Syriac schools was not sufficient for the new standards required by the rich sponsors of the translations, and translators accordingly invested time and effort into learning Greek well because by then it had become a lucrative profession.[5]

This observation is undoubtedly true from the perspective of Gutas's study of the larger process of the transmission of Greek literary and scientific culture to the Arabic-speaking world, but it leaves the mistaken impression that there were no philosophical interests among Syriac or Arabic-speaking Christians of the early Islamic period beyond the lucrative opportunity for translation he mentions. The fact is that these Christian scholars, albeit that they were newly primed by the serendipitous possibilities of financial gain, were also all building on earlier traditions in their own communities. They used their skills not only to translate but also to employ philosophical and logical thought in support of their faith commitments and to commend the philosophical life itself as a fruitful development that might provide the social possibility for harmony between Christians and Muslims in the caliphate. Accordingly, after a brief review of the earlier progress of Greek philosophy and logic, particularly that of Aristotle, in the intellectual concerns of the Christians of the Orient, in this chapter we shall focus our attention on several representative figures in the translation movement who were also significant Christian thinkers in the Arabic-speaking world of the Muslims.

Syrian Christian Philosophers

In earlier Christian history, and coming to fruition in the fourth century, Greek-speaking Christian intellectuals had already done their best to co-

---

in the Early Abbasid Period," *Bulletin of the Royal Institute for Inter-Faith Studies* 1 (1999): 25–44.

[5] Gutas, *Greek Thought, Arabic Culture*, 138.

opt Late Antique, Hellenic philosophy into what they sometimes called "Christian Philosophy" or the "Philosophy of Christ,"[6] a process that in effect created a new, hybrid intellectual discipline that some commentators have now dubbed simply "Christianism."[7] And it may well have been, at least in part, in reaction to this Christian co-optation of philosophy that in Athens and Alexandria in the fifth and sixth centuries Neoplatonist and other philosophers were determined to keep Christianity out of their discipline, at the same time that some of them resolutely defended traditional, Hellenistic/Egyptian religion, in ways obviously dictated by their reaction to the challenge of the then growing Christian religious establishment.[8]

The Neoplatonist school in Athens seems eventually to have fallen victim to the edict of the emperor Justinian I in the year 529 that prohibited non-Christians to teach philosophy or law.[9] But in Alexandria, some accommodation with the local Christian patriarch for the participation of Christians in the academy is said to have given the largely Neoplatonist institution a new lease on life that preserved it until at least the early Islamic period.[10] But here the Christian students of philosophy, in contrast to the ways of the Christian intellectuals of earlier generations, seem to have taken a different approach to their discipline; they did not so much co-opt traditional philosophy and its exercises into a new *paideia*, after the manner of Origen, Evagrius of Pontus, the Cappadocian Fathers, and other prominent Christianists of an earlier era. Rather, respecting the integrity of the philosophical enterprise in its own right, their purpose was to use their expertise in its traditional disciplines, and particularly in Aristotelian logic, reasonably to defend the credibility of the truth claims of divine revelation,

[6] See Anne-Marie Malingrey, *"Philosophia": Étude d'un groupe de mots dans la literature grecque, des Présocratiques au IVe siècle après J.-C.* (Paris: Librairie C. Klincksieck, 1961), esp. 289–301; Jaroslav Pelikan, *Christianity and Classical Culture: The Metamorphosis of Natural Theology in the Christian Encounter with Hellenism*, The Gifford Lectures, 1992/93 (New Haven, CT: Yale University Press, 1993), esp. 177–83.

[7] For the definition of the term "Christianism," see I. P. Sheldon-Williams, "The Greek Christian Platonist Tradition from the Cappadocians to Maximus and Eriugena," in *The Cambridge History of Later Greek and Early Medieval Philosophy*, ed. A. H. Armstrong, 425 and n. 3 (Cambridge: Cambridge University Press, 1967).

[8] See James A. Francis, *Subversive Virtue: Asceticism and Authority in the Second-Century Pagan World* (University Park: Pennsylvania State University Press, 1995); Anne Sheppard, "Philosophy and Philosophical Schools," in *The Cambridge Ancient History; Late Antiquity: Empire and Successors, A.D. 425–600*, ed. Averil Cameron et al., 14: 835–54 (Cambridge: Cambridge University Press, 2000).

[9] On this much-discussed matter, see Alan Cameron, "The Last Days of the Academy at Athens," *Proceedings of the Cambridge Philosophical Society* 195, n.s. 15 (1969): 7–29; H. J. Blumenthal, "529 and Its Sequel: What Happened to the Academy?" *Byzantion* 48 (1978): 369–85.

[10] See H. J. Blumenthal, "Alexandria as a Centre of Philosophy in Later Classical Antiquity," *Illinois Classical Studies* 18 (1993): 307–25.

and even to refine the expression of the religious claims themselves. Of course, this respect for the integrity of philosophy did not prevent Christian philosophers from taking issue, on philosophical grounds, with positions espoused by Aristotle and other non-Christians that they deemed to be in contradiction with positions they held on religious grounds. For example, and most notably, they defended the biblical doctrine of creation as opposed to the Aristotelian hypothesis of the eternity of the world.[11]

As it happened, there was an impressive number of Syrians with ties to Edessa and the Monophysite/Jacobite, or Syrian Orthodox, church who took up the practice of philosophy in Alexandria and elsewhere from the sixth century onward. They and their so-called Nestorian, or Church of the East, colleagues in Edessa, Nisibis, and the surrounding Syriac-speaking milieu in the eighth and ninth centuries made up the community of scholars in whose footsteps Arabic-speaking Christians such as Ḥunayn ibn Isḥāq (808–873) and Yaḥyā ibn ʿAdī (893–974) and their students would follow in the ninth and tenth centuries.[12]

The story begins back in the days of John Philoponos (ca. 490–ca. 570), a Jacobite Christian student of the Neoplatonist Ammonius, son of Hermeias, in Alexandria.[13] Philoponos functioned both as a philosopher and as a defender of Christianity. Indeed, one may make the case that his troubles with the Christian authorities over the issue of his perceived "Tritheism" and other dogmatic matters had their roots in his philosophical and logical concerns, rather than in any purely heretical, theological consider-

[11] The doctrine of creation was already well developed in the philosophical mode of "Christianism" in the works of the Cappadocian Fathers of the Byzantine church. See Pelikan, *Christianity and Classical Culture*, 90–106, 248–62. In the sixth century, Christian philosophers in the Neoplatonist tradition of Alexandria took up this issue in more straightforward philosophical terms. See, e.g., Christian Wildberg, trans., *John Philoponus: Against Aristotle on the Eternity of the World* (London: Duckworth, and Ithaca, NY: Cornell University Press, 1987). For more information on John Philoponus, see the bibliographical notes below. Later, in Islamic times, Arabic-speaking philosophers would again be struggling with the issue of the creation versus the eternity of the world. See the summary discussions in Joel L. Kraemer, *Philosophy in the Renaissance of Islam: Abū Sulaymān al-Sijistānī and His Circle* (Leiden: Brill, 1986), 198–200; Herbert A. Davidson, *Proofs for Eternity, Creation and the Existence of God in Medieval Islamic and Jewish Philosophy* (New York: Oxford University Press, 1987), esp. 86–116; Lenn Evan Goodman, *Islamic Humanism* (Oxford: Oxford University Press, 2003), esp., 122–60.

[12] Many of these earlier Syrian "Aristotelians" and their works were discussed already in Khalil Georr, *Les categories d'Aristote dans leurs versions syro-arabes* (Beirut: Institut Français de Damas, 1948), esp. 1–32. But see Henri Hugonnard-Roche, *La logique d'Aristote du grec au syriaque: Études sur la transmission des texts de l'Organon et leur interpretation philosophique*, Textes et Traditions, no. 9 (Paris: Librairie Philosophique J. Vrin, 2004).

[13] See H.-D. Saffrey, "Le chrétien Jean Philopon et la survivance de l'école d'Alexandrie au Vie siècle," *Revue des Études Grecques* 67 (1954): 396–410; Richard Sorabji, ed., *Philoponus and the Rejection of Aristotelian Science* (London: Duckworth, 1987).

ations.[14] In any event, there was a student of Philoponos in Alexandria, a fellow Jacobite, who later switched his allegiance to the Melkites; he was from the Syriac-speaking environs of Edessa, and his name was Sergius of Reshʿayna (d. 536). He became the first-known link between the enthusiasts for Aristotle in Neoplatonist Alexandria and the Syriac-speaking communities in northern Syria.[15] Subsequently, their numbers would increase to the point that a modern historian could marvel at how much an enthusiasm for classical Greek science, philosophy, and literature, and especially for the works of Aristotle, flourished in the Syriac-speaking community of the Jacobites, while at the same time they seemed to languish in neglect in contemporary, Greek-speaking Byzantium.[16]

In Syria the study of the works of "the Philosopher" and of other Greek thinkers always involved translation into Syriac as the first step in the enterprise. It went hand in hand with the wider project to translate Greek scriptural and theological texts, an undertaking that began in earnest in the sixth century as thinkers in the flourishing churches of the so-called Jacobites (Syrian Orthodox) and Nestorians (Assyrian Church of the East) were struggling to define their social and ecclesiastical identities,[17] largely in reaction to the doctrines and policies of the conciliar orthodoxy enforced in the Roman Empire from the time of the emperor Justinian I (r. 527–65) onward.[18] It is important to insist on this broader framework of the de-

[14] See Theresia Hainthaler, "John Philoponus, Philosopher and Theologian in Alexandria," in *Christ in Christian Tradition*, ed. Aloys Grillmeier and Theresia Hainthaler, vol. 2, *From the Council of Chalcedon (451) to Gregory the Great (590–604)*, part 4, "The Church of Alexandria with Nubia and Ethiopia after 451," trans. O. C. Dean, 107–46 (London: Mowbray and Louisville, KY: Westminster John Knox Press, 1996).

[15] See Henri Hugonnard-Roche, "Aux origines de l'exégèse orientale de la logique d'Aristote: Sergius de Reshʿayna (d. 536), médecin et philosophe," *Journal Asiatique* 277 (1989): 1–17; Hugonnard-Roche, "Note dur Sergius de Reshʿayna, traducteur du grec en syriaque et commentateur d'Aristote," in *The Ancient Tradition in Christian and Islamic Hellenism: Studies on the Transmission of Greek Philosophy and Sciences; Dedicated to J. J. Drossart Lulofs on His Ninetieth Birthday*, ed. Gerhard Endress and Remke Kruk, 121–43 (Leiden: Research School CNWS, School of Asian, African, and Amerindian Studies, 1997).

[16] See Lawrence I. Conrad, "Varietas Syriaca: Secular and Scientific Culture in the Christian Communities of Syria after the Arab Conquest," in *After Bardaisan: Studies on Continuity and Change in Syriac Christianity in Honour of Professor Han J. W. Drijvers*, ed. Gerrit J. Reinink, and A. C. Klugkist, 85–105, Orientalia Lovaniensia Analecta, 89 (Leuven, Belgium: Peeters, 1999).

[17] See especially Sebastian P. Brock, "From Antagonism to Assimilation: Syriac Attitudes to Greek Learning," in *East of Byzantium: Syria and Armenia in the Formative Period*, ed. Nina Garsoïan et al., 17–34, Dumbarton Oaks Symposium, 1980 (Washington, DC: Dumbarton Oaks, 1982); Brock, "Syriac Culture in the Seventh Century," *ARAM* 1 (1989): 268–80.

[18] In this connection see the important study in Aloys Grillmeier and Theresia Hainthaler, *Christ in Christian Tradition*, vol. 2, *From the Council of Chalcedon (451) to Gregory the Great (590–604)*, part 2, "The Church of Constantinople in the Sixth Century," trans. John Cawte

velopment of ecclesial identities as the context for the Syrian translation movement, often conducted in connection with intercommunal apologetic and polemical concerns and particularly in connection with the proper definition and deployment of the technical terms of the controversial theological and Christological formulas.[19] To discuss the translations in isolation from the larger spectrum of the intellectual preoccupations in connection with which they were in fact accomplished, as is often done in modern scholarly studies of the Syriac translations, is to leave them in a hermeneutical limbo where their only significance then seems unaccountably to be merely to prepare the way for the much better known Graeco-Arabic translation movement of early Islamic times. The practice of discussing the Syriac translations apart from the needs that prompted their production in the first place also lends support to the modern, stipulated separation and isolation of the claims of reason and revelation respectively in the minds of the translators and their associates. In fact, as we shall see, their efforts were most often to use the distinction of the one set of claims to bolster the verisimilitude of propositions drawn from the other one.

From the time of Sergius of Reshʿayna to that of Yaḥyā ibn ʿAdī, both Syriac-speaking Jacobites, more than four hundred years elapsed. Over that long period of time, in the careers of an impressive number of mostly other Jacobite scholars from the environs of Edessa, some with direct ties to the philosophical school in Alexandria, the fortunes of Aristotle and Greek philosophy and science more generally, grew steadily in the Syriac-speaking world. In this connection one might mention the names of Severus Sebokht (d. 666/7), Athanasius of Balad (d. 696), Jacob of Edessa (633–708), George, Bishop of the Arabs (d. 724), and Theophilus of Edessa (d. 785),[20] bringing the chain of scholarship well into Islamic times. This tradition of cultivating Greek learning in Syriac translation, flourishing in the Syrian churches well before the time of the early ʿAbbasid translation movement, formed the intellectual heritage of a Jacobite scholar such as Yaḥyā ibn ʿAdī's immediate scholarly predecessors in his hometown, the Jacobite enclave of Takrit in the Persian domain in the preceding century, in the careers and works of men such as Ḥabīb ibn Khidmah Abū Rāʾiṭah (d. before 850), the first Jacobite to write theological tracts in Arabic, and Nonnus of Nisibis (d. after 862), who wrote apologetic and exegetical works in both Syriac and Arabic.[21]

---

and Pauline Allen, esp. "The Theological Actions Undertaken by Justinian I," 317–475 (London: Mowbray and Louisville, KY: Westminster John Knox Press, 1995).

[19] See in this connection the remarks of D. S. Wallace-Hadrill, *Christian Antioch: A Study of Early Christian Thought in the East* (Cambridge: Cambridge University Press, 1982), esp. 96–116.

[20] On these scholars and their work, see Georr, *Les categories d'Aristote*, esp. 16–32; Brock, "From Antagonism to Assimilation," esp. 22–27; Hugonnard-Roche, *La logique d'Aristote.*

[21] For Abū Rā'iṭah, see Georg Graf, *Die Schriften des Jacobiten Ḥabīb ibn Khidma Abū*

In the meantime, in the Syriac-speaking community of the so-called Nestorian Church of the East, interest in Aristotle and the Greek sciences presumably did not lag far behind that of the Jacobites, although the chain of scholarly tradition over time is initially harder to follow.[22] Paul the Persian (fl. 531–78), who was a younger contemporary of the initially Jacobite Sergius of Reshʿayna, with similar ties to Alexandria, cultivated a strong interest in Aristotelian thought, but in the end he became a convert to Zoroastrianism in Persia, at the court of Khusrau Anūshirwān (r. 531–79).[23] While interest in Greek learning certainly flourished in the widespread Nestorian school system in the Syriac-speaking milieu, in centers such as Nisibis, al-Ḥīra, the monastery of Dayr Qunnā, and Jundīsābūr,[24] one does not find much mention of Aristotle or of the cultivation of Greek logic in Nestorian Syriac texts until the time of Patriarch Timothy I (727/8–823), who, as we have seen, in his letters in Syriac tells of his discussions with Aristotelian logicians at the court of the caliph al-Mahdī (r. 775–85) in Baghdad.[25] It is noteworthy in this connection that Patriarch Timothy had to make arrangements to borrow copies of Aristotle's *Topics* and parts of the *Organon* from the Jacobite monastery of Mar Mattai, between Mosul and Tagrit.[26] Nevertheless, by the mid-eighth century Nestorian scholars, such as members of the Bukhtīshū family, with their connections

Rāʾiṭa, CSCO, vols. 130 and 131 (Louvain, Belgium: Peeters, 1951); Sidney H. Griffith, "Ḥabīb ibn Khidmah Abū Rāʾiṭah, a Christian *mutakallim* of the First Abbasid Century," *Oriens Christianus* 64 (1980): 161–201. For Nonnus, see Albert van Roey, *Nonnus de Nisibe, Traité apologétique: Étude, texte et traduction*, Bibliothèque du Muséon, 21 (Louvain, Belgium: Peeters, 1948); Sidney H. Griffith, "The Apologetic Treatise of Nonnus of Nisibis," *ARAM* 3 (1991): 115–38.

22 See Raymond LeCoz, *Les médecins nestoriens au moyen âge: Les maîtres des arabes* (Paris: L'Harmattan, 2004).

23 See Dimitri Gutas, "Paul the Persian on the Classification of the Parts of Aristotle's Philosophy: A Milestone between Alexandria and Bagdad," *Der Islam* 60 (1983): 231–67, esp. 250. See also Javier Teixidor, "Science *versus* foi chez Paul le Perse; une note," in *From Byzantium to Iran: Armenian Studies in Honour of Nina G. Garsoïan*, ed. J.-P. Mahé and R. W. Thomson, 509–19 (Atlanta: Scholars Press, 1997); Teixidor, *Aristote en syriaque: Paul le perse, logician du VIe siècle* (Paris: CNRS, 2003).

24 On the Nestorian school system, beginning with the famous school of Nisibis, see Gerrit J. Reinink, "'Edessa Grew Dim and Nisibis Shone Forth': The School of Nisibis at the Transition of the Sixth-Seventh Century," in Drijvers and MacDonald, eds., *Centres of Learning*, 77–89. The Jacobite metropolitan, Marûthâ of Takrit (d. 649) wrote of how those whom he called Nestorians in his day, wanting to steal away the simple people to their own errors, sought to establish a school in every village, many of which, he says, were pedagogically excellent. See F. Nau, "Histoires d'Ahoudemmeh et de Marouta," *Patrologia Orientalis* 3 (1905): 65–66.

25 See Thomas R. Hurst, "Letter 40 of the Nestorian Patriarch Timothy I (727–823): An Edition and Translation" (master's thesis, Catholic University of America, 1981); Hanna Cheikho, *Dialectique du langage sur Dieu de Timothée I (728–823) à Serge* (Rome: Istituto Pontificale di Studi Orientali, 1983).

26 See Sebastian P. Brock, "Two Letters of the Patriarch Timothy from the Late Eighth Century on Translations from Greek," *Arabic Sciences and Philosophy* 9 (1999): 233–46.

with Jundīsābūr in Iran,[27] Ḥunayn ibn Isḥāq (808–873), who hailed from the Nestorian capital of the Lakhmids, al-Ḥīra in Iraq,[28] and Abū Bishr Mattā ibn Yūnus (d. 940), from the flourishing Nestorian monastery of Dayr Qunnā not far from Baghdad,[29] who became "the founder of the Aristotelian school in Baghdad early in the tenth century,"[30] would all come to be among the dominant Christian scholars in the Graeco-Arabic translation movement in early ʿAbbasid times. In fact, the Nestorian Abū Bishr Mattā, as we will see, would be one of the Jacobite Yaḥyā ibn ʿAdī's principal teachers.

Concomitantly, in Islamic intellectual circles associated with the caliph's court in Baghdad from the early ninth century onward, many theoretical concerns, not entirely dissimilar to those that had prompted the interest of Christian intellectuals in the study of Greek philosophy and science in earlier times, had already conspired to attract Muslim thinkers such as Abū Yūsuf Yaʿqūb ibn Isḥāq al-Kindī (c. 801–866) to the study of the logic and philosophy of Aristotle in its Alexandrian dress. Gerhard Endress says that for al-Kindī, "philosophy was to vindicate the pursuit of rational activity as an activity in the service of Islam."[31] When more Arabic translations of "the Philosopher's" works, initially done largely by Syriac-speaking Christians, became available, so in this same spirit were more Muslim thinkers attracted to them. A major case in point is provided by the career of Abū Naṣr al-Fārābī (ca. 870–950), who had studied Aristotelian logic with two Nestorian Christian scholars, Yuḥannā ibn Ḥaylān (d. 910) and Abū Bishr Mattā ibn Yūnus, mentioned above.[32] Al-Fārābī went on to become a world-class philosopher in his own right, and prominent among his concerns, in addition to his interest in political philosophy, was the relationship between reason and revelation.[33] In the present context what is immediately relevant

[27] See Gutas, *Greek Thought, Arabic Culture*, 118.

[28] See Myriam Salama-Carr, *La traduction à l'époque abbaside: L'école de Hunayn ibn Ishaq et son importance pour la traduction* (Paris: Didier, 1990).

[29] See Louis Massignon, "La politique islamo-chrétienne des scribes nestoriens de Deir Qunna à la cour de Bagdad au IXe siècle de notre ère," *Vivre et Penser* 2 (1942): 7–14, reprinted in L. Massignon, *Opera Minora*, 3 vols., ed. Y. Moubarac (Beirut: Dar al-Maaref, 1963), 1: 250–57.

[30] Gutas, *Greek Thought, Arabic Culture*, 14.

[31] Gerhard Endress, "The Circle of al-Kindī: Early Arabic Translations from the Greek and the Rise of Islamic Philosophy," in Endress and Kruk, eds., *The Ancient Tradition in Christian and Islamic Hellenism*, 50.

[32] On these two Christian scholars and their affiliations, see Joep Lameer, "From Alexandria to Baghdad: Reflections on the Genesis of a Problematical Tradition," in Endress and Kruk, eds., *The Ancient Tradition in Christian and Islamic Hellenism*, 181–91.

[33] On this important theme in the work of al-Fārābī, see Muhsin S. Mahdi, *Alfarabi and the Foundation of Islamic Political Philosophy* (Chicago: University of Chicago Press, 2001). See also Philippe Vallat, *Farabi et l'École d'Alexandrie: Des prémisses de la connaissance à la philosophie politique*, Études Musulmanes, 38 (Paris: Vrin, 2004).

is the fact that he too, a Muslim, along with his own logic tutor Abū Bishr Mattā, was one of the principal teachers of the Christian philosopher and theologian Yaḥyā ibn ʿAdī. Another important Muslim physician/philosopher of the period, a man who had taken Socrates as his model in the philosophical life, Muḥammad ibn Zakariyyāʾ ar-Rāzī (864–925),[34] and who lived for a decade or so in Baghdad during the time of the caliph al-Muʿtaḍid (892–902), is also sometimes named as one of Yaḥyā ibn ʿAdī's teachers.[35] The young Jacobite logician could hardly have had a more illustrious cast of mentors and tutors at a time when the translation movement in Baghdad was reaching its apogee.

According to Gerhard Endress, "The undisputed master of philosophy, for the Christian schools of late Hellenism as well as for the Muslim transmitters of this tradition, was Aristotle: founder of the paradigms of rational discourse, and of a coherent system of the world."[36] This is certainly a point of view shared by a medieval Syriac-speaking chronicler from the Jacobite community. At the point in the anonymous Syriac *Chronicon ad Annum Christi 1234 Pertinens* at which the chronicler comes to the discussion of what he calls the "era of the Greeks," by which he means the time of Alexander the Great (r. 356–23 BC) and his Seleucid successors in the Syriac-speaking frontier lands between the Roman and Persian empires, he has this to say about Aristotle and the importance of his works for the Christians:

> At this time, Aristotle, "the Philosopher," collected all the scattered kinds of philosophical doctrines and he made of them one great body, thick with powerful opinions and doctrines, since he separated the truth from falsehood. Without the reading of the book of logic [*mlîlûthâ*] that he made it is not possible to understand the knowledge of books, the meaning of doctrines, and the sense of the Holy Scriptures, on which depends the hope of the Christians, unless one is a man to whom, because of the excellence of his [religious] practice, the grace of the Holy Spirit is given, the one who makes all wise.[37]

[34] See Albert Z. Iskandar, "Al-Rāzī," in *Religion, Learning, and Science in the ʿAbbasid Period*, ed. M. J. L. Young et al., 370–77 (Cambridge: Cambridge University Press, 1990).

[35] This according to the historian Abū al-Ḥasan ʿAlī al-Masʿūdī (d. 956) in his *At-Tanbīh wa l-Ishrāf*, as reported by Endress, *The Works of Yaḥyā ibn ʿAdī*, 6. See also Lenn E. Goodman, "Muḥammad ibn Zakariyyāʾ al-Rāzā," in *History of Islamic Philosophy*, ed. Seyyed Hossein Nasr and Oliver Leaman, 198, Routledge History of World Philosophies, vol. 1 (London: Routledge, 1996); Marie-Thérèse Urvoy, *Traité d'éthique d'Abû Zakariyyâʾ Yahyâ ibn ʿAdi*, Études Chrétiennes Arabes (Paris: Cariscript, 1991), 32. One modern scholar very much doubts that al-Rāzī could have been Yaḥyā's teacher: Dominique Urvoy, *Les penseurs libres dans l'islam classique* (Paris: Albin Michel, 1996), 144.

[36] Endress, "The Circle of al-Kindī," in Endress and Kruk, eds., *The Ancient Tradition in Christian and Islamic Hellenism*, 52.

[37] I.-B. Chabot, ed., *Anonymi Auctoris Chronicon ad Annum Christi 1234 Pertinens*,

Fig. 4. Aristotle and Alexander the Great
Taken from the pages of a thirteenth-century Arabic manuscript now in the British Library and containing a work called *Animals and Their Uses*, by the Christian physician and scholar Ibn Bakhtishūʿ, the illustration shows Alexander the Great at the feet of his teacher Aristotle. Both Alexander and Aristotle were celebrated by Jewish, Christian, and Muslim scholars in ʿAbbasid Baghdad. (British Library Oriental Manuscript 2784, thirteenth-century Arabic, f. 96. Arabic translation of Aristotle's "Animals and Their Uses," by permission of the British Library.)

In ʿAbbasid times there were more Christian thinkers interested in the philosophies and sciences of the Greeks than just those Aristotelians among the Jacobites and the Nestorians who took their texts and commentaries from the Alexandrian tradition. And there were more Muslims whose philosophical and scientific interests reached well beyond a single-minded devotion to Aristotle. Nevertheless these were the Christian and Muslim philosophers who shaped the intellectual milieu in which Ḥunayn ibn Isḥāq and Yaḥyā ibn ʿAdī pursued their careers. And just as the Muslims among this generation of philosophers wanted "to vindicate the pursuit of rational activity as an activity in the service of Islam,"[38] so did Ḥunayn and Yaḥyā and their associates intend to vindicate with the same philosophy the doctrines and practices of the Christians and the Christology of the Nestorians and the Jacobites respectively. Indeed, one important reason for the sustained interest in Aristotelian thought among the Jacobites and Nestorians of the time, and a significant impetus behind their projects to translate texts from Greek into Syriac from the sixth century onward, and latterly into Arabic, was precisely the need for "the Philosopher's" definitions and distinctions of terms in the effort evermore clearly to differentiate and defend their confessional formulas, and hence their ecclesiastical identities. This process was still underway by the time of the Islamic occupation in the seventh century of the largely Syriac-speaking, Aramean homeland. It continued well into Islamic times, with the Muslims themselves now becoming new participants in the enterprise to find ways clearly to articulate and to defend their own distinctive religious identities. By the ninth century, Arabic-speaking Christian and Muslim philosophers in Baghdad were together commending the philosophical life as a workable model for interreligious *convivencia* in a city that by their time had a large and important Christian population.[39]

In this light then the Jacobite, Nestorian, and Muslim teachers in Greek logic and philosophy appear to have flourished at a time in Baghdad when interconfessional and interreligious interest in the works of the Alexandrian Aristotelians went hand in hand with a concern among both Christians and Muslims to show that their own religious traditions accorded best with the requirements of the life of reason lived in pursuit of the highest knowledge, and to argue that they and their coreligionists alone were the truest heirs of Aristotle. In this context, the Christians were concerned to refute the counter claims not only of Muslims, but of other Christian groups as well.

CSCO, vols. 82 and 109 (Paris: J. Gabalda, 1920 and Louvain: Imprimerie Orientaliste L. Durbecq, 1952), 82: 104–5 (Syriac), 109: 82 (Latin).

38 Endress, "The Circle of al-Kindī," 50.

39 See Michel Allard, "Les chrétiens à Baghdad," *Arabica* 9 (1962): 267–288; Jean Maurice Fiey, *Chrétiens syriaques sous les abbasides surtout à Bagdad (749–1258)*, CSCO, vol. 420 (Louvain, Belgium: Secrétariat du Corpus SCO, 1980), esp. 117–85.

Similarly, Muslim philosophers not only rejected the distinctive religious doctrines of the Christians, but they disdained the intellectual approach of the Muslim religious controversialists, the *mutakallimūn*, as well. In the end, in Baghdad in the tenth century, some Muslim and Christian philosophers shared a passion for the philosophical life that bound them together in ways that featured Christians such as the Nestorian Abū Bishr Mattā ibn Yūnus and the Jacobite Yaḥyā ibn ʿAdī championing the claims of philosophy against the methods of the Muslim *mutakallimūn*,[40] while Muslims such as Abū Yūsuf al-Kindī and Abū ʿIsā al-Warrāq (d. ca. 862) were taking issue from a philosophical perspective with the principal doctrines of the Christians.[41] At the same time, the Jacobite Christian Yaḥyā ibn ʿAdī used his expertise in Aristotelian logic and philosophy to defend Christian doctrines and practices both against the challenges posed by Muslims and to attack Nestorian Christological formulas, all the while using the same means to commend the veracity of Jacobite Christological teachings. But these Christian thinkers' engagement with the logic and philosophy of Aristotle was not limited to mounting rational or theoretical arguments against the positions of their doctrinal adversaries.

Like the philosophers of Late Antiquity from whom they borrowed so

[40] One thinks in this connection of the famous debate between the Christian logician Abū Bishr Mattā ibn Yūnus and the Muslim *mutakallim* Abū Saʿīd as-Sīrāfī, for which see D. S. Margoliouth, "The Discussion between Abū Bishr Mattā and Abū Saʿīd al-Sīrāfī," *Journal of the Royal Asiatic Society* (1905): 79–129; Muhsin Mahdi, "Language and Logic in Classical Islam," in *Logic in Classical Islamic Culture*, ed. G. E. von Grunebaum, 51–83, (Wiesbaden: Harrassowitz, 1970); Gerhard Endress, "The Debate between Arabic Grammar and Greek Logic in Classical Islamic Thought," *Journal for the History of Arabic Science* [Aleppo] 1 (1977): 320–23, 339–51; Endress, "Grammatik and Logik: Arabische Philologie und griechische Philosophie im Widerstreit," in *Sprachphilosophie in Antike und Mittelalter*, ed. Burkhard Mojsisch, 163–299, Bochumer Studien zur Philosophie, 3 (Amsterdam: Gruner, 1986). Similarly, Yaḥyā ibn ʿAdī himself wrote a treatise against the methods of the *mutakallimūn*; see Gerhard Endress, "Yaḥyā ibn ʿAdī: *Maqāla fī tabyīn al-faṣl bayna ṣināʿat al-manṭiq al-falsafī wa l-naḥw al-ʿarabi*," *Journal for the History of Arabic Science* [Aleppo] 2 (1978): 181–93, and he also attacked their doctrines; see, e.g., Shlomo Pines and Michael Schwarz, "Yaḥyā ibn ʿAdī's Refutation of the Doctrine of Acquisition (*iktisāb* in *Studia Orientalia Memoriae D. H. Baneth Dedicata* (Jerusalem: Magnes Press, Hebrew University of Jerusalem, 1979), 49–94; Emilio Platti, "Yaḥyā Ibn ʿAdī and the Theory of *Iktisāb* in Thomas, *Christians at the Heart of Islamic Rule*, 151–57.

[41] For al-Kindī, see Augustin Périer, "Un traité de Yahyâ ben ʿAdî: Defense du dogme de la trinité contre les objections d'al-Kindî," *Revue de l'Orient Chrétien* 3rd series, 2 (1920–21): 3–21; for al-Warrāq, see E. Platti, trans., *Abū ʿĪsā al-Warrāq, Yaḥyā ibn ʿAdī; de l'Incarnation*, CSCO, vols. 490 and 491 (Louvain, Belgium: Peeters, 1987); David Thomas, *Anti-Christian Polemic in Early Islam: Abū ʿĪsā al-Warrāq's "Against the Trinity,"* University of Cambridge Oriental Publications, 45 (Cambridge: Cambridge University Press, 1992); Thomas, *Early Muslim Polemic against Christianity: Abū ʿĪsā al-Warrāq's "Against the Incarnation,"* University of Cambridge Oriental Publications, 59 (Cambridge: Cambridge University Press, 2002).

much, Ḥunayn ibn Isḥāq and Yaḥyā ibn ʿAdī and the Muslim and Christian members of their circles of scholars in medieval Baghdad wanted to live the philosophical life as such, and to cultivate the practice of philosophically inspired "spiritual exercises,"[42] very much in the context of their Christian and Islamic religious commitments.

Ḥunayn ibn Isḥāq

The one Christian philosopher who on anyone's account played a major role in the early phase of the ʿAbbasid translation movement whose name many in the West might actually recognize is the already-mentioned Nestorian Ḥunayn ibn Isḥāq (808–873).[43] He was a contemporary of the first generation of Christian theologians who regularly wrote in Arabic, men like Theodore Abū Qurrah, Ḥabīb ibn Khidmah Abū Rāʾiṭah, and ʿAmmār al-Baṣrī, whose careers we have discussed in previous chapters. Ḥunayn was a member of the Arab Christian tribe of ʿIbād from al-Ḥīra, hence the sobriquet *al-ʿIbādī*, which we often find added to his name in the sources. By all accounts he was a precocious youth, the son of a pharmacist, who received his early medical training at the famous Persian school of Jundīsāpūr. Subsequently he traveled widely, both within the world of Islam and beyond it, even into Byzantine territory. A Syriac-speaker from birth, on his travels Ḥunayn was interested in perfecting his knowledge of languages such as Greek and Arabic, and he was constantly in search of manuscripts, especially scientific, medical, and philosophical texts. He says himself that in his youth he was already engaged in translating the works of the Greek physician Galen. Ḥunayn gained considerable fame in the caliphate as a physician and as a translator of Greek texts into Syriac and Arabic. In due course he became the chief physician of the caliph al-Mutawakkil (r. 847–61), and in his maturity, in conjunction with the officials at the famous library in Baghdad called Bayt al-Ḥikmah, or House of Wisdom, he administered a whole school of translators, including most famously his son Isḥāq, who worked with him especially on philosophical texts, and his nephew Ḥubaysh, his preferred collaborator on scientific works. In addition to translations of numerous philosophical, medical, and other scien-

[42] In this connection one is mindful of the studies of Pierre Hadot, *Philosophy as a Way of Life*, trans. Michael Chase (Oxford: Blackwell, 1995); Hadot, *What Is Ancient Philosophy?* trans. Michael Chase (Cambridge, MA: Harvard University Press, 2002).

[43] On Ḥunayn's life and works, see G. C. Anawati, "Ḥunayn ibn Isḥāq al-ʿIbādī, Abū Zayd," in *Dictionary of Scientific Biography*, vol. 15, supplement 1, ed. Charles Coulston Gillispie, 230–34 (New York: Charles Scribner's, 1980); Albert Z. Iskandar, "Ḥunayn the Translator," and "Ḥunayn the Physician," in Gillispie, *Dictionary of Scientific Biography*, 234–49.

tific texts produced by Ḥunayn and his school,[44] according to the reports that have come down to us, Ḥunayn himself was the translator of a number of the works of Aristotle into Syriac that his son Isḥāq then translated into Arabic, with Ḥunayn subsequently reviewing them.[45] But medicine and the translation of Greek texts were not Ḥunayn's only concerns, albeit that they were an important source of income for him and they are his major claim to fame in the eyes of most latter-day western scholars. He was also an active apologist for his Christian faith and a promoter of the philosophical way of life.

Some reports claim that Ḥunayn had a hand in the translation of the Septuagint Bible into Arabic. However that might be, he did compose some apologetic tracts, one on proofs for the existence of the one God, creator of all that is, and one on the ways and means of discerning the true religion, two themes that figure prominently in the works of contemporary Christian Arabic theologians. A later Christian writer, the thirteenth-century Copt, al-Muʿtaman ibn al-ʿAssāl, mentioned earlier, describes another work by Ḥunayn on the end of human life and the reckoning for one's freely chosen behavior in this world that each person will then face in the world to come.[46] But perhaps the most interesting text to mention in connection with Ḥunayn's involvement in religious apologetics is one that features his participation with another Christian scholar and translator in an exchange of letters with a Muslim acquaintance at the caliph's court who had addressed a letter to Ḥunayn in which he summons him to the profession of Islam.

Around the year 855, the astronomer ʿAlī ibn Yaḥyā al-Munajjim (d. 888) wrote a letter to Ḥunayn ibn Isḥāq in which he offers arguments framed in the manner of an Aristotelian logician to prove that Muḥammad was truly a prophet sent by God. Al-Munajjim proposes that consequently it is incumbent upon Ḥunayn as a reasonable man to convert to Islam. Ḥunayn replies with a letter of his own in which he points out from his logician's point of view the formal and material fallacies in al-Munajjim's syllogisms. Along the way Ḥunayn mentions reasons why one might consider Christianity to be the true religion. Then, almost a generation later, another Christian scholar, the Melkite Qusṭa ibn Lūqā (c. 830–912)[47] re-

[44] See the long list of texts translated in Salama-Carr, *La traduction à l'époque abbasside*, 69–75.

[45] See F. E. Peeters, *Aristoteles Arabus: The Oriental Translations and Commentaries on the Aristotelian Corpus* (Leiden: Brill, 1968).

[46] See Georg Graf, *Geschichte der christlichen arabischen Literatur*, vol. 2, Studi e Testi, 133 (Vatican City: Biblioteca Apostolica Vaticana, 1947), 122–29. See the edition of this treatise in Samir Khalil Samir, "Maqālah ʿfī l-ājālʾ liḤunayn ibn Isḥāq," *al-Machriq* 65 (1991): 403–25. This article also includes a comprehensive list of the works of Ḥunayn.

[47] Qusṭa ibn Lūqā's name, in the spelling Kusta Ben Luka, is given to William Butler Yeats's mysterious interlocutor in his esoteric work *A Vision*.

sponded once again to al-Munajjim's proposal with yet another letter, this time addressed to the astronomer's son, in which Qusṭa takes issue with the substance of al-Munajjim's arguments, particularly one in which he had put forward the Muslim doctrine of the inimitability of the Qur'ān as an evidentiary miracle in testimony to the veracity of the Islamic scripture. Qusṭa ibn Lūqā counters this claim with a disquisition on the nature of literary prosody and the observation that by its very nature it cannot sustain the comparison al-Munajjim's argument would demand of it. Sometime thereafter a presumably Christian editor assembled the three pieces of correspondence into a single publication that then circulated in Arabic-speaking Christian communities as part of the growing archive of popular apologetic literature.[48]

In the effort to commend the philosophical way of life among his contemporaries, Ḥunayn ibn Isḥāq composed a work that came eventually to enjoy a wide circulation among scholars in the Arabic-speaking world and even beyond it in translation. This was his *Kitāb ādāb al-falāsifah*, sometimes called *Nawādir al-falāsifah*, titles that mean roughly "gnomic sayings" or "instructive anecdotes" of the philosophers.[49] It is a collection of quotations by and about ancient wise men and philosophers that was meant to serve a practical purpose for people who would make the effort to inform their daily lives and the policies of their societies with the best moral insights philosophy had to offer. Indeed, Ḥunayn, like his contemporary the Muslim Aristotelian philosopher Yaʿqūb ibn Isḥāq al-Kindī (ca. 800—ca. 867), understood that in addition to offering the means to defend the credibility of divine revelation, philosophy was also a way of life, not just a mode of intellectual inquiry or scholarly discourse on abstruse topics. And in their day one of the ways in which people translated philosophy into daily life was by reading the biographies of wise men of the past and meditating on their words of wisdom. Ḥunayn and other Arabic Christian writers in

[48] See Paul Nwyia and Samir Khalil Samir, *Une correspondence islamo-chrétienne entre Ibn al-Munağğim, Ḥunayn ibn Isḥāq et Qusṭa ibn Lūqā*, Patrologia Orientalis, no. 185, vol. 40, fasc. 4 (Paris: Brepols, 1981). See also the study of this text by Wadi Z. Haddad, "Continuity and Change in Religious Adherence: Ninth-Century Baghdad," in *Conversion and Continuity: Indigenous Christian Communities in Islamic Lands; Eighth to Eighteenth Centuries*, ed. Michael Gervers and Ramzi Jibran Bikhazi, 33–53, Papers in Mediaeval Studies, 9 (Toronto: Pontifical Institute of Mediaeval Studies, 1990).

[49] See Abdurrahman Badawi, ed., *Ḥunain ibn Ishaq: Âdâb al-Falâsifa (Sentences des Philosophes)* [Arabic], (Safat, Kuwait: Éditions de l'Institut des Manuscrits Arabes, 1985). See also Graf, *Geschichte*, 2: 126. See in particular Karl Merkle, *Die Sittensprüche der Philosophen, "Kitāb ādāb al-falāsifa" von Honein ibn Isḥāq in der Überarbeitung des Muḥammad ibn ʿAlī al-Anṣārī* (Leipzig: Harrassowitz, 1921), reprinted in Fuat Sezgin, ed., *Ḥunain ibn Isḥāq: Tests and Studies*, Islamic Philosophy, vol. 17 (Frankfurt: Institute for the History of Arabic-Islamic Science at the Johann Wolfgang Goethe University, 1999). See also John K. Walsh, "Versiones peninsulares del *ʿKitāb ādāb al-falāsifa*ʾ de Ḥunayn ibn Isḥāq," *Al-Andalus* 41 (1976): 355–84.

ʿAbbasid times thought that the cultivation of the philosophical life in this manner in the Islamic milieu would dispose people in both the Muslim and the Christian communities to live harmoniously with one another for the common good of all members of society.

Yaḥyā ibn ʿAdī

While Ḥunayn ibn Isḥāq was undoubtedly the most well known Christian philosopher of Baghdad in the ninth century, when the effort was very much focused on the translation enterprise, in the tenth century in the caliphs' city, while translation was still an important undertaking, scholars were nevertheless by that time more concerned with matters of interpretation and commentary than previously was the case, and they were more given to composing philosophical treatises of their own. In this milieu the most important Christian figure was the Jacobite Yaḥyā ibn ʿAdī (893–974), who became the center of a philosophical circle in Baghdad that included Muslims as well as Christians of all denominations among his colleagues and disciples.[50]

Yaḥyā ibn ʿAdī was born in the city of Takrīt in Iraq. As a young man he moved to Baghdad where he studied with Abū Bishr Mattā ibn Yūnus (ca. 870–ca. 940),[51] a philosopher from the Church of the East who has been credited with founding the Baghdad school of Aristotelians. Yaḥyā was also the student of the now world-famous Muslim philosopher, Abū Nasr al-Farābī (ca. 870–950). By the mid-940s Yaḥyā ibn ʿAdī had become a major figure in his own right in a new generation of intellectuals in Baghdad. While he earned his living as a professional scribe, he became one of the leading exponents of the "Peripatetic" school of thought in the caliph's capital city,[52] in the process earning for himself the title *al-manṭiqī*, that is, "the logician." Yaḥyā's passion was for books of logic and philosophy; he not only searched for them and copied them, but he also translated them from Syriac into Arabic. In this enterprise, of course, he followed in the footsteps of a number of earlier Christian scribes and translators. But Yaḥyā was also a teacher and an author in his own right, with works to his credit in logic, philosophy, and theology.

[50] See Joel L. Kraemer, *Humanism in the Renaissance of Islam: The Cultural Revival during the Buyid Age* (Leiden: Brill, 1986), 104–39.

[51] See Gutas, *Greek Thought, Arabic Culture*, 14.

[52] See F. E. Peters, *Aristotle and the Arabs: The Aristotelian Tradition in Islam* (New York: New York University Press, 1968), 160–63. Dimitri Gutas says Yaḥyā ibn ʿAdī was the "head of the Baghdad Aristotelians in the mid-tenth century." Gutas, *Greek Thought, Arabic Culture*, 101.

As just a brief review of his bibliography shows,[53] Yaḥyā was much involved with both Aristotle's *Topics* and his *Physics*, the two works Dimitri Gutas has identified as of crucial interest in what he calls "the exigencies of inter-faith discourse" in the era of the translation movement.[54] In all his works on these and other philosophical topics, Yaḥyā seems to have stayed close to the teaching of Aristotle and his Alexandrian interpreters, a circumstance that earned him some obloquy in later years, when later Muslim philosophers such as Ibn Sīnā/Avicenna (d. 1037) and others voiced their disdain for the work of those whom they viewed as the staid and unadventuresome Aristotelians of Baghdad.[55]

In view of the clash between the philosopher-logicians and the more traditional Muslim religious thinkers in Baghdad in the ninth and tenth centuries, many modern commentators have said that for the philosophers in that milieu, including Yaḥyā ibn ʿAdī, the use of reason was deemed superior to religion in the search for answers to life's ultimate questions. In this connection Gutas has written, "Just as logic is superior to grammar in that it is universal and supralingual—so Abū Bishr Mattā's and Yaḥyā's argument in defense of logic ran—so also is philosophy, the use of reason, superior to religion in that it is universal and supranational (since each nation has its own religion)."[56] For Joel Kraemer, this view was a basic tenet of the philosophic humanism of the renaissance of Islam in the Buyid period, and he goes on to say that "the chief architects of this philosophic humanism in our period were the Christian philosopher Yaḥyā ibn ʿAdī and his immediate disciples."[57] For Kraemer, Yaḥyā was "first and foremost a philosopher,"[58] even in his theological treatises.

However, for the Christian theologians of the Baghdad milieu, Aristotelian logic had, by way of contrast with the case among Muslim religious thinkers, long been an auxiliary discipline. Yaḥyā and the other Christian apologists, like Ḥunayn ibn Isḥāq in the preceding century, were thinking and writing within a tradition that had long since learned to present the claims of their religious convictions in the Greek idiom of Aristotelian

[53] See Gerhard Endress, *The Works of Yaḥyā ibn ʿAdī: An Analytical Inventory* (Wiesbaden: Dr. Ludwig Reichert Verlag, 1977). See also the important additions and corrections to Endress's *Inventory* in the review by Samir Khalil Samir, "Yaḥyā ibn ʿAdī," *Bulletin d'Arabe Chrétien* 3 (1979): 45–63. An important collection of Yaḥyā's philosophical works has since appeared: Sahban Khalifat, *Yaḥyā ibn ʿAdī: The Philosophical Treatises; a Critical Edition with an Introduction* [Arabic] (Amman: University of Jordan, 1988).

[54] Gutas, *Greek Thought, Arabic Culture*, 61–74.

[55] See Dimitri Gutas, *Avicenna and the Aristotelian Tradition* (Leiden: Brill, 1988), 64–72.

[56] Gutas, *Greek Thought, Arabic Culture*, 103.

[57] Kraemer, *Humanism in the Renaissance of Islam*, 6.

[58] Ibid., 106–7.

logic, even when translated into Syriac or Arabic. What is more, the doctrinal positions that Yaḥyā and the other Christians defended in Syriac or Arabic were initially formulated in Greek philosophical and logical terms. They were constantly being defended by appeal to the logical requirements of the proper definitions of the originally Greek terms, even in their Syriac and Arabic versions. This agenda was still the operative one in the ninth and tenth centuries, in response to the religious claims of Islam, when the challenge for Christians was not so much reason versus revelation, but the development of an appropriately logical and philosophical, not to say theological, vocabulary in Arabic. And it is surely from this perspective that a thinker like Yaḥyā ibn ʿAdī would have found the categories of the philosophers far more congenial for his religious, apologetic purposes in Arabic than the methods peculiar to the contemporary Muslim *mutakallimūn*.

In addition to his work as a logician, philosopher, and translator, Yaḥyā was also a prolific writer in the area of Christian theology and apologetics.[59] In this connection, his concerns were not limited to the customary topics of the Christian apologetic agenda developed in the previous century; they extended to issues of public morality, as in his book on the reformation of public morals,[60] his treatise on sexual abstinence and the philosophical life,[61] and to the larger question of the general human pursuit of happiness and the avoidance of sorrow. But when all is said and done, the defense of the doctrines of the Trinity, and of the Jacobite Christology in the doctrine of the Incarnation, loom largest among Yaḥyā ibn ʿAdī's theological concerns. They are the primary topics in the more than sixty works Gerhard Endress lists under the heading of "Christian Theology" in his bibliography of Yaḥyā's works.[62] So effective were Yaḥyā ibn ʿAdī's apologetic works in the eyes of other Christian writers in Arabic that large portions of them were excerpted for inclusion in compilations of texts on doctrinal topics made by other Arabic-speaking apologists in later times.

[59] In this connection, see the numerous studies of Emilio Platti, in particular: "Deux manuscripts théologiques de Yaḥyā b. ʿAdī," *MIDEO* 12 (1974): 217–29; Platti, "Yaḥyā b. ʿAdī, philosophe et théologien," *MIDEO* 14 (1980): 167–84; Platti, Une cosmologie chrétienne," *MIDEO* 15 (1982): 75–118; Platti, *Yaḥyā ibn ʿAdī, philosophe chrétien et philosophe arabe: Sa théologie de l'incarnation*, Orientalia Lovaniensia Analecta, 14 (Leuven, Belgium: Katholieke Universiteit Leuven, Departement Orientalistiek, 1983); Platti, *La grande polémique antinestorienne (et la discussion avec Muḥammad al-Misrī)*, CSCO, vols. 427–28 (Louvain, Belgium: Peeters, 1981); Platti, *Abū ʿĪsā al-Warrāq, Yaḥyā ibn ʿAdī: De l'incarnation*, CSCO, vols. 490 and 491 (Louvain, Belgium: Peeters, 1987).

[60] Yaḥyā ibn ʿAdī, *The Reformation of Morals*, ed. Samir Khalil Samir, intro. and trans. Sidney H. Griffith, Eastern Christian Texts, vol. 1 (Provo, UT: Brigham Young University Press, 2002).

[61] Vincent Mistrih, "Traité sur la continence de Yaḥyā ibn ʿAdī; edition critique," *Studia Orientalia Christiana: Collectanea* 16 (1981): 1–137.

[62] See Endress, *Works of Yaḥyā ibn ʿAdī*, 99–123.

Particularly notable among them were the Coptic scholars of the thirteenth century, whom we mentioned in previous chapters.

Like Ḥunayn ibn Isḥāq before him, Yaḥyā ibn ʿAdī was devoted to the cultivation of the human mind and the pursuit of the philosophical life as the most humane way to promote a realm of public discourse in which both Christians and Muslims could participate. He was convinced that in the end reason could serve the interests of revelation, and devotion to philosophy could preserve the decencies of life in common. His argument on behalf of this position was based on the following principle: "Men are a single tribe (*qabīl*), related to one another; humanity unites them. The adornment of the divine power is in all of them and in each one of them, and it is the rational soul."[63]

On this basis Yaḥyā offered suggestions for how one might aim to become "a perfect human being" (*al-insān al-kāmil*) by extirpating vices and cultivating virtues in one's own life. For him the requisite perfection then consists in the acquisition of what he calls "true science" and "godly wisdom"; they bring one closest to God.[64] It is clear too that while he speaks much in the *Reformation of Morals* about kings, aristocrats, and the members of the ruling classes of the pluralistic Islamic society in Baghdad in his day, Yaḥyā's own favorite people are those whom he calls "scholars," "monks," and "ascetics." He says that "what is to be considered good for them is clothing of hair and coarse material, traveling on foot, obscurity, attendance at churches and mosques and so forth, and abhorrence for luxurious living."[65] Furthermore, he says, their task is to "give people an interest in eternal life."[66] Yaḥyā's talk of scholars, monks, and ascetics, and churches and mosques in the *Reformation of Morals* evokes his view of the Islamo-Christian milieu in which he lived and worked. It invites the supposition that in his pursuit of philosophy in the interreligious company of Muslim, Jacobite, Nestorian, and Melkite Christian teachers and students, Yaḥyā hoped to cultivate among them all a sense of "humanity." He called it *al-insāniyyah* in Arabic, a term best translated as "humane behavior," the cultivation of which Yaḥyā thought should foster the growth of a measure of mutual esteem between the upholders of religious convictions who are inherently critical of one another.

[63] Yaḥyā Ibn ʿAdī, *The Reformation of Morals*, 5:14, 106 and 107.

[64] See, e.g., Mistrih, "*Traité sur la continence*," 1.3–4, 33.2–3, and 34.5–7.

[65] Yaḥyā ibn ʿAdī, *The Reformation of Morals*, 3.43, 60.

[66] Ibid., 3.45, 62.

Colloquy between Christian and Muslim Philosophers

Muslim thinkers, too, were interested in fostering the philosophical way of life in society, and many of them, like Yaḥyā's own master al-Farābī, had much to say about the qualities of "the virtuous city" (*al-madīnah al-faḍīlah*), as he characterized the ideal society, and the role of religion in fostering its well being.[67] They also discussed the ascetic and spiritual exercises that would be best calculated to foster the life of reason and religion in such a society. For example, in Yaḥyā ibn ʿAdī's day a lively debate ensued between Christian and Muslim thinkers over the right parameters for the practice of sexual abstinence in the philosophical life, with Yaḥyā championing complete abstinence for those fit for it, as in the ancient Christian monastic life. His Muslim adversaries argued to the contrary that in this as in other such matters, right reason teaches that virtue stands in the middle, fostering moderation over complete abstinence, which they argued is harmful to individuals, injurious to society, and detestable to God.[68]

Already in the first generation of philosophy in the Islamic world, "the philosopher of the Arabs," al-Kindī (d. 867) had been concerned to commend the goods of the philosophical life to society at large in the matter of coping with normal human problems. He composed a small treatise, *On the Art of Dispelling Sorrows*,[69] in which he sought, not unlike the ancient Boethius (ca. 480–524/26),[70] to apply the consolations of philosophy to the alleviation of life's inevitable miseries. This small book caught the fancy of a number of Christian writers in the next generations, and three of them, Elias al-Jawharī (fl. 893) of the Church of the East, the Copt Severus ibn al-Muqaffaʿ (d. ca. 1000), and Elias of Nisibis (d. 1046) of the Church of the East, all wrote books in Arabic in answer to al-Kindī's treatise in which they named the Muslim philosopher and his work and quoted from it, but they proposed a very different approach. While all three Christian treatises are very different works on their own terms, they agree with al-Kindī in commending an attitude of long suffering in the face of human misery rather than one of engaging in rigorous rational argument. But unlike al-Kindī the three Christian writers may be said to have "theologized" the

[67] See Muhsin S. Mahdi, *Alfarabi and the Foundation of Islamic Political Philosophy* (Chicago: University of Chicago Press, 2001); Vallat, *Farabi et l'École d'Alexandrie.*

[68] See Mistrih, "Traité sur la continence." See also Sidney H. Griffith, "Yaḥyā ibn ʿAdī's Colloquy on Sexual Abstinence and the Philosophical Life," in *Arabic Theology, Arabic Philosophy; from the Many to the One: Essays in Celebration of Richard M. Frank*, ed. James Montgomery, 299–333, Orientalia Lovaniensia Analecta, 152 (Leuven, Belgium: Peeters, 2006).

[69] See Al-Kindī, *Le moyen de chaser les tristesses; et autres textes éthiques*, intro., trans., and notes, Soumaya Mestiri and Guillaume Dye (Paris: Fayard, 2004).

[70] See Thérèse-Anne Druart, "Philosophical Consolation in Christianity and Islam: Boethius and al-Kindī," *Topoi* 19 (2000): 25–34.

line of thinking they found in the work by al-Kindī, bringing it into the biblical realm of Christian thinking they proposed would provide a measure of natural fulfillment to his philosophical insights. In spite of the fact that the Christian writers thus introduced the dimension of divine revelation into the discussion, the leitmotif of these compositions of theirs remained the one set by al-Kindī. Their works and his then testify to the lively interchange between Muslim and Christian thinkers that the translation movement and the Christian and Muslim cultivation of philosophy made possible in Baghdad and its environs from the late eighth to the mid-eleventh centuries.[71]

Philosophy in Arabic in the Latin West

Unbeknownst to the Christian and Muslim translators and philosophers in Baghdad in the days of the ʿAbbasid translation movement, the fruits of their labors would in due course reach way beyond the limits of the Islamic world to foster the study of philosophy and the pursuit of the philosophical life in medieval Europe, where their Arabic versions of the works of Greek-speaking philosophers and scientists came into Latin translations and sparked yet another intellectual renaissance.[72] In al-Andalus in the twelfth century, Archbishop Raymond of Toledo (r. 1126–51) "was responsible for the initial patronage and organization of the loose body of scholars who made up the Toledo 'school of translators,'"[73] which "remained in operation well into the thirteenth century, attracting world-class scholars like Michael Scot and Herman [of Carinthia]."[74] And while Toledo was the epicenter of this new, western translation movement, translations were also made in a number of other places in Spain and Italy during these centuries, enlisting the services of famous translators such as Robert of Ketton, Adelard of Bath, Gerard of Cremona, Petrus Alfonsi, John of Segovia, and John of Salisbury to name only the most well

[71] See Sidney H. Griffith, "The Muslim Philosopher al-Kindī and His Christian Readers: Three Arab Christian Texts on 'The Dissipation of Sorrows,'" *Bulletin of the John Rylands University Library of Manchester* 78 (1996): 111–27.

[72] See Fernand van Steenberghen, *Aristotle in the West: The Origins of Latin Aristotelianism*, trans. Leonard Johnston (New York: Humanities Press, 1970); George Makdisi, *The Rise of Colleges: Institutions of Learning in Islam and the West* (Edinburgh: Edinburgh University Press, 1981); Makdisi, *The Rise of Humanism in Classical Islam and the Christian West* (Edinburgh: Edinburgh University Press, 1990).

[73] María Rosa Menocal, *The Ornament of the World: How Muslims, Jews, and Christians Created a Culture of Tolerance in Medieval Spain* (Boston: Little, Brown, 2002), 195.

[74] Richard E. Rubenstein, *Aristotle's Children: How Christians, Muslims, and Jews Rediscovered Ancient Wisdom and Illuminated the Middle Ages* (Orlando, FL: Harcourt, 2003), 19.

known.[75] Their efforts benefited not only scientists and philosophers in the Latin West, but they prompted a change in theology as well.[76]

Philosophical and scientific texts were not the only ones translated from Arabic into Latin in Spain. As in the East, the Christian translators were also interested in the texts that defended Christian faith in the context of the Islamic challenge. And so it happened that among the Arabic texts that the abbot of Cluny, Peter the Venerable (ca. 1094–1156), commissioned for translation during his visit to Toledo in the 1140s was the *Correspondence between al-Hāshimī and al-Kindī*, originally composed in Arabic by a Christian apologist and polemicist in the ninth century, perhaps in the environs of Baghdad.[77] As we mentioned in the previous chapter, it was one of the texts that had the widest circulation of all Arab Christian works in the early Islamic period. And just to be able to end where we began in the discussion of Christian theology in Arabic, we now know that there was also a Latin translation of Patriarch Timothy's account of his debate with the caliph al-Mahdī available in the West in the late thirteenth or early fourteenth century.[78] So through the efforts of the translators the "church in the shadow of the mosque" did bequeath to the church in the West a small portion of her more popular interreligious heritage along with the riches of the philosophy of Aristotle and the wider range of Greek science and philosophy.

[75] See Charles Burnett, "The Translating Activity in Medieval Spain," in *The Legacy of Muslim Spain*, 2 vols., ed. Salma Khadra Jayyusi, 2: 1036–58 (Leiden: Brill, 1994).

[76] See Jean Jolivet, *La théologie et les arabes* (Paris: Cerf, 2002).

[77] See James Kritzeck, *Peter the Venerable and Islam* (Princeton, NJ: Princeton University Press, 1964).

[78] See Thomas E. Burman, *Religious Polemic and the Intellectual History of the Mozarabs, c. 1050–1200*, Brill's Studies in Intellectual History, vol. 52 (Leiden: Brill, 1994), 96–97.

VI

WHAT HAS BAGHDAD TO DO WITH CONSTANTINOPLE OR ROME?

ORIENTAL CHRISTIAN SELF-DEFINITION IN THE WORLD OF ISLAM

Communal Identities

Church historians have normally told the story of the schisms in the Christian community resulting from the decisions of the councils of Ephesus in 431 and Chalcedon in 451 as having come about gradually, roughly during the century that elapsed between the time of the council of Chalcedon and the council of Constantinople II in 553. The latter council in particular gave definitive force to the policy of the Byzantine emperor Justinian I (r. 527–65) to enforce Chalcedonian orthodoxy throughout the Roman Empire. It is a story told almost exclusively from the point of view of Roman imperial orthodoxy, which even uses the denominational adjectives anachronistically, the polemically inspired epithets, Nestorian, Jacobite, and Melkite, and, of course, the entirely polemical designation Monophysite, as designations for what are then regarded as dissident churches.[1] But the fact is that none of the communities designated by these names existed as fully developed, ecclesial entities in the sixth century, albeit that the Christological controversies out of which they emerged were certainly in full spate at that time. It was not until almost fifty years later, after the time when the emperor Heraclius (r. 610–41) lost the territories of the so-called Oriental Patriarchates to the Islamic conquest at the battle of the Yarmuk in 636, that at the council of Constantinople III (681) Roman imperial orthodoxy found its own full doctrinal definition in formulas that would prove lasting. It was reaffirmed finally just over a century later, in connection with the Byzantine Iconoclast controversy, at the council of Nicea II in 787. But another forty-some years was wanted before the publication of the earlier forms of the *Synodicon of Orthodoxy* in 843, and the establishment of the Feast of Orthodoxy.[2] So in fact the ecclesial identities of the enduring

[1] See, e.g., Vincent Deroche, *Entre Rome et l'islam: Les chrétientés d'orient, 610–1054* (Paris: Éditions Sedes, 1996).

[2] See J. M. Hussey, *The Orthodox Church in the Byzantine Empire*, Oxford History of the Christian Church (Oxford: Clarendon Press, 1986), esp. 62–68.

churches in the East did not come to their maturity until well after the rise of Islam. This being the case, and since most of the non-Chalcedonian Christians lived under Muslim rule in the Oriental Patriarchates, one must consider the challenge of Islam as itself having been a factor in the Christian, community-building process. This was especially the case of the three communities who lived with the Muslims, the Nestorians, the Jacobites, and the Melkites, to use the troika of names one finds most frequently in Muslim sources for them. Actually, as we shall see, the communities of Christians in the Islamic world included more than just these three; from the beginning there were also the Copts, the Armenians, the Georgians, and the Maronites, not to mention the Greek Orthodox, the Latins, and the Mozarabs of Spain.

The Christians who lived in the world of Islam shaped their enduring ecclesial identities, both culturally and intellectually, within the context of several local determining circumstances: their encounter with the Muslims, their adoption of the Arabic language, and their isolation from other Christian communities outside of the Islamic world. They came to their maturity as separate church communities for the most part within the world of Islam and without interference from or significant contact for long periods of time with the patriarchal sees of either Constantinople or Rome. This was the case even for the Melkites, as we shall see, who professed the faith of Byzantine imperial orthodoxy; for a crucial period in their history they were cut off from easy access to Constantinople. The break in two-way communication between Constantinople and Jerusalem extended during the crucial century and a half from around the year 815 to the time following the Byzantine emperor John Tzimisces's (d. 976) "crusade" into Syria and Palestine in 975.[3] This was the very period of the effective Arabicization of church life in the caliphate and the first phase of Christian theological development in response to intellectual pressure from Muslim controversialists. These circumstances then, along with the concomitant doctrinal disagreements on the part of the Nestorians, the Jacobites, the Copts, and the Armenians with the Greek- and Latin-speaking churches, provided the historical situation of creedal and cultural estrangement that in turn produced the perception of alienation on the part of the Christians of the Islamic world from their brethren in the West. One might even take the appearance of this phenomenon to be the definitive moment in the his-

[3] See Sidney H. Griffith, "Byzantium and the Christians in the World of Islam: Constantinople and the Church in the Holy Land in the Ninth Century," *Medieval Encounters* 3 (1997): 231–65; Griffith, "What Has Constantinople to Do with Jerusalem? Palestine in the Ninth Century; Byzantine Orthodoxy in the World of Islam," in *Byzantium in the Ninth Century: Dead or Alive? Papers from the Thirtieth Spring Symposium of Byzantine Studies, Birmingham, March 1996*, ed. Leslie Brubaker, 181–94 (Aldershot, UK, and Brookfield, VT: Variorum, 1998).

torical transition in ecclesiastical history from Late Antiquity to the Middle Ages. In these circumstances the Nestorians, Jacobites/Copts, and Melkites, the classical denominations of the Christians in the Islamic world, can be seen emerging in their mature identities, formulating their differences in polemical reactions to one another in tracts most often written in Arabic.

Nestorians

The community that both Muslims and Christians have over the centuries regularly called the Nestorians are often said to trace their heritage back to Patriarch Nestorius of Constantinople (r. 428–31) and his refusal to accept the epithet Theotokos as a fitting title for Mary, the Mother of Jesus.[4] Their fate is said to have been determined at the Council of Ephesus in 431 when both Nestorius and his theological position were anathematized. From the historical point of view, this simplistic account of the origins of the church called Nestorian is false. Nestorius's theological struggle with Patriarch Cyril of Alexandria (d. 444) over the significance of the Marian title is something of a "red herring" as far as any true account of the origins of the so-called Nestorian church in Persia is concerned. Rather, the sociohistorical community lamentably misnamed Nestorian by their adversaries for polemical reasons had its origins not in Patriarch Nestorius's struggles with Patriarch Cyril in Byzantium, but in the Syriac-speaking, academic communities of Edessa and Nisibis in the days of the schoolman Narsai (d. 503) and Bishop Bar Sauma of Nisibis (d. before 496).[5] These scholarly churchmen and their associates cultivated an enthusiasm for the Greek works of Theodore of Mopsuestia (ca. 350–428), who, inspired by his own teacher Diodore of Tarsus (d. ca. 390), had rooted his theology in a close reading and interpretation of the literal text of the scriptures. Narsai and his followers, first in Edessa and then in Nisibis, under the leadership of Bishop Bar Sauma, began the task of translating the works of Theodore into Syriac. In the Syriac-speaking world, so-called Nestorian writers devotedly called Theodore of Mopsuestia "the blessed interpreter." In due course, his works would become the touchstone of right thinking for all those in communion with the Church of the East, whose patriarchal see was Seleucia/Ctesiphon in Persia.[6]

[4] See Sebastian P. Brock, "The 'Nestorian' Church: a Lamentable Misnomer," *Bulletin of the John Rylands University Library of Manchester* 78 (1996): 23–35.

[5] See Stephen Gero, *Barsauma of Nisibis and Persian Christianity in the Fifth Century*, CSCO, vol. 426 (Louvain, Belgium: Peeters, 1981).

[6] See D. S. Wallace-Hadrill, *Christian Antioch: A Study of Early Christian Thought in the East* (Cambridge: Cambridge University Press, 1982). See also Theresia Hainthaler, "Die 'an-

Already during his days in the school of Edessa, before his flight to Nisibis in 471, Narsai and his associates had parted company with his erstwhile friend, Jacob of Serug (ca. 451–521) and those who agreed with him over the exegetical authorities whose works should be considered normative in the catechetical school. The latter would not accept Theodore of Mopsuestia as their only master, and they paid allegiance more to the works of the Cappadocian Fathers and to those of Cyril of Alexandria.[7] This disagreement forced Narsai's move to Nisibis, there to found the school that would become well known in subsequent generations as the intellectual center for the burgeoning Church of the East, as the principal Christian community in Persia came to be called after the synods of Seleucia/Ctesiphon in the sixth and early seventh centuries had clearly defined its creedal identity.[8] For this community in its beginnings Narsai wrote a Syriac *mêmrâ* in which he celebrated the memory of the three "doctors" and "fathers" they venerated: Diodore, Theodore, and Nestorius.[9] The latter was included because in retrospect he could be seen to be of the same school of thought as Theodore, and his erstwhile companion, John Chrysostom (ca. 347–407), both of whom were students of Diodore. But what stands out in Narsai's *mêmrâ* in addition to the names of those he honors is the poignant recollection of the intellectual and social struggles between the partisans of two schools of thought in Syriac-speaking Edessa in the late fifth century. Arguably, what would later be called the Jacobite and Nestorian churches had their intellectual and sociological origins in the struggles between the masters in the schools of Edessa and Nisibis over the exegetical and theological traditions they would follow. Matters came to a head in the time of the Byzantine emperor Justinian I (r. 527–65), who after

tiochenische Schule' und theologische Schulen im Bereich des antiochenischen Patriarchats," in *Jesus der Christus im Glauben der Kirche*, ed. Aloys Grillmeier, 227–61, Band 2/3, "Die Kirchen von Jerusalem und Antiochien nach 451 bis 600" (Freiburg, Germany: Herder, 2002).

[7] See Tanios Bou Mansour, *La théologie de Jacques de Saroug*, 2 vols., Bibliothèque de l'Université Saint-Esprit, vols. 16 and 40 (Kaslik, Lebanon: Université Saint-Esprit, 1993 and 2000). See also Thomas Kollamparampil, *Jacob of Serugh: Select Festal Homilies* (Rome: Centre for Indian and Inter-Religious Studies and Bangalore: Dharmaram Publications, 1997); T. Kollamparampil, *Salvation in Christ According to Jacob of Serugh* (Bangalore: Dharmaram Publications, 2001).

[8] See Sebastian P. Brock, "The Christology of the Church of the East in the Synods of the Fifth to Early Seventh Centuries; Preliminary Considerations and Materials," in Sebastian Brock, *Studies in Syriac Christianity; History, Literature and Theology* (Aldershot, UK: Variorum/Ashgate, 1992), no. 12.

[9] See Fr. Martin, "Homélie de Narsai sur les trois docteurs nestoriens," *Journal Asiatique* 9th series, 14 (1899): 446–92; 15 (1900): 469–525. See also L. Ambramowski, "Das Konzil von Chalkedon in der Homilie des Narsai über die drei nestorianischen Lehrer," *Zeitschrift für Kirchengeschichte* 66 (1954–55): 140–43.

many confrontations forced the issue in the so-called Three Chapters controversy (543/4) that eventually resulted in the formal condemnation of Theodore of Mopsuestia, his works, and their supporters at the council of Constantinople II in 553.[10] Thereafter the decisions of the council of Chalcedon in 451 were accepted in Byzantium as articulating the official orthodox Christology of the church in the Roman Empire. Syriac-speaking dissenters from this policy found refuge in the frontier zones of their homeland, the borderlands between Rome and Persia.

The so-called Nestorian church can be seen coming into existence in its distinctive canonical and confessional identity outside the borders of the Roman Empire in Persia through the decisions of the series of councils in the sixth and early seventh centuries mentioned above, the collected acts of which have been published by a modern editor in the *Synodicon Orientale*, a collection of documents that reached its final form only in Islamic times. Its theological profile found its clearest statement in Syriac in an important work by Babai the Great (551/2–628), which in the West is most often called by its Latin title, *Liber de unione*. In this book Babai set out the distinctive Christology of the Church of the East in the carefully defined terms of the developed theology of Theodore of Mopsuestia.[11] But no sooner had this been accomplished than the Islamic conquest reached Seleucia/Ctesiphon in the year 645, and for the rest of its early history the so-called Nestorian Church of the East was left to define its sociological identity within the new circumstances provided by the world of Islam.[12] Her creedal and exegetical teachings were articulated in Syriac by writers who lived in Islamic times, men such as Patriarch Timothy I, Theodore bar Kônî, Ishôʿ bar Nûn, Ishôʿdad of Merv (ninth century) and others, all living in Islamic times. Her doctrines were defended in Arabic against both the challenges of Islam and the polemics of rival Christian denominations by writers such as ʿAmmār al-Baṣrī (fl. ca. 850), Elias al-Jawharī, ʿAbd Allāh Ibn aṭ-Ṭayyib (d. 1043), Elias of Nisibis (975–ca. 1046), and ʿAbd Īshûʿ bar Berîkâ (d. 1318), to name only those whose names are most prominent. These Syriac- and Arabic-speaking writers of Islamic times were the

[10] See Adelbert Davids, "The Person and Teachings of Theodore of Mopsuestia and the Relationship between Him, His Teachings and the Church of the East with a Special Reference to the Three Chapters Controversy," in *Syriac Dialogue: Third Non-Official Consultation on Dialogue within the Syriac Tradition*, ed. Alfred Stirnemann and Gerhard Wilflinger, 38–52 (Vienna: Foundation Pro Oriente, 1998).

[11] See Geevarghese Chediath, *The Christology of Mar Babai the Great* (Kottayam, India: Oriental Institute of Religious Studies and Paderborn, Germany: Ostkirchendienst, 1982).

[12] For a description of these postconquest circumstances, see Michael G. Morony, *Iraq after the Muslim Conquest* (Princeton, NJ: Princeton University Press, 1984); Chase F. Robinson, *Empire and Elites after the Muslim Conquest: The Transformation of Northern Mesopotamia* (Cambridge: Cambridge University Press, 2000).

ones who presented the Church of the East in what would be her enduring aspect.[13]

Due to the missionary activity of this Church of the East, Christianity spread not only into South Arabia and Iran but across the silk routes of Central Asia into China by the seventh century, and southward into India. Much earlier, certainly before the fourth century, Syriac-speaking Christians had already brought their faith across the Arabian ocean with the merchant fleets into the Malabar Coast and southern India generally, where to this day the so-called Thomas Christians still celebrate their Syrian heritage.[14]

Jacobites

When the teacher Jacob of Serug broke with his colleague Narsai in the school of Edessa in Syria in the late fifth century over the issue of what would be the authoritative exegetical and doctrinal traditions in the Syriac-speaking churches, his theological associates and heirs eventually gave their allegiance to Patriarch Severus of Antioch (ca. 465–538, r. 512–18), who clearly articulated the Christology of Cyril of Alexandria in his Cathedral homilies delivered in Greek, soon to be translated into Syriac, the only language in which they all survive; one of them being preserved in Coptic.[15] In the Syriac-speaking community in the environs of Edessa, the ground had already been prepared for their reception, especially in the monastic communities, by the works and influence of Philoxenus of Mabbug (ca. 440–523).[16] When the emperor Justinian's policies subsequently forced

[13] See Raymond LeCoz, *Histoire de l'église d'orient: Chrétiens d'Irak, d'Iran et de Turquie* (Paris: Cerf, 1995); Ian Gillman and Hans-Joachim Klimkeit, *Christians in Asia before 1500* (Ann Arbor: University of Michigan Press, 1999); Wilhelm Baum and Dietmar W. Winkler, *The Church of the East: A Concise History* (London and New York: Routledge Curzon, 2003).

[14] See Samuel H. Moffett, *A History of Christianity in Asia*, 2nd rev. and corrected ed. (Maryknoll, NY: Orbis Books, 1998—ca. 2005); Gillman and Klimkeit, *Christians in Asia*; Cardinal Eugene Tisserant, *Eastern Christianity in India: A History of the Syro-Malabar Church from the Earliest Time to the Present Day*, trans. E. R. Hambye, S.J. (Westminster, MD: Newman Press, 1957).

[15] See Joseph Lebon, *Le monophysisme severien: Étude historique, littéraire et théologique sur la resistance monophysite au Concile de Chalcedoine jusqu'a la constitution de l'église jacobite* (Louvain, Belgium: J. Van Linthout, 1909; repr. New York: AMS Press, 1978); Lebon, "La christologie du monophysisme syrien," in *Das Konzil von Chalkedon: Geschichte und Gegenwart*, ed. Aloys Grillmeier and Heinrich Bacht, 3 vols., 1: 425–580 (Würzburg: Echter Verlag, 1951–154); Aloys Grillmeier, *Christ in Christian Tradition*, vol. 2, part 2, trans. John Cawte and Pauline Allen (London: Mowbray, and Louisville, KY: Westminster John Knox Press, 1995), 21–173; Pauline Allen and C. T. R. Hayward, *Severus of Antioch* (London and New York: Routledge, 2004).

[16] For a quick overview of the thought and works of Jacob, Severus, and Philoxenus, see

public allegiance in Byzantium to the Chalcedonian Christological formula, those who followed the faith articulated by the long-deposed Patriarch Severus went underground. Their numbers and their perseverance were increased in the Syriac-speaking communities with the consecration of the sympathetic bishop Jacob Baradaeus (ca. 500–578), who was installed in Edessa in 542 at the behest of the leaders of the Ghassanid Arab tribal confederation who were important allies of Byzantine power on the Syrian and Arabian borders. Subsequently, due to the tireless clandestine activities of Bishop Jacob to support those who rejected Chalcedon and accepted the doctrine of the Patriarchs Cyril of Alexandria and Severus of Antioch, the whole community of them in the Syriac-speaking milieu came to be called Jacobites by their adversaries.[17] But still, sociologically speaking, in spite of the currency of epithets such as Jacobite or the even more polemical Monophysite to describe them, there was not yet a full-fledged ecclesial community, a hierarchically separate and independent Jacobite church. Byzantine emperors and churchmen, such as Zeno (r. 474–91) with the *Henoticon* in 482, and Heraclius with his support of the doctrines of Monenergism and Monotheletism and his *Ecthesis* of 638, were still looking for ways to accommodate those whom they considered Syrian dissidents within the communion of Byzantine orthodoxy well into Islamic times. Arguably, it was not until the late seventh century that political release from the control of the government of Byzantium provided the Syriac-speaking, Jacobite communities now living under Arab government the opportunity to consolidate their denominational identity with their own fully independent hierarchical structures.

It is evident in the Greek works of writers such as Anastasios of Sinai (d. ca. 710) and John of Damascus (d. ca. 749) that within the Islamic world already in the early eighth century controversy between the several Christian communities, the nascent Melkites, the Jacobites, and the Nestorians, was already high on the list of Christian intellectual concerns in the new sociopolitical circumstances in which they now found themselves. In this milieu, Jacob of Edessa (ca. 640–708), writing in Syriac, most effectively articulated Jacobite doctrine and practice in an idiom that would in due

Roberta Chesnut, *Three Monophysite Christologies* (Oxford: Oxford University Press, 1976). See also Tanios Bou Mansour, "Die Christologie des Jakob von Sarug," in Grillmeier, *Jesus der Christus im Glauben der Kirche*, 2/3, 449–99; André de Halleux, *Philoxène de Mabbog: Sa vie, ses écrits, sa théologie* (Louvain, Belgium: Imprimerie Orientaliste, 1963); T. Bou Mansour, "Die Christologie des Philoxenus von Mabbug," in Grillmeier, *Jesus der Christus im Glauben der Kirche*, 2/3, 500–569.

[17] See David Bundy, "Jacob Baradaeus: The State of Research: A Review of Sources and a New Approach," *Le Muséon* 91 (1978),: 45–86; T. Hainthaler, "Aufbau der antichalcedonischen Hierarchie durch Jakob Baradai," in Grillmeier, *Jesus der Christus im Glauben der Kirche*, 2/3, 197–203.

course become the standard expression of his church's theological identity.[18] Then, beginning in the ninth century, when writers from all three communities were bringing these intercommunal, Christian controversies into Arabic, the spokespersons for the Jacobites, who often wrote both in Syriac and Arabic, men such as Ḥabīb ibn Khidmah Abū Rā'iṭah (d. ca. 851), Nonnus of Nisibis, Yaḥyā ibn ʿAdī (893–974), Abū ʿAlī ʿĪsā ibn Zurʿa (943–1008), and Gregorius Abū l-Faraj ibn al-ʿIbrī (1225/6–1286), known in the West as Bar Hebraeus, all played a role in further defining the Jacobite religious identity not only in response to the challenges of their Christian adversaries but also in this very context, providing their responses to the religious challenges of the Muslims. These writers presented the Jacobite or Syrian Orthodox Church in what would be her enduring aspect.[19]

Copts and Armenians

There were two Christian communities in the world of Islam whose faith was the same as that of the Jacobites and who were in communion with them, but who preserved their own communal and ecclesial identities, with their own hierarchies, apart from the Syriac-speaking Jacobites. They are the Copts of Egypt and the Armenians. The Copts had their own early Christian heritage both in their own language, Coptic, and in Greek, the dominant language of learning in the ancient patriarchate of Alexandria and the language in which St. Cyril of Alexandria, the principal theological authority for the Copts, wrote his letters and treatises. From the tenth century on, they, like the other mainline denominations in the caliphate, also adopted Arabic. In fact, as we have mentioned earlier, in due course the center of Christian literary productivity in Arabic shifted from Iraq and Syria/Palestine to Egypt, and eventually the Copts produced more Christian texts in Arabic than all of the other Christian denominations living in the world of Islam put together. Because of their acceptance of Patriarch

[18] Much work remains to be done on Jacob of Edessa, a figure whose importance in the history of the Jacobites, the Syrian Orthodox Church, would be difficult to overstate. For now, see Han J. W. Drijvers, "Jakob von Edessa (633–708)," in *Theologische Realenzyklopädie*, vol. 16 (Berlin: De Gruyter, 1993), 468–70; Dirk Kruisheer and Lucas Van Rompay, "A Bibliographical *Clavis* to the Works of Jacob of Edessa," *Hugoye* 1 (1998), http://syrcom.cua.edu/Hugoye/Vol1No1/Clavis.html.

[19] See W. Hage, *Die syrisch-jakobitische Kirche in frühislamischer Zeit* (Wiesbaden: Otto Harrassowitz, 1966); Sebastian P. Brock and David G. K. Taylor, eds., *The Hidden Pearl: The Syrian Orthodox Church and Its Ancient Aramaic Heritage*, 4 vols. (Rome: Trans World Film Italia, 2001); Bas ter Haar Romeny, "From Religious Association to Ethnic Community: A Research Project on Identity Formation among the Syrian Orthodox under Muslim Rule," *Islam and Christian-Muslim Relations* 16 (2005): 377–99.

Severus of Antioch's concise presentation of Cyril of Alexandria's Christology in his Cathedral homilies, the Copts are often put together with the Jacobites in discussions of the denominational differences among the Christians in the world of Islam, albeit that they are the much larger community and have their own independent church structures.[20]

The Armenians too, for the most part, have professed the same faith as the Jacobites while retaining their own independent hierarchical structures and their own language and ecclesiastical literature and cultural traditions.[21] They have borrowed much from Syriac sources, but they have never adopted Arabic as a church language although they have lived in all parts of the Islamic world since the very beginnings of Islam and have long been fluent in Arabic for purposes of everyday life.[22] Also from the very beginnings of Islam there has been an important Armenian enclave in Jerusalem where they have persistently represented the Jacobite point of view in theological controversy with the local Melkites from the early years of this community's distinctive, ecclesial development. Interestingly, there is even some evidence that from the seventh century onward there was a group of Armenian Chalcedonians in Jerusalem engaged in theological activity and producing texts that had a considerable influence on ecclesiastical and political developments back home in Armenia.[23]

Melkites

While the Nestorian and Jacobite churches were already in the process of formation prior to the rise of Islam, albeit that they achieved the full expression of their enduring ecclesiastical identities only in the first centuries of the caliphate, the Melkite community as a sociologically distinct community of Christians came into existence only in Islamic times and in the world of Islam. They professed the faith of Byzantine orthodoxy, but very much in the Arabic-speaking milieu of the Islamic challenge to Christian

[20] See P. du Bourget, *Les Coptes*, 2nd ed. (Paris: Presses Universitaires de France, 1988); A. S. Atiya, ed., *The Coptic Encyclopedia*, 7 vols. (New York: Macmillan 1991); A. Gerhards and H. Brakmann, eds., *Die koptische Kirche: Einfürung in das ägyptische Christentum* (Stuttgart: Kohlhammer, 1994).

[21] See J.-P. Mahé, "L'église areménienne de 611 à 1066," in *Histoire du Christianisme*, ed. J. M. Mayeur, 4: 457–547 (Paris: Desclée, 1993); Nina Garsoïan, *L'église arménienne et le grand schisme d'Orient*, CSCO, vol. 574 (Louvain, Belgium: Peeters, 1999).

[22] See Edmund Schütz, "Armenia: A Christian Enclave in the Islamic Near East in the Middle Ages," in Michael Gervers and Ramzi Jibran Bikhazi, *Conversion and Continuity: Indigenous Christian Communities in Islamic Lands; Eighth to Eighteenth Centuries*, Papers in Mediaeval Studies, 9, 217–36 (Toronto: Pontifical Institute of Mediaeval Studies, 1990).

[23] See S. P. Cowe, "An Armenian Job Fragment from Sinai and Its Implications," *Oriens Christianus* 76 (1972): 123–57.

faith. The name Melkite seems first to have been used by Syriac-speaking Jacobites, and perhaps even by Maronites, to designate those Christians in the caliphate who accepted the teachings of the sixth ecumenical council of the Byzantine imperial church, Constantinople III (681).[24] Their most authoritative spokesperson was John of Damascus (d. ca. 749), who wrote in Greek.[25] But they were also the first of the Christian denominations to adopt Arabic as an ecclesiastical language.[26] The process of Arabicization began already in the second half of the eighth century, and the earliest Christian writer regularly to write in Arabic whose name we know was the Melkite Theodore Abū Qurrah (ca. 755–ca. 830), who wrote not only to respond to the religious challenge of Islam but also very much to state the claims of the Melkites over against those of the Jacobites and the Nestorians. The Melkites, like the others, argued with both Muslims and their fellow Christians that they were in their own view the only truly orthodox Christians. The see of Jerusalem and the monasteries of the Judean desert, particularly Mar Sabas, would remain the intellectual center for the Melkites, but members of their community were to be found throughout the Arabic-speaking world, from Alexandria in Egypt to Antioch in Syria and even in Baghdad.[27] Spokesmen for the Arabic-speaking Melkites in addition to Abū Qurrah included writers such as the now anonymous ninth-century author of the popular *Disputation of the Monk Abraham of Tiberias with an Emir in Jerusalem*, Qusṭā ibn Lūqā (ca. 830–912), the historian Saʿīd ibn Biṭrīq (877–933), also known as Patriarch Eutychius of Alexandria, Abū l-Fatḥ ʿAbd Allāh ibn al-Faḍl al-Anṭākī (fl. ca. 1050), and Paul of Antioch (ca. 1180). These major writers, among many others, presented

[24] See Sidney H. Griffith, "'Melkites,' 'Jacobites,' and the Christological Controversies in Arabic in Third/Ninth Century Syria," in *Syrian Christians under Islam: The First Thousand Years*, ed. David Thomas, 9–55 (Leiden: Brill, 2001).

[25] See Andrew Louth, *St. John Damascene: Tradition and Originality in Byzantine Theology*, Oxford Early Christian Studies (Oxford: Oxford University Press, 2002). In this excellent book, the author somewhat discounts the relevance of John of Damascus's theological synthesis to the situation of the local, Syro-Palestinian church community in which he actually lived. In this connection, see Sidney H. Griffith, "John of Damascus and the Church in Syria in the Umayyad Era: The Intellectual and Cultural Milieu of Orthodox Christians in the World of Islam," in *Giovanni di Damasco: Un Padre al Sorgere dell'Islam*, Atti del XIII Convegno Ecumenico Internazionale di Spiritualità Ortodossa, Sezione Bizantina, 11–13 settembre 2005 (Bose, Italy: Monastero di Bose, 2006), 21–52.

[26] See Sidney H. Griffith, "The Church of Jerusalem and the 'Melkites': The Making of an 'Arab Orthodox' Christian Identity in the World of Islam, 750–1050 CE," in *Christians and Christianity in the Holy Land: From the Origins to the Latin Kingdoms*, ed. Ora Limor and G. G. Stroumsa, 173–202 (Turnhout, Belgium: Brepols, 2006).

[27] See Sidney H. Griffith, "The *Life of Theodore of Edessa*: History, Hagiography, and Religious Apologetics in Mar Saba Monastery in Early Abbasid Times," in *The Sabaite Heritage in the Orthodox Church from the Fifth Century to the Present*, ed. Joseph Patrich, 147–69, Orientalia Lovaniensia Analecta, 98 (Leuven, Belgium: Peeters, 2001).

the profile of the Melkite church in what would be its enduring form in the Arabic-speaking world.[28]

But a further word must be said about the epithet Melkite. In its first and most appropriate usage it was not synonymous with the Greek Orthodox denomination; they were often called *ar-Rūm*, that is, the Romans, or the Byzantines, by Arabic-speaking Muslims and Christians alike, meaning the Greek Orthodox church of Byzantium. Rather, by contrast with the Greek Orthodox, the Melkites were Arabic-speaking Christians in the world of Islam who were nevertheless in communion with the Greek Orthodox whose faith they shared. If they were to be designated by an ethnic or linguistic label at all, which historically was never the case, they might well have been called the Arab Orthodox. The Crusaders called the Melkites *Syri* in Latin, for reasons which need not detain us now, but the fact that they used a distinctive name for them indicates that at that time they were still perceived to be a different community from the Greeks. After the time of the Crusades, and especially in Ottoman times, when the Greek Orthodox Church gained the upper hand over their coreligionists in the old Oriental Patriarchates, the Melkites were for all practical purposes subsumed into the Greek Orthodox Church. In modern times, adding to the terminological confusion, the old designation Melkite was co-opted after 1729 by the largely Arabic-speaking Melkite Greek Catholic Church, a community that in the eighteenth century came from the Orthodox Church into union with Rome.[29]

Maronites and Georgians

Along with the Melkites, whose theological and liturgical heritage was Greek and Aramaic/Syriac,[30] there was another Syriac-speaking community prominent in Syria/Palestine in the early Islamic period, the Maronites, whose heritage was the classical Edessan Syriac tradition. Like the Melkites, the Maronites also professed the faith of Chalcedon. But some Maronites, according to several early Melkite writers, at least for a time had

[28] See Joseph Nasrallah, *Histoire de movement littéraire dans l'église melchite du Ve au XXe siècle*, 4 vols. (Louvain, Belgium: Peeters, 1979–89).

[29] See Robert M. Haddad, *Syrian Christians in Muslim Society: An Interpretation* (Princeton, NJ: Princeton University Press, 1970); Haddad, "On Melkite Passage to the Unia: The Case of Patriarch Cyril al-Zaʿīm (1672–1720)," in *Christians and Jews in the Ottoman Empire*, ed. B. Braude and B. Lewis, 2: 67–90 (New York: Holmes and Meier, 1982); Haddad, "Conversion of Eastern Orthodox Christians to the Unia in the Seventeenth and Eighteenth Centuries," in Gervers and Bikhazi, *Conversion and Continuity*, 449–59.

[30] See Sidney H. Griffith, "From Aramaic to Arabic: The Languages of the Monasteries of Palestine in the Byzantine and Early Islamic Periods," *Dumbarton Oaks Papers* 51 (1997): 11–31.

also accepted the monothelitism supported by the emperor Heraclius's *Ecthesis* in force between the years 638 and 648.[31] However this may be, from the ecclesial point of view, albeit that they retained their own communal identity and hierarchical independence, the Maronites were coreligionists with the Melkites, and their theological positions were discussed in conjunction with those of the Melkites even by the Muslim commentators. In the twelfth century (1182), the Maronites formally entered into communion with the see of Rome, with whom they had in fact never been at odds. This move then provided the sociological criterion for considering them a separate community of Christians in the world of Islam.[32] But by this time the Melkites too were having identity problems, given their imminent absorption among the recently returned Greek Orthodox, as mentioned above.

Also in the Melkite milieu in the early Islamic period and sharing their creedal allegiance completely were the Georgians, like the Armenians a separate language community. They had a presence in the Holy Land from the middle of the fifth century onward. One of the most important contributions of the Georgian monks, particularly in the early Islamic period, was their activity as translators. Numerous texts, originally written in Greek and Arabic, have survived only because they have been preserved in Georgian translations.[33] One of the most important Georgian texts to come out of this milieu and to survive to modern times is the so-called Palestinian-Georgian *Calendar*.[34] It is a unique document in that it offers us a first-hand look at the liturgical practices of the see of Jerusalem in the period before the reassertion of Byzantine Greek influence in the area, in the course of which the Melkite ecclesial identity was gradually eclipsed by that of the Greek Orthodox, and the Jerusalem church adopted the reformed liturgy of Constantinople.

The Muslims and Christian Ecumenism

Muslim observers of the Christian churches in their midst did their best to describe and understand the differences between the Melkites, Jacobites,

[31] See Samir Khalil Samir, "Abū Qurrah et les Maronites," *Proche-Orient Chrétien* 41 (1991): 25–33.

[32] See Elias El-Hayek, "Struggle for Survival: The Maronites of the Middle Ages," in Gervers and Bikhazi, *Conversion and Continuity*, 407–21; Harald Suermann, *Die Grundungs Geschichte der Maronitischen Kirche*, Orientalia Biblica et Christiana, vol. 10 (Wiesbaden: Harrassowitz, 1998).

[33] See B. Peradze, "An Account of the Georgian Monks and Monasteries in Palestine," *Georgica* 4–5 (1937): 181–237.

[34] See G. Garitte, *Le Calendrier palestino-géorgien du Sinaiticus 34 (Xe siècle)* (Brussels: Société des Bollandistes, 1958).

Nestorians, and their associated ecclesial communities. Two writers in particular, Abū ʿĪsā al-Warrāq (d. ca. 860)[35] and the *Muʿtazilite* ʿAbd al-Jabbār al-Hamdhānī (d. 1025),[36] not to mention the Andalūsī scholar Ibn Ḥazm (994–1064),[37] and others too numerous to mention here, discussed the varying doctrines in great detail in the context of their refutations of Christian beliefs and practices. The Muslim commentators noted that the three mainline Christian denominations agreed with one another on almost every point of doctrine, and that their theological divisions were predicated almost solely on their differing confessional formulas in the expression of their several views about how the union of the divine and the human in Christ may the most truthfully be stated. Arabic-speaking Christian writers were well aware of the same issue, though most of them went to great lengths in their Arabic works, in full view of the Muslims, vigorously to defend the veracity of their own denomination's formulas against those of their Christian adversaries. And it was in this process that the several churches came to what would be the enduring expressions of their differences. Nevertheless, there were also some ecumenists among the Christian writers who thought that in the face of the multiple challenges from Islam it would behoove the Christians to look beyond their mutual differences for the sake of presenting a united defense of Christianity's claim to be the true religion.

In the tenth century, the Melkite Abū ʿAlī Naẓīf ibn Yumn (d. after 983) wrote a treatise in which he proposed the then novel idea that Christians living among Muslims should come to some accord among themselves, recognizing that they do in fact confess the same faith, while they express it in different confessional formulas. The Copt al-Muʾtaman ibn ʿAssāl then took up this idea in the thirteenth century, and in his magisterial work in Arabic, the *Summary of the Principles of Religion*, relying on the Melkite Ibn Yumn's suggestion, he explained how all the Christian communities and denominations in fact professed the same faith in Christ, albeit that they differed in their theologies.[38] Al-Muʾtaman also included quotations

[35] See David Thomas, *Anti-Christian Polemic in Early Islam: Abū ʿĪsā al-Warrāq's "Against the Trinity,"* University of Cambridge Oriental Publications, no. 45 (Cambridge: Cambridge University Press, 1992); D. Thomas, *Early Muslim Polemic against Christianity: Abū ʿĪsā al-Warrāq's "Against the Incarnation,"* University of Cambridge Oriental Publications, no. 59 (Cambridge: Cambridge University Press, 2002).

[36] See S. Stern, "ʿAbd al-Jabbār's Account of How Christ's Religion Was Falsified by the Adoption of Roman Customs," *Journal of Theological Studies* 19 (1968): 128–85; Wilferd Madelung, "Al-Qāsim ibn Ibrāhīm and Christian Theology," *ARAM* 3 (1991): 35–44. See Gabriel Said Reynolds, *A Muslim Theologian in the Sectarian Milieu: ʿAbd al-Jabbār and the Critique of Christian Origins*, Islamic History and Civilization, Studies and Texts, vol. 56 (Leiden: Brill, 2004).

[37] See Theodore Pulcini, *Exegesis as Polemical Discourse: Ibn Ḥazm on Jewish and Christian Scriptures* (Atlanta: Scholars Press, 1998).

[38] See Samir Khalil Samir, "Un traité du cheikh Abū ʿAlī Naẓīf ibn Yumn sur l'accord des

from other Christian ecumenist writers in Arabic, such as the shadowy ʿAlī ibn Dāwud al-Arfādī, of uncertain date and denomination, who had earlier written a treatise on the basic unanimity of creed among the several Christian denominations.[39]

Public Christian Worship

Just as different Christological formulas served as internal identity markers among the several communities of Christians in the world of Islam, so did certain patterns of public religious behavior serve as external markers between Christians and Muslims. One of these, which often aroused the disdain of Muslims in early Islamic times, was the Christian practice of venerating the cross and the icons of Christ and the saints. In fact, there is a story told about Ḥunayn ibn Isḥāq (d. 873), the Nestorian physician, philosopher, and translator, which nicely illustrates just how the practice of venerating icons could serve as a sure marker of a genuine Christian in the world of Islam. According to the story, which is presented as Ḥunayn's autobiography, Ḥunayn had an enemy at the caliph's court, a fellow Christian physician, Gabriel Bukhtīshūʿ who wanted to do him harm, so this enemy told the caliph al-Mutawakkil (r. 847–61) that in spite of his pretence to the contrary Ḥunayn really was not a practicing Christian but "an atheist who believes neither in the oneness of God nor in the Afterlife. He hides behind a mask of Christianity, but in fact denies God's attributes and repudiates the prophets."[40] Bukhtīshūʿ tells the caliph that the proof of it would be that Ḥunayn would actually be willing to spit on an icon of Jesus and his mother Mary. Bukhtīshūʿ then convinced Ḥunayn that the caliph, having been given such an icon, was tormenting the Christians with it by asking them, "What do you think of it? Isn't it the image of your god and his mother?"[41] Bukhtīshūʿ told Ḥunayn that to put an end to this provocation he simply spat on the icon and advised Ḥunayn to do the same. So when al-Mutawakkil then showed Ḥunayn the icon, according to Ḥunayn himself, the following exchange ensued:

> "Isn't this a wonderful picture, Ḥunayn?"
> "Just as you say, your Majesty."

---

chrétiens entre eux malgré leur disaccord dans l'expression," *Mélanges de l'Université Saint-Joseph* 51 (1990): 329–43; Samir, "Dhikr madhāhib an-naṣārā liMuʾtaman ad-dawlah ibn al-ʿAssāl," *al-Machriq* 66 (1992): 481–91.

[39] See Gérard Troupeau, "Le livre de l'unanimité de la foi de ʿAlī ibn Dāwud al-Arfādī," *Melto* 5 (1969): 197–219.

[40] Dwight F. Reynolds, ed., et al., *Interpreting the Self: Autobiography in the Arabic Literary Tradition* (Berkeley: University of California Press, 2001), 112.

[41] Reynolds, *Interpreting the Self*, 112.

"What do you think of it? Isn't it the image of your god and his mother?"
"God forbid, your Majesty! Is God Almighty an image, can He be depicted? This is a picture like any other."
"So this image has no power at all, either to help or to harm?"
"That's right, your Majesty."
"If it's as you say, spit on it."
I spat on it, and he immediately ordered me thrown in prison.[42]

While there are several narrative strands in the story, it is clear that the role of icon veneration in Christian life was certainly an issue between Christians and Muslims. Ḥunayn himself confirms it when in the sequel he says that the Nestorian patriarch, Theodosius I (r. 853–58), was summoned on that occasion and, "the moment he saw the icon, he fell upon it without even saluting the caliph and held it close, kissing it and weeping at length."[43] Then, according to Ḥunayn, the caliph gave the icon to Theodosius, but he says, "I want you to tell me how you deal with someone who spits on it." Theodosius gives the following reply:

> If he is a Muslim, then there is no punishment, since he does not recognize its sanctity. Nevertheless, he should be made aware of it, reprimanded, and reproached—in accordance with the severity of the offense—so that he never does it again. If he is a Christian and ignorant, people are to reproach and rebuke him, and threaten him with awful punishments, and condemn him, until he repents. At any rate, only someone totally ignorant of religion would commit such an act. But should someone in full command of his own mind spit on this image, he spits on Mary, the Mother of God and on our Lord Jesus Christ.[44]

Ḥunayn goes on in the narrative to tell of the punishments he endured and of how in the end he was saved from his ignominy. But his story eloquently testifies to the sanctity of the icons among the Christians in his day and to how readily the icons served as moments of confrontation between Muslims and Christians. It was customary for Muslim polemicists to charge Christians with idolatry on account of their veneration of crosses and icons. An early but anonymous Muslim controversialist put it as follows in his charge against a Christian correspondent:

> You extol the cross and the image. You kiss them, and you prostrate yourselves to them, even though they are what people have made with their own hands. They neither hear, nor see, nor do harm, nor bring

[42] Ibid., 113.
[43] Ibid.
[44] Ibid., 113–14.

> any advantage. The most estimable of them among you are made of gold and silver. Such is what Abraham's people did with their images and idols.[45]

There are archaeological evidences of the destruction and defacement of Christian images in the early Islamic period due to the conflict with Muslims they aroused. There is also some evidence that Christians themselves may have altered or defaced some images to avoid trouble with the Muslims in this matter.[46] And there were certainly Christians who because of the Muslim polemic against the veneration of crosses and icons began themselves to shy away from the practice out of a fear of public obloquy. Theodore Abū Qurrah himself wrote a tract in Arabic, drawing on the previous work of John of Damascus in his three discourses in Greek *Against the Calumniators of the Holy Icons*,[47] to combat this very development as a pressing pastoral problem among his fellow Melkites. As Abū Qurrah explained it, someone had informed him of the fact that in the Church of the Holy Icon of Christ in Edessa[48] there were Christians coming there to worship who were now unwilling to pay the customary veneration to the icon. He stated the problem this way:

> Many Christians are abandoning prostration to the image of Christ . . . and to the images of his saints . . . because non-Christians, and especially those who claim to be in possession of a scripture sent down from God, rebuke them for their prostration to these images, and because of it impute to them the worship of the idols, and the infringement of what God commanded in the Torah and the prophets, and they sneer at them.[49]

[45] D. Sourdel, "Un pamphlet musulman anonyme d'époque ʿabbāside contre les chrétiens," *Revue des Études Islamiques* 34 (1966): 29. See also Younus Mirza, "Abraham as an Iconoclast: Understanding the Destruction of 'Images' through Qurʾanic Exegesis," *Islam and Christian-Muslim Relations* 16 (2005): 413–28.

[46] See Robert Schick, *The Christian Communities of Palestine from Byzantine to Islamic Rule: A Historical and Archaeological Study*, Studies in Late Antique and Early Islam, 2 (Princeton, NJ: Darwin Press, 1995), 180–219; Susanna Ognibene, *Umm al-Rasas: La chiesa di Santo Stefano ed il "problema iconofobico"* (Rome: L'Erma di Bretschneider, 2002).

[47] See the new English translation, St. John of Damascus, *Three Treatises on the Divine Images*, trans. and intro. Andrew Louth (Crestwood, NY: St. Vladimir's Seminary Press, 2003).

[48] The Icon of Edessa, which had its own church in that city, was famous among the Christians of the Near East from well before Islamic times until the mid-tenth century when it was transported to Constantinople. See, most recently, Han J. W. Drijvers, "The Image of Edessa in the Syriac Tradition," in *The Holy Face and the Paradox of Representation*, ed. H. L. Kessler and G. Wolf, 6: 13–31, Villa Spelman Colloquia, Florence 1996 (Bologna: Nuova Alfa, 1998); Sebastian Brock, "Transformations of the Edessa Portrait of Christ," *Journal of Assyrian Academic Studies* 18 (2004): 46–56.

[49] Quoted from the translation in Sidney H. Griffith, "Theodore Abū Qurrah's Arabic Tract on the Christian Practice of Venerating Images," *Journal of the American Oriental So-*

Clearly the public obloquy of Muslims had induced a case of iconophobia in some Christians, and Abū Qurrah was called upon to counter it in the tract he wrote, geared to promote the idea that the veneration of the cross and the icons was a necessary part of the Christian witness in the Islamic milieu to the truth of their faith in the divinity of Christ and in the salvation won for them by his death on the cross. For the cross and the icons publicly declared those very points of Christian faith which the Qurʾān, in the Muslim view, explicitly denied: that Christ was the son of God (*al-Māʾidah* 5:17) and that he died on the cross (*an-Nisā* 6:157).[50]

In addition to the practice of venerating crosses, icons, and martyrs' relics, there were also other public religious behaviors that outwardly distinguished the Christians from the Muslims. Prominent among them was what in the context of life in the world of Islam one might call the Christian *qiblah*,[51] the direction the Christians faced when they prayed. Unlike the Muslims, who faced the *Kaʿbah* in Mecca when they prayed, and the Jews, who faced Jerusalem, Christians customarily faced east to pray. This distinctive, Christian behavior came up for discussion in virtually every apologetic tract in Syriac or Arabic written by a Christian in the early Islamic period. In their answers to the queries of the Muslims on the subject, Christian writers never failed to mention that the reason they prayed facing east was due to the fact that the Garden of Eden was planted in the east (Genesis 2:8) and that at the end of time, at the second coming, the Messiah would approach Jerusalem from the east.[52] Consequently, they insisted, all Christians face this direction when they pray. Following the Qurʾān, Muslims usually argued to the contrary that, "To Allāh belongs the East and the West. He guides whom He wills towards the right path" (*al-Baqarah* 2:142).

At various times during the long history of the *convivencia* of the Christians with the Muslims in the caliphate, when rulers insisted on the full ap-

---

ciety 105 (1985): 58. See Sidney H. Griffith, intro. and trans., *A Treatise on the Veneration of the Holy Icons Written in Arabic by Theodore Abū Qurrah, Bishop of Ḥarrān (ca. 755–ca. 830 AD); Translated into English with Introduction and Notes*, Eastern Christian Texts in Translation, 1 (Leuven, Belgium: Peeters, 1997).

50 In this connection, see G. R. D. King, "Islam, Iconoclasm, and the Declaration of Doctrine," *Bulletin of the School of Oriental and African Studies* 48 (1985): 267–77; Patricia Crone, "Islam, Judeo-Christianity, and Byzantine Iconoclasm," *Jerusalem Studies in Arabic and Islam* 2 (1980): 59–95.

51 On the meaning and importance of the *qiblah* for Muslims, to determine which they often engaged in some fairly complicated calculations, see A. J. Wensinck and D. A. King, "Ḳibla," *EI*, new ed., vol. 5, 82–88.

52 See, e.g., this matter discussed already in one of the earliest apologetic texts in Syriac, the dialogue of the monk of Bêt Ḥālê with a Muslim notable, Diyarbakir Syriac MS 95, f. 14. On this text see Sidney H. Griffith, "Disputing with Islam in Syriac: The Case of the Monk of Bêt Ḥālê and a Muslim Emir," *Hugoye* 3, no. 1 (2000), http://syrcom.cua.edu/Hugoye.

plication of the stipulations included in the Covenant of ʿUmar and other legal traditions that were meant to govern the statutory low profile the People of the Book were required to maintain in Islamic society after the payment of a special poll tax (*al-jizyah*, cf. *at-Tawbah* 9:29),[53] Christians and Jews were publicly marked off from the Muslims by a number of social disabilities, sometimes including even a distinctive attire and distinguishing badges they were required to wear.[54] Over time, these measures, which were seldom consistently or systematically enforced, nevertheless by their very theoretical currency must have contributed substantively to the development of a subaltern mentality among Christians in the world of Islam. They may well have played a significant role in the well-attested, gradual, demographic decline of Christians in much of the Islamic world,[55] which became precipitate in the Mamluk period (1254–1517), when in consequence of the harsh attitude against the *dhimmī* population on the part of the rigorist thinker Ibn Taymiyyah (1263–1328) and his colleagues about non-Muslims,[56] all significant intellectual colloquy between Christians and Muslims in the world of Islam seems gradually to have diminished to insignificance. At this time Ibn Taymiyyah, and others such as Ibn Qayyim al-Jawziyyah (1292–1350) and Taqī ad-Dīn as-Subkī (1274–1355), to name only the most prominent thinkers, revived the much earlier opinion of the historian, Qur'ān-commentator and traditionist, aṭ-Ṭabarī (839–923), according to which Jews and Christians should be expelled not only from Arabia proper, but from any Muslim dominated area

[53] See Yohanan Friedmann, *Tolerance and Coercion in Islam: Interfaith Relations in the Muslim Tradition*, Cambridge Studies in Islamic Civilization (Cambridge: Cambridge University Press, 2003), esp. 34–53. See also the important study by Albrecht Noth, "Abgrenzungsprobleme zwischen Muslimen und Nicht-Muslimen. Die ʿBedingungen ʿUmars (*aš-Šurūṭ al-ʿumariyya*)," *Jerusalem Studies in Arabic and Islam* 9 (1987): 290–315; the article is now published in an English translation, Albrecht Noth, "Problems of Differentiation between Muslims and non-Muslims: Re-Reading the 'Ordinances of ʿUmar' (*al-Šurūṭ al-ʿumariyya*), in *Muslims and Others in Early Islamic Society*, ed. Robert Hoyland, 18: 103–24, The Formation of the Classical Islamic World (Aldershot, UK: Ashgate, 2004).

[54] See the important article by Ḥabīb Zayyāt, "The Distinctive Signs of the Christians and Jews in Islam," [Arabic] *al-Machriq* 43 (1949): 161–252, and the discussion of these matters in Mark R. Cohen, *Under Crescent and Cross: The Jews in the Middle Ages* (Princeton, NJ: Princeton University Press, 1994), 52–74, esp. 61–64.

[55] See Jean-Pierre Valognes, *Vie et mort des chrétiens d'orient: Des origines à nos jours* (Paris: Fayard, 1994); Andrea Pacini, ed., *Christian Communities in the Arab Middle East: The Challenge of the Future* (Oxford: Clarendon Press, 1998).

[56] Thomas F. Michel, ed. and trans., *A Muslim Theologian's Response to Christianity: Ibn Taymiyya's al-jawāb al-sahih* (Delmar, NY: Caravan Books, 1984); Rifaat Ebied and David Thomas, eds., *Muslim-Christian Polemic during the Crusades: The Letter from the People of Cyprus and Ibn Abī Ṭālib al-Dimashqī's Response*, Muslim-Christian Polemic during the Crusades, no. 2 (Leiden: Brill, 2005).

in which the Muslims had no real need of the services of the *dhimmī* population.[57]

The very mention of the legal disabilities that theoretically applied to Christians living within the Islamic polity forcefully reminds one that the profession of Christian faith amid the sorrows of *Dhimmitude*, which Islamic law and practice imposed on Jews and Christians, was a costly witness, and at times it entailed real martyrdom. While Christian martyrologies in Syriac, Coptic, Arabic, and even Greek and Latin from the early Islamic period are not numerous, there are nevertheless some very important ones, which help the modern reader gain a better understanding of the sometimes precarious position of Christians in early Islamic society.

Christian Martyrs in the World of Islam

By the time of the Islamic conquest, Christians in the Roman Empire thought of the age of the martyrs as definitely in the past; it was the time before Constantine had taken the first step early in the fourth century in the process that would lead eventually to the establishment of Christianity as the religion of the empire. But with the establishment of Islam in the territories of the Oriental Patriarchates as a consequence of the Islamic conquest in the seventh century, Christians in fact came face to face with the first comprehensive, official rejection of the principal doctrines of their religion since the days of the anti-Christian polemicists, Celsus (fl. ca. 178), Prophyry (ca. 232–ca. 303), and Julian the Apostate (332–363), who had all written powerful works against Christian faith some four hundred years in the past.[58] And as was the case in the earlier instance in the Roman Empire, so too in Islamic times did the new, Muslim polemicists have the power of their government behind them. For example, it seems that the Muslim scholar Abū ʿUthmān Amr ibn Bahr al-Jāḥiẓ (777–868), who was also a prominent literary figure in his day, wrote his well-known essay, "Refutation of the Christians" (*Kitāb ar-radd ʿalā n-naṣārā*) expressly at the request of the caliph al-Mutawwakil (r. 847–61), who was one of the first ʿAbbasid caliphs systematically to promote specifically anti-Christian policies throughout the caliphate.[59] In these circumstances, conditions were

[57] See Seth Ward, "A Fragment from an Unknown Work by al-Ṭabarī on the Tradition 'Expel the Jews and Christians from the Arabian Peninsula (and the Lands of Islam),'" *Bulletin of the School of Oriental and African Studies* 53 (1990): 407–20.

[58] See Robert L. Wilken, *The Christians as the Romans Saw Them* (New Haven, CT: Yale University Press, 1984).

[59] See J. M. Fiey, *Chrétiens syriaques sous les Abbassides surtout à Bagdad, 749–1258*, CSCO, vol. 420 (Louvain, Belgium: Secrétariat du Corpus SCO, 1980), 83–105, 94–97.

once again ripe for deadly confrontations between Christians and the authorities of the government over matters of religious faith.

Unlike the case in the pre-Constantinian, late Roman Empire, there was no general persecution of Christians as such in the Islamic world. Rather, to the contrary there were even some legal protections for them as People of the Book, albeit that amid the sorrows of *Dhimmitude*, at various times and places in particular circumstances Christians and Jews were in fact victims of violence and massacre. On these occasions it was often the case that the causes of violence were an amalgam of social, political, economic, and even ethnic hostilities affecting the pursuit of power, and not religion as such, although religion may often have been an aggravating factor.[60] Sometimes in these circumstances, because of their perceived implication in these hostilities, local Christians and other People of the Book were deemed by some Muslim authorities to have forfeited the statutory protection (*dhimmah*) otherwise normally guaranteed to them in virtue of their payment of the special poll tax (*al-jizyah*) and general maintenance of a low social profile as the Qur'ān demands of them (*at-Tawbah* 9:29). So, while Christians were certainly sometimes the victims of atrocities at the hands of Muslims, which are a matter of historical record in the chronicles written in Syriac and Arabic in the early Islamic period, Christians were not normally subject to outright persecution in the world of Islam simply by reason of being Christian.[61] Nevertheless, there were Christian martyrs in early Islamic times who suffered at the hands of Muslim authorities; they are often called "neomartyrs" to distinguish them from those who underwent their trials during the earlier, pre-Constantinian Age of Martyrs.

One of the earliest neomartyrs whose story is preserved in Syriac chronicles was Cyrus of Ḥarrān (d. 770).[62] His situation is particularly instruc-

[60] See Youssef Courbage and Philippe Fargues, *Christians and Jews under Islam*, trans. Judy Mabro (London and New York: I. B. Tauris, 1997); Paul Fregosi, *Jihad in the West: Muslim Conquests from the 7th to the 21st Centuries* (Amherst, NY: Prometheous Books, 1998).

[61] The records of these atrocities have been brought to the fore in recent times in several publications by Bat Ye'or, *The Dhimmī: Jews and Christians under Islam* (Rutherford, NJ: Fairleigh Dickinson University Press, 1985); Ye'or, *The Decline of Eastern Christianity under Islam: From Jihad to Dhimmitude; Seventh–Twentieth Century* (Madison, NJ: Fairleigh Dickinson University Press, 1996); Ye'or, *Islam and Dhimmitude: Where Civilizations Collide* (Madison, NJ: Fairleigh Dickinson University Press, 2002). One must use these books with care due to the author's extreme anti-Islamic prejudice and consequent distortion of the facts of history and their interpretation. Nevertheless, it remains to Bat Ye'or's credit to have raised an important issue that historians have neglected, viz., systematic study of the effect of the Islamic legislation regarding the People of the Book on the factual diminution of Jewish and Christian communities in the world of Islam.

[62] See Amir Harrak, "Piecing Together the Fragmentary Account of the Martyrdom of Cyrus of Ḥarrān," *Analecta Bollandiana* 121 (2003): 297–328. See also Jean Maurice Fiey, *Saints Syriaques*, ed. Lawrence I. Conrad, 61, Studies in Late Antiquity and Early Islam, 6 (Princeton, NJ: Darwin Press, 2004).

tive, and illustrative, of the complications one often finds in the Christian martyrologies composed in the world of Islam, because it highlights the social ambiguities that commonly abound in these accounts. As was the case in other such narratives from a later time, it emerges from this story that from the point of view of the Muslim authorities, Cyrus was executed not for being a Christian but for having been an apostate from Islam, albeit that his testimony was cherished by Christians as that of a martyr because of his willingness to suffer even the penalty of death for his adherence to the Christian faith. It appears that earlier in his life, for reasons that are no longer clear, but that one account characterizes as due to "some passion,"[63] Cyrus had in fact become a Muslim, and this circumstance is what put his life in jeopardy with the Muslim authorities when he reconverted to Christianity. Since he refused to rectify his lapse from Islam, he was thereupon sentenced to death, the statutory penalty for apostasy in the Islamic legal system.[64] This situation in turn introduced a new consideration into the Christian conception of martyrdom, one that put the accent on the personal testimony of the martyr and his disparagement of Islam rather than on the persecutor's direct challenge to the martyr's Christian faith. It would become a standard feature of most Christian martyrologies from the Islamic world.

While Christian martyrologies written originally in Arabic are not numerous, there are a half-dozen of them surviving from the early period in Greek, Georgian, Armenian, and Arabic, mostly from the Melkite community in Syria/Palestine.[65] They are precious sources of information about the difficulties between Muslims and Christians in the early Islamic period. In all six of them, as in the case of the Syriac account of the ordeal of Cyrus of Ḥarrān, conversion from Islam to Christianity emerges as a central problem in the narratives. Three of the martyrs reportedly lost their lives precisely because they were apostates from Islam. In the accounts of the other three martyrs, the protagonists, in addition to reviling Islam, the Qur'ān, and Muḥammad, were all engaged in attempts to persuade Muslims to convert to Christianity, especially those who had recently apostatized from the church. And of course, independently of their historical verisimilitude, which by all accounts is very high, the narratives themselves became an important part of the effort on the part of the churchmen of the time to strengthen the faith of Christians tempted to convert to Islam. In the narratives that recount the martyrs' exploits there is usually a report

[63] Harrak, "Piecing Together the Fragmentary Account," 309.

[64] On the complicated procedures in cases of apostasy from Islam, see Friedmann, *Toleration and Coercion in Islam*, 121–59.

[65] See the early martyrologies reviewed in Robert Hoyland, *Seeing Islam as Others Saw It: A Survey and Evaluation of Christian, Jewish, and Zoroastrian Writings on Early Islam*, Studies in Late Antiquity and Early Islam, 13 (Princeton, NJ: Darwin Press, 1997), 336–86.

of an interview between the martyr and a caliph, an emir, or some other Muslim official, in which the martyr takes the opportunity of his moment in the public eye to give instructions on the rudiments of the Christian faith, along with a declaration of what he considers to be the shortcomings of Islam as a candidate to be the true religion.[66] It is tempting to think that these martyrs' speeches were in fact among the circumstances that enhanced the popularity of a distinct genre of apologetics among Christians in the early Islamic period that I call the Monk in the Emir's *majlis*; most of the widely distributed texts of popular apologetics in the early period were in this genre, or one closely related to it, and the earliest exemplars in Arabic have martyrological settings.[67]

One Christian martyr narrative from among the Melkites, surviving in both Greek and Arabic, from early ʿAbbasid times, is surely completely legendary. It tells of a king who converts from Islam to Christianity, and who loses his life in testimony to his new Christian faith. In the Arabic recension of the story he is identified as none other than the caliph al-Maʾmūn (r. 813–33).[68] The circulation of this story in the Christian community in the Islamic world reminds the modern reader that the martyr accounts served many purposes beyond just the memorial of the sufferings of individuals who gave their lives in testimony to their faith. In the communities in which they were read, such narratives also fulfilled the social function of strengthening the resolve and confidence of members of a social and religious minority by suggesting that in regard to their truth claims and their moral rectitude the martyrs and their coreligionists really were, all appearances to the contrary not notwithstanding, superior to those in power over them, a superiority that even members of the oppressor class were themselves sometimes depicted in the martyrologies as being willing to confess.

[66] See Sidney H. Griffith, "Christians, Muslims, and Neo-Martyrs: Saints' Lives and Holy Land History," in *Sharing the Sacred: Religious Contacts and Conflicts in the Holy Land: First–Fifteenth Centuries CE*, ed. Arieh Kofsky and Guy G. Stroumsa, 163–207 (Jerusalem: Yad Izhak Ben Zvi, 1998); Mark N. Swanson, "The Martyrdom of ʿAbd al-Masīḥ, Superior of Mount Sinai (Qays al-Ghassānī)," in *Syrian Christians under Islam: The First Thousand Years*, ed. David Thomas, 107–29 (Leiden: Brill, 2004); David H. Vila, "Rawḥ al-Qurayshī and the Development of an Arabic Christian Community," in *Christianity and Native Cultures: Perspectives from Different Regions of the World*, ed. Cyriac Pullapilly et al., 83–95 (South Bend, IN: Cross Cultural Publications, 2004). See also David H. Vila, "Christian Martyrs in the First Abbasid Century and the Development of an Apologetic against Islam" (PhD diss., St. Louis University, 1999), UMI Microform no. 9942830.

[67] See Sidney H. Griffith, "The Monk in the Emir's *Majlis*: Reflections on a Popular Genre of Christian Literary Apologetics in Arabic in the Early Islamic Period," in *The Majlis: Interreligious Encounters in Medieval Islam*, ed. Hava Lazarus-Yafeh et al., 13–65 (Wiesbaden: Harrassowitz Verlag, 1999).

[68] See Griffith, "The *Life of Theodore of Edessa*," 159–60. See also Mark N. Swanson, "The Christian al-Maʾmūn Tradition," in *Christians at the Heart of Islamic Rule: Church Life and Scholarship in ʿAbbasid Iraq*, ed. David Thomas, 63–92 (Leiden: Brill, 2003).

Another martyr's narrative with similar features, but from a different Islamic milieu from that of the Melkites, is the Bohairic account of the martyrdom of the Copt, John of Phanijōit, in Cairo in Ayyubid times.[69] Like a number of the other neomartyrs, John had converted to Islam and then, having repented, reconverted to Christianity, thereby making him liable in Muslim eyes to the death penalty for the crime of apostasy from Islam. From a Christian perspective, the author of the martyrology presents John as being acutely conscious of the moral pollution he had incurred in his life by his conversion to Islam. In his response to the queries of the sultan, who actively searches for ways to save John's life and who proposes a number of worldly inducements to secure a happy solution to the seeming legal impasse, John is reported to have replied, "I need neither gold nor garment nor horse nor wealth. Rather, I am a polluted man. May my lord the king purify me with his sword, or grant me the favor of my faith."[70]

In the account of John's arrest, trial, and execution, the Coptic author presented the story, embellished with details that highlight the martyr's Christian goodness and sincerity, and these qualities are portrayed as winning the admiration even of his Muslim captors and guards. Contrariwise, the narrative puts an accent on what Christians would regard as the negative moral qualities of Islamic life and religious practice. In this way the author provides the Christian reader with what Jason Zaborowski calls a "hidden transcript." He points out that this transcript articulates the narrative in Christian terms that effectively invert the dominant, Islamic ideology under which the Copts were living. It transforms the narrative into an expression of Coptic, Christian values that are shown to undercut the moral claims of Islam at the same time as it encourages Christians to be true to their faith, even under duress.[71] The text is therefore a particularly good example of the ways in which all the accounts of the neomartyrs written by Christians living within the world of Islam had the potential to reaffirm and shore up the sense of Christian solidarity in times and places in which their public confessional identity was almost submerged under the social and cultural weight of Islam.

The Martyrs of Cordoba

Perhaps the most well known of all the accounts of Christian martyrs in the world of Islam comes from a community we have not much discussed. It

[69] See Jason R. Zaborowski, *The Coptic Martyrdom of John of Phanijōit: Assimilation and Conversion to Islam in Thirteenth-Century Egypt*, The History of Christian-Muslim Relations, vol. 3 (Leiden: Brill, 2005).

[70] Zaborowski, *The Coptic Martyrdom*, 105.

[71] See the important introductory chapter in ibid., 11–34.

is the story of the martyrs of Cordoba in Spain, who suffered during the 850s. Their story is told in Latin by Eulogius of Cordoba/Toledo (ca. 859),[72] one who himself joined their number a short time after the events he recounted. We learn of the times and their challenges from Eulogius's friend and biographer, Paulus Alvarus (d. 860),[73] who described the cultural situation of the Christians in Islamic Spain in his own day as follows:

> My fellow Christians delight in the poems and romances of the Arabs; they study the works of Mohammadan theologians and philosophers not in order to refute them, but to acquire correct and elegant Arabic style. Where today can a layman be found who reads the Latin commentaries on Holy Scriptures? Who is there that studies the Gospels, the prophets, the Apostles? Alas, the young Christians who are most conspicuous for their talents have no knowledge of any literature or language save the Arabic. . . . The pity of it! Christians have forgotten their own tongue, and scarce one in a thousand can be found to be able to compose in fair Latin to a friend.[74]

Being painfully conscious of this high degree of enculturation into the life of the world of Islam on the part of their Christian contemporaries, in the decade of the 850s some fifty monks and others put themselves forward for martyrdom in Cordoba by publicly denouncing Islam, ridiculing the Qur'ān, and insulting the prophet Muḥammad. The Muslim authorities are portrayed in the accounts as being reluctant to impose the death penalty; they delay the proceedings and offer numerous opportunities for those determined to be martyrs to think better of their purposes. Nevertheless, in the end these Christians were executed. Their purpose in pressing the issue was publicly to affirm their faith and openly to reject Islam, as well as to impugn the claims to religious credibility of the Qur'ān and the prophet Muḥammad.[75] The martyrs' actions created controversy among the local Christians themselves, at least some of whom thought that forcing the issue in this way was contrary to the true spirit of the ancient martyrs, who had not sought confrontation with the pagan authorities, but when arrested and brought to trial had accepted death rather than to forswear their faith. Some Christians of Andalusia seem also to have thought that the actions of the Cordoba martyrs were counterproductive to the mis-

[72] See Maria Jesus Aldana Garcia, *La estructura narrativa del Memoriale Sanctorum de San Eulogio: Libros II–III* (Cordoba: Publicaciones Obra Social y Cultural Cajasur, 1995).

[73] See Feliciano Delgado Leon, *Alvaro de Cordoba y la polemica contra el Islam: El Indiculus Luminosus* (Cordoba: Publicaciones Obra Social y Cultural Cajasur, 1996).

[74] Quoted in the translation used by Andrew Wheatcroft, *Infidels: A History of the Conflict between Christendom and Islam* (New York: Random House, 2003), 75–76.

[75] See Edward P. Colbert, *The Martyrs of Córdoba (850–859): A Study of the Sources* (Washington, DC: Catholic University of America, 1962).

sion of the church in the difficult circumstances of life under Muslim rule.[76] Nevertheless, the testimony of the martyrs lived on to strengthen the sense of identity among the Christians of the Iberian Peninsula, and their memory was evoked to inspire the efforts of the *Reconquista* in later times.[77]

It seems that it was only by the middle of the ninth century that Spanish Christians took full cognizance of the religious challenge of Islam,[78] which became truly serious when large numbers of the previously Latin-speaking Christians began to adopt the Arabic language, as Paulus Alvarus noticed. For this reason, the Spanish Christians of the Islamic period have come to be called Mozarabs by modern scholars, from the Arabic term *mustaʿarib*, which has a range of connotations extending from assimilated Arab, pretend Arab, speaker of Arabic, to Arabist. But as a term for the Arabic-speaking Christians of al-Andalus in general it is a modern scholarly invention. One never finds it in this sense in Arabic texts. Rather, it is found "in Christian sources, from the 11th century onwards, as a pejorative term for Christians of Arabic origin living in the medieval Christian kingdoms, particularly Toledo"[79] after its reconquest in 1085. In al-Andalus itself, for as long as they lived with the Muslims, while many may have converted to Islam the ancestors of those who would later be called Mozarabs "remained Christians, worshipping according to the Visigothic rite, speaking a Romance dialect in addition to Arabic, and, among the clergy at least, cultivating some knowledge of Latin."[80] As for Christian Arabic literature in Spain, it seems to have had its beginnings in the second half of the ninth century. As mentioned in an earlier chapter, one of the writers whose name we know from this early period, Ḥafṣ ibn Albar al-Qūṭī (d. 889), as irony would have it, seems to have been the son of the very Paulus Alvarus whose

[76] See Kenneth Baxter Wolf, *Christian Martyrs in Muslim Spain* (Cambridge: Cambridge University Press, 1988); Wolf, "The Earliest Latin Lives of Muḥammad," in Gervers and Bikhazi, *Conversion and Continuity*, 88–101; Jessica Coope, *The Martyrs of Córdoba: Community and Family Conflict in an Age of Mass Conversion* (Lincoln: University of Nebraska Press, 1995).

[77] It may well have been the case that the Franciscans who sought martyrdom at the hands of Muslims in North Africa in the early thirteenth century were inspired by the martyrs of Cordoba. See John V. Tolan, *Saracens: Islam in the Medieval European Imagination* (New York: Columbia University Press, 2002), 214–21.

[78] See Kenneth Baxter Wolf, "The Earliest Spanish Christian Views of Islam," *Church History* 55 (1986): 281–293, expanded and updated in Kenneth Baxter Wolf, "Christian Views of Islam in Early Medieval Spain," in *Medieval Christian Perceptions of Islam*, ed. John Victor Tolan, Garland Medieval Casebooks, vol. 10, Garland Reference Library of the Humanities, 1768: 85–108 (New York: Garland, 1996). See also Ann Christys, *Christians in al-Andalus, (711–1000)* (Richmond, UK: Curzon, 2002).

[79] Mikel De Epalza, "Mozarabs: An Emblematic Christian Minority in Islamic al-Andalus," in *The Legacy of Muslim Spain*, 2 vols., ed. Salma Khadra Jayyusi, 1: 149 (Leiden: Brill, 1994).

[80] Thomas E. Burman, *Religious Polemic and the Intellectual History of the Mozarabs, c. 1050–1200*, Brill's Studies in Intellectual History, vol. 52 (Leiden: Brill, 1994), 14.

words bemoaning the progress of Arabic among talented young Christians have just been quoted above. For the rest, it seems that it was not until the eleventh and twelfth centuries, after the fall of Toledo in 1085, that Christians again wrote apologetic or polemic works in Arabic in Spain in response to the religious challenge of Islam. An interesting feature of these latter day texts is the debt they owe to the Arabic Christian literature of the East that seems to have been readily available to Christians in Spain at that time.[81] While we know of the existence of many more of them, barely a half-dozen of these Arabic Christian texts composed in Spain have come down to us, the rest having fallen victim, one supposes, to the vicissitudes of the religious and cultural antipathies of the *Reconquista* and its aftermath.

Christians in Islamic Spain shared many of the experiences of their coreligionists in the East, including the formation of a distinct social identity that afterward made them seem foreign and suspect to their own coreligionists living beyond the borders of Islam. This is one of the reasons why the heritage of the Arabic-speaking Christians has so often failed to come to the notice of western Christians over the centuries. But in the case of Muslim Spain, in spite of, or perhaps because of the failure of westerners to know much about the Christians of the world of Islam, a romantic legend about the glories of a harmonious and tolerant *convivencia* between Jews, Christians, and Muslims in Andalusia in Islamic times, and in Toledo after the Christian conquest of that city in 1085, has relatively recently captured the popular imagination.[82] In this connection, it is important to remember the observations of the historian who is reportedly the one who first used the felicitous term *convivencia* to describe the modes of mutual accommodation that obtained between Jews, Christians, and Muslims in Spain in Islamic times.[83] Américo Castro wrote that, "Each of the three peoples of the peninsula [Christians, Moors, Jews] saw itself forced to live for eight centuries together with the other two at the same time it pas-

[81] See Burman, *Religious Polemic*, esp. 14, 31, 35–37. See also, for the earlier period, Dominique Millet-Gérard, *Chrétiens mozarabes et culture islamique dans l'Espagne des VIIIe–IXe siècles* (Paris: Études Augustiniennes, 1984).

[82] See, e.g., María Rosa Menocal, *The Ornament of the World: How Muslims, Jews, and Christians Created a Culture of Tolerance in Medieval Spain* (Boston: Little, Brown, 2002); Roger Garaudy, *L'islam en occident: Cordue, capitale de l'esprit* (Paris: L'Harmattan, 1987). Some writers, while taking cognizance of the Christians' endurance of *Dhimmitude* in this milieu, nevertheless still somewhat wistfully speak of an age of enlightenment or of a dialogue of cultures. See Chris Lowney, *A Vanished World: Medieval Spain's Golden Age of Enlightenment* (New York: Free Press, 2005); Hans Küng, *Der Islam: Geschichte, Gegenwart, Zukunft* (Munich and Zurich: Piper, 2004), 461–63; Stephen O'Shea, *Sea of Faith: Islam and Christianity in the Medieval Mediterranean World* (New York: Walker, 2006).

[83] See Wheatcroft, *Infidels*, 67.

sionately desired their extermination."[84] Furthermore, Castro underlined the fact that the peaceful coexistence these communities enjoyed was very much determined by the stipulations of Islamic law regarding protected minorities. He wrote, "Those who did not disturb the peace of the Saracens were allowed to enjoy their own peace in the Saracen cities. . . . Spanish tolerance was the result of a *modus vivendi*, not of a theology."[85]

While the situation of the Christians in al-Andalus was a special one, and given the fact that Américo Castro used the concept of *convivencia* as a methodological principle for plotting the course of what he considered to be the determining factors in Spanish history, the term has nevertheless taken on a life of its own in the contemporary parlance of historians and those concerned with interreligious dialogue. To the degree that we may appropriate it to refer to the modes of accommodation reached between the dominant Islamic polity and the subaltern religious communities (Jews and Christians) in the wider world of Islam in ʿAbbasid times (750–1258), the term and concept of *convivencia* seems particularly apt to evoke the intellectual and social history of those Christians who not only came to a new expression of their own traditions in Arabic, but in the process also made essential contributions to the growth and development of the classical culture of Islam.

[84] Américo Castro, *The Structure of Spanish History*, trans. Edmund L. King (Princeton, NJ: Princeton University Press, 1954), 54–55. See the important historiographical study of Alex Novikoff, "Between Tolerance and Intolerance in Medieval Spain: An Historiographic Enigma," *Medieval Encounters* 11 (2005): 7–36.

[85] Castro, *Structure of Spanish History*, 223 and 225.

VII

BETWEEN THE CRESCENT AND THE CROSS

CONVIVENCIA, THE CLASH OF THEOLOGIES, AND INTERRELIGIOUS DIALOGUE

Intertwined Religious Discourses

When the Christians living in the territories that came under Islamic rule during the first century after the death of the prophet Muḥammad (ca. 570–632) eventually adopted the Arabic language, beginning for some of them as early as the second half of the eighth century, although they took up Arabic for their own purposes, they also by that very fact opened a public channel of communication with the Muslims about religion and culture. The ensuing conversation was both indirect and direct. It was indirect in the sense that Christian theology, and apologetics in Arabic addressed primarily to Christians, was nevertheless readily available to the perusal of Muslims by reasons of its being in the Arabic language. The conversation was direct in that among the Christian Arabic texts from the early Islamic period some of them were in fact openly addressed to Muslims.[1] Muslim scholars in their turn sometimes responded by name to texts written by Christian authors; and sometimes they wrote about Christian doctrines and practices and developed their own Islamic theology in ways that indicated they were very familiar with the Christian texts.[2] But communication between Christians and Muslims was not the only result of the adoption of Arabic by Christians. The use of the Arabic language also provided the opportunity for the development of Christian theology in a new key, within a new frame of reference and with new challenges for Christian apologists.

One of the most persistent problems to be faced by the Christian Arabic

[1] A major case in point is the record of Elias of Nisibis's (975–1046) discussions with the vizier Abū l-Qāsim al-Ḥusayn ibn ʿAlī al-Maghribī (981–1027) in 1026 and 1027, which Elias published and dedicated to al-Maghribī under the title *Kitāb al-majālis*. See Samir Khalil Samir, *Foi et culture en Irak au XIe siècle* (Aldershot, UK: Ashgate Publishing, 1996), 1: 259–67.

[2] The Muslim scholar al-Qāsim ibn Ibrāhīm (785–860), for example, clearly shows his familiarity with the Arabic writings of Theodore Abū Qurrah, although he does not cite him by name in his text. See Wilferd Madelung, "Al-Qāsim ibn Ibrāhīm and Christian Theology," *ARAM* 3 (1991): 35–44.

writers whose works were mentioned in earlier chapters was the challenge of how to express the distinctive teachings of Christianity in an Arabic idiom in which the religious vocabulary had already acquired strong Islamic overtones. As Kenneth Cragg so aptly put it, when Christians in the caliphate outside of the Arabian Peninsula began speaking Arabic, they found themselves "bound over to a language that is bound over to Islam."[3] In addition to this difficulty, there were also numerous accompanying problems in translating the technical terms of Christian theology from their original Greek and Syriac into Arabic.[4] The translators of Greek philosophical texts into Arabic faced similar problems, and in both instances the Arabic words and phrases chosen to render the technical terms took on nuances as translation terms that reached well beyond their usual ranges of meaning, and for this reason they were likely to be unintelligible to the general reader who would come across them in their new contexts.

Most Arabic Christian writers in the formative period of Islamic history strove to translate and to clarify the doctrines and distinctive confessional formulas of their several denominations in their Arabic treatises and tracts, rather than to rethink in the Islamic milieu how best to articulate the Christian message anew. Some modern Christian historians and theologians have faulted the early apologists for this option. These commentators view it as a lost opportunity on the part of the early Arabic Christian writers; they could have chosen to reformulate Gospel Christianity in the new Arabic idiom in view of the challenges of the Qur᾽ān, rather than to have imported the divisions and obscurities of an earlier Christian era into the new world order.[5] But as we have argued in the previous chapter, it was only in Islamic times that the several denominations of the Christians in the Middle East actually came into full and enduring expression of their identities as distinct Christian communities. So one must ask the question, did not the Arabicization of Christianity in the early Islamic period pave the way for a clash of theologies more than it offered the newly Arabic-speaking Christians an opportunity for new developments in the presentation and expression of their most basic doctrines?

On one level it is certainly true that a clash of theologies characterized the relationships between Muslims and Christians in the early Islamic period, in the sense that their shared reasoning issued in radically opposed

[3] Kenneth Cragg, *The Arab Christian: A History in the Middle East* (Louisville, KY: Westminster John Knox Press, 1991), 31.

[4] See this problem discussed in connection with terms in the Christian creed in Arabic in Sidney H. Griffith, "Theology and the Arab Christian: The Case of the 'Melkite' Creed," in *A Faithful Presence: Essays for Kenneth Cragg*, ed. David Thomas, 184–200 (London: Melisende, 2003).

[5] See, e.g., Cragg, *The Arab Christian*, where this point of view is one of the author's principal themes.

conclusions on major religious topics. But on another level it is also true that the dialogue between them, which the public culture they shared made possible, also allowed them to discuss together such issues as the ontological status of the divine attributes, or the effects of the acts of the divine will on human freedom, in ways that mutually influenced the shape of their communities' discourse on these and other topics on their shared discussion agenda. The early development of the Islamic *ʿilm al-kalām*, for example, certainly betrays its debt to earlier Christian topics and modes of discourse. But at the same time, early Christian apologetic texts in Arabic in their turn also clearly show their debt to the methods and manners of the Muslim *mutakallimūn* as well as to the list of their conventional topics of conversation.[6] So, on a deeper level, in the formative period of Islamic thought in the ʿAbbasid era, before the disruptive incursions into the Arab world from both the Mongol East and the Latin West in the twelfth and thirteenth centuries, there really was in some measure a community of discourse about religion between Muslims and Christians in spite of the clash of their theologies, and in spite of the civil and social disabilities under which the Christians, together with the Jews and other religious minorities, lived.[7]

Similarly, the early ʿAbbasid translation movement in which so many Christians participated, as well as the scientific and philosophical circles that flourished in Baghdad in the same and subsequent centuries, in which Christian and Muslim scholars so often worked together, were responsible for introducing into the intellectual fabric of the Islamic world a measure of Hellenism that would leave its permanent mark there. All of these developments testify to the important role Christians played in the elaboration of the classical culture of the Islamic world in its first flowering.[8] In

[6] See Shlomo Pines, "Some Traits of Christian Theological Writing in Relation to Moslem *Kalām* and to Jewish Thought," in Shlomo Pines, *Studies in the History of Arabic Philosophy*, The Collected Works of Shlomo Pines, vol. 3 (Jerusalem: Magnes Press, 1996), 105–25, [79–99]; C. H. Becker, "Christian Polemic and the Formation of Islamic Dogma," in *Muslims and Others in Early Islamic Society*, ed. Robert Hoyland, 18: 241–57, The Formation of the Classical Islamic World (Aldershot UK: Ashgate, 2004).

[7] See Munʾim A. Sirry, "Early Muslim-Christian Dialogue: A Closer Look at Major Themes of the Theological Encounter," *Islam and Christian-Muslim Relations* 16 (2005): 361–76. And see also the pertinent essays in Barbara Roggema et al., eds., *The Three Rings: Textual Studies in the Historical Trialogue of Judaism, Christianity, and Islam* (Leuven, Belgium: Peeters, 2005).

[8] See Adam Mez, *Die Renaissance des Islams* (Reprografischer Nachdruck der Ausdruck Heidelberg, 1922; repr., Hildesheim, Germany: G. Olms, 1968); Joel L. Kraemer, *Humanism in the Renaissance of Islam: The Cultural Revival during the Buyid Age* (Leiden: Brill, 1986); Dimitri Gutas, *Greek Thought, Arabic Culture: The Graeco-Arabic Translation Movement in Baghdad and Early ʿAbbasid Society (2nd–4th/8th–10th Centuries)* (London: Routledge, 1998); Lenn E. Goodman, *Islamic Humanism* (Oxford: Oxford University Press, 2003).

the early centuries of Islam, there was a certain community of interests between Jewish, Christian, and Muslim scholars on some levels, which bound them together in the deeper structures of their cultural and intellectual lives in spite of the clash of their theologies and the wall of *Dhimmitude*, which held them in different and even opposed social and religious allegiances.[9]

Already in the earliest phase of the process of Islam's self-definition in its distinct religious identity, the preexisting Jewish and Christian realms of discourse provided both the template and the foil for so much of what would become the characteristically Islamic exegetical and liturgical idiom.[10] Even earlier, the Qur'ān itself in its origins obviously participated in a dialogue of the scriptures, with the Torah, the Psalms, the Prophets, and the Gospel named in the Qur'ān as the partners of record in the conversation.[11] While the Qur'ān definitely offers a critique of Jews, Christians, and others in terms of the actual state of their religion, it also presumes in its audience a familiarity with biblical narratives, as well as with other aspects of Jewish and Christian lore, faith, and practice. In short, the Qur'ān and early Islam are literally unthinkable outside of the Judeo-Christian milieu in which Islam was born and grew to its maturity.

In spite of the clash of theologies that the Jewish and Christian adoption of Arabic in the early Islamic period made evident within the Islamic world itself, the underlying sibling relationship and history of commonality between the three communities of faith are also unmistakable. This history's claim to be the imperative ground for interreligious dialogue between Jews, Christians, and Muslims seems to be unimpeachable, especially since it is a fact that even through the long centuries of mutual hostilities the fortunes of the three communities have became, if anything, even more inextricably intertwined.[12]

[9] On this theme, see especially Roger Arnaldez, *À la croisée des trois momothéismes: Une communauté de pensée au Moyen Age* (Paris: Albin Michel, 1993). See also Arnaldez, *Three Messengers for One God*, trans. G. W. Schlabach et al. (Notre Dame, IN: University of Notre Dame Press, 1994).

[10] See John Wansbrough, *The Sectarian Milieu: Content and Composition of Islamic Salvation History* (Oxford: Oxford University Press, 1978); Uri Rubin, *Between Bible and Qur'ān: The Children of Israel and the Islamic Self-Image* (Princeton, NJ: Darwin Press, 1999).

[11] See John Reeves, ed., *Bible and Qur'ān: Essays in Scriptural Intertextuality*, Symposium Series, no. 24 (Atlanta: Society of Biblical Literature, 2003).

[12] The best single source and reference book for the history of Christian/Muslim relations is undoubtedly J. M. Gaudeul, *Encounters and Clashes: Islam and Christianity in History*, 2 vols., Collection "Studi arabo-islamici del PISAI" no. 15 (Rome: Pontificio Istituto di Studi Arabi e d'Islamistica, 2000).

The Qur'ān and Dialogue

The Qur'ān envisions a continuous dialogue between Muslims and Christians, and while dialogue, understood as simply conversation between two or more partners, is not always agreeable or friendly, it is nevertheless communication. Indeed, the Qur'ān presumes the priority of the Torah and the Gospel and insists that in reference to the earlier divine revelations it is itself "a corroborating scripture in the Arabic language to warn wrong doers and to announce good news to those who do well" (*al-Aḥqāf* 46:12). In the Qur'ān, God then advises the Muslims, "If you are in doubt about what We have sent down to you, ask those who were reading scripture before you" (*Yūnus* 10:94). Further, the Qur'ān assumes that the dialogue between Jews, Christians, and Muslims will sometimes even take the form of arguments about religion, for one passage says, "Do not dispute with the People of the Book save in the fairest way;[13] except for those who are evil doers. And say: 'We believe in what has been sent down to us and what has been sent down to you. Our God and your God are one and to Him we are submissive'" (*al-ʿAnkabūt* 29:46). In this context of dispute between Jews, Christians, and Muslims the Qur'ān foresees that the disputants will want to put forward proof-texts from the scriptures in support of their contentions. In this connection the Qur'ān has advice for the Muslims: "They say: 'None will enter Paradise except those who are Jews and Christians.' Such are their vain wishes. Say: 'Bring forth your proof (*burhānakum*) if you are truthful'" (*al-Baqarah* 2:111). Here the proof envisioned is precisely proof from scripture. These and similar passages are the texts that corroborate the presumption that the Qur'ān envisions a continuous interreligious conversation between the Muslims and the 'Scripture People' (*Ahl-al-kitāb*).

There is one Qur'ānic narrative in particular in which the occasion of the revelation of a passage, according to Islamic tradition, was the visit of some Christian notables from the south Arabian town of Najrān to Muḥammad in Medina.[14] On that occasion the discussion between them had turned to the subject of Jesus, the Messiah, and to the question of what is the truth concerning him. It reminds one of Jesus's own question to his disciples, "Who do men say that the Son of Man is?" (Matthew 16:13). According

[13] For a useful discussion of this Qur'ān passage, see Jane Dammen McAuliffe, "'Debate with them in the better way,' the Construction of a Qur'ānic Commonplace," in *Myths, Historical Archetypes and Symbolic Figures in Arabic Literature: Towards a New Hermeneutic Approach*, ed. Angelika Neuwirth et al., 163–88 (Beirut and Stuttgart: Franz Steiner Verlag, 1999).

[14] On the Christians of Najrān, see René Tardy, *Najrân: Chrétiens d'Arabie avant l'Islam*, Recherches, 8 (Beirut: Dar el-Machreq, 1999).

to the traditional account, on this occasion the following verses came down to Muḥammad:

> Jesus in God's sight is like Adam; He created him from dust, then said to him: "Be," and there he was. [This is] the truth from your Lord; so do not be one of the doubters. To those who dispute about it after the knowledge which has come to you, say: "Come now; let us call our sons and your sons, our wives and your wives, ourselves and yourselves. Then let us invoke a malediction (*nabtahil*) and so bring God's curse on those not telling the truth. (*l ʿImrān* 3:59–61)

This Qurʾānic evocation of the occasion of a Muslim/Christian encounter during Muḥammad's lifetime certainly does not reflect a friendly, interreligious dialogue. Rather, the conversation is confrontational and the prophet is instructed to issue a challenge to the visiting Christians of Najrān; it is an instance of the Qurʾān's critique of a central Christian doctrine, the doctrine of the Incarnation. And in that very capacity, it may serve as a Qurʾānic icon for the character of the Christian/Muslim dialogue that took place within the world of Islam after the Islamic conquest and after the Christians in the occupied territories adopted the Arabic language. In this milieu Muslims challenged and critiqued major points of Christian faith, and Christians responded vigorously in defense of their defining doctrines and practices. It is interesting to note in this connection that while the Qurʾān text invokes malediction and curse, it nevertheless also on the face of it, once the adversaries would have staked their lives and those of their loved ones on their own steadfastness in faith, leaves the judgment between the two parties in this matter in the hands of God.

According to Islamic tradition, the Christian deputation from Najrān turned away from the challenge to engage in the ancient ceremony of mutually and formally calling God's curse down (*mubāhalah*) upon whichever of the two parties was not speaking truthfully on that occasion in Medina when the question as to the true identity of the Messiah was put.[15] Louis Massignon (1883–1962) thought that St. Francis of Assisi restored the balance in this matter when in the *majlis* of the Ayyūbid sultan al-Malik al-Kāmil (r. 1218–38) at Damietta in 1219 he challenged the faith of the sultan and even underwent ordeals of fire unscathed, according to some tellings of the story.[16] But this interpretation overlooks the witness of

[15] See Louis Massignon, "La *Mubâhala* de Médine et l'hyperdulie de Fâtima," in Louis Massignon, *Parole donnée* (Paris: Éditions du Seuil, 1983), 147–67.

[16] See Leonardus Lemmens, "De Sancto Francisco Christum Praedicante coram Sultano Aegypti," *Archivum Franciscanum Historicum* 19 (1926): 559–78; J. Hoeberichts, *Francis and Islam* (Quincy, IL: Franciscan Press, 1997). See also Benjamin Z. Kedar, *Crusade and Mission: European Approaches toward the Muslims* (Princeton, NJ: Princeton University Press, 1984), 116–26.

Christian intellectual life in the intervening centuries in Syriac and Arabic in response to the religious challenge of Islam, as well as the testimonies of the Christian neomartyrs, who in Islamic times might also be considered to have taken up the Qur'ān's challenge to testify to the Gospel truth as they believed it to be.

The Religion of Abraham

The Qur'ān also puts forward a *theologoumenon* that many in modern times have taken to be a helpful one in the search for a foundation on which to build a certain solidarity of faith between the People of the Book, the Jews, the Christians, and the Muslims, which might prompt them to engage in interreligious dialogue with a sense of developing a relationship with one another that is warranted in scripture. It is the idea that the "religion of Abraham" that precedes them all in time, somehow also scripturally unites them. The Qur'ān asks, "Who has a better religious practice (*dīn*) than one who submits himself to God, does right and follows the true religion (*millah*) of Abraham the 'faithful gentile' (*ḥanīf*)?[17] God has taken Abraham as a friend (*khalīlan*)" (*an-Nisā'* 4:125). As it happens, one can find the epithet "God's friend" applied to Abraham in the scriptures of all three communities. In the Hebrew Bible there is the phrase, "But you, Israel, my servant, Jacob, whom I have chosen, offspring of Abraham my friend . . . " (Isaiah 41:8); and in the New Testament there is the statement, "You also see how the Scripture was fulfilled which says, 'Abraham believed God, and it was credited to him as justice' (Genesis 15:6); for this he received the title 'God's friend'" (James 2:23).

The Qur'ān says further, "Abraham was neither a Jew nor a 'Christian' (*naṣrāniyyan*), but a 'faithful gentile' (*ḥanīf*) and a *muslim*. And he was not one of the polytheists (*al-mushrikīn*)" (*Ā l ʿImrān* 3:67). In this passage, while the adjective *muslim* is transliterated with a lower case "m" to indicate that here it means "one who is submissive," and not that Abraham was a "Muslim," there is in fact no upper- or lowercase lettering in Arabic, and so many Muslims would naturally hear it to mean simply that the patriarch was a Muslim avant la lettre, in the same way that the early Chris-

[17] The Arabic term *ḥanīf* is a difficult one to understand and to translate accurately into English. Among Muslims it is generally understood to mean one who in the time before Islam was a true monotheist. In this sense it is often translated as "one inclining to the right religion," "true in faith." One problem in connection with the word is that its Syriac cognate *ḥanpâ* normally means "heathen," "pagan." My translation "faithful gentile" follows insights developed by François De Blois, "*Naṣrānī* (ναζωραιος) and *ḥanīf* (εθνικος): Studies on the Religious Vocabulary of Christianity and Islam," *Bulletin of the School of Oriental and African Studies* 65 (2002): 1–30.

tian historian Eusebius of Caesarea (ca. 260–ca. 340) considered Abraham a Christian, if not in name, then in fact, as he said.[18] Furthermore, it is clear already in the Qur'ān that the appeal to Abraham was used not to claim fellowship for Muslims with Jews and Christians but the opposite. The Qur'ān says, "They say: 'If you become Jews or Christians, you shall be well-guided.' Say: 'Rather, we follow the religion (*millah*) of Abraham, who was a 'faithful gentile' (*ḥanīfan*) and not one of the polytheists (*al-mushrikīn*)" (*al-Baqarah* 2:135) Strictly speaking, the Qur'ān's "religion of Abraham" is not that of the Jews or Christians. Nor for that matter is the Jewish idea of Abraham's religion or the Christian conception of Abraham as the man of faith really compatible with the Islamic idea of the "religion of Abraham" as we find it in the Qur'ān.[19]

Nevertheless, in spite of the very different ideas among Jews, Christians, and Muslims about the "religion (*millah*) of Abraham," the figure of Abraham clearly stands as a faithful monotheist in all three traditions and as a personal icon of right faith in all their scriptures. This more general concept is the one that underlies the popular use of such expressions as "the religions of Abraham," "the Abrahamic faiths," or "the children of Abraham" to include Judaism, Christianity, and Islam.[20] Some Christian scholars have even put the Abraham *theologoumenon* in one form or another at the heart of their promotion of interreligious dialogue with Muslims in the present day.[21] The French Islamicist Louis Massignon and his associates

[18] Eusebius wrote that, "Even if we are clearly new, and this really fresh name of Christians is recently known among all nations, nevertheless our life and method of conduct, in accordance with the precepts of religion, has not been recently invented by us, but from the first creation of man, so to speak, has been upheld by the natural concepts of the men of old who were the friends of God . . . especially Abraham. . . . If the line be traced back from Abraham to the first man, anyone who should describe those who have obtained a good testimony for righteousness, as Christians in fact, if not in name, would not shoot wide of the truth. . . . So that it must clearly be held that the announcement to all the Gentiles, recently made through the teaching of Christ, is the very first and most ancient and antique discovery of true religion by Abraham and those lovers of God who followed him. . . . Facts show that at the present moment it is only among Christians throughout the whole world that the manner of religion which was Abraham's can actually be found in practice." Eusebius of Caesarea, *The Ecclesiastical History*, trans. Kirsopp Lake and J. E. L. Oulton, ed. H. J. Lawlor, The Loeb Classical Library, 2 vols. (Cambridge, MA: Harvard University Press, 1980), 1: iv, 41–45.

[19] See Uri Rubin, "*Ḥanīfiyya* and Kaʿba: An Inquiry into the Arabian Pre-Islamic Background of *Dīn Ibrāhīm*," *Jerusalem Studies in Arabic and Islam* 13 (1990): 85–112.

[20] Current popular examples are Bruce Feiler, *Abraham: A Journey to the Heart of Three Faiths* (New York: William Morrow/HarperCollins, 2002); David Klinghoffer, *The Discovery of God: Abraham and the Birth of Monotheism* (New York: Doubleday, 2003); F. E. Peters, *The Children of Abraham: Judaism, Christianity, Islam*, new rev. ed. (Princeton, NJ: Princeton University Press, 2004).

[21] See Sidney H. Griffith, "Sharing the Faith of Abraham: The 'Credo' of Louis Massignon," *Islam and Christian-Muslim Relations* 8 (1997): 193–210; Karl-Josef Kuschel, *Abraham: Sign of Hope for Jews, Christians, and Muslims*, trans. John Bowden (New York:

and disciples in particular have sought to trace the relationships of the first Arab Muslims, the Ishmaelites as the Christians called them, to the biblical sons of Ishmael and through their genealogies to posit a measure of participation in the blessings promised to the descendants of Abraham through his son Ishmael as recorded in the book of Genesis (16:11–12; 21:18; 25:12–18).[22] This biblical connection could then, they submit, be considered a scriptural warrant for a more positive estimation on the part of Christians of Muḥammad's participation in the charism of prophecy, of the Qur'ān's role as a transmitter of revelation, and of Islam's mission to proclaim faith in the one God, Creator of the heavens and the earth.[23] Most recently, Hans Küng, having reviewed much of the previous thinking on the Abraham *theologoumenon*, speaks of it as building "eine Art abrahamischer Ökumene," among Jews, Christians, and Muslims that cannot be obliterated in spite of all the hostility that has beset the historical relations between these communities.[24]

While western thinkers in recent times have thus made much of the Qur'ān's idea of the "religion of Abraham" and of its potential as a theological foundation for dialogue between Muslims and Christians, the Christian writers in Syriac and Arabic who lived in the world of Islam in the heyday of its classical culture, by way of contrast made use of the Abraham theme largely to highlight the clash between Christian and Muslim theologies. It is true that Patriarch Timothy I, in his conversations with Muslims in the court of Caliph al-Mahdī (r. 775–85), was willing to compare the religious experiences of Abraham and Muḥammad, in that both of them turned away from idols to become preachers of the one God.[25] But most often Christian apologists made the point that Muslims misinterpreted the role of Abraham in salvation history. One finds this motif already in one of the earliest apologetic texts, the Syriac account of the dialogue between a monk of Bêt Ḥālê and a Muslim notable in the early eighth century.

According to the frame story, the monk was attending to the needs of

Continuum, 1995); Louis Massignon, *Les trois prières d'Abraham*, Patrimoines (Paris: Cerf, 1997); Reinhard G. Kratz and Tilman Nagel, eds., *"Abraham, unser Vater": Die gemeinsamen Wurzeln von Judentum, Christentum, und Islam* (Göttingen: Wallstein Verlag, 2003).

[22] See, e.g., Y. Moubarac, *Abraham dans le Coran* (Paris: Vrin, 1958); Michel Hayek, *Le mystère d'Ishmael* (Paris: Mame, 1964). See also the strong objection to this line of thinking in R. Dagorn, *La geste d'Ismaël d'après l'onomastique et la tradition arabes* (Geneva: Froz, 1981).

[23] See Massignon, *Les trois prières*, esp. "L'Hégire d'Ismaël," 59–118.

[24] See Hans Küng, *Der Islam: Geschichte, Gegenwart, Zukunft* (Munich and Zurich: Piper, 2004), 78–90, esp. 89.

[25] See Samir Khalil Samir, "The Prophet Muḥammad as Seen by Timothy I and Other Arab Christian Authors," in *Syrian Christians under Islam: The First Thousand Years*, ed. David Thomas, 95 (Leiden: Brill, 2001).

the Muslim notable who had come to the monastery to recover from his injuries. After some hesitation the monk agreed to answer the Muslim's queries about religion and about the religion of the Christians in particular. The very first question the Muslim poses to the monk is this one: "Why do you not acknowledge Abraham and his commandments? He is the father of the prophets and the kings, and scripture attests to his righteousness." The following exchange ensues:

> The monk said, "What acknowledgement of Abraham do you require of us? What are his commands you want us to carry out?"
>
> The Arab said, "Circumcision and sacrifices, because he received them from God."
>
> The monk said, "Truly the fact that Abraham is the father of the prophets and kings, and even his righteousness, is manifest to all readers of the scriptures. But as the shadow is in relationship to the body, and the word in regard to the deed, so is the career of our father Abraham in regard to the new things the Messiah accomplished for the redemption of our lives."[26]

In the sequel, the monk explains how from the Christian point of view the story of Abraham and his commandments, circumcision and sacrifice, served as types or emblems in the Old Covenant narrative for what God would bring to pass in reality in Christ, as it is proclaimed in the New Covenant. On the monk's reading, circumcision marked out the sons of Abraham in the way that Baptism would mark the true Christians; the scriptural account of Abraham's aborted sacrifice of his son (Genesis 22) prefigured the actual sacrifice of Christ on the cross. In this way, the author of the dialogue between the monk and the Muslim emir, and other Christian apologists of the same milieu who took up the same challenge in other works in Syriac and Arabic, all viewed the figure of Abraham from a distinctly Christian perspective,[27] and in the process they implicitly discounted the Qur'ān's claims about the "religion of Abraham." Clearly their views were from a different perspective from the one adopted by modern theologians who search the Qur'ān for mutually agreeable points of common faith from which to promote interreligious dialogue with Muslims. In this matter, as in others, the Christian writers in Syriac and Arabic

[26] Syriac MS Diyarbakir 95, ff. 4–5. On this manuscript and the still unpublished text, see Sidney H. Griffith, "Disputing with Islam in Syriac: The Case of the Monk of Bêt Ḥālê and a Muslim Emir," *Hugoye* 3 (January 2000), http://syrcom.cua.edu/Hugoye/Vol3No1/HV3V1Griffith.html.

[27] For more on this topic, see Martin Tamcke, "'Wir sind nicht von Abrahams Samen!': Deutungen Abrahams in der ostsyrischen Literatur," in Kratz and Nagel, *"Abraham unser Vater,"* 112–32.

in the early Islamic period had their own, very different, approaches to the Qur'ān.

Arab Christians and the Qur'ān

The Qur'ān was obviously a major text in the world of the Arabophone Christians, and in their works one can distinguish two levels of its presence. On the one hand, and without any pertinent comment by them on the phenomenon, their Christian Arabic texts are replete with words and phrases from the Qur'ān that had entered the common parlance of the Arabic-speaking people long before the time when Christians living in the conquered territories adopted the Arabic language. On the other hand, some Arab Christian writers explicitly discussed the Qur'ān and quoted from it. Some of them depicted the Qur'ān as a flawed scripture, and they detailed its shortcomings. Others, in the course of their arguments with Muslims, appealed to texts from the Qur'ān, sometimes citing it by name, sometimes not; they cited it both in witness of the truth of their polemics against Islam, and even in testimony to the truth of the Christian positions they were defending.

Two texts of the ninth century in particular present the Qur'ān in its canonical form as an incredible scripture. One of them, the ingenious Christian legend of the monk Baḥīrā, in both its Syriac and Arabic versions, suggests that the Qur'ān was originally a Christian book that an errant monk had dictated to Muḥammad. At one point, at the end of one section of the narrative, the monk says:

> Many other things I wrote for him, too numerous to mention, by which I sought to turn him to a belief in the truth and a recognition of the coming of the Messiah into the world, and the condemnation of the Jews in regard to that which they say of our Lord, the true Messiah.[28]

In the sequel, the writer says that Jews ultimately subverted the monk's original intentions, and he accuses the renowned, early Jewish convert to Islam, Kaʿb al-Aḥbār,[29] of having distorted the original Christian text of the Qur'ān into the canonical Islamic one, which is therefore flawed and unreliable. In this way the author of the legend sought to reverse the customary Islamic charge against the Jews and Christians of the distortion and

[28] Richard Gottheil, "A Christian Bahira Legend," *Zeitschrift für Assyriologie* 15 (1900): 64 (Arabic); 17 (1903): 141 (English).

[29] See M. Schmitz, "Kaʿb al-Akhbār," *EI*, new ed., vol. 4 (1978), 316–17.

corruption (*at-taḥrīf*) of the Torah and the Gospel, and in the process he also explains why the Qur'ān is now an incredible scripture.[30]

On a more directly polemical note, another Arab Christian writer of the ninth century, the author of the legendary correspondence between al-Hīshimī, the Muslim, and al-Kindī, the Christian,[31] building on the allegations contained in the Christian Baḥīrā legend, engaged in a comprehensive polemic against the Qur'ān that was designed to demonstrate its utter failure as a credible divine scripture. He discussed its origins, its collection after the death of Muḥammad, and the claims made by early Muslim writers about the inimitability of its text (*i'jāz al-Qur'ān*).[32] Of all the Arab Christian works that have come down to us, this anonymous polemic contains the most negative attack against the authenticity and the credibility of the Qur'ān as a prophetic text.[33] With this work in the background, it may then come as a surprise for the modern reader to learn that other Christian writers in the early Islamic period actually quoted the Qur'ān in their apologetic works for its probative value.

In one of the earliest Christian Arabic texts we know, the work its modern editor called *On the Triune Nature of God*,[34] a text composed some time in the second half of the eighth century, the now unknown author evoked the Qur'ān in two remarkable ways. First of all, he composed an introduction to his own work, in which he modeled his Arabic diction on the prosody of the Qur'ān, interweaving unmistakably Qur'ānic themes and expressions into the text. Second, in the section of the work in which he cited passages from the scriptures in witness of the veracity of the Christian doctrine of the Trinity he included quotations from the Qur'ān, without

[30] For more on this tantalizing legend, see Sidney H. Griffith, "Muḥammad and the Monk Baḥīrā: Reflections on a Syriac and Arabic Text from Early Abbasid Times," *Oriens Christianus* 79 (1995): 146–74; Barbara Roggema, "A Christian Reading of the Qur'ān: The Arabic Version of the Legend of Sergius-Baḥīrā and Its Use of Qur'ān and Sīrā," in Thomas, *Syrian Christians under Islam*, 57–73.

[31] On this work, which was briefly discussed in an earlier chapter, see Bénédicte Landron, *Chrétiens et Musulmans en Irak: Attitudes Nestoriennes vis-à-vis de l'Islam*, Études Chrétiennes Arabes (Paris: Cariscript, 1994), 78–89.

[32] On this issue, in the context of interreligious controversy, see Richard C. Martin, "The Role of the Basrah Mu'tazilah in Formulating the Doctrine of the Apologetic Miracle," *Journal of Near Eastern Studies* 39 (1980): 175–89.

[33] There is a record that Abū Nūḥ al-Anbārī, a contemporary and supporter of Patriarch Timothy I, wrote a "Refutation of the Qur'ān" (*Tafnīd al-Qur'ān*). While this work was reportedly examined at the turn of the twentieth century, in a manuscript of the late thirteenth century in the Sbath collection, no more has since been heard of it in the scholarly literature. See Landron, *Chrétiens et Musulmans en Irak*, 53–54.

[34] See Margaret Dunlop Gibson, *An Arabic Version of the Acts of the Apostles and the Seven Catholic Epistles, with a Treatise on the Triune Nature of God*, Studia Sinaitica, 7 (London: C. J. Clay and Sons, 1899), 74–107 (Arabic), 2–36 (English).

any qualification, as if its testimony were in his mind on a par with the Bible passages he had just quoted.[35] Clearly, without any overt validation of the Qur'ān's status as a book of divine revelation, this author's intention was nevertheless to enlist the probative value of the Islamic scripture, in the context of the Arabic-speaking milieu in which he wrote, on behalf of the credibility of the Christian doctrine he was defending.

Numerous other Christian Arabic works quote passages from the Qur'ān as proof-texts in defense of the veracity of Christian doctrines.[36] Perhaps the passage most often cited in them is the following verse from *sūrah* 4 *an-Nisā'* 171: "The Messiah, Jesus, son of Mary, is only Allāh's Messenger (*rasūl Allāh*) and His Word (*kalimatuhu*), which He imparted to Mary, and is a spirit from Him (*rūḥun minhu*)." What attracted the Christian apologists' attention to this verse is what they perceived to be its potential on the face of it to affirm both the doctrine of the Trinity ("God, His Word, and a spirit from Him") and the doctrine of the Incarnation ("His Word which He imparted to Mary"). As one of the apologists put it to his Muslim addressee, "Your own scripture (*kitāb*), your own Qur'ān has taught you the truth about God's hypostases (*aqānīm*) when it spoke of 'the Messiah, ʿĪsā ibn Maryam, as the Messenger of God, and His Word that He cast into Maryam, and a spirit from Him.'"[37]

Another case in point is furnished by the Melkite writer, Paul of Antioch, who attempted in his "Letter to a Muslim Friend" to interpret the passages of the Qur'ān that refer to the Nazarenes/Christians (*an-naṣārā*) as demonstrating that the Christians of his own day should not be numbered among the "polytheists" (*mushriqūn*) or "infidels" (*kuffār*), as some contemporary Muslim controversialists were arguing should be the case.[38] Numerous other instances of such references to the Qur'ān on the part of Christian writers could be cited here, some of them quite ingenious in their interpretations. For example, to mention just one more instance, in the

[35] See Mark N. Swanson, "Beyond Proof-Texting: Approaches to the Qur'ān in Some Early Arabic Christian Apologies," *The Muslim World* 86 (1998): 297–319.

[36] See, e.g., the texts discussed in Sidney H. Griffith, "The Qur'ān in Arab Christian Texts; the Development of an Apologetical Argument: Abū Qurrah in the *Majlis* of al-Ma'mūn," *Parole de l'Orient* 24 (1999): 203–33.

[37] Sinai Arabic MS 434, f. 174r. On the text from which this passage is quoted, see Sidney H. Griffith, "Answers for the Shaykh: A 'Melkite' Arabic Text from Sinai and the Doctrines of the Trinity and the Incarnation in 'Arab Orthodox' Apologetics," in *The Encounter of Eastern Christianity with Early Islam*, ed. Emmanouela Grypeou, Mark Swanson, and David Thomas, 277–309 (Leiden: Brill, 2006).

[38] See L. Buffat, "Lettre de Paul, évêque de Saïda, moine d'Antioche, à un musulman de ses amis demeurant a Saïda," *Revue de l'Orient Chrétien* 8 (1903): 388–425; Paul Khoury, *Paul d'Antioche, évêque melkite de Sidon (XIIe s.)*, Recherches de l'Institut de Lettres Orientales de Beyrouth, t. 24 (Beirut: Impr. catholique, 1964), 169–87 (French), 59–83 (Arabic).

course of their arguments to show the truth of the doctrine of the Incarnation, a number of Melkite writers evoked the following verse of the Qurʾān: "It is not given to any mortal that Allāh should speak to him, except by revelation or from behind a veil (*min warāʾi ḥijābin*) (*ash-Shūrā* 42:51). The apologists suggested that the veil the Qurʾān mentions is none other than the human nature of the Messiah, from behind which the Son of God, God the Word, addressed mankind.[39]

Christian apologists were certainly aware that Muslim scholars put entirely different interpretations upon the quotations from the Qurʾān, which the Christians appropriated for use in their arguments in support of the credibility of Christian doctrines. But the apologists could nevertheless suggest, at least to their own coreligionists, that on the face of it, the Qurʾān's text, when taken out of its own Islamic hermeneutical frame of reference, could bear alternate interpretations, which could plausibly be advanced from a Christian perspective. This exercise did not involve the presumption on the part of the Christian writers in Arabic in the early Islamic period that the Qurʾān was in their view a genuine scripture, containing divine revelation on the level of the Bible. Nevertheless, they could and did make use of its authority in the Arabic-speaking milieu to commend the veracity of the Christian doctrines that were in dispute between themselves and their Muslim interlocutors.

Christian Belles Lettres in Arabic

We have heretofore spoken almost exclusively of the religious, philosophical, and theological components of Christian Arabic culture in the early Islamic period. While these concerns are the dominant ones in the surviving literature, one must not forget to mention in passing that Christians also composed works of a literary character in Arabic. The earliest and most famous of these are undoubtedly the poems of Ghiyāth ibn Ghawth ibn Ṣalt al-Akhṭal (ca. 640–ca. 710), a Christian Arab of the tribe of Taghlīb whose language echoed that of the pre-Islamic Arabic poets.[40] He flourished in the milieu of the Umayyad caliphs, whose praises he sang in his verses.[41] While in hagiographic sources al-Akhṭal is reported to have had an association with the younger St. John of Damascus (d. ca. 749), his po-

[39] See the discussion of the allusions to this verse in Melkite texts in Swanson, "Beyond Proof-Texting," and Griffith, "Answers for the Shaykh."

[40] See R. Blachère, "Al-Akhṭal," *EI*, new ed., vol. 1, 331.

[41] See Henri Lammens, "Le chantre des Omiades: Notes biographiques et littéraires sur le poète arabe chrétien Aḫṭal," *Journal Asiatique* n.s. 4 (1894): 94–241, 381–459.

etry reveals little if any religious concern, be it Christian or Muslim; he was a panegyrist whose colleagues were the early Muslim court poets.[42] Nevertheless, al-Akhṭal may be claimed as one of the earliest, if not the earliest, Arab Christian writer whose name we know. Unlike most of the later Christian Arabic writers, his work has a permanent place in the larger canon of classical Arabic literature.

Another Christian poet, from a much later time, whose Arabic works are now available for modern readers, is the Palestinian Sulaymān al-Ghazzī, who flourished during the last years of the tenth and the early years of the eleventh century.[43] Along with more conventional works of Melkite theology, Sulaymān composed haunting poems of grief and religious fervor, which often evoke memories of the Holy Land and pilgrimage to the biblical *loca sancta*. Unfortunately, none of his works has been translated into a modern western language, a circumstance that highlights the neglect that continues to plague the memory of the Christians of the world of Islam among their coreligionists outside of the Middle East.

In addition to poetry, Christian authors also composed works in other literary genres. One of the most popular of these is the Arabic *maqāmah*, a prose work of fiction that usually focuses on the exploits of a single, tricksterlike character whose wit and hidden wisdom exposes the foibles of rich, learned, or well-placed members of society. It came into prominence in the eleventh century, its most popular representations being found in the well-known works of the slightly later writer, Muḥammad al-Qāsim al-Ḥarīrī (d. 1122).[44] But already in the early days of the genre's popularity, Ibn Buṭlān (d. 1066), a disciple of the famed Nestorian physician, monk, and theologian Abū l-Faraj ʿAbd Allāh ibn aṭ-Tayyib (d. 1043),[45] was composing *maqāmāt* in what would become the classical style; two of them achieved a considerable fame, the *Banquet of the Physicians* and the *Banquet of the Priests.* The latter composition is available for modern western readers in a French translation.[46]

[42] See Roger Allen, *An Introduction to Arabic Literature* (Cambridge: Cambridge University Press, 2000), 87–90.

[43] See Néophytos Edelby, ed., *Sulaymān al-Ghazzī*, Patrimoine Arabe Chrétien, vols. 7, 8, and 9 (Jounieh, Lebanon: Librairie Saint Paul and Rome: Pontificio Istituto Orientale, 1984–86).

[44] See Allen, *Introduction to Arabic Literature*, 162–67.

[45] On Ibn Buṭlān, see Georg Graf, *Geschichte der christlichen arabischen Literatur*, vol. 2, Studi e Testi, 133 (Vatican City: Biblioteca Apostolica Vaticana, 1947), 191–95; Raymond Le Coz, *Les médecins nestoriens au moyen âge: Les maîtres des Arabes* (Paris: L'Harmattan, 2004), 200–202.

[46] See Joseph Dagher and Gérard Troupeau, trans., *Ibn Buṭlān: Le banquet des prêtres; une maqāma chrétien du XIe siècle* (Paris: Geuthner, 2004).

The Local Christian Languages

While Christians were writing in Arabic already in the eighth century, as we have seen, and have continued to do so to the present day, they also continued to employ the indigenous languages of their several communities. Among them, Greek was the first to disappear from daily use, probably because it was largely an ecclesiastical and scholarly language. It enjoyed a continued currency in Melkite church circles, but even there the community also continued to produce translations from Greek into Christian Palestinian Aramaic well into the twelfth century.[47] And in Jerusalem, Georgian-speaking monks translated texts from both Greek and Arabic into their own language, sometimes thereby preserving texts that otherwise would have been lost to posterity. A remarkable case in point is the valuable liturgical calendar of the Melkites that preserves the memory of the old Jerusalem liturgy from the time before the Byzantine reforms; the Arabic original has not survived.[48]

Syriac has persisted in use, especially among the Maronites, Jacobites, and Nestorians, even enjoying something of a renaissance in the thirteenth century,[49] when bilingual writers such as the Jacobite Gregory Abū l-Faraj, known as Bar Hebraeus, (1225–1286), who wrote in both Syriac and Arabic, could confidently draw on the works of both the traditional Christian masters and Muslim thinkers such as Ibn Sīna (980–1037) and al-Ghazālī (1058–1111).[50] Some in the Syriac-speaking communities have even used the script of their language to write in Arabic, a writing commonly called Garshūnī, which is in general use among Christians to this day, especially, but not exclusively, in liturgical texts.[51]

Much controversy surrounds the issue of the fate of the Coptic language among the largely Arabic-speaking Christians of Egypt. It seems gradually to have faded from common use after the thirteenth century, but it is important to note that at the beginning of that century a martyrology featuring a confrontation between a Christian and the Muslim authori-

[47] See Sidney H. Griffith, "From Aramaic to Arabic: The Languages of the Monasteries of Palestine in the Byzantine and Early Islamic Periods," *Dumbarton Oaks Papers* 51 (1997): 11–31.

[48] See Gérard Garitte, ed. and trans., *Le calendrier palestino-géorgien de Sinaiticus 34 (Xe siècle)*, Subsidia Hagiographica, no. 30 (Brussels: Société des Bollandistes, 1958).

[49] See the remarkable work of Patriarch Ignatius Aphram I Barsoum, *The History of Syriac Literature and Sciences*, trans. Matti Moosa (Pueblo, CO: Passeggiata Press, 2000).

[50] See H. G. B. Teule, "Bar Hebraeus' *Ethikon*; al-Ghazālī and Ibn Sīnā," *Islamochristiana* 18 (1992): 73–86.

[51] A. Mingana, "Garshūnī or Karshūnī," *Journal of the Royal Asiatic Society* (1928): 891–93; G. Troupeau, "Karshūnī," *EI*, rev. ed., vol. 4, 671–72.

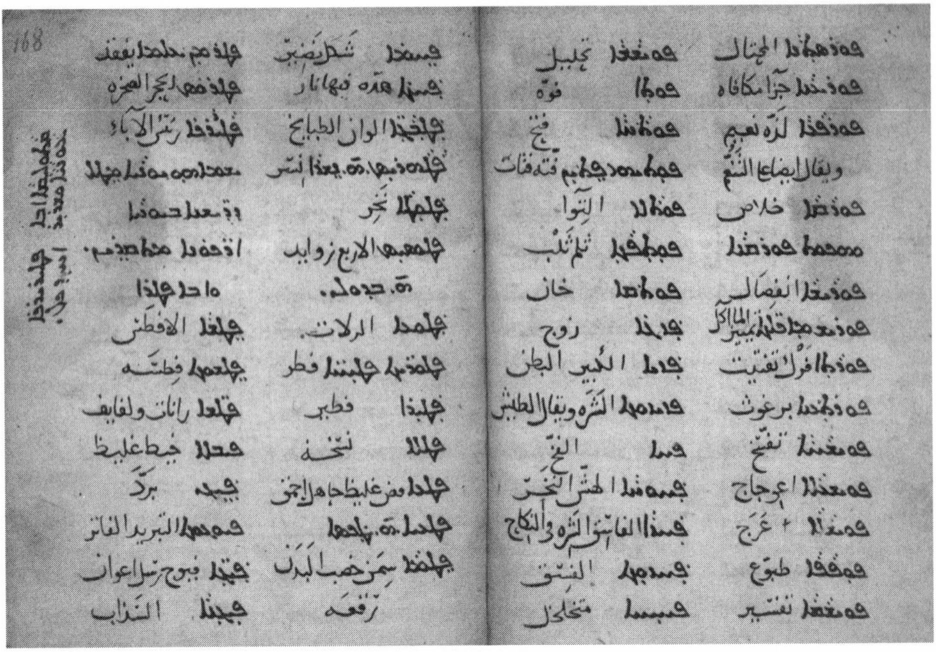

Fig. 5. Syriac-Arabic Word List
This page from a mini Syriac-Arabic Lexicon of the fourteenth to sixteenth century, Hyvernat Syriac MS 13 in the collections of the Institute of Christian Oriental Research at the Catholic University of America, shows the Arabic equivalents for Syriac words and phrases. Such word lists were common tools for scholars and scribes in the bilingual and bicultural Christian communities in the Levant in early Islamic times. (Hyvernat Syriac Manuscript 13, f. 168, fourteenth–sixteenth century. Courtesy of the Institute of Christian Oriental Research, the Catholic University of America, Washington, DC.)

ties, presumably intended for a popular audience, could still be written in Coptic.[52]

Armenian Christians have been constantly present in the world of Islam and on its immediate borders from early Islamic times onward.[53] While

[52] See the discussion in Jason R. Zaborowski, *The Coptic Martyrdom of John of Phanijōit: Assimilation and Conversion to Islam in Thirteenth-Century Egypt* (Leiden: Brill, 2005).

[53] For an account of the Armenian church as it relates to the history of the churches discussed in this book, see Nina Garsoïan, *L'Église arménienne et le grand schisme d'orient*, CSCO, vol. 574 (Louvain, Belgium: Peeters, 1999).

Fig. 6. The Gospel in Coptic and Arabic
This illustration of the Flight into Egypt and the Massacre of the Innocents occupies a page in an undated, medieval manuscript in the British Library that features the Gospel text in Bohairic Coptic and Arabic. Such bilingual texts of the scriptures were common in Egypt in early Islamic times, reflecting the dual culture of the local Christians. (British Library Oriental Manuscript 1316, f. 5v. "The Four Gospels in Coptic and Arabic," by permission of the British Library.)

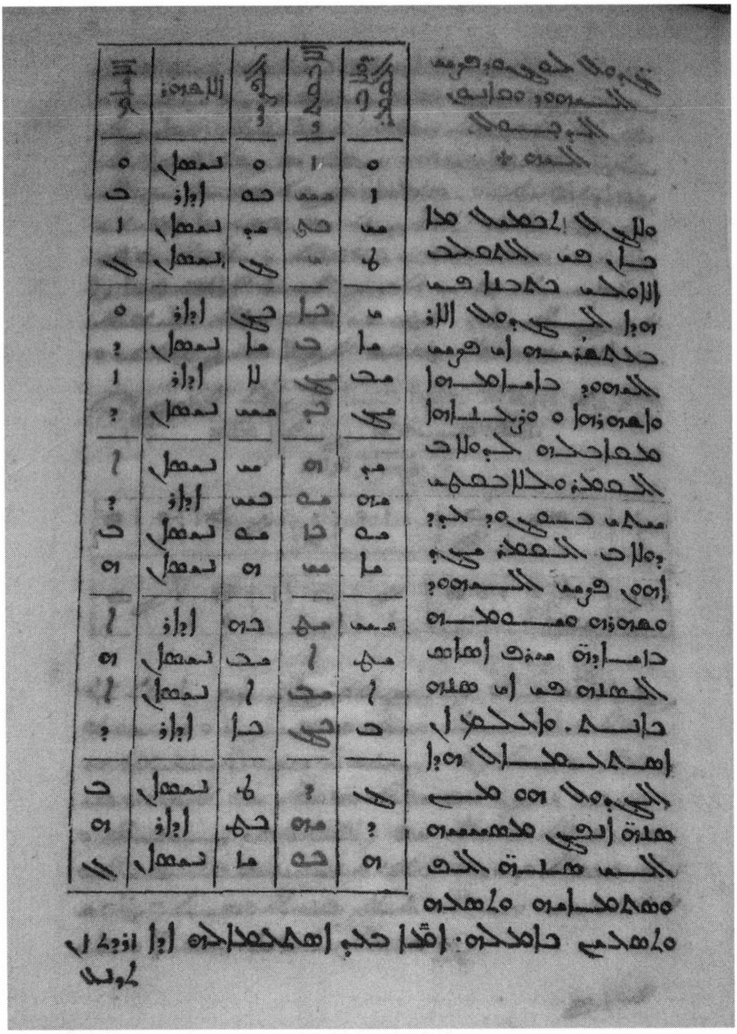

Fig. 7. Garshūnī Text
This page from a book on the liturgical calendar of the Syro-Chaldeans, brought into harmony with the reformed, Gregorian calendar of Pope Gregory XIII (r. 1572–85), was printed in Rome in 1583. It is in Arabic, written in Syriac characters, a scribal practice called "Garshūnī" writing. This practice, which graphically reflects the dual culture of Christians in the world of Islam, persisted in use in liturgical books well into modern times. (Michaele Hesronita, *Qalandarios*, Romae: S. Cong. de Fide, 1637. Courtesy of the Institute of Christian Oriental Research, the Catholic University of America, Washington, DC.)

there is a rich literature in Armenian, there has not been much modern scholarly study of the treatment of Islam in Armenian texts.[54] Yet we know that Armenian historians took notice of the apologetic and polemical exchanges between Muslims and Christians. For example, an Armenian translation of a portion of the so-called Correspondence between the caliph ʿUmar II (r. 715–20) and the Byzantine Emperor Leo III (r. 717–41) is included in the Armenian historian Ghevond's (d. ca. 790) account of the Arab conquest.[55] This Correspondence features a Christian apologist's response (Leo) to an anti-Christian text by a Muslim writer (ʿUmar); scholars are still uncertain about the original language of the letter of Leo. It may have been written originally in Arabic; the Arabic text of the ʿUmar side of the correspondence has been published, but the Arabic text of the Leo portion remains unedited and unstudied, although its existence in a Sinai Arabic manuscript is reported.[56] The immediate point is to highlight the Armenian writer's attention to this correspondence, suggesting that such literature would have caught the interest of a broad spectrum of Armenian readers.

All of the Christian communities who lived within the world of Islam in the early Islamic period strove to cultivate good relations with Muslims at the same time that both in Arabic and in their own languages they clearly marked the differences between the two creeds. Their immediate purpose in much of their writing about Islam was to forestall Christian conversions to Islamic faith. Nevertheless, their acculturation into the Arabic-speaking, Islamic commonwealth inevitably resulted in a measure of Arabicization and even of Islamicization in their diction, both in Arabic and in their native languages, as they strove to find a common discourse between themselves and those who posed the major local challenge to their faith. These developments in turn, along with a number of theological issues, seem to have played a role in the estrangement of Oriental Christians from their coreligionists in the West and outside of the world of Islam.

[54] For the earlier period, see the inclusion of Armenian sources in the study of Robert Hoyland, *Seeing Islam as Others Saw It: A Survey and Evaluation of Christian, Jewish, and Zoroastrian Writings on Early Islam* (Princeton, NJ: Darwin Press, 1997).

[55] See Arthur Jeffery, "Ghevond's Text of the Correspondence between ʿUmar II and Leo III," *Harvard Theological Review* 37 (1944): 269–332.

[56] For discussion and bibliography, see Hoyland, *Seeing Islam*, 490–501; J. M. Gaudeul, trans., *La correspondence de ʿUmar et Leon (vers 900)*, Studi arabo-islamici del PISAI, no. 6 (Rome: Pontificio Istituto di Studi Arabi e d'Islamistica, 1995); Gaudeul, *Encounters and Clashes: Islam and Christianity in History*, 2 vols. (Rome: Pontificio Istituto di Studi Arabi e d'Islamistica, 2000), 1: 81–86.

Today's Muslim/Christian Dialogue

Western Christian thinkers engaged in interreligious dialogue with Muslims in the modern world, and those who have in recent times been concerned with comparative theology in the study of Christianity and Islam,[57] have seldom if ever taken any useful cognizance of the intellectual history of the Christians who lived for centuries in the world of Islam and who wrote Christian philosophy and theology in Syriac and Arabic. When the Christians of the Islamic world claimed their attention at all, modern western scholars have contented themselves with offering denominational histories of the dwindling communities, with little or no mention of their intellectual and cultural engagement with Muslims or of their scholarly accomplishments in the era of the growth and development of the classic cultures of Islam.[58] Even those scholars who have offered in-depth studies of Islamic and Christian theologies in comparison with each other have restricted themselves on the Christian side to the works of the major thinkers of the medieval West, such as Peter Abelard (1079–1142/3), Thomas Aquinas (1225–1274), or Nicholas of Cusa (1401–1464), just to name the most well known among them. The one notable exception in this general pattern of western scholarly neglect of the Christian East is the attention westerners have paid to the contributions of the Christian translators of Greek philosophical and scientific texts into Arabic in early ʿAbbasid times.[59] In this connection alone one finds some ready name recognition among modern scholars for individual Arabophone Christians such as Ḥunayn ibn Isḥāq (808–873) or Yaḥyā ibn ʿAdī (893–974). Otherwise, the Christian thinkers of the Islamic world with whom we have been concerned are known only to a small group of specialists. It is time to factor their thought into today's dialogue between Christians and Muslims and to include their works on the reading lists of the comparative theologians.

[57] In this connection one thinks the most immediately of the pioneering work of James W. Sweetman, *Islam and Christian Theology: A Study of the Interpretation of Theological Ideas in the Two Religions*, 2 vols. in 4 (London: Lutterworth Press, 1954–67).

[58] To name just the most widely available studies, see Aziz Suryal Atiya, *A History of Eastern Christianity* (Notre Dame, IN: University of Notre Dame Press, 1968); Jean-Pierre Valognes, *Vie et mort des chrétiens d'Orient: Des origines à nos jours* (Paris: Fayard, 1994); Bernard Heyberger, *Les chrétiens du Proche-Orient: Au temps de la réforme catholique (Syrie, Liban, Palestine, XVIIe–XVIIIe siècles)* (Rome: École Française de Rome, 1994); Antonie Wessels, *Arab and Christian? Christians in the Middle East* (Kampen, the Netherlands: Kok Pharos Publishing House, 1995); Andrea Pacini, ed., *Christian Communities in the Arab Middle East* (Oxford: Clarendon Press, 1998); Betty Jane Bailey and J. Martin Bailey, *Who Are the Christians in the Middle East* (Grand Rapids, MI: William B. Eerdmans, 2003).

[59] See most comprehensively, Dimitri Gutas, *Greek Thought, Arabic Culture: The Graeco-Arabic Translation Movement in Baghdad and Early ʿAbbasid Society (2nd–4th/8th–10th Centuries)* (London and New York: Routledge, 1998).

It should readily become apparent that when the works of the early Arab Christian apologists are read in conjunction with those of the best of today's Christian theologians writing in dialogue with Muslims,[60] the testimony of the earlier thinkers enriches the discourse, much in the way that in Christian theology more generally patristic literature continues to provide a *resourcement* for the modern theological enterprise.

In this age of religious pluralism, one often hears it said that the works of early Christian writers in the Islamic world such as those we have been discussing here are too polemical to reward the efforts of today's scholars of the Muslim world to master them. This wrongheaded idée fixe prevents those who harbor it from noticing how adroitly the major Arabic-speaking apologists for Christianity in the early Islamic period tailored their arguments to the modes of thinking and even the Arabic diction of the developing Islamic sciences in their day. It also prevents students of the early phases of the growth and development of Islamic religious thinking from taking cognizance of one of the major intellectual frameworks within which Muslim thinkers in the formative period unfolded what would become the master confessional narratives of Islamic faith.

After the formative period of Islamic thought, the end of which William Montgomery Watt dated as early as the year 950,[61] the main lines of Christian thought in the Arabic-speaking, Islamic milieu had also already been drawn. As we have seen, later Arabophone Christian writers and thinkers, up to the twelfth and thirteenth centuries in Egypt, collected, fine-tuned, and synthesized the apologetic and theological discourse of earlier Christian authors. After their time, and up to the twentieth century for all practical purposes, the Arabic idiom of Christians under Muslim rule in the Middle East remained constant, but not frozen. There were notable writers and major cultural figures among these Christians during the long centuries of the communities' decline into demographic insignificance. But the vocabulary and even the parameters of their Christian discourse in Arabic remained remarkably stable. During these centuries the concerns of Christians had more to do with survival and with establishing relationships with Christian churches outside of the Islamic world. This latter process, which involved the arrival of numerous Christian missionaries from the West in the Middle East, in the end brought even more drastic changes, multiplying divisions within the indigenous churches and adding entirely new ecclesial communities with little or no connection to the histories of the Christian churches which, as it were, had grown up with Islam. Meanwhile,

[60] In this connection, see the interesting work of Mark Beaumont, *Christology in Dialogue with Muslims: A Critical Analysis of Christian Presentations of Christ for Muslims from the Ninth and Twentieth Centuries* (Oxford: Regnum Books International, 2005).

[61] See W. Montgomery Watt, *The Formative Period of Islamic Thought* (Edinburgh: Edinburgh University Press, 1973; repr., Oxford: One World, 1998), 316.

from at least the thirteenth century onward, a state of continuous war between Muslim states and western Christian nations continued to embitter Muslim/Christian relations.

In the Middle East the early promise of more harmonious common life between Muslims, Christians, and Jews, as in the intercommunal salons/*majālis* of tenth-century Baghdad, gave way, especially after the Mongol devastations of 1258,[62] to the harsher views of non-Muslims propagated by scholars such as Ibn Taymiyya (1263–1328) and many subsequent Muslim teachers.[63] It may well have been the case that the demographic diminishment of *dhimmī* communities from the fourteenth century onward, reducing the political and social power of Jews and Christians in Islamic society, contributed substantially to the atmosphere that favored the harsher views of these minorities. In Andalusia, visions of an always-fragile *convivencia* gave way after the full success of the *Reconquista* to the definite embitterment of exile for Jews and Muslims, and the persecuting zeal of the victors who seemed eventually to want to erase every trace of Judaism and Islam from the population.[64] Thereafter, in the wider world of Islam, wherever Christians have lived in close association with a Muslim majority, with few exceptions, such as in Jordan, Syria, and Iraq until recently and for a season in Lebanon, intercommunal hostilities have abounded, often with attendant violence between Muslims and Christians. One need only mention the names of the places still featured in the nightly news to make the point: Egypt, Iraq, the Sudan, Nigeria, Algeria, East Timor, the Philippines, Indonesia, Malaysia, and Pakistan, to mention only the locations of the most prominent, recent flash points.

Outside of the Islamic world, for a millennium and more, up until the middle of the twentieth century, constant states of war, and subsequent colonialism and imperialism have deeply embittered Muslims and Christians against each other and so made efforts at religious rapprochement almost unthinkable for most of this period. The combination of religious animosity, cultural disdain, and military hostility that obtained between Muslim and Christian polities for well over a millennium produced on both sides a large literature of mutual rejection.[65] The virulence of this literature seemed to increase with time, especially after the Ottoman encroachments into Eastern Europe from the fifteenth century onward, combining

[62] See Paul Heck, "*Jihād* Revisited," *Journal of Religious Ethics* 32 (2004): 95–128.

[63] See Thomas F. Michel, ed. and trans., *A Muslim Theologian's Response to Christianity: Ibn Taymiyya's al-Jawab al-Sahih* (Delmar, NY: Caravan Books, 1984).

[64] See David Coleman, *Creating Christian Granada: Society and Religious Culture in an Old-World Frontier City, 1492–1600* (Ithaca, NY: Cornell University Press, 2003).

[65] See Rollin Armour Sr., *Islam, Christianity, and the West: A Troubled History*, Faith Meets Faith Series (Maryknoll, NY: Orbis Books, 2002).

cultural, religious, and political attacks.[66] Over the course of time the mutual demonization of the other became almost subconscious. It was relieved only occasionally by intellectual borrowings, and sometimes by a romantic, intercultural fascination on the part of some westerners for the Arab East.[67] As for the Muslims, until Ottoman times they seldom showed much interest in the civilization of western Christians; when they did they found it sorely wanting.[68] By the dawn of the twentieth century, and well up into the century, the levels of religious animosity and the vicissitudes of almost continuous warfare between Muslim and Christian countries would not have made many people think that efforts at some measure of rapprochement were in the offing. But in the West, Christian thinkers with a broad experience beyond the borders of their homelands were already, early in the twentieth century, beginning to have a change of heart and mind. Many of them had participated in early missionary efforts in Islamic lands, efforts that had the net effect not of converting Muslims but, as mentioned above, of splintering the remaining Christian communities in the Islamic world even further than they had been before the arrival of the missionaries. In the Roman Catholic Church the newer considerations in the field of missiology and the experiences of several influential pioneers in interreligious dialogue in the early years of the twentieth century would ultimately find expression in the revolutionary statements of Vatican II (1963–65). Similar statements have been issued by many other Christian churches. Now it is time for westerners to consider the lessons to be learned from the experience of the Christians who have lived in the world of Islam for centuries.

[66] Recent studies of these developments include Richard Fletcher, *The Cross and the Crescent: Christianity and Islam from Muhammad to the Reformation* (New York: Viking, 2003); Andrew Wheatcroft, *Infidels: A History of the Conflict between Christendom and Islam* (New York: Random House, 2004).

[67] See, e.g., Dorothee Metlitzki, *The Matter of Araby in Medieval England* (New Haven, CT: Yale University Press, 1977).

[68] See, e.g., Bernard Lewis, *The Muslim Discovery of Europe* (New York: W. W. Norton, 1982).

BIBLIOGRAPHY

Abū ʿAbd Allāh al-Ḥumaydī. *Jadhwat al-Muqtabis*. Edited by Muḥammad ibn Tāwīt al-Ṭanjī. Cairo: Dār al-Miṣrīyyah, 1953.

ʿAbd al-Jabbār al-Hamdhānī. *Al-Mughnī fī abwāb at-tawḥīd wa-l-ʿadl*. 14 vols. Cairo: al-Dār al-Miṣriyya li l-Taʾlīf wa l-Tarjama, 1958–65.

Accad, Martin. "Did the Later Syriac Fathers Take into Consideration Their Islamic Context When Reinterpreting the New Testament?" *Parole de l'Orient* 23 (1998): 13–32.

———. "The Gospels in the Muslim Discourse of the Ninth to the Fourteenth Centuries: An Exegetical Inventorial Table." *Islam and Christian-Muslim Relations* 14 (2003): 67–91, 205–20, 337–52, 459–79.

Adamson, Peter, and Richard C. Taylor, eds. *The Cambridge Companion to Arabic Philosophy*. Cambridge: Cambridge University Press, 2005.

Aldana Garcia, Maria Jesus. *La estructura narrativa del Memoriale Sanctorum de San Eulogio: Libros II–III*. Cordoba: Publicaciones Obra Social y Cultural Cajasur, 1995.

Alexander, Paul J. *The Byzantine Apocalyptic Tradition*. Berkeley: University of California Press, 1985.

Al-Faruqi, Ismail Raji. *Islam and Other Faiths*. Edited by Ataullah Siddiqui. Leicester, UK: The Islamic Foundation, and Herndon, VA: The International Institute of Islamic Thought, 1998.

Alfeyev, Hilarion. *The Spiritual World of Isaac the Syrian*. Cistercian Studies, no. 175. Kalamazoo, MI: Cistercian Publications, 2000.

Al-Kindī, Abū Yūsuf Yaʿqūb ibn Isḥāq. *Le moyen de chasser les tristesses; et autres textes éthiques*. Introduction, translation, and notes by Soumaya Mestiri and Guillaume Dye. Paris: Fayard, 2004.

Allard, Michel. "Les chrétiens à Baghdad." *Arabica* 9 (1962): 375–88.

Allen, Pauline, and C. T. R. Hayward. *Severus of Antioch*. London and New York: Routledge, 2004.

Al-Muʾtaman Ibn al-ʿAssāl. *Summa dei Principi della Religione*. Edited by A. Wadi. Studia Orientalia Christiana Monographiae, 6a–b and 7a–b. Cairo: The Franciscan Centre of Christian Oriental Studies, 1998–99.

Altmann, A., and S. M. Stern. *Isaac Israeli: A Neoplatonic Philosopher of the Tenth Century; His Works Translated with Comments and an Outline of His Philosophy*. Scripta Judaica, vol. 1. London: Oxford University Press, 1958.

Ambramowski, L. "Das Konzil von Chalkedon in der Homilie des Narsai über die drei nestorianischen Lehrer," *Zeitschrift für Kirchengeschichte* 66 (1954–1955): 140–143.

Anawati, G. C. "Ḥunayn ibn Isḥāq al-ʿIbādī, Abū Zayd." In Gillispie, *Dictionary of Scientific Biography*, 230–34.

Armour, Rollin, Sr. *Islam, Christianity and the West: A Troubled History*. Faith Meets Faith Series. Maryknoll, NY: Orbis Books, 2002.

Arnaldez, Roger. *À la croisée des trois monotheismes: Une communauté de pensée au Moyen Age*. Paris: Albin Michel, 1993.

———. *Three Messengers for One God.* Translated by G. W. Schlabach et al. Notre Dame, IN: University of Notre Dame Press, 1994.

Atiya, Aziz Suryal. *The Coptic Encyclopedia.* 7 vols. New York: Macmillan, 1991.

———. *A History of Eastern Christianity,* Notre Dame, IN: University of Notre Dame Press, 1968.

Auzepy, M.-F. "De la Palestine à Constantinople (VIIIe—IXe siècles): Étienne le Sabaïte et Jean Damascène." *Travaux et Mémoires* 12 (1994): 183–218.

Ayoub, Mahmoud. "Dhimmah in Qur'an and Hadith." *Arab Studies Quarterly* 5 (1983): 172–82.

Bacha, Constantine. *Les oeuvres arabes de Theodore Abou-Kurra, évêque d'Haran.* Beirut: Maṭbaʿat al-Fawāʾid li-Ṣāḥibih Ḥalīl al-Badawī, 1904.

———. *Un traité des oeuvres arabes de Theodore Abou-Kurra, évêque de Haran.* Tripoli, Syria: L'Évêché Grec-Catholique, and Rome: Procureur des Basiliens de Saint-Sauveur, 1905.

Bacha, Ḥabīb, ed. *Ḥawāshī (Notes) d'ibn al-Maḥrūma sur le ʿTanqīḥ' d'ibn Kammūna.* Patrimoine Arabe Chrétien, 6. Jounieh: Librairie Saint-Paul, and Rome: Pontificio Istituto Orientale, 1984.

Badawi, Abdurrahman. *Hunain ibn Ishaq: Âdâb al-Falâsifa (Sentences des Philosophes)* (Arabic). Safat, Kuwait: Éditions de l'Institut des Manuscrits Arabes, 1985.

Bailey, Betty Jane, and J. Martin Bailey. *Who Are the Christians in the Middle East?* Grand Rapids, MI: William B. Eerdmans, 2003.

Baneth, David, and Haggai Ben-Shammai, eds. *Kitāb ar-radd wa d-dalīl fī d-dīn adh-dhalīl (al-kitāb al Khazarī).* Jerusalem: Magnes Press, 1977.

Baum, Wilhelm, and Dietmar Winkler. *The Church of the East: A Concise History.* New York: Routledge Curzon, 2003.

Beaumont, Mark. *Christology in Dialogue with Muslims: A Critical Analysis of Christian Presentations of Christ for Muslims from the Ninth and Twentieth Centuries.* Oxford: Regnum Books International, 2005.

Becker, C. H. "Christian Polemic and the Formation of Islamic Dogma." In *Muslims and Others in Early Islamic Society,* edited by Robert Hoyland, 241–57. The Formation of the Classical Islamic World, vol. 18. Aldershot, UK: Ashgate, 2004.

———. "Christliche Polemik und islamische Dogmenbildung." *Zeitschrift für Assyriologie* 25 (1911): 175–95.

Bekkum, Wout Jac. Van. "The *Kuzari* of Judah Halevi and Its Reflection on Life, Faith, and Philosophy." In Roggema, *The Three Rings,* 3–18.

Beltran, Miguel. "Los atributos divinos en Juan de Damasco y su influencia en el islam." *Collectanea Christiana Orientalia* 2 (2005): 25–42.

Ben Shammai, Haggai. "Qirqisani on the Oneness of God." *Jewish Quarterly Review* 73 (1982): 105–11.

Berkey, Jonathan P. *The Formation of Islam: Religion and Society in the Near East, 600–1800.* Cambridge: Cambridge University Press, 2003.

Bidawid, Raphael. *Les lettres du patriarche nestorien Timothée.* Studi e Testi, 187. Vatican City: Biblioteca Apostolica Vaticana, 1956.

Blau, Joshua. *The Emergence and Linguistic Background of Judaeo-Arabic: A Study of the Origins of Neo-Arabic and Middle Arabic.* Jerusalem: Ben-Zvi Institute, 1999.

———. *A Grammar of Christian Arabic*. CSCO, vols. 267, 276, and 279. Louvain, Belgium: Peeters, 1966–67.

Blumenthal, H. J. "Alexandria as a Centre of Philosophy in Later Classical Antiquity." *Illinois Classical Studies* 18 (1993): 307–25.

———. "529 and Its Sequel: What Happened to the Academy?" *Byzantion* 48 (1978): 369–85.

Bobzin, Hartmut. "'A Treasury of Heresies': Christian Polemics against the Koran." In *The Qur'ān as Text*, edited by Stefan Wild, 157–75. Leiden: Brill, 1996.

Bosworth, C. E. "The Concept of *dhimma* in Early Islam." In *Christians and Jews in the Ottoman Empire: The Functioning of a Plural Society*, 2 vols., edited by B. Braude and B. Lewis, 1: 37–51. New York and London: Holmes and Meier, 1982).

———. "The 'Protected Peoples' (Christians and Jews) in Medieval Egypt and Syria." *Bulletin of the John Rylands University Library of Manchester* 62 (1979): 11–36.

Bottini, Laura. *Al-Kindī: Apologia del Cristianesimo; traduzione dall'arabo, introduzione*. Patrimonio Culturale Arabo Cristiano, 4. Milan: Jaca Book, 1998.

Bouamama, Ali. *La littérature polémique musulmane contre le christianisme depuis ses origins jusqu'au XIIIe siècle*. Algiers: Enterprise Nationale du Livre, 1988.

Bourget, P. du. *Les Coptes*, 2nd ed. Paris: Presses Universitaires de France, 1988.

Brock, Sebastian P. "Christians in the Sasanid Empire: A Case of Divided Loyalties." In *Religion and National Identity*, edited by Stuart Mews, 1–19. Studies in Church History, 18. Oxford: Oxford University Press, 1982.

———. "The Christology of the Church of the East in the Synods of the Fifth to Early Seventh Centuries: Preliminary Considerations and Materials." In Sebastian Brock, *Studies in Syriac Christianity; History, Literature and Theology*, no. 12. Aldershot, UK: Variorum/Ashgate, 1992.

———. "From Antagonism to Assimilation: Syriac Attitudes to Greek Learning." In *East of Byzantium: Syria and Armenia in the Formative Period*, edited by Nina Garsoïan et al., 17–34. Dumbarton Oaks Symposium, 1980. Washington, DC: Dumbarton Oaks, 1982.

———. "The 'Nestorian' Church: A Lamentable Misnomer." *Bulletin of the John Rylands University Library of Manchester* 78 (1996): 23–35.

———. "North Mesopotamia in the Late Seventh Century: Book XV of John Bar Penkāyō's *Rīš Mellō*." *Jerusalem Studies in Arabic and Islam* 9 (1987): 51–75.

———. "Syriac Culture in the Seventh Century." *ARAM* 1 (1989): 268–80.

———. "Transformations of the Edessa Portrait of Christ." *Journal of Assyrian Academic Studies* 18 (2004): 46–56.

———. "Two Letters of the Patriarch Timothy from the Late Eighth Century on Translations from Greek." *Arabic Sciences and Philosophy* 9 (1999): 233–46.

———, and David G. K. Taylor et al. *The Hidden Pearl: The Syrian Orthodox Church and Its Aramaic Heritage*. Rome: Trans World Film Italia, 2001.

Buffat, L. "Lettre de Paul, évêque de Saïda, moine d'Antioche, à un musulman de ses amis demeurant a Saïda." *Revue de l'Orient Chrétien* 8 (1903): 388–425.

Bulliet, Richard W. *The Case for Islamo-Christian Civilization*. New York: Columbia University Press, 2004.

———. *Conversion to Islam in the Medieval Period: An Essay in Quantitative History*. Cambridge, MA: Harvard University Press, 1979.

Bundy, David. "Jacob Baradaeus: The State of Research: A Review of Sources and a New Approach." *Le Muséon* 91 (1978): 45–86.

Burman, Thomas E. *Religious Polemic and the Intellectual History of the Mozarabs, c. 1050–1200*. Leiden: Brill, 1994.

Burnett, Charles. "Arabic into Latin: The Reception of Arabic Philosophy into Western Europe." In *The Cambridge Companion to Arabic Philosophy*, edited by Peter Adamson and Richard C. Taylor, 370–404. Cambridge: Cambridge University Press, 2005.

———. "The Translating Activity in Medieval Spain." In *The Legacy of Muslim Spain*, 2 vols., edited by Salma Khadra Jayyusi, 2: 1036–58. Leiden: Brill, 1994.

Bushrui, Suheil B. "Yeats' Arabic Interests." In *In Excited Reverie: A Centenary Tribute to William Butler Yeats, 1856–1939*, edited by A. Norman Jeffares and K. G. W. Cross. London: Macmillan, 1965.

Busse, Heribert. "Monotheismus und islamische Christologie in der Bauinschrift der Felsendoms in Jerusalem." *Theologische Quartalschrift* 161 (1981): 168–78.

———. " ʿOmar b. al-Ḫaṭṭāb in Jerusalem," *Jerusalem Studies in Arabic and Islam* 5 (1984): 73–119.

———. " ʿOmar's Image as the Conqueror of Jerusalem." *Jerusalem Studies in Arabic and Islam* 8 (1986): 149–68.

———. "Die ʿUmar-Moschee im östlichen Atrium der Grabeskirche." *Zeitschrift des deutschen Palästina-Vereins* 109 (1993): 73–82.

———. "Zur Geschichte und Deutung der frühislamischen *Ḥaram*bauten in Jerusalem." *Zeitschrift des deutschen Palästina-Vereins* 107 (1991): 144–54.

Butterworth, C. E., et al. *The Introduction of Arabic Philosophy into Europe*. Studien und Texte zur Geistesgeschichte des Mittelalters, vol. 39. Leiden: Brill, 1997.

Cameron, Alan. "The Last Days of the Academy at Athens." *Proceedings of the Cambridge Philosophical Society* 195, n.s. 15 (1969): 7–29.

Cameron, Averil, and Lawrence I Conrad, eds. *The Byzantine and Early Islamic Near East I: Problems in the Literary Source Material*. Studies in Late Antiquity and Early Islam, 1. Princeton, NJ: Darwin Press, 1992.

Carali, Paul. *Le Christianisme et l'Islam: Controverse attribuée au moine Georges du Couvent de St. Siméon (Séeucie) soutenue devant le Prince El-Mouchammar Fils de Saladin en 1207*. Beit Chebab. Lebanon: Imprimerie Al-Alam, 1933.

Caspar, Robert. "Les versions arabes du dialogue entre le Catholicos Timothée I et le calife al-Mahdī (IIe/VIIIe siècle). *Islamochristiana* 3 (1977): 150 (Arabic).

———, et al., eds. "Bibliographie du dialogue-islamo-chrétien." *Islamochristiana* 1 (1975)—7 (1981).

Cassarino, Mirella. *Traduzioni e Traduttori Arabi dall' VIII all' XI Secolo*. Rome: Salerno Editrice, 1998.

Castro, Américo. *The Structure of Spanish History*. Translated by Edmund L. King. Princeton, NJ: Princeton University Press, 1954.

Chabot, I.-B., ed. and trans. *Anonymi Auctoris Chronicon ad Annum Christi 1234 Pertinens*. CSCO, vols. 82 and 109. Paris: J. Gabalda, 1920; repr. Louvain, Belgium: Imprimerie Orientaliste L. Durbecq, 1952.

Chediath, Geevarghese. *The Christology of Mar Babai the Great.* Kottayam, India: Oriental Institute of Religious Studies, and Paderborn, Germany: Ostkirchendienst, 1982.

Cheikho, Hanna. *Dialectique du langage sur Dieu de Timothée I (728–823) à Serge.* Rome: Pont. Institutum Studiorum Orientalium, 1983.

Cheikho, Louis. "Majālis Ilīyā Muṭrān Nusaybīn." *al-Machriq* 20 (1922): 33–44, 112–17, 117–22, 267–70, 270–72, 366–77, 425–34.

———. "Mīmar li Tadūrūs Abū Qurrah fī wujūd al-Khāliq wa d-dīn al-qawīmm." *al-Machriq* 15 (1912): 757–74; 825–42.

———. *Seize traités théologiques d'auteurs arabes chrétiens.* Beirut: Dar al-Machreq, 1906.

———. *Vingt traités théologiques d'auteurs arabes chrétiens.* Beirut: Dar al-Machreq, 1920.

Chesnut, Roberta. *Three Monophysite Christologies.* Oxford: Oxford University Press, 1976.

Chiesa, Bruno, and Wilfrid Lockwood, eds. and trans. *Ya'qūb al-Qirqisānī on Jewish Sects and Christianity.* Frankfurt: Peter Lang, 1984.

Choksy, Jamsheed K. *Conflict and Cooperation: Zoroastrian Subalterns and Muslim Elites in Medieval Iranian Society.* New York: Columbia University Press, 1997.

Christys, Ann. *Christians in al-Andalus (711–1000).* Richmond, UK: Curzon Press, 2002.

Cohen, Mark R. *Under Crescent and Cross: The Jews in the Middle Ages.* Princeton, NJ: Princeton University Press, 1994.

Colbert, Edward P. *The Martyrs of Córdoba (850–859): A Study of the Sources.* Washington, DC: Catholic University of America, 1962.

Coleman, David. *Creating Christian Granada: Society and Religious Culture in an Old-World Frontier City, 1492–1600.* Ithaca, NY: Cornell University Press, 2003.

Conrad, Lawrence I. "Varietas Syriaca: Secular and Sientific Culture in the Christian Communities of Syria after the Arab Conquest." In *After Bardaisan: Studies on Continuity and Change in Syriac Christianity in Honour of Professor Han J. W. Drijvers,* edited by G. J. Reinink and A. C. Klugkist, 85–105. Orientalia Lovaniensia Analecta, 89. Leuven, Belgium: Peeters, 1999.

Constable, Olivia Remie. *Housing the Stranger in the Mediterranean World: Lodging, Trade, and Travel in Late Antiquity and the Middle Ages.* Cambridge: Cambridge University Press, 2003.

Cook, Michael. *Early Muslim Dogma,* Cambridge: Cambridge University Press, 1981.

———. "The Origins of Kalam." *Bulletin of the School of Oriental and African Studies* 43 (1980): 32–43.

Coope, Jessica A. *The Martyrs of Córdoba: Community and Family Conflict in an Age of Mass Conversion.* Lincoln: University of Nebraska Press, 1995.

Courbage, Youssef, and Philippe Fargues. *Christians and Jews under Islam.* Translated by Judy Mabro. London and New York: I. B. Tauris, 1997.

Cowe, S. P. "An Armenian Job Fragment from Sinai and Its Implications." *Oriens Christianus* 76 (1972): 123–57.

Cragg, Kenneth. *The Arab Christian: A History in the Middle East.* London: Mowbray, 1992.

———. *Faith and Life Negotiate: A Christian Story-Study.* Norwich: Canterbury Press, 1994.

———. *Muhammad and the Christian: A Question of Response.* London: Darton, Longman and Todd, and Maryknoll, NY: Orbis Books, 1984.

Crone, Patricia. *God's Rule: Government and Islam.* New York: Columbia University Press, 2004.

———. "Islam, Judeo-Christianity, and Byzantine Iconoclasm." *Jerusalem Studies in Arabic and Islam* 2 (1980): 59–95.

Dagher, Joseph, and Gérard Troupeau. *Ibn Buṭlān: Le banquet des prêtres; une maqāma chrétien du XIe siècle.* Paris: Geuthner, 2004.

Dagorn, R. *La geste d'Ismaël d'après l'onomastique et la tradition arabes.* Geneva: Froz, 1981.

Daiber, Hans. "Masā'il wa-Adjwiba." *EI*, 2nd ed., vol. 4, 636–39.

Daniel, Norman. *Islam and the West: The Making of an Image.* Edinburgh: Edinburgh University Press, 1960; published in a revised edition, Oxford: One World, 1993.

Davids, Adelbert. "The Person and Teachings of Theodore of Mopsuestia and the Relationship between Him, His Teachings and the Church of the East with a Special Reference to the Three Chapters Controversy." In *Syriac Dialogue: Third Non-Official Consultation on Dialogue within the Syriac Tradition,* edited by Alfred Stirnemann and Gerhard Wilflinger, 38–52. Vienna: Foundation Pro Oriente, 1998.

Davidson, Herbert A. *Moses Maimonides: The Man and His Works.* Oxford: Oxford University Press, 2005.

———. *Proofs for Eternity, Creation, and the Existence of God in Medieval Islamic and Jewish Philosophy.* New York: Oxford University Press, 1987.

De Blois, François. "*Naṣrānī* (ναζωραιος) and *ḥanīf* (εθνικος): Studies on the Religious Vocabulary of Christianity and Islam." *Bulletin of the School of Oriental and African Studies* 65 (2002): 1–30.

De Epalza, Mikel. "Mozarabs: An Emblematic Christian Minority in Islamic al-Andalus." In *The Legacy of Muslim Spain,* 2 vols., edited by Salma Khadra Jayyusi, 1: 149. Leiden: Brill, 1994.

Delgado Leon, Feliciano. *Alvaro de Cordoba y la polemica contra el Islam: El Indiculus Luminosus.* Cordoba: Publicaciones Obra Social y Cultural Cajasur, 1996.

Dennett, Daniel C. *Conversion and the Poll Tax in Early Islam.* Cambridge, MA: Harvard University Press, 1950.

Deroche, Vincent. *Entre Rome et l'islam: Les chrétientés d'orient, 610–1054.* Paris: Éditions Seuil, 1996.

———. "La polémique anti-judaique au Ve et au VIIe siècle: Un memento inédit, les *Képhalia.*" *Travaux et Mémoires* 11 (1991): 275–312.

Destremau, C., and J. Moncelon. *Massignon.* Paris: Plon, 1994.

Dick, Ignace. "Un continuateur arabe de saint Jean Damascène: Théodore Abuqurra, évêque melkite de Harran." *Proche-Orient Chrétien* 12 (1962): 209–23, 319–32; 13 (1963): 114–29.

———. "Deux écrits inédits de Théodore Abuqurra." *Le Muséon* 72 (1959): 53–67.

———. *La discussion d'Abū Qurrah avec les ulémas musulmans devant le calife al-Ma'mūn: Étude et edition critique.* Aleppo, Syria: Privately printed, 1999.

———. *Théodore Abuqurra, Traité de l'existence du createur et de la vraie religion; introduction et texte critique.* Patrimoine Arabe Chrétien, 3. Jounieh, Lebanon: al-Maktabah al-Būlusīyah, and Rome: al-Maʿhad al-Bābawī al-Sharqī, 1982.

———. *Théodore Abuqurra, Traité du culte des icons; introduction et texte critique.* Patrimoine Arabe Chrétien, 10. Jounieh, Lebanon: al-Maktabah al-Būlusīyah, and Rome: al-Maʿhad al-Bābawī al-Sharqī, 1986.

Dodge, Bayard, ed. and trans. *The Fihrist of al-Nadīm: A Tenth-Century Survey of Muslim Culture.* 2 vols. New York: Columbia University Press, 1970.

Donner, Fred M. *The Early Islamic Conquests*, Princeton, NJ: Princeton University Press, 1981.

———. "From Believers to Muslims: Confessional Self-Identity in the Early Islamic Community." *Al-Abhath* 50–51 (2002–3): 9–53.

———. *Narratives of Islamic Origins: The Beginnings of Islamic Historical Writing.* Princeton, NJ: Darwin Press, 1998.

Drijvers, Han J. W. "The Gospel of the Twelve Apostles: A Syriac Apocalypse from the Early Islamic Period." In Cameron and Conrad, *Byzantine and Early Islamic Near East I*, 189–213.

———. "The Image of Edessa in the Syriac Tradition." In *The Holy Face and the Paradox of Representation*, edited by H. L. Kessler and G. Wolf, 6: 13–31. Villa Spelman Colloquia, Florence 1996. Bologna: Nuova Alfa, 1998.

———. "Jakob von Edessa (633–708)." In *Theologische Realenzyklopädie,* 16: 468–470. Berlin: De Gruyter, 1993.

———. "The Testament of Our Lord: Jacob of Edessa's Response to Islam." *ARAM* 6 (1994): 104–14.

———, and A. A. MacDonald, eds. *Centres of Learning: Learning and Location in Pre-Modern Europe and the Near East.* Brill's Studies in Intellectual History, vol. 61. Leiden: Brill, 1995.

Druart, Thérèse-Anne. "Philosophical Consolation in Christianity and Islam: Boethius and al-Kindī." *Topoi* 19 (2000): 25–34.

Ducellier, Alain. *Chrétiens d'Orient et Islam au Moyen Age; VIIe–XVe siècle.* Paris: Armand Colin/Masson, 1996.

Dunlop, D. "Ḥafṣ b. Albar—the Last of the Goths?" *Journal of the Royal Asiatic Society* (1954): 136–51.

———. "Sobre Ḥafṣ ibn Albar al-Qūṭī al-Qurṭubī." *Al-Andalus* 20 (1955): 211–13.

Ebied, R., and D. Thomas, eds. *Muslim-Christian Polemic during the Crusades: The Letter from the People of Cyprus and Ibn Abī Ṭālib al-Dimashqī's Response.* History of Christian-Muslim Relations, vol. 2. Leiden: Brill, 2005.

Edelby, Néophytos. *Sulaiman al-Ghazzī: Écrits.* Patrimoine Arabe Chrétien, vols. 7, 8, 9. Jounieh, Lebanon: Librairie Saint Paul, and Rome: Pontificio Istituto Orientale, 1984–86.

Eid, Hadi. *Lettre du calife Hârûn al-Rašîd à l'empereur Constantin VI: Texte présenté, commenté et traduit.* Études Chrétiennes Arabes. Paris: Cariscript, 1992.

El Hassan bin Talal. *Christianity in the Arab World.* Amman: Royal Institute for Inter-Faith Studies, 1995.

El-Hayek, Elias. "Struggle for Survival: The Maronites of the Middle Ages." In Gervers and Bikhazi, *Conversion and Continuity*, 407–21.

Endress, Gerhard. "The Circle of al-Kindī: Early Arabic Translations from the Greek and the Rise of Islamic Philosophy." In Endress and Kruk, eds. *The Ancient Tradition in Christian and Islamic Hellenism*, 43–76.

———. "The Debate between Arabic Grammar and Greek Logic in Classical Islamic Thought." *Journal for the History of Arabic Science* (Aleppo) 1 (1977): 320–23, 339–51.

———. "Grammatik and Logik: Arabische Philologie und griechische Philosophie im Widerstreit." In *Sprachphilosophie in Antike und Mittelalter*, edited by Burkhard Mojsisch, 163–299. Bochumer Studien zur Philosophie, 3. Amsterdam: Gruner, 1986.

———. *The Works of Yaḥyā ibn ʿAdī: An Analytical Inventory.* Wiesbaden: Reichert, 1977.

———. "Yaḥyā ibn ʿAdī: *Maqāla fī tabyīn al-faṣl bayna sīnāʿat al-manṭiq al-falsafī wa l-naḥw al-ʿarabī.*" *Journal for the History of Arabic Science* (Aleppo) 2 (1978): 181–93.

———, and Remke Kruk, eds. *The Ancient Tradition in Christian and Islamic Hellenism: Studies on the Transmission of Greek Philosophy and Sciences.* Leiden: Research School CNWS, School of Asian, African, and Amerindian Studies, 1997.

Eusebius of Caesarea. *The Ecclesiastical History.* Translated by Kirsopp Lake and J. E. L. Oulton, edited by H. J. Lawlor. The Loeb Classical Library. 2 vols. Cambridge, MA: Harvard University Press, 1980.

Fakhry, Majid. *A History of Islamic Philosophy*, 3rd ed. New York: Columbia University Press, 2004.

Fattal, A. *Le statut legal des non-musulmans en pays d'Islam.* Beirut: Imprimerie Catholique, 1958.

Feiler, Bruce. *Abraham: A Journey to the Heart of Three Faiths.* New York: William Morrow/HarperCollins, 2002.

Feldtkeller, Andreas. *Die 'Mutter der Kirchen' im 'Haus des Islam': Gegenseitige Wahrnehmung von arabischen Christen und Muslimen im West-und Ostjordanland.* Erlangen, Germany: Erlanger Verlag für Mission und Ökumene, 1998.

Fenton, Paul B. "Judaeo-Arabic Literature." In *Religion, Learning and Society in the ʿAbbasid Period*, edited by M. J. L. Young et al., 461–76. The Cambridge History of Arabic Literature. Cambridge: Cambridge University Press, 1990.

———. "Sa'adyā ben Yūsuf." *EI*, new ed., 7 (1993): 661–62.

Fiey, Jean Maurice. *Chrétiens syriaques sous les Abbasides surtout à Bagdad (749–1258).* Corpus Scriptorum Christianorum Orientalium, vol. 420. Louvain, Belgium: Secrétariat du Corpus SCO, 1980.

———. *Saints Syriaques.* Edited by Lawrence I. Conrad. Studies in Late Antiquity and Early Islam, 6. Princeton, NJ: Darwin Press, 2004.

Flannery, Austin, ed. *Vatican Council II: The Conciliar and Post Conciliar Documents.* Vatican Collection, vol. 1, rev. ed. Northport, NY: Costello Publishing, 1975 and 1984.

Fletcher, Richard. *The Cross and the Crescent: Christianity and Islam from Muhammad to the Reformation*, New York: Viking, 2003.

Flusin, Bernard. "L'Esplanade du temple a l'arrivée des arabes, d'après deux récits byzantins." In *Bayt al-Maqdis: ʿAbd al-Malik's Jerusalem*, part 1, edited by Julian Raby and Jeremy Johns, 17–31. Oxford: Oxford University Press, 1992.

Fontaine, Resianne. "Abraham ibn Daud's Polemics against Muslims and Christians." In Roggema, *The Three Rings*, 19–34.

Fowden, Garth. *Empire to Commonwealth: Consequences of Monotheism in Late Antiquity*. Princeton, NJ: Princeton University Press, 1993.

Francis, James A. *Subversive Virtue: Asceticism and Authority in the Second-Century Pagan World*. University Park: Pennsylvania State University Press, 1995.

Frank, Richard M. *Beings and Their Attributes: The Teaching of the Basrian School of the Muʿtazila in the Classical Period*. Albany: State University of New York Press, 1978.

———. "The Science of Kalām." *Arabic Science and Philosophy* 2 (1992): 9–37.

Fregosi, Paul. *Jihad in the West: Muslim Conquests from the 7th to the 21st Centuries*. Amherst, NY: Prometheus Books, 1998.

Friedman, Yohanan. "Classification of Unbelievers in Sunnī Muslim Law and Tradition." *Jerusalem Studies in Arabic and Islam* 22 (1998): 163–195.

———. *Tolerance and Coercion in Islam: Interfaith Relations in the Muslim Tradition*. Cambridge: Cambridge University Press, 2003.

Fritsch, Erdman. *Islam und Christentum im Mittelalter*. Breslau: Müller and Seiffert, 1930.

Fück, J. W. "Some Hitherto Unpublished Texts on the Muʿtazilite Movement from Ibn-al-Nadim's Kitāb-al-Fihrist." In *Professor Muhammad Shafi Presentation Volume*, edited by S. M. Abdullah, 62. Lahore: Punjab University Press, 1955.

Gallez, Édouard-Marie. *La messie et son prophète: Aux origines de l'islam*. 2 vols. Studia Arabia 1 and 2, 2nd ed. Paris: Éditions de Paris, 2005.

Gallo, Maria, trans. *Palestinese anonimo: Omelia arabo-cristiana dell'VIII secolo*. Rome: Città Nuova Editrice, 1994.

Garaudy, Roger. *L'islam en occident: Cordue, capitale de l'esprit*. Paris: L'Harmattan, 1987.

Garitte, G., *Le Calendrier palestino-géorgien du Sinaiticus 34 (Xe siècle)*. Brussels: Société des Bollandistes, 1958.

Garsoïan, Nina, *L'église arménienne et le grand schisme d'Orient*. CSCO, vol. 574. Louvain, Belgium: Peeters, 1999.

Gaudeul, Jean-Marie, and Robert Caspar. *La correspondence de ʿUmar et Leon (vers 900)*. Studi arabo-islamici del PISAI, no. 6. Rome: Pontificio Istituto di Studi Arabi e d'Islamistica, 1995.

———. *Encounters and Clashes: Islam and Christianity in History*. 2 vols., rev. ed. Rome: Pontificio Istituto di Studi Arabi e Islamici, 2000.

———. *Riposte aux Chrétiens*. Rome: Pontifical Institute of Arabic and Islamic Studies, 1995.

———. "Textes de la tradition musulmane concernant le *taḥrīf* (falsification) des écritures." *Islamochristiana* 6 (1980): 61–104.

Geiger, Abraham, *Was hat Mohammed aus dem Judenthume aufgenommen?* Eine von der Königliche preussischen Rheinuniversität gekrönte Presschrift. 2nd ed. Leipzig: M. W. Kaufmann, 1902.

Georr, Khalil. *Les categories d'Aristote dans leurs versions syro-arabes.* Beirut: Institut Français de Damas, 1948.

Gerhards, A., and H. Brakmann, eds. *Die koptische Kirche: Einfürung in das ägyptische Christentum.* Stuttgart: Kohlhammer, 1994.

Gero, Stephen. *Barsauma of Nisibis and Persian Christianity in the Fifth Century.* CSCO, vol. 426. Louvain, Belgium: Peeters, 1981.

Gervers, Michael, and Ramzi Jibran Bikhazi, eds. *Conversion and Continuity: Indigenous Christian Communities in Islamic Lands; Eighth to Eighteenth Centuries.* Papers in Medieval Studies, 9. Toronto: Pontifical Institute of Medieval Studies, 1990.

Gibson, Margaret Dunlop. *An Arabic Version of the Acts of the Apostles and the Seven Catholic Epistles, with a Treatise on the Triune Nature of God.* Studia Sinaitica, 7. London: C. J. Clay and Sons, 1899.

Gil, Ioannes, ed. *Corpus Scriptorum Muzarabicorum.* 2 vols. Madrid: Instituto Antonio de Nebrija, 1973.

Gil, Moshe. *A History of Palestine, 634–1099.* Cambridge: Cambridge University Press, 1992.

Gilliot, Claude. "Les 'informateurs' juifs et chrétiens de Muḥammad" *Jerusalem Studies in Arabic and Islam* 22 (1998): 84–126.

Gillispie, Charles Coulston. *Dictionary of Scientific Biography,* vol. 15, supplement 1. New York: Charles Scribner's, 1980.

Gillman, Ian, and Hans-Joachim Klimkeit. *Christians in Asia before 1500.* Ann Arbor: University of Michigan Press, 1999.

Gimaret, Daniel. *Les noms divins en Islam: Exégèse lexicographique et théologique.* Paris: Cerf, 1988.

Golb, Norman, ed. *Judeo-Arabic Studies: Proceedings of the Founding Conference of the Society for Judaeo-Arabic Studies.* Studies in Muslim-Jewish Relations, 3. Amsterdam: Harwood Academic Publishers, 1997.

Goodman, Lenn E., trans. and commentator. *The Book of Theodicy: Translation and Commentary on the Book of Job by Saddiah ben Joseph al-Fayyūmī.* Yale Judaica Series. New Haven, CT: Yale University Press, 1988.

———. *Islamic Humanism.* Oxford: Oxford University Press, 2003.

———. "Muḥammad ibn Zakariyyā' al-Rāzī." In Nasr and Leaman, *History of Islamic Philosophy,* 1: 198–215.

———. "Saadiah Gaon al-Fayyumi." In Nasr and Leaman, *History of Islamic Philosophy,* 2: 696–711.

Gottheil, Richard. "A Christian Bahira Legend." *Zeitschrift für Assyriologie* 13 (1898): 189–242; 14 (1899): 203–68; 15 (1900): 56–102; 17 (1903): 125–66.

Goussen, H. *Die christlich-arabische Literatur der Mozaraber.* Beiträge zur christlich-arabischen Literaturgeschichte, Heft, 4. Leipzig: Harrassowitz, 1909.

Grabar, Oleg. *The Shape of the Holy: Early Islamic Jerusalem.* Princeton, NJ: Princeton University Press, 1996.

Graf, Georg. *Die arabischen Schriften des Theodor Abu Qurra, Bischofs von Ḥarrān (ca. 740–820).* Paderborn, Germany: Ferdinand Schöningh, 1910.

———. "Christliche-arabische Texte: Zwei Disputationen zwischen Muslimen und Christen." In *Griechische, koptische und arabische Texte zur Religion und religiösen Literatur in Ägyptens Spätzeit*, edited by Friedrich Bilabel and Adolf Grohmann, 1–31. Heidelberg: Verlag der Universitätsbibliothek, 1934.

———. *Geschichte der christlichen arabischen Literatur.* 5 vols. Studi e Testi, 118, 133, 146, 147, 172. Vatican City: Biblioteca Apostolica Vaticana, 1944–53.

———. "Die Koptische Gelehrtenfamilie der *Aulād al-ʿAssāl* und ihr Schrifttum." *Orientalia* n.s. 1 (1932): 34–56, 129–48, 193–204.

———. *Die Schriften des Jacobiten Ḥabīb Ibn Ḫidma Abū Rāʾiṭa.* CSCO, vols. 130 and 131. Louvain, Belgium: Peeters, 1951.

———. *Des Theodor Abu Kurra Traktat über den Schöpfer und die wahre Religion.* Beiträge zur Geschichte der Philosophie des Mittelalters, Texte und Untersuchungen, Band 14, Heft 1. Münster: W. Aschendorf, 1913.

Griffith, Sidney H. " ʿAmmār al-Baṣrī's *Kitāb al-burhān*: Christian *Kalām* in the First Abbasid Century." *Le Muséon* 96 (1983): 145–81.

———. "Anastasios of Sinai, the *Hodegos* and the Muslims." *Greek Orthodox Theological Review* 32 (1987): 341–58.

———. "Answers for the Shaykh: A 'Melkite' Arabic Text from Sinai and the Doctrines of the Trinity and the Incarnation in 'Arab Orthodox' Apologetics." In *The Encounter of Eastern Christianity with Early Islam*, edited by Emmanouela Grypeou, Mark Swanson, and David Thomas, 277–309. Leiden: Brill, 2006.

———. "Anthony David of Baghdad, Scribe and Monk of Mar Sabas: Arabic in the Monasteries of Palestine." *Church History* 58 (1989): 7–19.

———. "The Apologetic Treatise of Nonnus of Nisibis." *ARAM* 3 (1991): 115–38.

———. "Apologetics and Historiography in the Annals of Eutychios of Alexandria: Christian Self-Definition in the World of Islam." In *Studies on the Christian Arabic Heritage*, edited by R. Ebied and H. Teule, 65–89. Eastern Christian Studies, 5. Leuven, Belgium: Peeters, 2004.

———. "Arab Christian Culture in the Early Abbasid Period." *Bulletin of the Royal Institute for Inter-Faith Studies* 1 (1999): 25–44.

———. *Arabic Christianity in the Monasteries of Ninth-Century Palestine.* Collected Studies Series, 380. Aldershot, UK: Variorum/Ashgate, 1992.

———. "Arguing from Scripture: The Bible in the Christian/Muslim Encounter in the Middle Ages." In *Scripture and Pluralism: Reading the Bible in the Religiously Plural Worlds of the Middle Ages and Renaissance*, edited by T. J. Heffernan and T. E. Burman, 29–58. Studies in the History of Christian Traditions, 123. Leiden: Brill, 2006.

———. *The Beginnings of Christian Theology in Arabic: Muslim-Christian Encounters in the Early Islamic Period.* Collected Studies Series, 746. Aldershot, UK: Variorum/Ashgate, 2002.

———. "Byzantium and the Christians in the World of Islam: Constantinople and the Church in the Holy Land in the Ninth Century." *Medieval Encounters* 3 (1997): 231–65.

———. *Byzantium and the Early Islamic Conquests.* Cambridge: Cambridge University Press, 1992.

———. "Chapter Ten of the Scholion: Theodore bar Kônî's Apology for Christianity." *Orientalia Christiana Periodica* 47 (1981): 158–88.

———. "Christians, Muslims, and Neo-Martyrs: Saints' Lives and Holy Land History." In *Sharing the Sacred: Religious Contacts and Conflicts in the Holy Land; First-Fifteenth Centuries CE*, edited by Arieh Kofsky and Guy G. Stroumsa, 163–207. Jerusalem: Yad Izhak Ben Zvi, 1998.

———. "The Church of Jerusalem and the 'Melkites': The Making of an 'Arab Orthodox' Christian Identity in the World of Islam, 750–1050 CE." In *Christians and Christianity in the Holy Land: From the Origins to the Latin Kingdoms*, edited by Ora Limor and G. G. Stroumsa, 173–202. Turnhout, Belgium: Brepols, 2006).

———. "Comparative Religion in the Apologetics of the First Christian Arabic Theologians." *Proceedings of the PMR Conference: Annual Publication of the Patristic, Mediaeval and Renaissance Conference* 4 (1979): 63–87.

———. "The Concept of *al-uqnūm* in ʿAmmār al-Baṣrī's Apology for the Doctrine of the Trinity." In *Actes du premier congrès international d'études arabes chrétiennes (Goslar, septembre 1980)*, edited by Samir Khalil Samir, 169–91. Orientalia Christiana Analecta, 218. Rome: Pontificium Institutum Studiorum Orientalium, 1982.

———. "The Controversial Theology of Theodore Abū Qurrah: A Methodological, Comparative Study in Christian Arabic Literature." PhD diss., Catholic University of America, 1978, 86–133.

———. "Disputes with Muslims in Syriac Christian Texts: From Patriarch John (d. 648) to Bar Hebraeus (d. 1286)." In *Religionsgespräche im Mittelalter*, edited by B. Lewis and F. Niewöhner, 257–59. Wolfenbütteler Mittelalter-Studien, 4. Wiesbaden: Harrassowitz, 1992.

———. "Disputing with Islam in Syriac: The Case of the Monk of Bêt Ḥālê with a Muslim Emir." *Hugoye* 3.1 (January, 2000), http://Syrcom.cua.edu/Hugoye/Vol3No1/HV3N1/Griffith.html.

———. "Faith and Reason in Christian Kalām: Theodore Abū Qurrah on Discerning the True Religion." In *Christian Arabic Apologetics during the Abbasid Period (750–1258)*, edited by S. Kh. Samir and J. S. Nielsen, 1–43. Studies in the History of Religions, vol. 63. Leiden: Brill, 1994.

———. "From Aramaic to Arabic: The Languages of the Monasteries of Palestine in the Byzantine and Early Islamic Periods." *Dumbarton Oaks Papers* 51 (1997): 11–31.

———. "The Gospel in Arabic: An Inquiry into Its Appearance in the First Abbasid Century." *Oriens Christianus* 69 (1985): 126–67.

———. "Greek into Arabic: Life and Letters in the Monasteries of Palestine in the 9th Century: The Example of the *Summa Theologiae Arabica*." *Orientalia Christiana Analecta* 226 (1986): 123–41.

———. "Ḥabīb ibn Ḫidmah Abū Rāʾiṭah, a Christian *mutakallim* of the First Abbasid Century." *Oriens Christianus* 64 (1980): 161–201.

———. "Images, Islam, and Christian Icons: A Moment in the Christian/Muslim Encounter in Early Islamic Times." In *La Syrie de Byzance à l'Islam VIIe–VIIIe siècles. Actes du Colloque International Lyon-Maison de l'Orient Mediterranéen, Paris—Institut du Monde Arabe, 11–15 Septembre 1990*, edited by P. Canivet and J.-P. Rey-Coquais, 121–38. Damascus: Institut Français de Damas, 1992.

———. "Islam and the Summa Theologiae Arabica; *Rabīʿ* I, 264 A.H." *Jerusalem Studies in Arabic and Islam* 13 (1990): 225–64.
———. "Jews and Muslims in Christian Syriac and Arabic Texts of the Ninth Century." *Jewish History* 3 (1988): 65–94.
———. "John of Damascus and the Church in Syria in the Umayyad Era: The Intellectual and Cultural Milieu of Orthodox Christians in the World of Islam." In *Giovanni di Damasco: Un Padre al Sorgere dell'Islam.* Atti del XIII Convegno Ecumenico Internazionale di Spiritualità Ortodossa, Sezione Bizantina, 11–13 settembre 2005. Bose, Italy: Monastero di Bose, 2006, 21–52.
———. "Kenneth Cragg on Christians and the Call to Islam." *Religious Studies Review* 20 (1994): 29–35.
———. "The *Kitāb miṣbāḥ al-ʿaql* of Severus ibn al-Muqaffaʿ: A Profile of the Christian Creed in Arabic in Tenth Century Egypt." *Medieval Encounters* 2 (1996): 15–42.
———. "The *Life of Theodore of Edessa*: History, Hagiography, and Religious Apologetics in Mar Saba Monastery in Early Abbasid Times." In *The Sabaite Heritage in the Orthodox Church from the Fifth Century to the Present*, edited by Joseph Patrich, 147–69. Orientalia Lovaniensia Analecta, 98. Leuven, Belgium: Peeters, 2001.
———. "Melkites, Jacobites, and the Christological Controversies in Arabic in Third/Ninth-Century Syria." In *Syrian Christians under Islam: The First Thousand Years*, edited by David Thomas, 9–55. Leiden: Brill, 2001.
———. "The Monk in the Emir's *Majlis*: Reflections on a Popular Genre of Christian Literary Apologetics in Arabic in the Early Islamic Period." In *The Majlis: Interreligious Encounters in Medieval Islam*, edited by Hava Lazarus-Yafeh et al., 4: 13–65. Studies in Arabic Language and Literature. Wiesbaden: Harrassowitz, 1999.
———. "The Monks of Palestine and the Growth of Christian Literature in Arabic." *The Muslim World* 78 (1988): 1–28.
———. "Muḥammad and the Monk Baḥîrâ: Reflections on a Syriac and Arabic Text from Early Abbasid Times." *Oriens Christianus* 79 (1995): 146–74.
———. "The Muslim Philosopher al-Kindī and His Christian Readers: Three Arab Christian Texts on 'The Dissipation of Sorrows.'" *Bulletin of the John Rylands University Library of Manchester* 78 (1996): 111–27.
———. "Muslims and Church Councils: The Apology of Theodore Abū Qurrah." In *Studia Patristica*, edited by E. A. Livingstone, 25: 270–99. Louvain, Belgium: Peeters, 1993.
———. "A Ninth Century *Summa Theologiae Arabica*." In *Actes du Deuxième Congrès International d'Études Arabes Chrétiennes (Oosterhesselen, septembre 1984)*, edited by S. K. Samir, 123–41. Orientalia Christiana Analecta, 226. Rome: Pontificio Istituto degli Studii Orientali, 1986.
———. "The Prophet Muḥammad, His Scripture and His Message According to the Christian Apologies in Arabic and Syriac from the First Abbasid Century." In *La vie du prophète Mahomet; colloque de Strasbourg—1980*, edited by T. Fahd, 118–22. Paris: Presses Universitaires de France, 1983.
———. "The Qurʾān in Arab Christian Texts: The Development of an Apologet-

ical Argument: Abū Qurrah in the *Maǧlis* of al-Ma'mūn." *Parole de l'Orient* 24 (1999): 203–33.

———. "Reflections on the Biography of Theodore Abū Qurrah." *Parole de l'Orient* 18 (1993): 143–70.

———. "Sharing the Faith of Abraham: The 'Credo' of Louis Massignon." *Islam and Christian-Muslim Relations* 8 (1997): 193–210.

———. "The Signs and Wonders of Orthodoxy: Miracles and Monks' Lives in Sixth-Century Palestine." In *Miracles in Jewish and Christian Antiquity: Imagining Truth*, edited by John Cavadini, 139–68. Notre Dame Studies in Theology, vol. 3. Notre Dame: IN: University of Notre Dame Press, 1999.

———. "Some Unpublished Arabic Sayings Attributed to Theodore Abū Qurrah." *Le Muséon* 92 (1979): 29–35.

———. "Stephen of Ramlah and the Christian Kerygma in Arabic in Ninth-Century Palestine." *Journal of Ecclesiastical History* 36 (1985): 23–45.

———. *Syriac Writers on Muslims and the Religious Challenge of Islam*. Mōrān 'Ethʾō, 7. Kottayam, India: St. Ephraem Ecumenical Research Institute, 1995.

———. "Theodore Abū Qurrah's Arabic Tract on the Christian Practice of Venerating Images." *Journal of the American Oriental Society* 105 (1985): 58.

———. "Theodore bar Kônî's Apology for Christianity." *Orientalia Christiana Periodica* 47 (1981): 158–88.

———. "Theodore bar Kônî's *Scholion*: A Nestorian *Summa contra Gentiles* from the First Abbasid Century." In *East of Byzantium: Syria and Armenia in the Formative Period*, edited by N. Garsoïan, T. Mathews, and R. Thomson, 53–72. Washington, DC: Dumbarton Oaks, 1982.

———. "Theology and the Arab Christian: The Case of the 'Melkite' Creed." In *A Faithful Presence: Essays for Kenneth Cragg*, edited by David Thomas, 184–200. London: Melisende, 2003.

———. "The View of Islam from the Monasteries of Palestine in the Early ʿAbbāsid Period." *Islam and Christian-Muslim Relations* 7 (1996): 9–28.

———. "What Has Constantinople to Do with Jerusalem? Palestine in the Ninth Century; Byzantine Orthodoxy in the World of Islam." In *Byzantium in the Ninth Century: Dead or Alive? Papers from the Thirtieth Spring Symposium of Byzantine Studies, Birmingham, March 1996*, edited by Leslie Brubaker, 181–94. Aldershot, UK, and Brookfield, VT: Variorum, 1998.

———. "Yaḥyā ibn ʿAdī's Colloquy on Sexual Abstinence and the Philosophical Life." In *Arabic Theology, Arabic Philosophy; from the Many to the One: Essays in Celebration of Richard M. Frank*, edited by James E. Montgomery. Orientalia Lovaniensia Analecta. Leuven, Belgium: Peeters, 2006, 299–333.

———, intro. and trans. *A Treatise on the Veneration of the Holy Icons Written in Arabic by Theodore Abū Qurrah, Bishop of Ḥarrān; Translated into English, with Introduction and Notes.* Eastern Christian Texts in Translation, 1. Leuven, Belgium: Peeters, 1997.

Grillmeier, Aloys, and Theresia Hainthaler. *Christ in Christian Tradition*, vol. 2, "From the Council of Chalcedon (451) to Gregory the Great (590–604), part 2, The Church of Constantinople in the Sixth Century." Translated by John Cawte and Pauline Allen. London: Mowbray, and Louisville, KY: Westminster John Knox Press, 1995.

———. *Christ in Christian Tradition*, vol. 2, "From the Council of Chalcedon (451) to Gregory the Great (590–604), part 4, The Church of Alexandria with Nubia and Ethiopia after 451. Translated by O. C. Dean. London: Mowbray, and Louisville, KY: Westminster John Knox Press, 1996.

———, et al. *Jesus der Christus im Glauben der Kirche*, Band 2/3, "Die Kirchen von Jerusalem und Antiochien nach 451 bis 600." Freiburg: Herder, 2002.

Gude, Mary Louise, *Louis Massignon: The Crucible of Compassion*. Notre Dame, IN: University of Notre Dame Press, 1996.

Guillaume, Alfred, "A Debate between Christian and Muslim Doctors." *Journal of the Royal Asiatic Society*, Centenary Supplement (October 1924): 233–44.

———. *The Life of Muhammad: A Translation of Ibn Ishaq's Sirat Rasul Allah*. Karachi: Oxford University Press, 1978.

———. "Theodore Abu Qurra as Apologist." *The Moslem World* 15 (1925): 42–51.

Gutas, Dimitri. *Avicenna and the Aristotelian Tradition*. Leiden: Brill, 1988. 64–72.

———. *Greek Thought, Arabic Culture: The Graeco-Arabic Translation Movement in Baghdad and Early ʿAbbāsid Society (2nd–4th/8th–10th Centuries)*. London and New York: Routledge, 1998.

———. "Paul the Persian on the Classification of the Parts of Aristotle's Philosophy: A Milestone between Alexandria and Bagdad." *Der Islam* 60 (1983): 231–67, esp. 250.

Haddad, Rachid. *La trinité divine chez les théologiens arabes (750–1050)*. Paris: Beauchesne, 1985.

Haddad, Robert M. "Conversion of Eastern Orthodox Christians to the Unia in the Seventeenth and Eighteenth Centuries." In Gervers and Bikhazi, *Conversion and Continuity*, 449–59.

———. "On Melkite Passage to the Unia: The Case of Patriarch Cyril al-Zaʿīm (1672–1720)." In *Christians and Jews in the Ottoman Empire*, 2 vols., edited by B. Braude and B. Lewis, 2: 67–90. New York: Holmes and Meier, 1982.

———. *Syrian Christians in Muslim Society: An Interpretation*. Princeton, NJ: Princeton University Press, 1970.

Haddad, Wadi Z., "Continuity and Change in Religious Adherence: Ninth-Century Baghdad." In Gervers and Bikhazi, *Conversion and Continuity*, 33–53.

Hadot, Pierre, *Philosophy as a Way of Life*. Translated by Michael Chase. Oxford: Blackwell, 1995.

———. *What Is Ancient Philosophy?* Translated by Michael Chase. Cambridge, MA: Harvard University Press, 2002.

Hage, W., *Die syrisch-jakobitische Kirche in frühislamischer Zeit*. Wiesbaden: Harrassowitz, 1966.

Hainthaler, Theresia. "Die 'antiochenische Schule' und theologische Schulen im Bereich des antiochenischen Patriarchats." In Grillmeier et al., *Jesus der Christus im Glauben der Kirche*, Band 2/3, 227–61.

———. "Aufbau der antichalcedonischen Hierarchie durch Jakob Baradai." In Grillmeier, *Jesus der Christus im Glauben der Kirche*, Band 2/3, 197–203.

———. "John Philoponus, Philosopher and Theologian in Alexandria." In Grillmeier and Hainthaler, *Christ in Christian Tradition*, vol. 2, part 4, 107–46.

Halleux, André de. *Philoxène de Mabbog: Sa vie, ses écrits, sa théologie*. Louvain, Belgium: Imprimerie Orientaliste, 1963.

Harper, George Mills. *The Making of Yeats's* A Vision: *A Study of the Automatic Script.* 2 vols. Carbondale and Edwardsville: Southern Illinois University Press, 1987.

Harpigny, G. *Islam et christianisme selon Louis Massignon.* Homo Religiosus, 6. Louvain-La-Neuve, Belgium: Centre d'Histoire des Religions, 1981.

Harrak, Amir, trans. *The Chronicle of Zuqnīn: Parts III and IV; A.D. 488–775.* Mediaeval Sources in Translation, 36. Toronto: Pontifical Institute of Mediaeval Studies, 1999.

———. "Piecing Together the Fragmentary Account of the Martyrdom of Cyrus of Ḥarrān." *Analecta Bollandiana* 121 (2003): 297–328.

Harvey, Steven. "Islamic Philosophy and Jewish Philosophy." In Adamson and Taylor, *The Cambridge Companion to Arabic Philosophy*, 349–69.

Hayek, Michel. ʿAmmr *al-Baṣrī; apologie et conroverses.* Beirut: Dar el-Machreq, 1977.

———. *Le mystère d'Ishmael.* Paris: Mame, 1964.

Heck, Paul L. "*Jihād* Revisited." *Journal of Religious Ethics* 32 (2004): 95–128.

Heijer, Johannes den. *Mawhūb ibn Manṣūr ibn Mufarrij et l'historiographie copto-arabe: Étude sur la composition de l'Histoire des Patriarches d'Alexandrie.* CSCO, vol. 513. Louvain, Belgium: Peeters, 1989.

Henninger, J. "Spuren christlicher Glaubenswahrheiten im Koran." *Neue Zeitschrift für Missionswissenschaft/Nouvelle Revue de science missionaire* 1 (1945): 135–40, 304–14; 2 (1946): 56–65, 109–22, 289–304; 3 (1947): 128–40, 290–301; 4 (1948): 129–41, 284–93; 5 (1949): 127–40, 290–300; 6 (1950): 207–17, 284–97.

Hespel, R., and R. Draguet. *Theodore bar Koni Livre des Scolies.* CSCO, vols. 431 and 432. Louvain, Belgium: Peeters, 1981 and 1982.

Heyberger, Bernard. *Les Chrétiens du Proche-Orient: Au temps de la réforme catholique (Syrie, Liban, Palestine, XVIIe–XVIIIe siècles).* Rome: École Française de Rome, 1994.

Hoeberichts, J. *Francis and Islam.* Quincy, IL: Franciscan Press, 1997.

Holmberg, Bo. "Notes on a Treatise on the Unity and Trinity of God Attributed to Yaḥyā ibn ʿAdī." In *Actes du deuxième congrès international d'études arabes chrétiennes,* edited by Samir Khalil Samir, 235–45. Orientalia Christiana Analecta, 226. Rome: Pont. Institutum Studiorum Orientalium, 1986.

———. *A Treatise on the Unity and Trinity of God by Israel of Kashkar (d. 872).* Lund, Sweden: Plus Ultra, 1989.

Hourani, Albert. *A History of the Arab Peoples.* New York: Warner Books, 1992.

Hoyland, Robert G. *Seeing Islam as Others Saw It: A Survey and Evaluation of Christian, Jewish, and Zoroastrian Writings on Early Islam.* Studies in Late Antiquity and Early Islam, 13. Princeton, NJ: Darwin Press, 1997.

Hugonnard-Roche, Henri. *La logique d'Aristote du grec au syriaque: Études sur la transmission des texts de l'Organon et leur interpretation philosophique.* Textes et Traditions, no. 9. Paris: Librairie Philosophique J. Vrin, 2004.

———. "Note dur Sergius de Reshʿayna, traducteur du grec en syriaque et commentateur d'Aristote." In Endress and Kruk, *The Ancient Tradition in Christian and Islamic Hellenism*, 121–43.

———. "Aux origines de l'exégèse orientale de la logique d'Aristote: Sergius de Reshʿayna (d. 536), médecin et philosophe." *Journal Asiatique* 277 (1989): 1–17.

Huntington, Samuel. *The Clash of Civilizations and the Remaking of World Order.* New York: Touchstone, 1996.

———. "Islam and the Clash of Civilizations." *Foreign Affairs* 72 (1993): 245–61.

Hurst, Thomas R. "Letter 40 of the Nestorian Patriarch Timothy I (727–823): An Edition and Translation." Master's thesis, Catholic University of America, 1981.

———. "The Syriac Letters of Timothy I (727–823): A Study in Christian-Muslim Controversy." PhD diss., Catholic University of America, 1986.

Hussey, J. M. *The Orthodox Church in the Byzantine Empire.* Oxford History of the Christian Church. Oxford: Clarendon Press, 1986.

Hyman, Arthur. "Jewish Philosophy in the Islamic World." In Nasr and Leaman, *History of Islamic Philosophy*, 1: 677–95.

Iskandar, Albert Z. "Al-Rāzī." In *Religion, Learning, and Science in the ʿAbbasid Period*, edited by M. J. L. Young et al., 370–77. Cambridge: Cambridge University Press, 1990.

———. "Ḥunayn the Translator," and "Ḥunayn the Physician." In Gillispie, *Dictionary of Scientific Biography*, vol. 15, supplement 1, 234–49.

Jager, Peter. "Intended Edition of a Disputation between a Monk of the Monastery of Bet Ḥālê and One of the Ṭayôyê." In Drijvers, *IV Symposium Syriacum*, 401–2.

Jolivet, Jean. *La théologie et les arabes.* Paris: Cerf, 2002.

Kaegi, Walter E. *Byzantium and the Early Islamic Conquests.* Cambridge: Cambridge University Press, 1992.

———. *Heraclius, Emperor of Byzantium.* Cambridge: Cambridge University Press, 2003.

———. "Initial Byzantine Reactions to the Arab Invasions." *Church History* 10 (1969): 139–49.

Keating, Sandra Toenies. "Dialogue between Muslims and Christians in the Early 9th Century: The Example of Ḥabīb ibn Khidmah Abū Rāʾiṭah al-Takrītī's Theology of the Trinity." PhD diss., Catholic University of America, 2001.

———. "Ḥabīb ibn Khidma Abū Rāʾiṭa al-Takrītī's 'The Refutation of the Melkites concerning the Union [of the Divinity and Humanity in Christ].'" In Thomas, *Christians at the Heart of Islamic Rule*, 39–53.

Kedar, Benjamin Z. *Crusade and Mission: European Approaches toward the Muslims.* Princeton, NJ: Princeton University Press, 1984.

Kegley, Charles W., Jr., ed. *The New Global Terrorism: Characteristics, Causes, Controls.* Upper Saddle River, NJ: Prentice-Hall, 2003.

Kellermann-Rost, M. "Ein pseudoaristotelischer traktat über die Tugend: Edition und Übersetzung der arabischen Fassungen des Abū Qurra und des Ibn aṭ-Ṭayyib." Unpublished PhD diss., Erlangen, 1965.

Kennedy, Hugh. "The Decline and Fall of the First Muslim Empire." *Der Islam* 81 (2004): 3–30.

Kessler, Christel. "ʿAbd al-Malik's Inscription in the Dome of the Rock: A Reconsideration." *Journal of the Royal Asiatic Society* (1970): 2–14.

Khalifat, Sahban. *Yaḥyā ibn ʿAdī: The Philosophical Treatises; a Critical Edition with an Introduction* (Arabic). Amman: University of Jordan, 1988.

Khalifé, A., and W. Kutsch. "Ar-radd ʿalā n-naṣārā de ʿAlī aṭ-Ṭabarī." *Mélanges de l'Université de Saint Joseph*, 36 (1959): 115–48.

Khoury, Adel-Théodore. "Apologétique Byzantine contre l'Islam." *Proche Orient Chrétien* 29 (1979): 242–300; 30 (1980): 132–74; 32 (1982): 14–49.

———. *Apologétique Byzantine contre l'Islam; VIIIe–XIIIe siècles*. Altenberge, Germany: Verlag für christlich-islamisches Schrifttum, 1982.

———. *Les théologiens byzantins et l'Islam: Textes et Auteurs, VIIIe–XIIIe's*. Leuven, Belgium: Nauwelaerts, 1969.

———. *Polémique Byzantine contre l'Islam*. Leiden: Brill, 1972.

Khoury, Paul, *Matériaux pour servir à l'étude de la controverse théologique islamo-chrétienne de langue arabe du VIIIe au XII siècle*. 4 vols. Religionswissenschaftliche Studien, 11: 1–4. Würzburg and Altenberge: Echter and Oros Verlag, 1989–99.

———. *Paul d'Antioche: Évêque melkite de Sidon*. Beirut: Imprimerie Catholique, 1964.

Kilpatrick, Hilary. "Monasteries through Muslim Eyes: The *Diyārāt* Books." In Thomas, *Christians at the Heart of Islamic Rule*, 19–37.

King, G. R. D. "Islam, Iconoclasm, and the Declaration of Doctrine." *Bulletin of the School of Oriental and African Studies* 48 (1985): 267–77.

Kiser, John W. *The Monks of Tibhirine: Faith, Love, and Terror in Algeria*. New York: St. Martin's Press, 2002.

Klinghoffer, David. *The Discovery of God: Abraham and the Birth of Monotheism*. New York: Doubleday, 2003.

Kollamparampil, Thomas. *Jacob of Serugh: Select Festal Homilies*. Rome: Center for Indian and Inter-Religious Studies, and Bangalore: Dharmaram Publications, 1997.

———. *Salvation in Christ according to Jacob of Serugh*. Bangalore: Dharmaram Publications, 2001.

Koningsveld, Pieter Sjoerd van. "La literature cristiano-árabe de la España Medieval y el significado de la transmission textual en árabe de la Collectio Conciliorum." In *Concilio III de Toledo: XIV Centenario, 589–1989*, 695–710. Toledo: Arzobispado de Toledo, 1991.

Kraemer, Joel L. *Humanism in the Renaissance of Islam: The Cultural Revival during the Buyid Age*. Leiden: Brill, 1986.

———. *Philosophy in the Renaissance of Islam: Abū Sulaymān al-Sijistānī and His Circle*. Leiden: Brill, 1986.

Kratz, Reinhard G., and Tilman Nagel, eds. *'Abraham, unser Vater': Die gemeinsamen Wurzeln von Judentum, Christentum und Islam*. Göttingen: Wallstein Verlag, 2003.

Krtizeck, James. *Peter the Venerable and Islam*. Princeton, NJ: Princeton University Press, 1964.

Kruisheer, Dirk, and Lucas Van Rompay. "A Bibliographical *Clavis* to the Works of Jacob of Edessa." *Hugoye* 1 (1998), http://syrcom.cua.edu/Hugoye/Vol1No1/Clavis.html.

Küng, Hans. *Der Islam: Geschichte, Gegenwart, Zukunft.* Munich and Zurich: Piper, 2004.

Lamb, Christopher. *The Call to Retrieval: Kenneth Cragg's Christian Vocation to Islam.* London: Gray Seal, 1997.

Lameer, Joep. "From Alexandria to Baghdad: Reflections on the Genesis of a Problematical Tradition." In Endress and Kruk, *The Ancient Tradition in Christian and Islamic Hellenism,* 181–91.

Lammens, Henri. "Le chantre des Omiades: Notes biographiques et littéraires sur le poète arabe chrétien Aḫṭal." *Journal Asiatique* n.s. 4 (1894): 94–241, 381–459.

Lamoreaux, John C. "The Biography of Theodore Abū Qurrah Revisited." *Dumbarton Oaks Papers* 56 (2002): 25–40.

———. *Theodore Abū Qurrah.* Provo, UT: Brigham Young University Press, 2006.

Landauer, Samuel, ed. *Kitāb al-amânât wa l-itiqâdât von Sa'adja b. Jûsuf al-Fajjûmî.* Leiden: Brill, 1880.

Landron, Bénédicte. "Les chrétiens arabes et les disciplines philosophiques." *Proche Orient Chrétien* 36 (1986),: 23–45.

———. *Chrétiens et musulmans en Irak: Attitudes Nestoriennes vis-à-vis de l'Islam.* Paris: Cariscript, 1994.

Lasker, Daniel J. "Rabbinism and Karaism: The Contest for Supremacy." In *Great Schisms in Jewish History,* edited by R. Jospe and S. M. Wagner, 47–72. New York: Ktav Publishing House, 1981.

———, and Sarah Stroumsa, eds. and trans. *The Polemic of Nestor the Priest: Qiṣṣat Mujādalat al-Usquf and Sefer Nestor Ha-Komer.* 2 vols. Jerusalem: Ben Zvi Institute, 1996.

Lazarus-Yafeh, Hava. *Intertwined Worlds: Medieval Islam and Bible Criticism.* Princeton, NJ: Princeton University Press, 1992.

———, et al., eds. *The Majlis: Interreligious Encounters in Medieval Islam.* Studies in Arabic Language and Literature, vol. 4. Wiesbaden: Harrassowitz, 1999.

Le Batelier, Nasreddin. *Le statut des moines en islam.* Beirut: Éditions el-Safina, 1997.

Lebon, Joseph. "La christologie du monophysisme syrien." In *Das Konzil von Chalkedon: Geschichte und Gegenwart,* 3 vols., edited by Aloys Grillmeier and Heinrich Bacht, 1: 425–580. Würzburg: Echter Verlag, 1951–54.

———. *Le monophysisme severien: Étude historique, littéraire et théologique sur la resistance monophysite au Concile de Chalcedoine jusqu'a la constitution de l'église jacobite.* Louvain, Belgium: J. Van Linthout, 1909; repr., New York: AMS Press, 1978.

Le Coz, Raymond. *Histoire de l'église d'orient: Chrétiens d'Irak, d'Iran et de Turquie.* Paris: Cerf, 1995.

———. *Les médecins nestoriens au moyen âge: Les maîtres des arabes.* Paris: L'Harmattan, 2004.

———, ed. *Jean Damascène: Écrits sur Islam.* Sources Chrétiens, 383. Paris: Cerf, 1992.

Lemmens, Leonardus, "De Sancto Francisco Christum Praedicante coram Sultano Aegypti." *Archivum Franciscanum Historicum* 19 (1926): 559–78.

Lewis, Bernard. *The Crisis of Islam: Holy War and Unholy Terror*. New York: Modern Library, 2003.

———. *Cultures in Conflict: Christians, Muslims, and Jews in the Age of Discovery*. New York: Oxford University Press, 1995.

———. *From Babel to Dragomans: Interpreting the Middle East*. Oxford and New York: Oxford University Press, 2004.

———. *Islam and the West*. New York: Oxford University Press, 1993.

———. *The Jews of Islam*. Princeton, NJ: Princeton University Press, 1984.

———. *The Middle East: 2000 Years of History from the Rise of Christianity to the Present Day*. London: Weidenfeld and Nicholson, 1995.

———. *The Multiple Identities of the Middle East*. New York: Schocken Books, 1998.

———. *The Muslim Discovery of Europe*. New York: W. W. Norton, 1982.

———. *What Went Wrong?: The Clash between Islam and Modernity in the Middle East*. New York: Perennial, 2003.

Littmann, Giselle. *See* Ye'or, Bat.

Louth, Andrew. "St. John Damascene: Preacher and Poet." In *Preacher and Audience: Studies in Early Christian and Byzantine Homiletics*, edited by P. Allen and M. Cunningham, 249. Leiden: Brill, 1998.

———. *St. John Damascene: Tradition and Originality in Byzantine Theology*. Oxford Early Christian Studies. Oxford: Oxford University Press, 2002.

———, trans. and intro. *Three Treatises on the Divine Images: St. John of Damascus*. Crestwood, NY: St. Vladimir's Seminary Press, 2003.

Lowney, Chris. *A Vanished World: Medieval Spain's Golden Age of Enlightenment*. New York: Free Press, 2005.

Luxenberg, Christoph. *Die syro-aramäische Lesart des Koran*. Berlin: Das arabische Buch, 2000.

Madelung, Wilferd. "Al-Qāsim ibn Ibrāhīm and Christian Theology," *ARAM* 3 (1991): 35–44.

Mahdi, Muhsin. *Alfarabi and the Foundation of Islamic Political Philosophy*. Chicago: University of Chicago Press, 2001.

———. "Language and Logic in Classical Islam." In *Logic in Classical Islamic Culture*, edited by E. von Grunebaum, 51–83. Wiesbaden: Harrassowitz, 1970.

Mahé, J.-P. "L'église areménienne de 611 à 1066." In *Histoire du Christianisme*, edited by J. M. Mayeur, 4: 457–547; Paris: Desclée, 1993.

Makdisi, George. *The Rise of Colleges: Institutions of Learning in Islam and the West*. Edinburgh: Edinburgh University Press, 1981.

———. *The Rise of Humanism in Classical Islam and the Christian West: With Special Reference to Scholasticism*. Edinburgh: Edinburgh University Press, 1990.

Malingrey, Anne-Marie. *"Philosophia": Étude d'un groupe de mots dans la literature grecque, des Présocratiques au IVe siècle après J.-C.* Paris: Librairie C. Klincksieck, 1961.

Mansour, Tanios Bou. "Die Christologie des Jakob von Sarug." In Grillmeier, *Jesus der Christus im Glauben der Kirche*, Band 2/3, 449–99.

———. *La théologie de Jacques de Saroug*. 2 vols. Bibliothèque de l'Université Saint-Esprit, vols. 16 and 40. Kaslik, Lebanon: Université Saint-Esprit, 1993 and 2000.

Marcuzzo, Giacinto Bulus. *Le dialogue d'Abraham de Tibériade avec ʿAbd al-Raḥmān al-Hāšimī à Jérusalem vers 820.* Textes et Études sur l'Orient Chretien, 3. Rome: Pontificio Istituto Orientale, 1986.

Margoliouth, D. S. "The Discussion between Abū Bishr Mattā and Abū Saʿīd al-Sīrāfī." *Journal of the Royal Asiatic Society* (1905): 79–129.

Martin, Fr. "Homélie de Narsai sur les trois docteurs nestoriens." *Journal Asiatique* 9th ser. 14 (1899): 446–92; 15 (1900): 469–525.

Martin, Richard. "The Role of the Basrah Muʿtazilah in Formulating the Doctrine of the Apologetic Miracle." *Journal of Near Eastern Studies* 39 (1980): 175–89.

Martínez, Francisco Javier. "La literatura apocalíptica y las primeras reacciones cristianas a la conquista islámica en Oriente." In *Europa y el Islam*, edited by Gonzalo Anes y Álvarez de Castrillón, 143–222. Madrid: Real Academia de la Historia, 2003.

Mason, Herbert. *Memoir of a Friend: Louis Massignon.* Notre Dame, IN: University of Notre Dame Press, 1988.

Massignon, Louis. "La *Mubâhala* de Médine et l'hyperdulie de Fâtima," In Louis Massignon, *Parole donnée*, 147–67. Paris: Éditions du Seuil, 1983.

———. *Opera Minora.* Edited by Y. Moubarac. 3 vols. Beirut: Dar al-Maaref, 1963.

———. "La politique islamo-chrétienne des scribes nestoriens de Deir Qunna á la cour de Bagdad au IXe siècle de notre ère." *Vivre et Penser* 2 (1942): 7–14.

———. *Les trois prières d'Abraham.* Paris: Cerf, 1997.

Mathews, Basil. *Young Islam on Trek: A Study in the Clash of Civilizations.* Boston: Houghton Mifflin, 1923.

McAuliffe, Jane Dammen. "Christians in the Qurʾān and Tafsīr." In Waardenburg, *Muslim Perceptions*, 105–21.

———. "'Debate with them in the better way': The Construction of a Qurʾānic Commonplace." In *Myths, Historical Archetypes and Symbolic Figures in Arabic Literature: Towards a New Hermeneutic Approach*, edited by Angelica Neuwirth et al., 163–88. Beirut: In Kommission bei Franz Steiner Verlag Stuttgart, 1999.

———. *Qurʾānic Christians: An Analysis of Classical and Modern Exegesis.* Cambridge: Cambridge University Press, 1991.

Melitzki, Dorothee. *The Matter of Araby in Medieval England.* New Haven, CT: Yale University Press, 1977.

Merkle, Karl. *Die Sittensprüche der Philosophen, "Kitâb Âdâb al-Falâsifa."* Leipzig: Harrosswitz, 1921.

Mez, Adam. *Die Renaissance des Islams.* Reprografischer Nachdruck der Ausdruck Heidelberg, 1922. Reprint, Hildesheim, Germany: G. Olms, 1968.

Menocal, María Rosa. *The Ornament of the World: How Muslims, Jews, and Christians Created a Culture of Tolerance in Medieval Spain.* Boston: Little, Brown, 2002.

Michel, Thomas F., ed. and trans. *A Muslim Theologian's Response to Christianity: Ibn Taymiyya's al-Jawāb al-Ṣaḥīḥ.* Delmar, NY: Caravan Books, 1984.

Millet-Gérard, Dominique. *Chrétiens mozarabes et culture islamique dans l'Espagne des VIIIe—Ixe siècles.* Paris: Études Augustiniennes, 1984.

Mimouni, Simon C. "Les Nazoréens: Recherche étymologique et historique." *Revue Biblique* 105 (1998): 208–65.

Mingana, Alphonse. "The Apology of Timothy the Patriarch before the Caliph al-Mahdī." *Bulletin of the John Rylands Library* 12 (1928): 137–226.

———. *The Book of Religion and Empire: A Semi-Official Defense and Exposition of Islam Written by Order at the Court and with the Assistance of the Caliph Mutawakkil (A.D. 847–861)*. Manchester: Manchester University Press, and New York: Longmans Green, 1922.

———. *Kitāb ad-dīn wa d-dawlah.* Beirut: Dār al-Afāq al-Jadīdah, 1982.

———. "Timothy's Apology for Christianity." *Woodbrooke Studies: Christian Documents in Syriac, Arabic, and Garshuni; Edited and Translated with a Critical Apparatus*, 2: 1–162. Cambridge: Heffer, 1928.

Mirza, Younus. "Abraham as an Iconoclast: Understanding the Destruction of 'Images' through Qur'anic Exegesis." *Islam and Christian-Muslim Relations* 16 (2005): 413–28.

Mistrih, Vincent. "Traité sur la continence de Yaḥyā ibn ʿAdī; édition critique." *Studia Orientalia Christiana: Collectanea* 16 (1981): 1–137.

Moffett, Samuel H. *A History of Christianity in Asia.* Vol. 1, 2nd rev. and corrected ed. Maryknoll, NY: Orbis Books, 1998 and 2005.

Morony, Michael G. "History and Identity in the Syrian Churches." In van Ginkell et al., *Redefining Christian Identity*, 1–33.

———. *Iraq after the Muslim Conquest.* Princeton, NJ: Princeton University Press, 1984.

Moubarac, Y. *Abraham dans le Coran.* Paris: Vrin, 1958.

Murphy-O'Connor, Jerome. "The Location of the Capitol in Aelia Capitolina." *Revue Biblique* 101 (1994): 407–15.

Muslim-Christian Research Group. *The Challenges of the Scripture: The Bible and the Qur'ān.* Maryknoll, NY: Orbis Books, 1989.

Nasr, Seyyed Hossein, and Oliver Leaman, eds. *History of Islamic Philosophy.* Routledge History of World Philosophies, 2 vols. London and New York: Routledge, 1996.

Nasrallah, Joseph. *Histoire de movement littéraire dans l'église melchite du Ve au XXe siècle.* 4 vols. Louvain, Belgium: Peeters, 1979–89.

Nau, F., "Cinq letters de Jacques d'Édesse à Jean le Stylite (traduction et analyse)." *Revue de l'Orient Chrétien* 14 (1909): 427–40.

———. "Un colloque du patriarche Jean avec l'émir des Agaréens." *Journal Asiatique* 11th ser., 5 (1915): 225–79.

———. "Histoires d'Ahoudemmeh et de Marouta." *Patrologia Orientalis* 3 (1905): 65–66.

———. "Traduction des letters XII et XIII de Jacques d'Édesse." *Revue de l'Orient Chrétien* 10 (1905): 197–208, 258–82.

Newman, N. A. *The Early Christian-Muslim Dialogue: A Collection of Documents from the First Three Islamic Centuries (632–900 A.D.). Translations with Commentary.* Hatfield, PA: Interdisciplinary Biblical Research Institute, 1993.

Nicoll, Alex. "Account of a Disputation between a Christian Monk and Three Learned Mohammedans on the Subject of Religion." In *The Edinburgh Annual Register for 1816*, vol. 9, parts 1 and 2, ccccv–ccccxlii. Edinburgh: A. Richbald Constable, 1820.

Noth, Albrecht. "Abgrenzungsprobleme zwischen Muslimen und Nicht-Muslimen.

Die Bedingungen ʿUmars (*al-Šurūṭ al-ʿumariyya*)." *Jerusalem Studies in Arabic and Islam* 9 (1987): 290–315.

———. "Problems of Differentiation between Muslims and Non-Muslims: Re-Reading the 'Ordinances of ʿUmar' (*al-Šurūṭ al-ʿumariyya*). In *Muslims and Others in Early Islamic Society*, edited by Robert Hoyland, 103–24. The Formation of the Classical Islamic World, vol. 18. Aldershot, UK: Ashgate, 2004.

Novikoff, Alex. "Between Tolerance and Intolerance in Medieval Spain: An Historiographic Enigma." *Medieval Encounters* 11 (2005): 7–36.

Nursi, Bediuzzaman Said. *Risale-I Nur Kulliyati*. 2 vols. Istanbul: Nesil Yayinlari, 1996.

Nwyia, Paul, and Samir Khalil Samir. *Une correspondence islamo-chrétienne entre Ibn al-Munağğim, Ḥunayn ibn Isḥāq et Qusṭa ibn Lūqā*. Patrologia Orientalis, no. 185, vol. 40, fasc. 4. Paris: Brepols, 1981.

Ognibene, Susanna. *Umm al-Rasas: La chiesa di Santo Stefano ed il 'problema iconofobico.'* Rome: L'Erma di Bretschneider, 2002.

Olster, David M. *Roman Defeat, Christian Response, and the Literary Construction of the Jew*. Philadelphia: University of Pennsylvania Press, 1994.

O'Shea, Stephen. *Sea of Faith: Islam and Christianity in the Medieval Mediterranean World*. New York: Walker, 2006.

Pacini, Andrea, ed. *Christian Communities in the Arab Middle East: The Challenge of the Future*. New York: Oxford University Press, 1998.

Palmer, Andrew, ed. *The Seventh Century in the West-Syrian Chronicles*. Translated Texts for Historians, vol. 15. Liverpool: Liverpool University Press, 1993.

Peeters, F. E. *Aristotle and the Arabs: The Aristotelian Tradition in Islam*. New York: New York University Press, 1968.

———. *Aristoteles Arabus: The Oriental Translations and Commentaries on the Aristotelian Corpus*. Leiden: Brill, 1968.

Pelikan, Jaroslav. *Christianity and Classical Culture; the Metamorphosis of Natural Theology in the Christian Encounter with Hellenism*. The Gifford Lectures, 1992/93. New Haven, CT: Yale University Press, 1993.

Penn, Michael. "Syriac Sources for the Study of Early Christian-Muslim Relations." *Islamochristiana* 29 (2003): 59–78.

Peradze, B. "An Account of the Georgian Monks and Monasteries in Palestine." *Georgica* 4–5 (1937): 181–237.

Peri, Oded. *Christianity under Islam in Jerusalem: The Question of the Holy Sites in Early Ottoman Times*. Leiden: Brill, 2001.

Périer, Augustin. "Un traité de Yahyâ ben ʿAdî: Defense du dogme de la trinité contre les objections d'al-Kindî." *Revue de l'Orient Chrétien* 3rd ser., 2 (1920–21): 3–21.

Perlmann, Moshe, ed. *Sa'd B. Manṣūr ibn Kammūna's Examination of the Inquiries into the Three Faiths: A Thirteenth-Century Essay in Comparative Religion*. Berkeley: University of California Press, 1967.

———, trans. *Ibn Kammūna's Examination of the Three Faiths: A Thirteenth-Century Essay in the Comparative Study of Religion; Translated from the Arabic, with an Introduction and Notes*. Berkeley: University of California Press, 1971.

Peters, F. E. *The Children of Abraham: Judaism, Christianity, Islam*. New rev. ed. Princeton, NJ: Princeton University Press, 2004.

Piccirillo, Michele. *L'Arabia Cristiana; dalla Provincia Imperiale al Primo Periodo Islamico*. Milan: Jaca Book, 2002.

Pines, Shlomo. "Some Traits of Christian Theological Writing in Relation to Moslem *Kalām* and to Jewish Thought." In Shlomo Pines, *Studies in the History of Arabic Philosophy*, The Collected Works of Shlomo Pines, 3: 105–25 [79–99]. Jerusalem: Magnes Press, 1996.

———, trans. *Moses Maimonides: The Guide of the Perplexed*. 2 vols. Chicago: University of Chicago Press, 1963.

———, and Michael Schwarz. "Yaḥyā ibn ʿAdī's Refutation of the Doctrine of Acquisition (*iktisāb*)." In *Studia Orientalia Memoriae D. H. Baneth Dedicata*, 49–94. Jerusalem: Magnes Press, Hebrew University of Jerusalem, 1979.

Platti, Emilio. "Une cosmologie chrétienne." *MIDEO* 15 (1982): 75–118.

———. "Deux manuscripts théologiques de Yaḥyā ibn ʿAdī." *MIDEO* 12 (1974): 217–29

———. *La grande polémique antinestorienne (et la discussion avec Muḥammad al-Misrī)*. CSCO, vols. 427–28. Louvain, Belgium: Peeters, 1981.

———. "Islam et Occident: '*Choc de theologies*'?" *Mélanges*, 347–79. Institut Dominicain d'Études Orientales du Caire. Louvain, Belgium: Peeters, 2000.

———. "Yaḥyā ibn ʿAdī and the Theory of *Iktisāb*." In Thomas, *Christians at the Heart of Islamic Rule*, 151–57.

———. "Yaḥyā ibn ʿAdī, philosophe et théologien." *MIDEO* 14 (1980): 167–84.

———. *Yaḥyā ibn ʿAdī: Théologien chrétien et philosophe arabe; sa théologie de l'incarnation*. Orientalia Lovaniensia Analecta, 14. Leuven, Belgium: Katholieke Universiteit Leuven, Departement Orientalistiek, 1983.

———, trans. *Abū ʿĪsā al-Warrāq, Yaḥyā ibn ʿAdī; de l'Incarnation*. CSCO, vols. 490 and 491. Louvain, Belgium: Peeters, 1987.

Poliack, Meira. "Rethinking Karaism: Between Judaism and Islam." *AJS Review* 30 (2006): 67–93.

Pontifical Council for Interreligious Dialogue. *Guidelines for Dialogue between Christians and Muslims*. Interreligious Documents, 1. Prepared by Maurice Borrmans, translated by R. Marston Speight. New York: Paulist Press, 1990.

———. *Recognize the Spiritual Bonds Which Unite Us: 16 Years of Christian-Muslim Dialogue*. Vatican City: Pontifical Council for Interreligious Dialogue, 1994.

Pritz, Ray A. *Nazarene Jewish Christianity: From the End of the New Testament Period until Its Disappearance in the Fourth Century*. Jerusalem: Magnes Press, and Leiden: E. J. Brill, 1988.

Pulcini, Theodore. *Exegesis as Polemical Discourse: Ibn Ḥazm on Jewish and Christian Scriptures*. Atlanta: Scholars Press, 1998.

Putman, Hans. *L'église et l'islam sous Timothée I (780–823): Étude sur l'église nestorienne au temps des premiers ʿAbbāsides avec nouvelle édition et traduction du dialogue entre Timothée et al-Mahdī*. Beirut: Dar el-Machreq, 1975.

Raby, Julian, and Jeremy Johns, eds. *Bayt al-Maqdis: ʿAbd al-Malik's Jerusalem*, part 1. Oxford: Oxford University Press, 1992.

Ramadan, Tariq. *Western Muslims and the Future of Islam*. Oxford: Oxford University Press, 2004.

Reeves, John, ed. *Bible and Qurʾān: Essays in Scriptural Intertextuality*. Symposium Series, no. 24. Atlanta: Society of Biblical Literature, 2003.

Regan, Geoffrey. *First Crusader: Byzantium's Holy Wars.* Stroud, UK: Sutton, 2001.

Reinink, G. J. "The Beginnings of Syriac Apologetic Literature in Response to Islam." *Oriens Christianus* 77 (1993): 165–87.

———. "'Edessa Grew Dim and Nisibis Shone Forth'; The School of Nisibis at the Transition of the Sixth-Seventh Century." In Drijvers and MacDonald, *Centres of Learning*, 77–89.

———. "Ps.-Methodius: A Concept of History in Response to the Rise of Islam." In Cameron and Conrad, *The Byzantine and Early Islamic Near East I*, 149–87.

———. *Die syrische Apokalypse des Pseudo-Methodios.* Corpus Scriptorum Christianorum Orientalium, vols. 540 and 541. Louvain, Belgium: Peeters, 1993.

Reynolds, Dwight F., ed., et al. *Interpreting the Self: Autobiography in the Arabic Literary Tradition.* Berkeley: University of California Press, 2001. 112.

Reynolds, Gabriel Said. *A Muslim Theologian in the Sectarian Milieu: ʿAbd al-Jabbār and the Critique of Christian Origins.* Islamic History and Civilization, Studies and Texts, vol. 56. Leiden: Brill, 2004.

Riad, Eva. *Studies in the Syriac Preface.* Studia Semitica Upsaliensia, 11. Uppsala, Sweden Almqvist and Wiksell, 1988.

Rissanen, Seppo. *Theological Encounter of Oriental Christians with Islam during Early Abbasid Rule.* Åbo: Åbo Adademis Förlag-Åbo Adademi University Press, 1993.

Robinson, Chase F. *Empire and Elites after the Muslim Conquest: The Transformation of Northern Mesopotamia.* Cambridge: Cambridge University Press, 2000.

Rocalve, P. *Louis Massignon et l'Islam.* Témoignages et documents, 2. Damascus: Institut Français, 1993.

Roey, Albert van. "Une apologie syriaque attribuée à Elie de Nisibe." *Le Muséon* 59 (1946): 381–97.

———. *Nonnus de Nisibe, traité apologétique: Étude, texte et traduction.* Bibliothèque du Muséon, 21. Louvain, Belgium: Peeters, 1948.

Roggema, Barbara. "A Christian Reading of the Qurʾān: The Legend of Sergius-Baḥīrā and Its Use of the Qurʾān and Sīra." In Thomas, *Syrian Christians under Islam*, 57–73.

———. "Epistemology as Polemics: Ibn Kammūna's Examination of the Apologetics of the Three Faiths." In Roggema, *The Three Rings*, 47–68.

———, et al., eds. *The Three Rings: Textual Studies in the Historical Trialogue of Judaism, Christianity and Islam.* Leuven, Belgium: Peeters, 2005.

Roisse, Philippe. "La circulation du savoir des Arabes chrétiens en Méditerranée médiévale: Approche des sources manuscrites." *Collectanea Christiana Orientalia* 1 (2004): 185–231.

Romeny, Bas ter Haar. "From Religious Association to Ethnic Community: A Research Project on Identity Formation among the Syrian Orthodox under Muslim Rule." *Islam and Christian-Muslim Relations* 16 (2005): 377–99.

Rosenblatt, Samuel, trans. *Saadia Gaon: The Book of Beliefs and Opinions.* Yale Judaica Series. New Haven, CT: Yale University Press, 1948.

Rubenson, Samuel. "Translating the Tradition: Some Remarks on the Arabicization of the Patristic Heritage in Egypt." *Medieval Encounters* 2 (1996): 4–14.

Rubenstein, Richard E. *Aristotle's Children: How Christians, Muslims, and Jews Rediscovered Ancient Wisdom and Illuminated the Middle Ages.* Orlando, FL: Harcourt, 2003.

Rubin, Milka Levy. "Arabization vers Islamization in the Palestinian Melkite Community during the Early Muslim Period." In *Sharing the Sacred: Religious Contacts and Conflicts in the Holy Land*, edited by Arieh Kofsky and Guy G. Stroumsa, 149–62. Jerusalem: Yad Izhak Ben Zvi, 1998.

———. "*Shurūṭ ʿUmar* and Its Alternatives: The Legal Debate on the Status of the *Dhimmīs*." *Jerusalem Studies in Arabic and Islam* 30 (2005): 170–206.

Rubin, Uri, *Between Bible and Qurʾān: The Children of Israel and the Islamic Self-Image.* Princeton, NJ: Darwin Press, 1999.

———. *The Eye of the Beholder: The Life of Muḥammad as Viewed by the Early Muslims; a Textual Analysis.* Studies in Late Antiquity and Early Islam, 5. Princeton, NJ: Darwin Press, 1995.

———. "*Ḥanīfiyya* and Kaʿba: An Inquiry into the Arabian Pre-Islamic Background of *Dīn Ibrāhīm*." *Jerusalem Studies in Arabic and Islam* 13 (1990): 85–112.

Saffrey, H.-D. "Le chrétien Jean Philopon et la survivance de l'école d'Alexandrie au Vie siècle." *Revue des Études Grecques* 67 (1954): 396–410.

Sahas, Daniel J. *Icon and Logos: Sources in Eighth-Century Iconoclasm.* Toronto Medieval Texts and Translations, 4. Toronto: University of Toronto Press, 1986.

———. *John of Damascus on Islam: The "Heresy of the Ishmaelites."* Leiden: Brill, 1972.

Salama-Carr, Myriam. *La traduction à l'époque abbaside: L'école de Hunayn ibn Ishaq et son importance pour la traduction.* Paris: Didier, 1990.

Samir, Samir Khalil. "Abū Qurrah et les Maronites." *Proche-Orient Chrétien* 41 (1991): 25–33.

———. "Dhikr madhāhib an-naṣārā liMuʾtaman ad-dawlah ibn al-ʿAssāl." *al-Machriq* 66 (1992): 481–91.

———. "The Earliest Arab Apology for Christianity (c. 750)." In Samir and Nielsen, *Christian Arabic Apologetics during the Abbasid Period*, 57–114.

———. "Entretien d'Elie de Nisibe avec le vizir Ibn ʿAlī al-Maghribī, su l'Unité et la Trinité." *Islamochristiana* 5 (1979): 31–117.

———. *Foi et culture en Irak au XIe siècle: Elie de Nisibe et l'Islam.* Collected Studies Series, 544. Aldershot, UK: Variorum/Ashgate, 1996.

———. "Maqālah Ḥunayn ibn Isḥāq fī kayfiyyah idrāk ḥaqīqah ad-diyānah." *al-Machriq* 71 (1997): 345–63.

———. "The Prophet Muḥammad as Seen by Timothy I and Some Other Arab Christian Authors." In Thomas, *Syrian Christians under Islam*, 75–106.

———. "Qui est l'interlocuteur musulman du patriarche syrien Jean III (631–648)?" In *IV Symposium Syriacum—1984*, edited by H. J. W. Drijvers et al., 387–400. Orientalia Christiana Analecta, 229, Rome: Pont. Institutum Studiorum Orientalium, 1987.

———. "La 'Somme des aspects de la foi': Oeuvre d'Abū Qurrah?" In *Actes du Deuxième Congrès International d'Études Arabes Chrétiennes (Oosterhesselen, septembre 1984)*, edited by K. Samir, 93–121. Orientalia Christiana Analecta, 226. Rome: Pontificio Istituto degli Studii Orientali, 1986.

———. *Le traité de l'unité de Yaḥyā ibn ʿAdī (893–974)* (Arabic). Patrimoine Arabe Chrétien, 2. Jounieh, Lebanon: Librairie Saint Paul, and Rome: Pontificio Istituto Orientale, 1980.

———. "Un traité du cheikh Abū ʿAlī Naẓīf ibn Yumn sur l'accord des chrétiens entre eux malgré leur disaccord dans l'expression." *Mélanges de l'Université Saint-Joseph* 51 (1990): 329–43.

———. "Yaḥyā ibn ʿAdī." *Bulletin d'Arabe Chrétien* 3 (1979): 45–63.

———, ed. *Miṣbāḥ az-ẓulma fī īḍāḥ al-khidma.* Cairo: Maktabat al-Kārūz, 1971.

———, and Paul Nwyia. *Une correspondance islamo-chrétienne entre ibn al-Munaggim, Ḥunayn ibn Isḥāq et Qusṭā ibn Lūqā.* Patrologia Orientalis, vol. 40, fasc. 4, no. 185. Turnhout, Belgium: Brepols, 1981.

———, and Jørgen S. Nielsen, eds. *Christian Arabic Apologetics during the Abbasid Period (750–1258).* Studies in the History of Religions, vol. 63. Leiden: Brill, 1994.

Samuelson, Norbert M., ed. and trans. *The Exalted Faith: Abraham ibn Daud.* Rutherford, NJ: Fairleigh Dickinson University Press, 1986.

Saritoprak, Zeki, and Sidney H. Griffith. "Fethullah Gülen and the 'People of the Book'; A Voice from Turkey for Interfaith Dialogue." *The Muslim World* 95 (2005): 329–40.

Sayyid, Fuʾad. *Fihris al-Makhṭūṭāt al-muṣawwarah*, part 2, *at-tāʾrīkh.* Cairo: Maṭbaʿat as-Sunnah al-Muḥammadiyyah, 1954.

Sbath, P. Paul. *Vingt traités philosophiques et apologétiques d'auteurs arabes chrétiens du IXe au XIVe siècle.* Cairo: H. Friedrich, 1929.

Scher, Addai. *Theodorus bar Kônî Liber Scholiorum.* CSCO, vols. 55 and 69. Paris: E Typographeo Reipublicae, 1910 and 1912, vol. 69.

Schick, Robert. *The Christian Communities of Palestine from Byzantine to Islamic Rule: A Historical and Archaeological Study.* Studies in Late Antique and Early Islam, 2. Princeton, NJ: Darwin Press, 1995.

Schmitz, M. "Kaʿb al-Akhbār." *EI*, new ed., 4 (1978): 316–17.

Schoeler, Gregor. *Écrire et transmettre dans les débuts de l'islam.* Paris: Presses Universitaires de France, 2002.

Schönborn, Christoph von. *Sophrone de Jérusalem: Vie monastique et confession dogmatique.* Paris: Beauchesne, 1972.

Schütz, Edmund. "Armenia: A Christian Enclave in the Islamic Near East in the Middle Ages." In Gervers and Bikhazi, *Conversion and Continuity*, 217–36.

Scruton, Roger. *The West and the Rest: Globalization and the Terrorist Threat.* Wilmington, DE: ISI Books, 2002.

Segal, J. G. *Edessa, "the Blessed City."* Oxford: Oxford University Press, 1970.

Sen, Amartya. *The Argumentative Indian: Writings on Indian History, Culture, and Identity.* New York: Farrar, Straus and Giroux, 2005.

Sendino, Jose Muñoz. "Al-Kindi, Apologia del Christianismo." *Miscelanea Comillas* 11 and 12 (1949): 339–460.

Sezgin, Fuat, ed. *Ḥunain ibn Isḥāq: Texts and Studies.* Islamic Philosophy, vol. 17. Frankfurt: Institute for the History of Arabic-Islamic Science at the Johann Wolfgang Goethe University, 1999.

Shahid, Irfan. *Byzantium and the Arabs in the Fifth Century.* Washington, DC: Dumbarton Oaks, 1989.

———. *Byzantium and the Arabs in the Fourth Century*. Washington, DC: Dumbarton Oaks, 1984.

———. *Byzantium and the Arabs in the Sixth Century*. Washington, DC: Dumbarton Oaks, 1995.

———. *Rome and the Arabs: A Prolegomenon to the Study of Byzantium and the Arabs*. Washington, DC: Dumbarton Oaks, 1984.

Shedd, W. A. *Islam and the Oriental Churches: Their Historical Relations*. Philadelphia: Presbyterian Board of Publication and Sabbath-School Work, 1904; repr., Piscataway, NJ: Gorgias Press, 2004.

Sheldon-Williams, I. P. "The Greek Christian Platonist Tradition from the Cappadocians to Maximus and Eriugena." In *The Cambridge History of Later Greek and Early Medieval Philosophy*, edited by A. H. Armstrong, 425 and n. 3. Cambridge: Cambridge University Press, 1967.

Sheppard, Anne. "Philosophy and Philosophical Schools." In *The Cambridge Ancient History; Late Antiquity: Empire and Successors, A.D. 425–600*, vol. 14, edited by Averil Cameron et al., 835–54. Cambridge: Cambridge University Press, 2000.

Sirry, Munʾim A. "Early Muslim-Christian Dialogue: A Closer Look at Major Themes of the Theological Encounter." *Islam and Christian-Muslim Relations* 16 (2005): 361–76.

Sklare, David. "Responses to Islamic Polemics by Jewish Mutakallimūn in the Tenth Century." In Lazarus-Yafeh, *The Majlis*, 135–61.

Sorabji, Richard, ed. *Philoponus and the Rejection of Aristotelian Science*. London: Duckworth, 1987.

Sourdel, D. "Un pamphlet musulman anonyme d'époque ʿabbāside contre les chrétiens." *Revue des Études Islamiques* 34 (1966): 29

Steenberghen, Fernand van. *Aristotle in the West: The Origins of Latin Aristotelianism*. Translated by Leonard Johnston. New York: Humanities Press, 1970.

Steinschneider, Moritz. *Die arabische Literatur der Juden: Ein Beitrag zur Literaturgeschichte der Araber; grossenteils aus handschriftlichen Quellen*. Frankfurt: J. Kaufmann, 1902.

———. *Polemische und apologetische Literatur in arabischen Sprache zwischen Muslimen, Christen und Juden*. Leipzig: Brockhaus, 1877.

Stern, S. "ʿAbd al-Jabbār's Account of How Christ's Religion Was Falsified by the Adoption of Roman Customs." *Journal of Theological Studies* 19 (1968): 128–85.

Stillman, Norman. *The Jews of Arab Lands: A History and Source Book*. Philadelphia: Jewish Publication Society of America, 1979.

Strauss, Leo. *Persecution and the Art of Writing*. Chicago: University of Chicago Press, 1952.

Stroumsa, Sarah. *Freethinkers of Medieval Islam, Ibn al-Rāwandī, Abū Bakr al-Rāzī and Their Impact on Islamic Thought*. Leiden: Brill, 1999.

———. "Jewish Polemics against Islam and Christianity in the Light of Judaeo-Arabic Texts." In Golb, *Judaeo-Arabic Studies*, 241–50.

———, ed. and trans. *Dāwūd ibn Marwān al-Muqammiṣ's Twenty Chapters*

(*ʿIshrūn Maqālah*). Études sur le Judaïsme Médiéval, vol. 13. Leiden: Brill, 1989.

Studer, Basil. *Die theologische Arbeitsweise des Johannes von Damaskus*. Studia Patristica et Byzantina, 2. Ettal: Buch-Kunstverlag, 1956.

Suermann, Harald. *Die geschichtstheologische Reaktion auf die einfallenden Muslime in der edessenischen Apokalyptic des 7. Jahrhunderts*. Frankfurt: Peter Lang, 1985.

———. *Die Grundungs Geschichte der Maronitischen Kirche*. Orientalia Biblica et Christiana, vol. 10. Wiesbaden: Harrassowitz, 1998.

Swanson, Mark. "Arabic as a Christian Language?" and "Early Christian-Muslim Theological Conversation among Arabic-speaking Intellectuals," available at http://www.luthersem.edu/faculty/fac_home.asp?contact_id=mswanson.

———. "Are Hypostases Attributes? An Investigation into the Modern Egyptian Christian Appropriation of the Medieval Arabic Apologetic Heritage." *Parole de l'Orient* 16 (1990–91): 239–50.

———. "Beyond Proof-Texting: Approaches to the Qurʾān in Some Early Arabic Christian Apologies." *The Muslim World* 88 (1998): 297–319.

———. "The Christian al-Maʾmūn Tradition." In Thomas, ed., *Christians at the Heart of Islamic Rule*, 63–92.

———. "The Martyrdom of ʿAbd al-Masīḥ, Superior of Mount Sinai (Qays al-Ghassānī)." In Thomas, *Syrian Christians under Islam*, 107–29.

———. "Some Considerations for the Dating of *Fī tathlīth Allāh al-wāḥid* (Sinai Ar. 154) and *Al-Jāmiʿ wujūh al-imān* (London British Library Or. 4950)." In *Actes du quatrième congrès international d'études arabes chrétiennes*, edited by Samir Khalil Samir, published in *Parole de l'Orient* 18 (1993): 117–41.

Sweetman, James W. *Islam and Christian Theology: A Study of the Interpretation of Theological Ideas in the Two Religions*. 2 vols. in 4. London: Lutterworth Press, 1954–67.

Tamcke, Martin. "'Wir sind nicht von Abrahams Samen!': Deutungen Abrahams in der ostsyrischen Literatur." In Kratz and Nagel, "*Abraham unser Vater*," 112–32.

Tardy, René. *Najrân: Chrétiens d'Arabie avant l'Islam*. Recherches, 8. Beirut: Dar el-Machreq, 1999.

Tartar, Georges. *Dialogue islamo-chrétien sous le calife al-Maʾmūn; les épîtres d'al-Hashimî et d'al-Kindî*. 2 vols. Combes-la-Ville: Centre Évangélique de Témoignage et de Dialogue, 1982.

Teixidor, Javier. *Aristotle en syriaque: Paul le perse, logician du Vie siècle*. Paris: CNRS, 2003.

———. "Science *versus* foi chez Paul le Perse: Une note." In *From Byzantium to Iran: Armenian Studies in Honour of Nina G. Garsoïan*, edited by J.-P. Mahé and R. W. Thomson, 509–19. Atlanta: Scholars Press, 1997.

Thomas, David, *Anti-Christian Polemic in Early Islam: Abū ʿĪsā al-Warrāq's "Against the Trinity."* University of Cambridge Oriental Publications, no. 45. Cambridge: Cambridge University Press, 1992.

———. *Early Muslim Polemic against Christianity: Abū ʿĪsā al-Warrāq's "Against the Incarnation."* University of Cambridge Oriental Publications, no. 59. Cambridge: Cambridge University Press, 2002.

———. "Ṭabarī's Book of Religion and Empire." *Bulletin of the John Rylands Library*, 69 (1986): 1–7.

———, ed. *Christians at the Heart of Islamic Rule: Church Life and Scholarship in ʿAbbasid Iraq.* The History of Christian-Muslim Relations, vol. 1. Leiden: Brill, 2003.

———. *A Faithful Presence: Essays for Kenneth Cragg.* London: Melisende, 2003.

———. *Syrian Christians under Islam: The First Thousand Years*, Leiden: Brill, 2001.

Tisserant, Eugene Cardinal. *Eastern Christianity in India: A History of the Syro-Malabar Church from the Earliest Time to the Present Day.* Translated by E. R. Hambye, S.J. Westminster, MD: Newman Press, 1957.

Tolan, John V. *Saracens: Islam in the Medieval European Imagination.* New York: Columbia University Press, 2002.

Trimingham, J. Spencer. *Christianity among the Arabs in Pre-Islamic Times.* London and New York: Longman, 1979.

Tritton, A. S. *The Caliphs and Their Non-Muslim Subjects: A Critical Study of the Covenant of ʿUmar.* London: Oxford University Press, 1930.

Troupeau, Gérard. "Les couvents chrétiens dans la literature arabe musulman." *La Nouvelle Revue de Caire* 1 (1975): 265–79.

———. *Études sur le christianisme arabe au Moyen Age.* Collected Studies Series, 515. Aldershot, UK: Variorum/Ashgate, 1995.

———. "Le livre de l'unanimité de la foi de ʿAlī ibn Dāwud al-Arfādī." *Melto* 5 (1969): 197–219.

———. "Le role des Syriaques dans la transmission et l'exploitation du patrimoine philosophique et scientifique grec." *Arabica* 38 (1991): 1–10.

Ünal, Ali, ed. and trans., and Alphonse Williams, ed. *Advocate of Dialogue: Fethullah Gülen.* Fairfax, VA: The Fountain, 2000.

Ursinus, M. O. H. "Millet." In *The Encyclopaedia of Islam: New Edition*, edited by C. E. Bosworth et al., 7: 61–64. Leiden: Brill, 1993.

Urvoy, Dominique. *Les penseurs libres dans l'islam classique.* Paris: Albin Michel, 1996.

Urvoy, Marie-Thérèse. "La culture et la littérature arabe des chrétiens d'al-Andalus." *Bulletin de Littérature Ecclésiastique* 92 (1991): 259–75.

———. *Traité d'éthique d'Abû Zakariyyâʾ Yahyâ ibn ʿAdi.* Études Chrétiennes Arabes. Paris: Cariscript, 1991.

Uthemann, Karl-Heinz. *Anastasii Sinaitae Viae Dux.* Corpus Christianorum, Series Graeca, 8. Leuven, Belgium: University Press, 1981.

Vajda, Georges. "Le milieu juif à Baghdad." *Arabica* 9 (1962): 389–93.

Vallat, Philippe. *Farabi et l'École d'Alexandrie: Des prémisses de la connaissance à la philosophie politique.* Études Musulmanes, 38. Paris: Vrin, 2004.

Valognes, Jean-Pierre. *Vie et mort des chrétiens d'Orient: Des origines à nos jours.* Paris: Fayard, 1994.

Van Ess, Josef. *Theologie und Gesellschaft im 2. und 3. Jahrhundert Hidschra.* 6 vols. Berlin: De Gruyter, 1991–97.

Van Ginkel, J. J., H. L. Murre-Van Den Berg, and T. M. Van Lint, eds. *Redefining Christian Identity: Cultural Interaction in the Middle East since the Rise of Islam.* Orientalia Lovaniensia Analecta, 134. Leuven, Belgium: Peeters, 2005.

Vila, David H. "Christian Martyrs in the First Abbasid Century and the Development of an Apologetic against Islam." Unpublished PhD diss., St. Louis University, 1999. UMI Microform no. 9942830.

———. "Rawḥ al-Qurayshī and the Development of an Arabic Christian Community." In *Christianity and Native Cultures: Perspectives from Different Regions of the World*, edited by Cyriac Pullapilly et al., 83–95. South Bend, IN: Cross Cultural Publications, 2004.

Waardenburg, Jacques. *Muslim Perceptions of Other Religions.* New York and Oxford: Oxford University Press, 1999.

———, ed. *Muslim-Christian Perceptions of Dialogue Today: Experiences and Expectations.* Leuven, Belgium: Peeters, 2000.

Wadi, A. *Studio su al-Muʾtaman Ibn al-ʿAssāl* (Arabic). Studia Orientalia Christiana Monographiae, 5. Cairo and Jerusalem: Franciscan Centre of Christian Oriental Studies/Franciscan Printing Press, 1997.

Wallace-Hadrill, D. S. *Christian Antioch: A Study of Early Christian Thought in the East.* Cambridge: Cambridge University Press, 1982.

Walsh, John K. "Versiones peninsulares del '*Kitāb ādāb al-falāsifa*' de Ḥunayn ibn Isḥāq." *Al-Andalus* 41 (1976): 355–84.

Wansbrough, John E. *The Sectarian Milieu: Content and Composition of Islamic Salvation History.* Oxford: Oxford University Press, 1978.

Ward, Seth. "A Fragment from an Unknown Work by al-Ṭabarī on the Tradition 'Expel the Jews and Christians from the Arabian Peninsula (and the Lands of Islam).'" *Bulletin of the School of Oriental and African Studies* 53 (1990): 407–20.

Wasserstrom, Steven M. *Between Muslim and Jew: The Problem of Symbiosis under Early Islam.* Princeton, NJ: Princeton University Press, 1995.

Watt, John W. "Eastward and Westward Transmission of Classical Rhetoric." In Drijvers and MacDonald, *Centres of Learning*, 63–76.

Watt, W. Montgomery. *The Formative Period of Islamic Thought.* Edinburgh: Edinburgh University Press, 1973; repr., Oxford: One World, 1998.

Wensinck, A. J., and D. A. King. "Ḳibla." *EI*, new ed., vol. 5, 82–88.

Wessels, Antonie. *Arab and Christian? Christians in the Middle East.* Kampen, The Netherlands: Kok Pharos Publishing House, 1995.

Wheatcroft, Andrew. *Infidels: A History of the Conflict between Christendom and Islam.* New York: Random House, 2003.

Wildberg, Christian, trans. *John Philoponus: Against Aristotle on the Eternity of the World.* London: Duckworth, and Ithaca, NY: Cornell University Press, 1987.

Wilken, Robert L. *The Christians as the Romans Saw Them.* New Haven, CT: Yale University Press, 1984.

———. *The Land Called Holy: Palestine in Christian History and Thought.* New Haven, CT: Yale University Press, 1992.

Winters, Paul A., ed. *Islam: Opposing Viewpoints.* San Diego, CA: Greenhaven Press, 1995.

Wolf, Kenneth Baxter. *Christian Martyrs in Muslim Spain.* Cambridge: Cambridge University Press, 1988.

———. "Christian Views of Islam in Early Medieval Spain." In *Medieval Christian Perceptions of Islam*, edited by John Victor Tolan, 85–108. Garland Medieval

Casebooks, vol. 10, Garland Reference Library of the Humanities, vol. 1768. New York: Garland, 1996.

———. "The Earliest Latin Lives of Muḥammad." In Gervers and Bikhazi, *Conversion and Continuity*, 88–101.

———. "The Earliest Spanish Christian Views of Islam." *Church History* 55 (1986): 281–93.

Wolfson, Harry A. "The Muslim Attributes and the Christian Trinity." *Harvard Theological Review* 49 (1956): 1–18.

Yaḥyā ibn ʿAdī. *The Reformation of Morals*. Edited by Samir Khalil Samir, translated by Sidney H. Griffith. Eastern Christian Texts, 1. Provo, UT: Brigham Young University Press, 2002.

Yeats, William Butler. *A Vision*. London: Macmillan, 1937.

Ye'or, Bat [Giselle Littman]. *The Decline of Eastern Christianity under Islam: From Jihad to Dhimmitude; Seventh–Twentieth Century*. Madison, NJ: Fairleigh Dickinson University Press, 1996.

———. *The Dhimmī: Jews and Christians under Islam*. Rutherford, NJ: Fairleigh Dickinson University Press, 1985.

———. *Islam and Dhimmitude: Where Civilizations Collide*. Madison, NJ: Fairleigh Dickinson University Press, 2002.

Yousif, Ephrem-Isa. *Les philosophes et traducteurs syriaques; d'Athènes à Bagdad*. Paris and Montreal: L'Harmattan, 1997.

Zaborowski, Jason R. *The Coptic Martyrdom of John of Phanijōit: Assimilation and Conversion to Islam in Thirteenth-Century Egypt*. The History of Christian-Muslim Relations, vol. 3. Leiden: Brill, 2005.

Zayyāt, Ḥabīb. "The Distinctive Signs of the Christians and Jews in Islam" (Arabic). *al-Machriq* 43 (1949): 161–252.

Zebiri, Kate. *Muslims and Christians Face to Face*. Oxford: One World, 1997.

INDEX

Abba Isaac. *See* Isaac (Abba Isaac) of Mount Sinai, 51
Abelard of Bath, 127
Abelard, Peter, 176
Abraham, 37, 78, 104; and the Abraham *theologoumenon*, 162, 163–64; religion of, 162–66, 163n18
Abraham of Tiberias, 79
Abramios, 51
ibn ʿAdī, Yahyā, 3, 62, 64, 66, 71, 73, 91, 110, 112, 117, 136, 176; as an Aristotelian philosopher, 123; and the concept of *al-insāniyyah* (humane behavior), 125; defense of Christian doctrines by, 118; education of, 122; effectiveness of his Christian apologetics, 124–25; as proponent of the "Peripatetic school" of thought, 122; and the pursuit of the philosophical life, 125; teachers of, 114, 115
Against Abū Qurrah, the Christian (ibn Ṣubayḥ al-Murdār), 63
Against ʿAmmār the Christian, in Refutation of the Christians (al-ʿAllāf, Abū Hudhayl), 63
Against the Calumniators of the Holy Icons (John of Damascus), 144
al-Aḥbār, Kaʿb, 166–67
al-Akhṭal, 169–70
ibn Albar al-Qūṭī, Ḥafṣ, 67, 153–54
Alexandria, 11, 24, 51, 109, 110, 112, 117
Alfonsi, Petrus, 127
al-Akhṭal, Ghiyāth ibn Ghawth ibn Ṣalt, 169–70
al-ʿAllāf, Abū Hudhayl, 63, 100
Allāh, 31, 58, 145, 168, 169
Ammonius, 110–11
Anastatios of Sinai, 28–29, 30, 51, 135; on Islam as a type of Christian heresy, 30–31
al-Anbāri, Abū Nūḥ, 47
Annals (Eutychius of Alexandria), 65
Anthony David, 51
Antioch, 11, 24, 51
apocalypse, 32–35
Apocalypse of Pseudo-Methodius, The, 33–35, 38
Aquinas, Thomas, 176
Arabia, 19–20
Arabic/Arabic texts, 2, 50n17, 70–71, 105, 106, 156; Arabic Christian texts composed in Spain, 153–54; "church books," 51; ecclesiastical, 48–53; and the formalities of letter writing, 88; "old South Palestinian" manuscripts, 50–51; *risālah*, 89, 98, 100. *See also* translation movements
Arabs, 27; Christian names for ("Saracens," "Hagarenes," or "Ishmaelites"), 24, 24n6; Christian responses to Arab theology, 28–32; incursions of into Roman and Persian territories, 23–25
Arabicization, 48, 157
Aristotle, 107, 110, 113, 123; importance of his work to Christians, 115, 117
Aristotelian logic, 109, 123–24
Aramaic, 12, 50, 51
Armenia, 8
Armenian/Armenian texts, 39, 172, 175
Armenians, 12, 21, 130, 136–37
ibn al-ʿAssāl, al-Muʿtaman, 120
Athanasius of Alexandria, 51
Athanasius of Balad, 112
Athens, 109
Awlād al-ʿAssāl, 65, 73

Babai the Great, 12, 133
Baghdad, 12, 51, 68, 125; as a center of philosophical thought, 117–19; intercommunal salons (*majālis*) of, 178
Baḥīrā (Sergius Baḥīrā), 38, 166
Banquet of the Physicians (ibn at-Tayyib), 170
Banquet of the Priests (ibn at-Tayyib), 170
Baradaeus, Jacob, 135
Basil of Caesarea, 51
al-Baṣrī, ʿAmmār, 3, 61–62, 83–85, 91, 133; on unworthy motives for espousing a religion, 98
al-Baṣrī, Ḥasan, 40
Bayt al-Ḥikmah (House of Wisdom), 119
bar Berîkâ, ʿAbd Īshû, 133
Bêt Ḥālê, 36–38, 39
Bible, 162, 168; Arabic translations of, 50

Kitāb al-burhān ("Book of Proof" [Peter of Bayt Ra's]), 91, 98
Kitāb al-majālis ("Book of Sessions"), 80
Kitāb al-masā'il wa l-ajwibah, 83–85, 91, 100
knowledge theory, 46
bar Kônî, Theodore, 43–44, 76, 77, 81–82, 133
Kraemer, Joel, 123
Küng, Hans, 164
Kuzari (al-Ḥasan), 72

Lamp in the Darkness (Ibn Kabar), 66
Leo III (emperor of Byzantium), 86, 175
"Letter to a Muslim Friend" (Paul of Antioch), 168–69
Levant, Arab occupation of, 11–13
Liber de unione (Babai the Great), 133
Liber Denudationis (Burman), 67–68
ibn Lūqā al-Baʿalbakī, Qusṭā, 3
ibn Lūqā, Qusṭā, 86, 88, 120–21, 138

al-Mahdī (Caliph al-Mahdī), 47, 76, 113, 128
ibn al-Maḥrūma, Abū l-Ḥasan, 74
Maimonides, Moses, 3, 73
al-Malik, ʿAbd, 14–15, 32, 37
al-Ma'mūn (caliph al-Maʾmūn), 80, 87, 87n39, 100
Manichaeans, 42
ibn Manṣūr ibn Kammūna, Saʿd, 73–74
Mar Chariton Monastery, 52, 57
Mār Mattī Monastery, 47
Mar Sabas Monastery, 51, 57, 138
Maronites, 130, 138, 139–40, 171
martyrs, Christian, 147–51; of Cordoba, 151–55; Cyrus of Ḥarrān, 148–49; John of Phanijōit, 151
Marûthâ of Takrit, 113n24
ibn Marwān al-Muqammiṣ, Dāwūd, 69
Mary, 29, 31–32, 83, 131, 168
Massignon, Louis, 161, 163–64
Mattā, Abū Bishr, 114, 115, 123
Melkite Greek Catholic Church, 139
"Melkites"/Melkite communities, 8, 13, 34, 41, 42, 43, 57, 62, 91, 137–39; ecclesial identity and writings of, 49–51, 53; origin of, 138; usage of the term "Melkite," 139
Mesopotamia, 11, 19
Methodius of Olympus, 33–34
Monenergism, 135
Monophysites, 28, 64, 110, 129. *See also* Jacobites (Monophysites)
Monotheletism, 135
Moschus, John, 26
Mozarabs (Spanish Christians), 130, 153
Muḥammad (the Prophet), 4, 9n9, 14, 23, 37, 42, 78, 80–81, 164; earliest Christian reference to, 25; as a king pleasing to God, 104; ridicule of by Christians, 152; as the "seal of the prophets," 104; and *Sīrah* (biography) literature, 92–93; as a teenager, 38; view of as a "false prophet," 24–25; as worthy of praise by all, 104–5
ibn Muḥammad al-Ḥumaydī, Abū ʿAbd Allāh, 63
ibn Munabbih, Wahb, 40
ibn al-Munajjim, Abū ʿIsa Yaḥyā, 86, 88, 120, 121
ibn al-Muqaffa, Severus, 65, 91, 126
Muslim/Christian relations, 3–4, 5
Muslims, 15, 20, 22, 42, 178–79; anti-Christian policies of, 20–21; and Christian ecumenism, 140–42; equality of, 15; as *ḥanpê*, 82; as the "new Jews," 46, 70; as "pagans," 43n62; as readers of Christian apologists, 100–103; responses of to Christian apologists, 62–64; Sunni, 64
mutakallimūn, 73, 85, 90, 93, 95, 96, 97, 124; debt of Christian apologetics to, 158; philosophical reactions against the methods of, 118
al-Muʿtaman, ibn al-ʿAssāl, 3, 65, 66, 141–42

Narsai, 131–32
Nawādir al-falāsifah (Ḥunayn ibn Isḥāq), 121
"Nazarenes/Nazoreans," (*an-Naṣārā*), 7–8, 8n6, 10
Nestorian Church of the East, 110, 112, 132; missionary activity of, 134
Nestorians, 8, 12, 42, 62, 130, 131–34, 138, 171; apologists for, 91; Christology of, 117, 133–34; intellectual and social origins of, 132–33; Nestorian scholars, 113–14; school system of, 113, 113n24
Nestorius of Constantinople, 131, 132
Newman, John Henry, 21
Nicholas of Cusa, 176
Nonnus of Nisibis, 112, 136